2nd Workshop on the Use of Computational Methods in the Study of Endangered Languages 2017 (ComputEL-2)

Honolulu, Hawaii, USA
6 – 7 March 2017

ISBN: 978-1-5108-4213-7

ComputEL-2

Proceedings of the

2nd Workshop on the Use of Computational Methods in the Study of Endangered Languages

March 6–7, 2017
Honolulu, Hawai'i, USA

Support:

Social Sciences and
Humanities Research
Council of Canada

Conseil de recherches
en sciences humaines
du Canada

Canada

UNIVERSITY
of HAWAI'I
MĀNOA

Preface

These proceedings contain the papers presented at the 2nd Workshop on the Use of Computational Methods in the Study of Endangered languages held in Honolulu, March 6–7, 2017. The workshop itself was co-located and took place after the 5th International Conference on Language Documentation and Conservation (ICLDC) at the University of Hawai'i at Mānoa. As the name implies, this is the second workshop held on the topic—the previous meeting was co-located with the ACL main conference in Baltimore, Maryland in 2014.

The workshop covers a wide range of topics relevant to the study and documentation of endangered languages, ranging from technical papers on working systems and applications, to reports on community activities with supporting computational components.

The purpose of the workshop is to bring together computational researchers, documentary linguists, and people involved with community efforts of language documentation and revitalization to take part in both formal and informal exchanges on how to integrate rapidly evolving language processing methods and tools into efforts of language description, documentation, and revitalization. The organizers are pleased with the range of papers, many of which highlight the importance of interdisciplinary work and interaction between the various communities that the workshop is aimed towards.

We received 39 submissions as long papers, short papers, or extended abstracts, of which 23 were selected for this volume (59%). In the proceedings, all papers are either short (≤ 5 pages) or long (≤ 9 pages). In addition, the workshop also features presentations from representatives of the National Science Foundation (NSF). Two panel dicussions on the topic of interaction between computational linguistics and the documentation and revitalization community as well as future planning of ComputEL underlined the demand and necessity of a workshop of this nature.

The organizing committee would like to thank the program committee for their thoughtful input on the submissions, as well as the organizers of ICLDC. We are also grateful to the NSF for funding part of the workshop (awards #1404352 and #1550905), and the Social Sciences and Humanities Research Council (SSHRC) of Canada for supporting the workshop through their Connections Outreach Grant #611-2016-0207.

ANTTI ARPPE
JEFF GOOD
MANS HULDEN
JORDAN LACHLER
ALEXIS PALMER
LANE SCHWARTZ

Organizing Committee:

Antti Arppe (University of Alberta)
Jeff Good (University at Buffalo)
Mans Hulden (University of Colorado)
Jordan Lachler (University of Alberta)
Alexis Palmer (University of North Texas)
Lane Schwartz (University of Illinois at Urbana-Champaign)

Program Committee:

Steve Abney (University of Michigan)
Dorothee Beermann (Norwegian University of Science and Technology)
Emily Bender (University of Washington)
Martin Benjamin (Kamusi Project International)
Damir Cavar (Indiana University)
Chris Cox (Carleton University)
Joel Dunham (The University of British Columbia)
Judith Klavans (University of Maryland)
Terry Langendoen (National Science Foundation)
Lori Levin (Carnegie Mellon University)
Will Lewis (Microsoft Research)
Worthy Martin (University of Virginia)
Michael Maxwell (Center for Advanced Study of Language)
Detmar Meurers (University of Tübingen)
Steve Moran (University of Zurich)
Sebastian Nordhoff (Glottotopia)
Kevin Scannell (Saint Louis University)
Gary Simons (SIL International)
Richard Sproat (Google, Inc.)
Trond Trosterud (University of Tromsø—The Arctic University of Norway)

Table of Contents

Conference Program

16:45–18:30: Poster session and late afternoon buffet

Converting a comprehensive lexical database into a computational model: The case of East Cree verb inflection
Antti Arppe, Marie-Odile Junker and Delasie Torkornoo

Instant annotations in ELAN corpora of spoken and written Komi, an endangered language of the Barents Sea region
Ciprian Gerstenberger, Niko Partanen and Michael Rießler

Inferring Case Systems from IGT: Enriching the Enrichment
Kristen Howell, Emily M. Bender, Michel Lockwood, Fei Xia and Olga Zamaraeva

Case Studies in the Automatic Characterization of Grammars from Small Wordlists
Jordan Kodner, Spencer Kaplan, Hongzhi Xu, Mitchell P. Marcus and Charles Yang

Endangered Data for Endangered Languages: Digitizing Print dictionaries
Michael Maxwell and Aric Bills

A computationally-assisted procedure for discovering poetic organization within oral tradition
David Meyer

Improving Coverage of an Inuktitut Morphological Analyzer Using a Segmental Recurrent Neural Network
Jeffrey Micher

Click reduction in fluent speech: a semi-automated analysis of Mangetti Dune !Xung
Amanda Miller and Micha Elsner

DECCA Repurposed: Detecting transcription inconsistencies without an orthographic standard
C. Anton Rytting and Julie Yelle

Jejueo talking dictionary: A collaborative online database for language revitalization
Moira Saltzman

Computational Support for Finding Word Classes: A Case Study of Abui
Olga Zamaraeva, František Kratochvíl, Emily M. Bender, Fei Xia and Kristen Howell

Tuesday, March 7th, 2017

08:45–09:00   Arrival, breakfast & chat

09:00–09:30   Q&A on National Science Foundation funding and application process (Colleen Fitzgerald and Terry Langendoen)

09:30–10:00   *Waldayu and Waldayu Mobile: Modern digital dictionary interfaces for endangered languages*
Patrick Littell, Aidan Pine and Henry Davis

10:00–10:30   *Connecting Documentation and Revitalization: A New Approach to Language Apps*
Alexa N. Little

10:30–11:00   Break: coffee and tea available

11:00–11:30   *Developing a Suite of Mobile Applications for Collaborative Language Documentation*
Mat Bettinson and Steven Bird

11:30–12:00   *Cross-language forced alignment to assist community-based linguistics for low resource languages*
Timothy Kempton

12:00–12:30   *A case study on using speech-to-translation alignments for language documentation*
Antonios Anastasopoulos and David Chiang

12:30–14:00   Lunch

14:00–15:00   ComputEL-3: Planning for the future

A Morphological Parser for Odawa

Dustin Bowers
Antti Arppe
Jordan Lachler
University of Alberta
4-32 Assiniboia Hall, University of Alberta
Edmonton, Alberta, Canada T6G 2E7
dabowers@ualberta.ca
arppe@ualberta.ca
lachler@ualberta.ca

Sjur Moshagen
Trond Trosterud
Department of Language and Culture
The Arctic University of Norway
Box 6050 Langnes
N-9037 Tromsø, Norway
sjur.n.moshagen@uit.no
trond.trosterud@uit.no

Abstract

Language communities and linguists conducting fieldwork often confront a lack of linguistic resources. This dearth can be substantially mitigated with the production of simple technologies. We illustrate the utility and design of a finite state parser, a widespread technology, for the Odawa dialect of Ojibwe (Algonquian, United States and Canada).

1 Credits

We would like to thank Rand Valentine, Mary Ann Corbiere, Alan Corbiere, Lena Antonsen, Miikka Silfverberg, Ryan Johnson, Katie Schmirler, Sarah Giesbrecht, and Atticus Harrigan for fruitful discussions during the development of this tool. We would also like to thank two anonymous reviewers for their helpful comments. This work was supported by a Partnership Development Grant (890-2013-0047) from the Social Sciences and Humanities Research Council of Canada and a Research Cluster Grant from the Kule Institute for Advanced Study at the University of Alberta.

2 Introduction

Language communities and linguists conducting grammatical or documentary fieldwork often confront a lack of linguistic resources. There may be incomplete prior grammatical descriptions of a language, an absence of written texts, or little infrastructure to help produce them. However, even with very few resources, linguistic technology can be produced to facilitate resource production. Building on prior work (see Trosterud 2005, Snoek et al 2014), the Alberta Language Technology laboratory (ALT-lab[1]) at the University of Alberta has produced a finite state model of the Odawa dialect of Ojibwe (otw, Algonquian, United States and Canada).[2] The production of this tool opens the door to faster editing and grammatical annotation of written texts, increases usability of electronic dictionaries, and provides a simple way to produce and check paradigms. We here summarize key features of the model of Odawa, and highlight some applications in which it is being used.

3 Basics of Finite State Machines

Finite state machines are a popular representation for a simple class of formal languages known as regular languages (Jurafsky and Martin 2000, Beesley and Karttunen 2003). Most importantly for our purposes, the phonology and morphology of natural languages may be productively modeled as regular languages (Johnson 1972, Koskenniemi 1983, Kaplan and Kay 1994). That is, the set of legal words of a natural language can be compactly represented with a finite state machine.

To take a simple example, we illustrate a finite state grammar for parsing the Odawa word for 'sacred stories' *aadsookaanan* into the stem and plural morpheme *aadsookaan-an* (doubled vowels indicate long vowels). Reading from left to right, the first step is to recognize *aadsookaan* 'sacred story' as an existing Odawa noun stem (indeed, a legal word), which in this case is followed by the plural morpheme *-an*, after which the word may not be further inflected and must end. This parse, and any other exhaustive segmentation of the string, is returned. This sequential decision process is straightforwardly mirrored in finite-state machines, where morpheme bound-

---

[1]http://altlab.artsrn.ualberta.ca/

[2]A similar model is under development by the Biigtigong Language Project (Kevin Scannell and John Paul Montano), see http://github.com/jpmontano/fst.

Proceedings of the 2nd Workshop on the Use of Computational Methods in the Study of Endangered Languages, pages 1–9,
Honolulu, Hawai'i, USA, March 6–7, 2017. ©2017 Association for Computational Linguistics

aries in a word correspond to states, and morphemes form the transitions between states. This can be represented as a directed graph, where states are nodes and morphemes are placed on arcs between nodes, with the phonological and syntactic components of the morpheme separated by a colon (e.g. *aadsookaan:N*).[3] The machine starts from a beginning state, labeled '0', and paths corresponding to legal words end in final states, marked with a double boundary. Hence, the finite state machine that parses *aadsookaan-an*, appears in Figure 1.

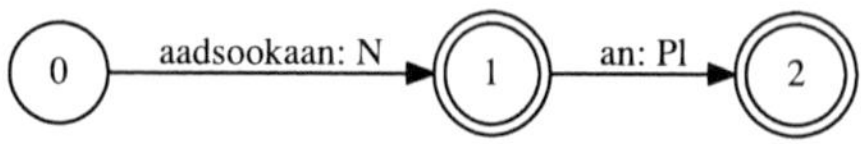

Figure 1: Finite state machine that recognizes the language containing *aadsookaan* and *aadsookaanan*.

4 Odawa Description

Odawa is a dialect of Ojibwe spoken mostly in the Great Lakes region of the United States and Canada. The dialect is endangered, as natural inter-generational transmission of the language ceased during or before the 1960's. Precise numbers of first-language speakers are difficult to come by, though Golla (2007) estimates that there are no more than two thousand speakers. There are efforts to revitalize the language, with immersion and non-immersion programs for children and adults in several communities. The language is predominately written in a romanization called the Fiero double-vowel system. Individual authors vary in whether they explicitly spell phonological processes like word-final devoicing or word-final short vowel lowering.

Ojibwe is a comparatively well-resourced language, as there was a tradition of missionary linguistics dating to the seventeenth century, which culminated in works by Baraga (1878b; 1878a) and Cuoq (1886). Odawa itself has also been the subject of sustained investigation, as seen in the works of Bloomfield (1957), Piggott, Kaye and Tokaichi (1971), Piggott and Kaye (1973),

Rhodes (1985a), Valentine (2001), and Corbiere and Valentine (2016).

4.1 Odawa Morphology

Like all Algonquian languages, Odawa has concatenative morphology that is easily represented with finite state machines. Setting aside a full discussion of the inflectional morphology (see Nichols 1980, Valentine 2001), nouns and verbs may be preceded by person prefixes, which may be followed by zero to six adverbial/adjectival prefixes. The full range of available suffixes varies between nouns and sub-classes of verbs, but they all have slots for realizing number, mood/aspect, and a second number slot specifically for arguments indexed by prefixes. Example (1) illustrates these slots for nouns (example from Valentine 2001:207).

(1)   g-makko-waa-bn-iin
      2-box-2.PL-PRF-PL
      'your folks' former boxes'

Nouns have additional slots for diminutive/contemptive suffixes, a pejorative suffix, and an optional possessive suffix. These suffixes are exemplified in the following synthesized example.

(2)   g-makk-oons-sh-im-waa-bn-iin
      2-box-DIM-PEJ-POS-2.PL-PRF-PL
      'your folks' former darn little boxes'

The verbal suffix template includes a position for negation, and in the case of transitive verbs with animate objects, a slot for object agreement (called a 'theme-sign' in the Algonquianist tradition, Brittain 1999, McGinnis 1999). Example (3a) illustrates the major verbal slots with a verb that subcategorizes for an animate object (example synthesized, see Valentine 2001:293), whereas example (3b) shows a verb with two adverbial prefixes ('preverbs' in the Algonquianist tradition, example courtesy of Alan Corbiere).

(3) a. n-waabm-aa-swaa-mnaa-dgen-ag
         1-see-3.OBJ-NEG-1.PL-DUB-3.PL
         'Perhaps we (excl.) don't see them'

      b. n-gii-zhi-bgosenm-aa-naan-ig
         1-PST-thus-beg-3.OBJ-1.PL-3.PL
         'We (excl.) did thus beg of them'

The examples in (3) illustrate the inflection of verbs in matrix clauses ('independent order' in Algonquianist terminology). The slot order

---

[3]This makes the machine a transducer rather than a standard automaton.

and phonological spell-out changes significantly in embedded clauses ('conjunct order' in Algonquianist terminology), an example of which is provided in (4). For simplicity, we will henceforth restrict attention to matrix clause forms.

(4) waabm-aa-siiw-angi-dwaa-wenh
     see-3.OBJ-NEG-1.PL-3.PL-DUB

     'Perhaps we (excl.) don't see them'

4.1.1 Long-Distance Dependencies

As mentioned in the previous section, number suffixes occur in different slots than the affixes for realizing person information. This is most clearly seen in how each person prefix subcategorizes for distinct sets of number suffixes. For instance, the first person prefix *n-* in (3a) is compatible with *-mnaa* '1.PL', but not with the suffix *-waa* '2.PL' seen in (1).

By contrast, the second person prefix *g-* is compatible with both *-mnaa* '1.PL' and *-waa* '2.PL', as seen in (5).[4]

(5) a. g-waabm-aa-mnaa-dgen-ag
         2-see-3.OBJ-1.PL-DUB-3.PL

         'Perhaps we (incl.) see them'

     b. g-waabm-aa-waa-dgen-ag
         2-see-3.OBJ-2.PL-DUB-3.PL

         'Perhaps you folks see them'

Finally, third person prefixes are not compatible with *-mnaa* '1.PL', but are compatible with *-waa* '2.PL'. This is shown in (6).[5]

(6) w-waabm-aa-waa-dgen-an
     3-see-3.OBJ-NEG-2.PL-DUB-3.OBV

     'Perhaps they see him'

These interactions between non-adjacent slots are important to track when developing a finite-state model, since finite state machines standardly have no memory, and thus cannot recall what a previous affix was. Without extensions to augment the power of the grammar, discussed in section 5.3.1, these dependencies can result in very large and difficult to maintain machines.

---

[4]As the examples in this section show, glosses for these number suffixes are somewhat imprecise, as their distribution indicates that their meaning is closer to "plural not including first person" (*-waa*) or "plural including first person" (*-mnaa*).

[5]The attentive reader may notice that the final suffix in (6) is *-an* '3.OBV'. This suffix marks obviation, which is required when two animate third persons are in the same clause. Functionally, obviation serves to allow predications with two third person participants to be expressed despite a general ban on arguments with the same person values.

4.2 Odawa Phonology

Algonquian languages commonly have uncontroversial phonology, with small phoneme inventories, simple syllable structure and few paradigmatic alternations. Much of Odawa phonology is no different, with many processes centering around adjusting consonant clusters or vowel hiatus in typologically unsurprising ways. For instance, the animate plural morpheme *-ag*, as in *daabaan-ag* 'cars', loses its vowel when preceded by a long vowel, as seen in *aamoo-g* 'bees'.

Odawa phonology recently became substantially more intricate. In the early part of the twentieth century, unstressed vowels became radically reduced or deleted (Bloomfield 1957:5). Since stress was assigned by left-to-right iambs, and person prefixes were incorporated into the phonological word, this resulted in paradigmatic alternations like those in (7):

(7) 'shoe'   'my shoe'
     makizin   ni-makizin   UR
     (makí)(zín)   (nimá)(kizín)   Stress
     (m_kí)(zín)   (n_má)(k_zín)   Deletion
     mkizin   nmakzin   SR

The innovation of the unstressed vowel deletion process has triggered an ongoing period of phonological changes, most saliently including the rise of novel prefix allomorphs and a decline in the use of stem-internal alternations (Rhodes 1985b, Bowers 2015:Ch 5). For instance, while *n-makzin* 'my shoe' is still recognized as a legal form of 'shoe', speakers also productively use *ndoo-mkizin* 'my shoe' (Rhodes 1985a). Indeed, person prefixes now appear in a variety of forms that are used interchangeably. In addition to *n-* and *ndoo-* for first person, we also find *nda-* and *ndi-*. Parallel allomorphy is seen for second person and third person prefixes, see Valentine (2001:62) and Bowers (2015:ch 5) for descriptions of how these prefixes arose.

There appear to be other changes as well, since the paradigms elicited from a native speaker of the language by Valentine (2001) often include some forms that cannot be derived by the unstressed vowel deletion process from the hypothesized underlying representations. The examples in (8) illustrate some of the forms that differ from their expected surface values, given Valentine's URs (Valentine 2001:233, 259).

(8)   a. 'you folks arrive'
          gi-dagoshin-am   UR
          (gidá)(goshí)(nám)   Stress
          (g_dá)(g_shí)(nám)   Deletion
          gdagshinam   Expected
          gdagoshnam   Listed

      b. 'they don't taste good'
          minopogod-sin-oon   UR
          (minó)(pogód)(sinóon) Stress
          (m_nó)(p_gód)(s_nóon) Deletion
          mnopgosnoon   ds→s
          mnopgosnoon   Expected
          mnopgsnoon   Listed

The full scope of these changes is currently being investigated. For the time being, our model implements the prefix changes and paradigm leveling innovations, but still enforces unstressed vowel deletion as if no exceptions had arisen.

5   Odawa Model

5.1   Design considerations

Our finite state model of Odawa has been written in *lexc*, a widely used programming language for writing finite state machines, which is recognized by the *xfst*, *hfst* and *foma* compilers (Beesley and Karttunen 2003, Lindén et al 2011, Huldén 2009). Additional processing of the output of the morphological module is carried out with *xfst* scripts. Our source code may be accessed at `https://victorio.uit.no/langtech/trunk/langs/otw/src/`.

Finite state machines allow morphological structure to be encoded in a variety of ways. As stated in section 3, a natural representation of concatenative morphology maps morpheme slots to states, and morphemes to the labels of arcs between the states. This is not, however, the only possible representation. Developers may choose to treat sequences of affixes, or even whole words, as unanalyzed wholes (often referred to as 'chunking'). Such an approach may be particularly useful if combinations of morphemes have non-compositional semantics, if segmentation of morphemes is difficult, or if pre-existing resources (like a database) already treat morphology in this way.

Another modeling decision concerns whether one deals with morphophonological alternations at stem-affix junctures by dividing stems into subtypes which are each associated with their own inflectional affix sets that can simply be glued onto the stem, or whether one models such morphophonological alternations using using context-based rewrite rules (roughly of the SPE type), or some combination of these approaches. In our case, we have chosen to model such morphophonological alternations entirely with rewrite rules, thus requiring no stem subtypes but the marking some orthographemes at the stem-suffix juncture with special characters to control the triggering of these rules.

Furthermore, morphosyntactic features need not perfectly mirror the target language. This is especially relevant in languages like Odawa where notionally related features like person and number are realized in possibly multiple disjoint locations, or if the morphological realization of a category like subject or object agreement varies between paradigm types.[6] In such cases, it can be convenient for non-specialist use of the parser, as well as for integration with other software applications, to depart from a close mapping between the target language and the model. See section 5.3.2 for further discussion.

In the case of Odawa, the concatenative, compositional nature of the morphology lends itself to a splitting approach, though a brute-force listing of entire suffix sequences may be attractive to avoid having to deal with the potentially disjoint multiple exponents of e.g. person/number features (cf. Arppe et al., fc). Splitting the morphemes has resulted in a concise and general description, which allows our model to generate inflected forms even if the cell of the paradigm was not enumerated in our source material.

Furthermore, Rand Valentine (p.c.) indicates that Ojibwe dialects often differ not in entire suffix chunks, but in the use of specific suffixes. Avoiding a redundant brute-force listing of suffix sequences thus positions our model to be easily extended to other dialects of Ojibwe, as the individual morpheme changes can be easily identified and carried out.

5.2   Phonology Module

As indicated in section 4.2, the model needs a phonological module to map the representation /gi-makakw-waa-bany-an/ 'your folks' former boxes' (Figure 2) to the actually observed

---

[6]This is the case in Odawa, where subject and object agreement occur in different morphological slots for verbs in matrix or embedded clauses.

4

gmakkowaabniin (example 1). We use a cascade of finite state transducers that are formally identical to *SPE*-style phonological rewrite rules (Chomsky and Halle 1968). This phonological module is composed with the morphological model, so that the morphological strings are modified by the phonology until they match surface forms of the language.

5.3 Morphological Module

The morphological module follows the slot structure of the language quite closely. That is, as each morpheme is encountered, a morphological feature is emitted. For instance, the section of the machine that handles example (1) corresponds to Figure (2). Finally, 14,237 lexical entries, drawn from Corbiere and Valentine (2016), make up the lexical content of our model.

5.3.1 Long Distance Modelling

Section 4.1.1 illustrated some of the long-distance dependencies that occur in Odawa. Recall that these relationships can make a standard finite state machine quite large and cumbersome to maintain and develop. The machine can be substantially compressed, at some cost in parsing speed, by introducing limited memory into the model with the flag diacritic extensions in *lexc*. When a morpheme m that interacts non-locally with another morpheme n is encountered, this information is stored in memory. When morpheme n is encountered, the information is retrieved, and if m is compatible with n, the parse continues.

To see this, consider Figure 3, which diagrams the person-number interaction for noun possession. In the figure, stored information is signaled with a flag diacritic of the form *!P.Per.X*, or 'positively set the person feature to X', while accessed information is signaled with *!D.Per.X*, or 'deny if the person feature is X'. Hence, if the first person prefix *ni-* is read, the machine will rule out following it with *-waa* '2.PL', which is incompatible with the first person feature.

5.3.2 Unifying Person and Number

As discussed in section 4.1.1, person and number information are not realized in the same, or even adjacent, slots in Odawa. The separation of person and number information is most extreme in transitive verbs with animate objects, where person and number of both subject and object are discontinuous. This can be seen in (3a), reproduced here with first person/number affixes bolded and third person/number affixes underlined, as in ***n**-waabm-<u>aa</u>-swaa-**mnaa**-dgen-<u>ag</u>* 'perhaps we don't see them'.

The separation of person and number can be inconvenient for non-specialist use of the analyzer, since it is customary to refer to person-number combinations as atomic entities (e.g. first person plural form), or impractical in its integration with other software applications, which may need to know only the set of morphological features, in some standard form and order, expressed by a word-form, instead of its exact morphological break-down. To address this, we have produced a second version of our model that translates the low-level analyses from the core model into a form with a standardized set of morphological features presented in a canonical order.

5.4 Model Behavior Examples

To summarize, in effect we have created two models, a basic one that provides a what-you-see-is-what-you-get parse of the morphology, and another that interprets the basic parse into a more condensed form. Both versions of our model carry out the full set of phonological mappings, including the vowel deletion process mentioned above. Concretely, this means that our models return the indicated analyses for the examples in (9), where the first analysis is the basic analysis and the second is the abstracted one.[7]

(9) a. bgizo
      swim-3
      swim-3.SG

      'He swims'

   b. bgiz-wi-bn-iig
      swim-3-PRF-3.PL
      swim-PRF-3.PL

      'They have swum'

   c. n-bagiz
      1-swim
      swim-1.SG

      'I swim'

   d. n-bagzo-mnaa-ba
      1-swim-1.PL-PRF
      swim-PRF-1.PL

      'We (excl.) have swum'

---

[7]Strictly speaking, our models return a lemma, rather than an English translation. Also, the full translated analyses include overt specification of default, unmarked features, like +Pos for verbs with positive polarity. These are suppressed here for brevity

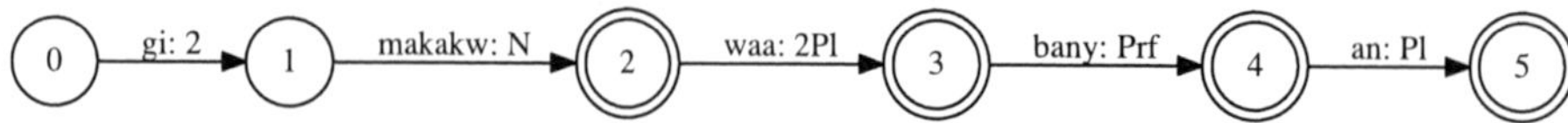

Figure 2: Finite state machine corresponding to path in Odawa model that recognizes *gmakkowaabniin* 'your folks' former boxes'. Further phonological processing allows the morpheme sequence in the model to match the actually attested form.

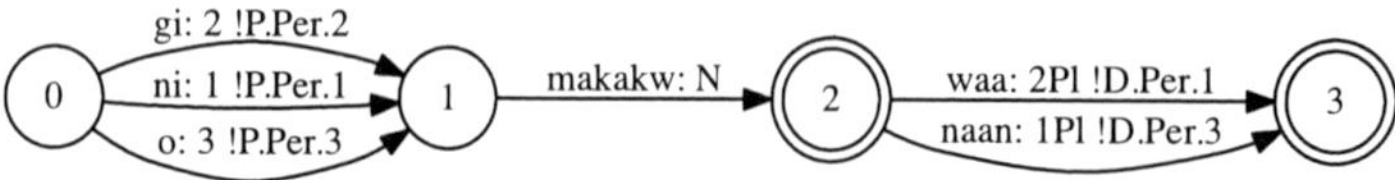

Figure 3: Finite state machine with memory to enforce co-occurrence restrictions between prefixes and suffixes.

As can be seen in (9), subject information appears string-finally in parses produced by the more abstract model. The only exception to this is in transitive verbs, which inflect for person and number of both subjects and objects. In this case, object information occurs string-finally and is marked with an explicit object marker. This is exemplified in (10), which reproduces (3a).

(10) n-waabm-aa-swaa-mnaa-dgen-ag
      1-see-3.OBJ-NEG-1.PL-DUB-3.PL
      see-NEG-DUB-1.PL-3.PL.OBJ

'Perhaps we (excl.) don't see them'

Note also that Algonquian languages are characterized by an imperfect correspondence between morphological slots and subject-object agreement. That is, while (10) shows agreement with a first person plural exclusive subject with *ni-…-mnaa* '1-…-1.PL', these same morphemes index object features in (11).

(11) n-waabm-ig-sii-mnaa-dgen-ag
      1-see-3.SUB.PRE=OBJ-NEG-1.PL-DUB-3.PL
      see-NEG-DUB-3.PL-1.PL.OBJ

'Perhaps they don't see us (excl.)'

Our translation module manages the distinction between (10) and (11) by identifying which morpheme occurs in the post-root slot (called a 'theme-sign' in the Algonquianist tradition). Hence, in our examples, if the suffix is *-aa*, then the object is third person and the subject is indexed by the prefix, while if it is */-igo/*, the subject is third person and the object is indexed by the prefix.[8] Such an approach allows our model to avoid global computations of the alignment of person hierarchies and grammatical role hierarchies commonly discussed in the descriptive literature (e.g. Valentine 2001:267-272).

5.5 Performance

We tested our core model against a small corpus (7,578 tokens, 2,685 types) of written Odawa. Our corpus consists of narratives and sentences collected in 1937 by Leonard Bloomfield (1957), less 45 unassimilated English loan types. This collection of texts is a somewhat atypical testing ground for language model development. First, Valentine (2001), the description which our model is based on, draws heavily from the collection, making it

---

[8]For the curious reader, the unabridged output for (10) appears below for the basic and translated versions, respectively:

```
1+waabmaa+VTA+ThmDir+Neg+1+Pl+Dub+3+Pl
waabmaa+VTA+Ind+Neg+Dub+1Pl+3PlO
```

For (11) the model outputs are:

```
1+waabmaa+VTA+ThmInv+Neg+1+Pl+Dub+3+Pl
waabmaa+VTA+Ind+Neg+Dub+3Pl+1PlO
```

In both versions '+VTA' is a common Algonquianist abbreviation for transitive verb with an animate object, in the basic model '+ThmDir' and '+ThmInv' are notations for third person object agreement and third person subject agreement, respectively (abbreviating Algonquianist 'direct theme' and 'inverse theme'). In the translated tags '+Ind' signals that the verb is a matrix clause form (Algonquianist 'independent order').

impossible to truly withhold data for use in testing. Furthermore, though Valentine (2001) draws many examples from the text collection, Andrew Medler, Bloomfield's consultant, spoke a dialect that differs slightly from the phonology of modern Odawa described in Valentine (2001). Finally, while the spelling system in the texts has been updated, no attempt was made to correct subphonemic effects in Bloomfield's transcription.

With small changes to compensate for deviations of Medler's speech from the modern dialects described by Valentine (2001), the core model recognized 84% of types in our corpus. To date, our corpus has no hand-verified analyses, making it impossible to provide precision or recall statistics.

A preliminary survey of errors indicated that the errors are distributed as shown in (12). Errors were identified as 'lexical' if a lexical item needed to be added or modified for successful parsing, 'morphological' if the error was a result of a missing morphological process, 'phonological' if a phonological rule had misapplied or was absent, 'orthographical' if the error resulted from an orthographic convention (these were overwhelmingly the misuse of apostrophes or the omission of interconsonantal *n*), 'dialectal' if the error resulted from dialect differences, and 'other' if the above categories did not apply.

(12)

Type	% of Errors
orthography	30%
morphology	28%
lexicon	20%
phonology	13%
dialect	5%
other	2%

Our core model parsed the full 7,578 word corpus in an average of 0.653 seconds over 15 runs on an Intel core i7@2.9 GHz processor, which equals a parsing speed of 11,605 words per second.

6 Applications

Morphological parsers, while useful for linguists, enable the creation of many downstream applications that have usefulness for a much broader audience. In our experience, one of the greatest benefits is found by being able to augment an electronic dictionary with the parser, creating an "intelligent" dictionary (Johnson et al. 2013). It has long been noted that, for languages with rich inflectional morphology, a morphologically non-aware dictionary can be extremely cumbersome to use, especially for speakers, learners and others lacking many years of linguistic training.

With a morphological parser, however, users may input any inflected form of a word, and be redirected to the appropriate lemma (cf. `http://www.nishnaabemwin.atlas-ling.ca`). While the user still may need to grapple with understanding some amount of linguistic terminology in order to fully benefit from the parse (e.g. identifying a particular form as the '2nd person plural dubitative negative' is still less than completely helpful for many users), at least they will be directed to the correct lexical entry, and so will be able to retrieve the appropriate lexical content of the word, even if its grammatical specifications are still somewhat opaque.

Moreover, even the grammatical information in the parse can itself be presented in a more user-friendly form. The same '2nd person plural dubitative negative' form could equally well be presented as the 'you folks perhaps do not X' form. Thus, although the inner workings of the electronic dictionary and parser remain highly technical, the view presented to the user can be made much more welcoming.

Furthermore, the morphological parser can also be used in reverse to generate individual word-forms expressing some desired combination of morphological features. Naturally, this can be scaled up to present collections of inflected forms (e.g. core word-forms or the full inflectional paradigm).

Morphological parsers can also facilitate the use and production of texts (cf. `http://altlab.ualberta.ca/korp/`). In the Odawa communities we work with, there is high demand from students for lemmatization of texts. The linking of an inflected word to the lemma in an electronic dictionary uses the same mechanism as lemmatization of texts, making this operation straightforward (`http://altlab.ualberta.ca/kidwinan/`). If the text is in an electronic format, the parser can even provide an on-the-fly analysis of the morphology of a word.

The benefits of an application of this sort are manifold. In particular, it allows learners (and newly-literate speakers) the chance to explore a wide range of texts, challenging their reading abilities and discovering new words on their own. This is especially valuable in languages which lack graded readers, and where people may be motivated to engage with texts that are above their proficiency levels in order to extract culturally-relevant information contained within. While the on-the-fly lemmatization is no substitute for a fully-annotated interlinear gloss, it is still a powerful aid in the development of written comprehension, which itself may increase the demand for more and better texts to be produced in the language.

Furthermore, parsers define a set of legal words, and therefore underlie important tools like spell-checkers and grammar checkers. Such tools can be helpful for literacy programs and speed the creation and proofing of high-quality texts in the language. Where communities are attempting to promulgate a particular written form of the language as standard, such tools can help in the codification and enforcement of those standards.

It is a short leap from the applications described above to classroom applications as well. Foremost among these are intelligent computer-aided language learning (or I-CALL) applications (Antonsen et al. 2013). The combination of a lexicon, a morphological parser and some simple grammatical rules can allow for the creation of an essentially infinite number of language drills of various types.

Because of the morphological knowledge that the parser contains, it is possible to give students feedback on their responses that goes well beyond "right" and "wrong". For example, an I-CALL application can recognize that although the drill is calling for the first person plural form of the verb to be provided, the student has instead offered the second person singular form. The application could then provide that feedback to the student, letting them know that although the form they gave was incorrect, it was in fact a valid form in the language.

In the longer term, the application can keep track of the students' responses, allowing the developers to analyze the patterns of correct and incorrect answers. This provides invaluable information for curriculum developers as they field-test new courses. This is especially important for developers working with endangered languages, where there is typically little to no pedagogical tradition to follow. Being able to apply quantitative measures to questions such as "Is it better to teach declarative forms before imperative forms, or the other way around?" has great potential for improving the efficacy of language teaching programs. Given the vital role that such programs play in the long-term resurgence of endangered languages, the potential benefits of these applications should not be discounted.

7 Conclusion

The ALT-lab group at the University of Alberta is developing language technology for First Nations languages. Our most recent project is a morphological parser of the Odawa dialect of Ojibwe, which is currently in an advanced beta stage. This parser comes in two versions, one which closely follows the morphology of the language, and another which interprets and reorganizes the morphology into a more user-friendly format. The development of a parser opens the door to exciting new research and opportunities for community applications.

References

Antonsen, L., T. Trosterud, and H. Uibo (2013). Generating modular grammar exercises with finite-state transducers. In *Proceedings of the second workshop on NLP for computer-assisted language learning at NODALIDA 2013. NEALT Proceedings Series 17 / Linkping Electronic Conference Proceedings 86*, pp. 2738.

Arppe, A., C. Harvey, M.-O. Junker, and J. R. Valentine (fc.). Algonquian verb paradigms. a case for systematicity and consistency. In *Algonquian Conference 47*.

Baraga, F. (1878a). *A Dictionary of the Otchipwe Language: Explained in English* (Second ed.). Beauchemin and Valois.

Baraga, F. (1878b). *A Theoretical and Practical Grammar of the Otchipwe Language* (Second ed.). Beauchemin and Valois.

Beesley, K. R. and L. Karttunen (2003). *Finite State Morphology*. CSLI Publications.

Bloomfield, L. (1957). *Eastern Ojibwa: Grammatical Sketch, Texts and Word List*. Ann Arbor: University of Michigan Press.

Bowers, D. (2015). *A System for Morphophonological Learning and its Consequences for Language Change*. Ph. D. thesis, UCLA.

Brittain, J. (1999). A reanalysis of transitive animate theme signs as object agreement: Evidence from western naskapi. In *Papers of the 30th Algonquian Conference*.

Chomsky, N. and M. Halle (1968). *The Sound Pattern of English*. Harper and Row.

Corbiere, M. A. and J. R. Valentine (2016). Nishnaabemwin: Odawa and Eastern Ojibwe online dictionary.

Cuoq, J. A. (1886). *Lexique de la langue Algonquine*. J Chapleau et fils.

Golla, V. (2007). North America. In *Encyclopedia of the World's Endangered Languages*. Routledge.

Huldén, M. (2009). Foma: A finite state toolkit and library. In *Proceedings of the 12th Conference of the European Chapter of the Association for Computational Linguistics*, pp. 29–32.

Johnson, C. D. (1972). *Formal Aspects of Phonological Description*. Mouton.

Johnson, R., L. Antonsen, and T. Trosterud (2013). Using finite state transducers for making efficient reading comprehension dictionaries. In S. Oepen, K. Hagen, and J. B. Johannessen (Eds.), *Proceedings of the 19th Nordic Conference of Computational Linguistics (NODALIDA 2013). NEALT Proceedings Series 16*, pp. 59–71.

Jurafsky, D. and J. Martin (2000). *Speech and Language Processing: An Introduction to Natural Language Processing, Computational Linguistics, and Speech Recognition*. Prentice-Hall.

Kaplan, R. M. and M. Kay (1994). Regular models of phonological rule systems. *Computational Linguistics 20*, 331–378.

Koskenniemi, K. (1983). *Two-Level Morphology: A General Computational Model for Word-Form Recognition and Production*. University of Helsinki.

Lindén, K., E. Axelson, S. Hardwick, M. Silfverberg, and T. Pirinen (2011). Hfst: Framework for compiling and applying morphologies. In *Proceedings of the Second International Workshop on Systems and Frameworks for Computational Morphology*, pp. 67–85.

McGinnis, M. (1999). Is there syntactic inversion in Ojibwa? In L. Bar-el, R. Dechaine, and C. Reinholtz (Eds.), *Papers from the Workshop on Structure & Constituency in Native American Languages*, Volume MIT Occasional Papers in Linguistics 17, pp. 101–118.

Nichols, J. D. (1980). *Ojibwe Morphology*. Ph. D. thesis, Harvard.

Piggott, G. L. and J. Kaye (1973). Odawa language project: Second report. Technical report, University of Toronto.

Piggott, G. L., J. Kaye, and K. Tokaichi (1971). Odawa language project: First report. Technical report, University of Toronto.

Rhodes, R. (1985a). *Eastern Ojibwa-Chippewa-Ottawa Dictionary*. Mouton.

Rhodes, R. (1985b). Lexicography and Ojibwa Vowel Deletion. *The Canadian Journal of Linguistics 30*(4), 453–471.

Snoek, C., D. Thunder, K. Lõo, A. Arppe, J. Lachler, S. Moshagen, and T. Trosterud (2014). Modeling the noun morphology of Plains Cree. In *Proceedings of the 52nd Annual Meeting of the Association for Computational Linguistics*.

Trosterud, T. (2005). Grammatically based language technology for minority languages. In *Lesser-Known Languages of South Asia: Status and Policies, Case Studies and Applications of Information Technology*, pp. 293–316. Mouton de Gruyter.

Valentine, J. R. (2001). *Nishnaabemwin Reference Grammar*. Toronto: University of Toronto Press, Inc.

Creating lexical resources for polysynthetic languages—the case of Arapaho

Ghazaleh Kazeminejad and **Andrew Cowell** and **Mans Hulden**
Department of Linguistics
University of Colorado
{ghazaleh.kazeminejad,james.cowell,mans.hulden}@colorado.edu

Abstract

This paper discusses the challenges in creating pedagogical and research resources for the Arapaho language. Because of the complex morphology of this language, printed resources cannot provide the typical useful functions that they can for many other languages. We discuss the challenges faced by most learners and researchers working with polysynthetic languages, of which Arapaho is an excellent example, as well as some currently implemented solutions in creating computer resources for this language, including a lexical database, a morphological parser, and a concordancer. The construction of the finite-state morphological parser which many downstream tasks rely on will be discussed in some detail.

1 Introduction

Of the approximately 6,000 languages spoken in the world today, at least half are critically endangered, and the death of a language often corresponds to the death of the culture of the speakers of that language (Minett and Wang, 2008). One of the strategies to preserve this heritage to some extent is documenting such languages through linguistic fieldwork. However, revitalization of an endangered language does not occur solely by documenting it in a book. What is required is sufficient motivation and practical means for the descendants of these cultures that help them in learning and using the language, which automatically leads to revitalization of that language.

Arapaho (ISO 639-3:arp) is one of the critically endangered languages in the Algonquian family (Cowell and Moss Sr., 2008; Lewis et al., 2009). Like all languages in the family, it is both polysynthetic and agglutinating. The learners and speak-

ers of the language are disproportionately disadvantaged by limiting themselves to printed media in comparison with more isolating languages such as the Indo-European ones. On the other hand, considering properties of this language which will be explained in section 2.1 below, electronic resources are indispensable for providing useful dictionaries and lexicons.

In the current project, the focus has been on the lexicon and morphology of Arapaho and developing computational tools mainly to support pedagogical purposes. Using the documented grammar (Cowell and Moss Sr., 2008) and the collected corpus of Arapaho, we have constructed an online lexical database (containing audio files), a morphological parser, and a concordancer implemented in the dictionary.

Section 2.1 briefly describes the current situation of the Arapaho language, in addition to some of its prominent phonological features, along with its verbal system which is the current focus of the parser, that being the most complex part of the morphology. Section 2.2 explains the necessity of creating such online resources rather than relying on traditional printed ones. Section 3 describes the design issues and technical details of each of the developed resources and tools, and section 4 discusses the reasons behind the decisions to develop such tools for a language like Arapaho.

2 Background

2.1 Arapaho

Arapaho is an Algonquian language currently spoken in two dialects: Northern Arapaho which has less than 200 native speakers all in their late fifties in the Wind River Indian Reservation in Wyoming, and Southern Arapaho which is spoken by only a handful of people all near eighty or older in western Oklahoma (Cowell and Moss Sr., 2008). After World War II, children began to be raised speaking

Proceedings of the 2nd Workshop on the Use of Computational Methods in the Study of Endangered Languages, pages 10–18,
Honolulu, Hawai‘i, USA, March 6–7, 2017. ©2017 Association for Computational Linguistics

English rather than Arapaho. However, the Northern Arapaho have attempted to maintain their language through documentation (both written and taped) and pedagogical efforts (producing extensive curricular materials). The standard orthography for Arapaho was developed in the late 1970s.

In general, the Northern Arapaho have a positive attitude toward the language, and the tribal government spends money on preservation efforts. A large transcribed and annotated spoken corpus has been created, parts of which are available in the Endangered Languages Archive.[1] Many young people take classes and show interest in the language. However, there are various economic and pedagogical limitations, and also the learners tend to not allot sufficient time to learn the language effectively. This work has largely relied on on locally produced ad-hoc curriculum and on the Arapaho Language Project website[2].

Arapaho has no fixed word order; pragmatic factors largely determine word order. It's a highly polysynthetic language, which incorporates as much information as possible into complex verbs. Consequently, many Arapaho sentences consist only of a verb. Roughly speaking, the following is the order of elements in the verb:

1. PROCLITIC

2. PERSON MARKER PREFIX

3. TENSE/ASPECT/MODE PREVERB

4. LEXICAL PREVERB

5. VERB STEM

6. DIRECTION OF ACTION THEME

7. PERSON/NUMBER SUFFIX

8. MODAL SUFFIX

The proclitics have modal and evidential functions. The person inflections mark first, second, and third person. Preverbs indicate tense and aspect, as well as negation and content questions. The verb stem is itself typically internally complex. The theme occurs with transitive verb stems and indicates the direction of action when multiple arguments are marked on the verb (i.e., who is acting on whom). Singular and plural are marked as well. The term *mode* in Arapaho refers to markers that indicate iterative and subjunctive constructions.

There are four classes of verb stems in Arapaho: transitive verbs with animate objects (TA) or with inanimate objects (TI), for which two arguments are obligatorily marked on the verb inflectionally, and intransitive verbs with animate subjects (AI) or with inanimate subjects (II), for which one argument is marked on the verb inflectionally.

A second key feature of Arapaho inflectional morphology is the existence of four different verbal orders: affirmative order (used primarily in affirmative independent clauses), non-affirmative (used primarily in negative and interrogative independent clauses), conjunct (used primarily in subordinate clauses), and imperative (used in imperative and prohibitive commands). The inflectional morphology used with any given verb stem varies according to the particular verbal order in question.

Expressing nominal arguments is not obligatory in Arapaho as long as the referents are clearly marked on the verb. Thus one could say:[3]

(1) **ne'-nih-'ii'-cesis-oowooceineti-3i'**
that-PAST-when-begin-lower self by rope-3PL
'that's when they started lowering themselves on the rope.'

The underlying polysynthetic verb stem in this expression is **hoowooceineti-**, "lower oneself by rope," and the verb stem itself is internally complex, consisting of **hoow-oocei-n-eti-**, down-rope-TRANSITIVE-REFLEXIVE. Thus, the overall expression has nine morphemes, four in the verb stem, four as prefixes, and one as a suffix. Such an expression is not exceptional, but is in fact a fairly common Arapaho word/sentence.

In addition to its extremely complex verbal morphology, Arapaho feature a rich array of phonological processes as well. These phonological alternations include phenomena such as progressive and regressive vowel harmony with non-parallel effects and distribution, allophonic rules, vowel epenthesis, consonant deletion, vowel reduction, vowel lengthening, and consonant mutation. Arapaho also has a complex pitch accent system, with a related system of vowel syncope. One of the very pervasive morphophonological processes found in Arapaho is an initial change that serves grammat-

---

[1] http://elar.soas.ac.uk/deposit/0194
[2] http://www.colorado.edu/csilw/alp/

[3] The orthography used for Arapaho largely corresponds to the International Phonetic Alphabet equivalents, except the symbols y = /j/, c = /tʃ/, ' = /ʔ/ and 3 = /θ/.

ically to indicate either present ongoing or present perfect in affirmative order and conjunct iterative verbs. In such tense/aspect combinations, the verb stem undergoes an initial change: for verb stems whose first syllable's nucleus is a short vowel, the vowel is lengthened; and for verb stems whose first syllable's nucleus is a long vowel, an infix /en/ or /on/ (depending on vowel harmony) is inserted between the initial consonant and the long vowel.

2.2 Necessity of Creating Computer Resources

It is immediately obvious that using an Arapaho dictionary—attempting to find or look up **hoowooceineti-** in particular—would be an extremely difficult task for anyone without linguistic training, and the audience of these resources would not be an exception, as they are neither linguists, nor Arapaho native speakers. Locating the actual stem among the many prefixes and suffixes requires fairly advanced knowledge of the morphosyntax of the language, and the underlying stem does not appear as such in the surface word form, due to loss of the initial /h/ following a consonant, so a knowledge of morphophonemic changes would also be required to successfully find the stem. These latter changes can be much more variable than simply loss of initial /h/. If we take the stem **ni'eenow-** "like s.o.", we find that surface forms are **nii'eenow-o'** "I like him/her," but **nii'eeneb-e3en** "I like you." The initial vowel is lengthened (due to lack of a preceding prefix), the final consonant mutates from /w/ to /b/ prior to a front vowel, and the final vowel of the stem shifts due to vowel harmony. Working backwards, a user would have to go from **nii'eeneb-** to **ni'eenow-**. In many cases, a stem has a half dozen or more allostems due to these types of changes.

A language such as Arapaho produces severe problems for a producer of print dictionaries. Is one to list all the different allostems, and refer the user back to a single base stem? If so, a base listing of 10,000 verbs (very quickly obtainable for a polysynthetic language) will produce a need for perhaps 50,000+ individual entries, most of them 'empty' cross-references. In addition, for transitive verbs with animate grammatical objects, the number of potential inflections is in the dozens (**-e3en** = 1S/2S, **-e3enee** = 1S/2P, **-o'** = 1S/3S, **-ou'u** = 1S/3P, **-een** = 1P/2S, etc.[4]). Since Ara-

---

[4] 1S/2P: 1SG Agent, 2PL Patient

paho verbs cannot appear without an inflection in most cases, the underlying stem never actually appears in discourse. One must thus list an inflected form for the user to show actual pronunciation. But clearly, dozens of different inflected forms occur for each transitive verb with an animate object, and even intransitive verbs have five different person marking suffixes, plus number suffixes and an exclusive/inclusive distinction with 1P. To top off the problems, when the verbs are used for negations and questions, a different set of markers— primarily prefixes—are used for person and number. Thus, each transitive verb has something approaching 100 common inflections, prior to the addition of any tense, aspect, modal or other prefixes or suffixes. Listing one or two of these may not be much help to a beginning learner.

The Algonquian languages are in this regard similar to several other language families in North America, including Iroquoian, Athabaskan (and the larger Na-Dene phylum) and Inuit-Aleut. The issues raised by Arapaho for dictionary users (as well as for those attempting to examine a textual corpus for a given morpheme or verb stem) are thus highly relevant for many different languages. Similar points to the ones above have been raised in previous basic computational work for morphologically complex and polysynthetic languages (Cox et al., 2016; Gasser, 2011; Hulden and Bischoff, 2008; Rios, 2011; Snoek et al., 2014).

3 Creating Computer Resources for Arapaho

3.1 Morphological Parser

The best first-step solution for many of the typical problems faced by polysynthetic and agglutinating languages such as Arapaho is a morphological parser. Similar efforts has taken place for another Algonquian language, Plains Cree (Snoek et al., 2014). Having developed a finite-state morphological parser for a morphologically complex language, developing a spell checker (or even corrector), a lemmatizer, or e-dictionary tools would be more accessible for any language (Alegria et al., 2009; Pirinen and Hardwick, 2012). This is much more crucial for languages with a heavy use of morphology, such as the Algonquian languages. Since in heavily agglutinating languages one word contains what in more isolating languages is equal to several isolated words (or maybe even a full sentence), access to a morphological analyzer for such languages is indispensable, and furthermore a prerequisite for other NLP tasks such as dependency parsing (Wagner et al., 2016).

We used the *foma* finite-state toolkit (Hulden, 2009) to construct a finite state transducer (FST)—the standard technology for producing morphological analyzers—which is bidirectional and able to simultaneously parse given surface forms and generate all possible forms for a given stem (Beesley and Karttunen, 2003). All the concatenative morphological rules as well as irregularities of the morphology of the language were taken care of using a finite-state lexicon compiler within *foma*, or *lexc*, which is a separate component in the system with a high-level declarative language for streamlining lexicon creation modeled as finite transducers (Beesley and Karttunen, 2003; Karttunen, 1993).

In the next step, the full set of Arapaho morphophonological rules were implemented as a set of morphophonological rewrite rules that perform context-conditioned sound/morpheme changes, so that the generated forms do not merely consist of a number of morphemes put together (the underlying form), but undergo the necessary alternations before the surface forms are generated. These transducers are essentially a series of phonological rewrite rules to move between an input strings (the analysis form, providing the grammatical information encoded within that form) and an output string (a surface form). For this purpose, the FSTs produce intermediate representations which are not visible after all the participating transducers have been combined together by transducer composition. Figure 1 is a schema of how our FST is designed to generate and parse word forms. Combining the lexicon transducer with the individual morphophonological rule transducers through transducer composition produces as output a single monolithic finite state transducer that can be used for both generation and parsing.

For example, **nonoohóbeen** is a surface form in Arapaho. Given to the parser, it is correctly parsed as

```
[VERB][TA][ANIMATE-OBJECT][AFFIRMATIVE]
[PRESENT][IC]noohow[1PL-EXCL-SUBJ][2SG-OBJ]
```

This simply interprets the given surface form as the verb stem **noohow** (*to see someone*) which is a transitive verb with an animate subject ([TA]) in the affirmative order ([AFFIRMATIVE]) order

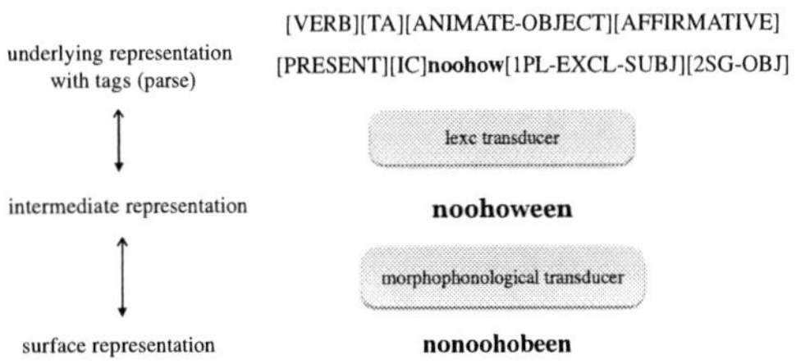

Figure 1: Composition in an FST illustrating the underlying (input) forms and the resulting surface (output) forms after mapping morpheme tags to concrete morphemes and subsequently undergoing morphophonological alternations.

and in present tense ([PRESENT]) (and therefore undergoing an initial change), with exclusive first person plural agent and second person singular patient. Note that the parse also shows an [IC] tag, which stands for Initial Change as described in section 2.1. It could be therefore translated as "We are seeing you.".

In the first step to design the parser, all the verb stems were automatically extracted from our lexical database (c.f. section 3.2), and each was flagged with its stem type (II, AI, TI, or TA) based on its part of speech in the lexical database. Some verbs were considered irregular by the grammar with regards to their inflectional markings. These were marked as irregular in a pre-processing step.

To enforce agreement constraints between non-adjacent morphemes, we use the formalism of flag diacritics within the grammar. These allow morpheme—and segments in general—to carry feature-setting and feature-unification operations and enable the FST to remember earlier paths taken, allowing for the grammar writer to enforce compatibility constraints between parts of a word (Beesley and Karttunen, 2003, p. 339).

In the next step, the lexicon compiler (*lexc*) file was designed using the *lexc* formalism to tag each stem with all its possible parses, connecting the input and output levels of the transducer with a colon (:). The part of speech and stem type were extracted from the lexical database in the preprocessing step, and the verbs receive all the possible inflections and we filter out inappropriate combinations using flag diacritics to control co-occurrence. For instance, a negative verb should be blocked from inflecting in anything but the non-affirmative. Or a past tense verb which has been prefixed by the past tense morpheme can not be

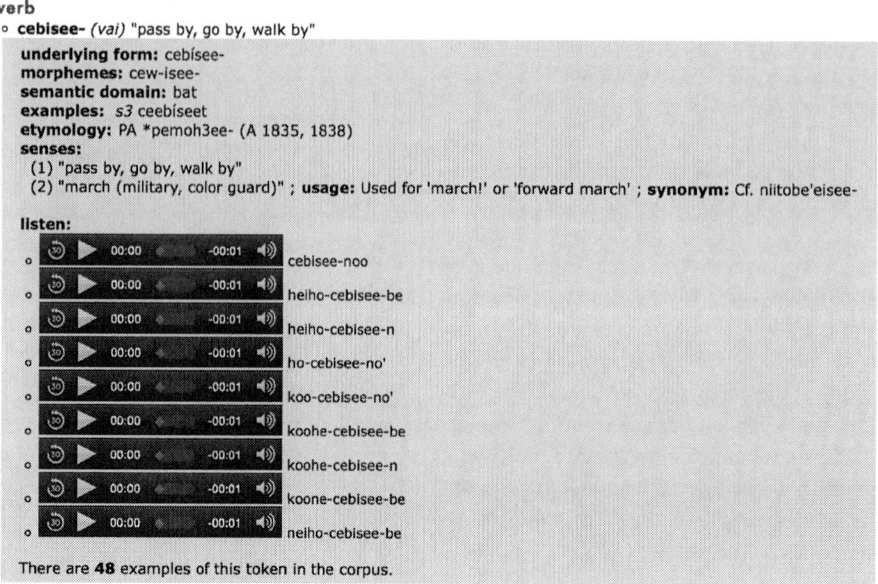

Figure 2: View of the Arapaho Dictionary.

simultaneously inflected for present tense by another morpheme.

One of the most important issues in designing the *lexc* component is the ordering of the morphemes. It may seem trivial to put the morphemes in order since the grammar book has (Cowell and Moss Sr., 2008) explicitly provided the ordering, but this still presents challenges once we get reach the specifics of each element. Person/number markers, for instance, are circumfixes for some verb orders. In order to prevent an AI (i.e. intransitive verb with animate subject) verb stem prefixed with, say, first person singular marker **ne-**, it needs to be flagged specifically with its person-number-stemType so that it is blocked from combining with random person-number suffixes.

In the final step, the *lexc* file is read into the *foma* system where all the morphophonological rewrite rules are applied to the intermediate forms created by the *lexc* file. The flag diacritics are very critical in this step as well, as we use the flag symbols as triggers for certain morphophonological changes. For example, the initial change process that marks present tense affirmative order forms is taken care of in this step. The following rewrite rule (in Xerox formalism) is one of the four rules required to apply this alternation to any word.

```
def IC1 i -> i i , o -> o o , u -> u u ,
e -> e e || "@U.IC.Yes@" \Alphabet*
```

```
"@U.StemInitial.Yes@" \Alphabet*
Consonant _ Consonant ;
```

The above rule indicates the initial change process where the present tense affirmative verbs with a short vowel in the first syllable of the stem would be lengthened. Using the `@U.IC.Yes@` flag in the conditioning environment forces the application of this vowel-lengthening rule only to those intermediate forms which contain this flag, where the vowel of the first syllable (hence `@U.StemInitial.Yes@` preceding it) is short.

The regressive vowel harmony rule (e∼o) applies to only a subset of verbal inflections. To model this, we introduce a blocking condition to the appropriate rewrite rule in form of flag diacritics, so that the rewrite rule for regressive vowel harmony doesn't apply to the person-number-stemType combinations that don't undergo vowel harmony.

The negative marker **ihoow-** poses an exception when no other morpheme precedes it. Normally in Arapaho, when a word is vowel-initial, an /h/ is inserted word-initially. For the negative marker, however, only the initial 'i' drops and the **hoow-** part remains. For instance, we expect the negative 3PL subject for the verb stem **towoti-** to be **ihoow-towoti-no**, but in fact what we get in the surface form is **hoowtowotino**. This exception is also covered using a flag in the *lexc* file that marks negative morphemes, which is later remembered in the *foma* file to be treated appropriately.

As mentioned above, the verb stems themselves may have a complex underlying form. Some verb stems with specific endings (such as *-oti*) in their underlying form show some irregularities in their inflection. Such issues are also accounted for in the lexicon description.

All the rewrite rules are individually defined at first, and then are applied to the intermediate forms defined in the *lexc* file. Using standard transducer composition, the defined rules are combined with the lexicon description, i.e. output of the *lexc* compilation, in the appropriate order. As is often the case when developing such grammars, care needs to be taken to assure that the alternations are applied in the correct order.

We have evaluated the parser against verb tables provided in the Arapaho Language reference grammar (Cowell and Moss Sr., 2008). The current recall of the parser is 98.2%.

3.2 Lexical Database

The lexical database software (which is also implemented online) was designed to include an annotation system where authorized annotators (linguists who know the Arapaho language) annotate words elicited from the existing Arapaho corpus with its relevant linguistic features such as the underlying form, gloss, part of speech, semantic domain, etc. and update the system, followed by the work of an adjudicator who accepts, rejects, or updates the annotation before the change applies to the lexical database.

The database also contains sound files associated with some word. For verbs, this includes different inflections for a verb stem uttered by an Arapaho native speaker. The sound files can be viewed in the publicly accessible online Arapaho-English dictionary[5] that we have developed, where for each verb stem queried, multiple fields of information are displayed in addition to a simple gloss. Figure 2 shows the dictionary entry for a verb stem, which contains all the sound files related to this stem along with the transcription of each uttered word in front of the corresponding sound file.

The morphological parser, used in conjunction with both a lexical and text database, solves sev-

eral problems simultaneously for users. First, we have automatically generated all possible allostems of each verb using the morphological parser (they are fully predictable), and written these into a subfield in our lexical database for /allostem. For example **hiine'etii-** 'to live' has allostems **iine'etii-**, **'iine'etii-** and **heniine'etii-**. Each allostem is linked to a parent stem. We can then direct that any lexical query to the database query both the /stem field and the /allostem field in the lexical database. If a user query involves an allostem, then the user is automatically referred (via the search function) to the base stem. Thus the user can enter any possible surface/spoken stem in the query field and find the appropriate base form, without needing to have knowledge of Arapaho morphophonemic processes.

When and if a print dictionary is eventually produced, we would likely use only the base stem as an entry. This arrangement of database fields and subfields prevents the possibility of 50,000 separate entries for 10,000 verbs; or if we choose to actually print all these allostems, it would be trivial to simply include a subheading such as "variant of…" in the gloss field to redirect the user.

3.3 Concordancer

Conversely, a user might want to find examples of a given stem in actual usage. For that purpose, we have developed a concordancer which is implemented inside the dictionary. The users have the option to specify the number of examples desired, and the dictionary will return the relevant sentence examples if the corpus contains them. The Arapaho corpus underlying this concordancer currently contains around 80,000 sentences (with an eventual goal of 100,000 sentences).

Performing lemmatization in Arapaho is not as easy as for isolating languages, and the listed base form of a stem is often not the most common alloform of the stem to occur in actual discourse. However, we have designed the concordance query function so that when a user asks for occurrences of the base stem, the search function searches simultaneously for all occurrences of allostems as well. Thus, the concordance reports back all instances of the stem in usage, without the user having to perform searches allostem by allostem. Indeed, the user does not even need to be able to predict or derive the possible allostems. Because the concordancer also reports back the

---

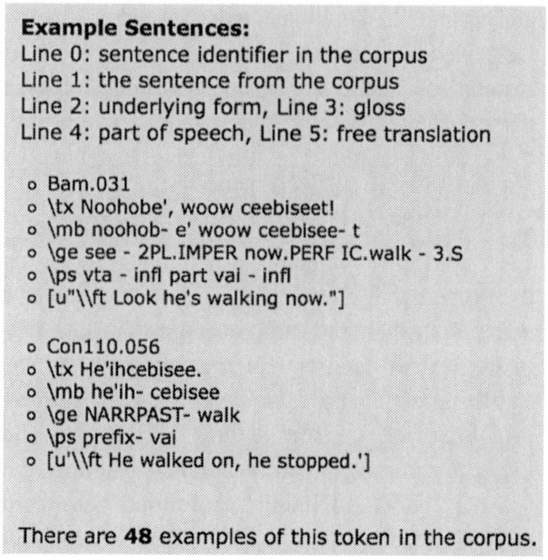

The figure at the top left is a reproduction of a text interface showing example sentences.

Example Sentences:
Line 0: sentence identifier in the corpus
Line 1: the sentence from the corpus
Line 2: underlying form, Line 3: gloss
Line 4: part of speech, Line 5: free translation

```
o Bam.031
o \tx Noohobe', woow ceebiseet!
o \mb noohob- e' woow ceebisee- t
o \ge see - 2PL.IMPER now.PERF IC.walk - 3.S
o \ps vta - infl part vai - infl
o [u"\\ft Look he's walking now."]

o Con110.056
o \tx He'ihcebisee.
o \mb he'ih- cebisee
o \ge NARRPAST- walk
o \ps prefix- vai
o [u'\\ft He walked on, he stopped.']
```

There are **48** examples of this token in the corpus.

Figure 3: Example sentences retrieved through the concordance Function in the Arapaho lexical database interface.

total number of instances of the stem and its allostems in the text database, it constitutes a valuable pedagogical resource, as it allows teachers to determine the relative frequency of all verb stems in the database. Figure 3 shows the example sentences retrieved through the concordance function and displayed in the dictionary, with a guideline on top indicating how to read the lines from the corpus.

4 Discussion

One question that often arises is the following: why have we not designated the most common form of a stem as the base form, since this is normal practice in linguistics with allophones and allomorphs, and one might logically expect that this is the form users would most often search for? The reason we have not done this is because of the polysynthetic nature of Arapaho. In English, we may find a verb 'walk' which can occur in collocations such as 'walk down', 'walk up', 'walk around' and so forth. In Arapaho, all of these occur as different verb stems: **hoowusee-** 'walk down', **noh'ohusee-** 'walk up', **noo'oesee-** 'walk around' (the bound morpheme **-see-** indicates 'walk'). The result of this is that Arapaho has far more verb stems in a given large chunk of text than English does. There are dozens of different 'walk' verb stems for example. A secondary result of this is that a given verb stem will occur much

less commonly across tens of thousands of lines of discourse than is the case in English. While our text corpus of (eventually) 100,000 lines (less than one million words) is not tiny in size, it certainly does not approach the several-billion-word corpora in English that one can access through resources such as The Sketch Engine (Kilgarriff et al., 2004). Thus, for any uncommon Arapaho verb stem, the combination of a relatively small overall text corpus and multiple allostems results in very low frequencies of occurrence per allostem (low single digits in many cases). As a result, chance factors can play a significant role in what is the 'most frequent' allostem. Moreover, once one starts getting **hiine'etii-** as the most common form for 'live', but some other h-initial verb stem turns out to be most common as **'iten-** (from base **hiten-** 'get, take') and another as **iisiiten-** (from base **hiisiiten-** 'grab, catch, seize'), then our morphological parsing ability would collapse. The parser is built to produce all allostems from a uniform base stem, with uniform phonology (all final **b/w** stem alternations take the **w** form as the base form, for example, and list the **b** stem as an allostem). Listing stems under the 'most common form' would destroy this uniformity.

Furthermore, in our design we decided to assign separate entries in the dictionary to some derived forms even though they include a productive morpheme. This happens only for the derived forms that occur in the corpus, and we included them in the dictionary to facilitate glossing. In addition however, productive morphemes such as the causative or benefactive morphemes sometimes produce derived forms with idiosyncratic meaning. For instance, combining **hiicoo-** 'smoke' with the causative suffix **-h** does not give a prototypical causative meaning, rather it means giving a cigarette and allowing one to smoke. There is also cognitive evidence from more recent studies (Cowell et al., 2017) suggesting that many of the morphologically complex stems are in fact part of the lexicon rather than the result of syntactic movement phenomena. So we definitely need to list such verbs in separate lexical entries.

Moreover, since our resources are primarily pedagogical and our audience are primarily beginning learners, we need to put a minimum burden on them in designing pedagogical resources. Since identifying and correctly implementing morphemes is a daunting and confusing task for beginning learners (and more so for the learners of a polysynthetic language), including them in the dictionary as far as they occur in the corpus seems to be a reasonable idea and not a redundant task.

In summary, the morphological parser when applied to stems allows us to point the user from allostems to a main stem in the lexical database, and from a main stem to all the allostems in the text database, in a way which requires no linguistic knowledge from the user, at least in terms of morphophonemics. This ability resolves the single most problematic issue with dictionaries of polysynthetic, agglutinating languages. This is also not a functionality available in commonly-used linguistic interlinearizing software such as Toolbox[6] or FLEx[7]. As a second stage of the project, we have also applied the morphological parser to generate all possible inflected forms of each verb. When a user finds a stem in the lexical database, that person can simply request, via a single query, that all inflections of the verb (with morphophonemic changes applied) be generated in a list. The list gives both the inflected form, its linguistic labels/parse, and a gloss ('I am [verb]ing'), for users without linguistic knowledge. Thus all one hundred or so forms of the transitive verbs with animate objects can be produced automatically, in a way impossible in a print dictionary with its space limitations.

The generated inflected surface forms for all verb stems are, in the next step, going to occupy another subfield in the dictionary (say, /inflstem). Thus, a user could enter a query for a word in the search field, and the database will be directed to search all /stem fields, all /allostem fields, and all /inflstem fields for a match. This will make the search function much more powerful, since not only does the average user not have the ability to do morphophonemic analysis, but he or she may often, at least initially, not be able to recognize all inflectional prefixes and suffixes, and thus enter an inflected form into the search field rather than just a stem. This is again the common problem with trying to use a dictionary with a polysynthetic agglutinating language. And again, due to the issue of allostems as well as morphophonemics, common linguistic dictionaries and annotation software have very imperfect functionality.

[6]http://www.sil.org/computing/toolbox/
[7]http://fieldworks.sil.org/flex/

5 Future Work

The next step in this process, which we have not yet implemented, will be to extend the morphological parser so that it generates all possible temporal, aspectual and modal forms of a verb. Currently the analyzer is only able to generate and parse verb forms in the present and past tense, and perfective and present-ongoing aspect. Continuing with our example of **hiine'etii-** 'to live', past tense is **nih'iine'etiinoo** 'I lived', the future tense is **heetniine'etiinoo**, the imperfective aspect is **niine'etiinoo**, and so forth. Since all 100 different inflections of a transitive verb can surface with around a dozen different Tense-Aspect-Mood forms, plus reduplicated forms, plus forms with lexical prefixes, the numbers quickly rise to the thousands or even millions of possible forms for any base verb stem. At this point, we encounter a separate problem (which is not the focus of this paper): that multiple base stems can generate the same surface inflected stem form via a process of random convergence, and a disambiguation component thus becomes necessary. The more powerful the parser, and the farther one moves beyond the stem itself, the more likely this is to become a problem. Although relatively simple statistical methods using weighted automata in the analyzer can be used to reliably filter out improbable analyses, if enough labeled data is given for training such a model. Such a disambiguator has been implemented for Plains Cree in Arppe et al. (2017), and we assume the same model would also be applicable to Arapaho. However, it is undeniable that at this point syntax becomes the fundamental problem, and that not all disambiguation can be performed by analyzing the plausibility of a particular morpheme combination. With the availability of much more labeled data, deep learning methods also become applicable for context-sensitive disambiguation (Shen et al., 2016). This problem in general then becomes a problem of syntactic disambiguation, as in NLP applications for more isolating languages such as English. Unlike English, however, in this case the syntax is internal to a single verbal form, rather than occurring across multiple words, and at this point some equivalent of the English VerbNet system (Schuler, 2005) could be to be used, though it will have to be more like a "StemNet," combined with "Prefix/SuffixNet."

References

Inaki Alegria, Izaskun Etxeberria, Mans Hulden, and Montserrat Maritxalar. 2009. Porting Basque morphological grammars to foma, an open-source tool. In *International Workshop on Finite-State Methods and Natural Language Processing*, pages 105–113. Springer.

Antti Arppe, Katherine Schmirler, Miikka Silfverberg, Mans Hulden, and Arok Wolvengrey. 2017. What are little Cree words made of? Insights from computational modelling of the derivational structure of Plains Cree stems. In *Papers of the 48th Algonquian Conference*.

Kenneth R. Beesley and Lauri Karttunen. 2003. Finite-state morphology: Xerox tools and techniques. *CSLI, Stanford*.

Andrew Cowell and Alonzo Moss Sr. 2008. *The Arapaho Language*. University Press of Colorado.

Andrew Cowell, Gail Ramsberger, and Lise Menn. 2017. Dementia and grammar in a polysynthetic language: An Arapaho case study. *Language*, 93(1).

Christopher Cox, Mans Hulden, Miikka Silfverberg, Jordan Lachler, Sally Rice, Sjur N. Moshagen, Trond Trosterud, and Antti Arppe. 2016. Computational modeling of the verb in Dene languages—the case of Tsuut'ina. In *Dene Languages Conference*.

Michael Gasser. 2011. Computational morphology and the teaching of indigenous languages. In *Indigenous Languages of Latin America—Actas del Primer Simposio sobre Enseñanza de Lenguas Indígenas de América Latina*, pages 52–61.

Mans Hulden and Shannon T. Bischoff. 2008. An experiment in computational parsing of the Navajo verb. *Coyote Papers: Working Papers in Linguistics*.

Mans Hulden. 2009. Foma: a finite-state compiler and library. In *Proceedings of the 12th Conference of the European Chapter of the Association for Computational Linguistics*, pages 29–32. Association for Computational Linguistics.

Lauri Karttunen. 1993. *Finite-state lexicon compiler*. Xerox Corporation. Palo Alto Research Center.

Adam Kilgarriff, Pavel Rychlý, Pavel Smrž, and David Tugwell. 2004. The Sketch Engine. In *Proceedings of the Eleventh EURALEX International Congress*, pages 105–116.

M. Paul Lewis, Gary F. Simons, and Charles D. Fennig. 2009. *Ethnologue: Languages of the world*, volume 16. SIL international Dallas, TX.

James W. Minett and William S-Y. Wang. 2008. Modelling endangered languages: The effects of bilingualism and social structure. *Lingua*, 118(1):19–45.

Tommi A. Pirinen and Sam Hardwick. 2012. Effect of language and error models on efficiency of finite-state spell-checking and correction. In *Proceedings of the 10th International Workshop on Finite State Methods and Natural Language Processing (FSMNLP)*, pages 1–9, Donostia–San Sebastin, July. Association for Computational Linguistics.

Annette Rios. 2011. Spell checking an agglutinative language: Quechua. In *5th Language and Technology Conference: Human Language Technologies as a Challenge for Computer Science and Linguistics*, pages 51–55.

Karin Kipper Schuler. 2005. *VerbNet: A broad-coverage, comprehensive verb lexicon*. Ph.D. thesis, University of Pennsylvania.

Qinlan Shen, Daniel Clothiaux, Emily Tagtow, Patrick Littell, and Chris Dyer. 2016. The role of context in neural morphological disambiguation. In *Proceedings of COLING 2016*, pages 181–191, Osaka, Japan, December.

Conor Snoek, Dorothy Thunder, Kaidi Lõo, Antti Arppe, Jordan Lachler, Sjur Moshagen, and Trond Trosterud. 2014. Modeling the noun morphology of Plains Cree. In *Proceedings of the 2014 Workshop on the Use of Computational Methods in the Study of Endangered Languages*, pages 34–42, Baltimore, Maryland, USA, June. Association for Computational Linguistics.

Irina Wagner, Andrew Cowell, and Jena D. Hwang. 2016. Applying universal dependency to the Arapaho language. In *Proceedings of LAW X—The 10th Linguistic Annotation Workshop*, pages 171–179. Association for Computational Linguistics.

From Small to Big Data:
paper manuscripts to RDF triples of
Australian Indigenous Vocabularies

Nick Thieberger
School of Languages and Linguistics,
University of Melbourne, Parkville,
Vic 3010, Australia
thien@unimelb.edu.au

Conal Tuohy
322 Henson Rd, Salisbury, Queensland
4107, Australia
conal.tuohy@gmail.com

Abstract

This paper discusses a project to encode archival vocabularies of Australian indigenous languages recorded in the early twentieth century and representing at least 40 different languages. We explore the text with novel techniques, based on encoding them in XML with a standard TEI schema. This project allows geographic navigation of the diverse vocabularies. Ontologies for people and place-names will provide further points of entry to the data, and will allow linking to external authority. The structured data has also been converted to RDF to build a linked data set. It will be used to calculate a Levenshtein distance between wordlists.

1 Introduction

Of the several hundred languages spoken in Australia over millennia before European settlement, less than fifty are currently learned by new generations of Aboriginal children. Records of the languages that are no longer spoken everyday are thus extremely valuable, both for those wanting to relearn their own heritage language, and for the broader society who want to know about indigenous knowledge systems. In this paper we discuss current work to encode vocabularies collected by Daisy Bates for a number of indigenous Australian languages, mainly from Western Australia in the early 1900s. These papers have been in the public domain since 1936 and as a collection of manuscripts held in Australian state libraries. We outline the process of creation and naming of the digital images of this paper collection, then show how we have encoded parts of this material, and created novel views based on the encoded formats, including page images with facsimile text. As the project develops we expect to build a model that can be applied to further sections of the collection that are not as well structured as the vocabularies. This work is offered as one way of encoding manuscript collections to provide access to what were otherwise paper artefacts[1].

2 The task

The complex problem of using historical records of Australian languages has benefited from the cooperation of a linguist (NT) with a technology expert (CT). The dataset has been constructed according to the TEI Guidelines[2], to embody both a (partial) facsimile of the original set of typescripts and a structured dataset to be used as a research collection. This material will be open to reuse, in particular providing access for indigenous people in remote areas to vocabularies of their ancestral languages. The model will also be an exemplar of how a text and document-based project, typical of humanities research, can benefit from new methods of encoding for subsequent reuse. For more on the content of the collection see [3].

By processing the wordlists and making them accessible online, we have prepared material that will be of use to indigenous Australians today, as well as creating an open research dataset which may be linked to and from other data. We believe that new digital methods can enrich the metadata and the interpretation of primary records in this collection. There are some 23,000 images on microfilm, and the first task has been to rename all files. Analysis of the texts identified three types of document, the 167 original questionnaires (around 100 pages each), 142 typescript versions of those questionnaires (each made up of varying numbers of pages), and 84 handwritten manu-

---

[1] The current alpha version is at http://bates.org.au/

[2] http://www.tei-c.org/Guidelines/P5/ (Accessed 2016-09-17).

Proceedings of the 2nd Workshop on the Use of Computational Methods in the Study of Endangered Languages, pages 19–23,
Honolulu, Hawai‘i, USA, March 6–7, 2017. ©2017 Association for Computational Linguistics

scripts that could be either questionnaires or additional material.

Any given word in a typescript comes from a predictable location in the associated questionnaire, and so can be assigned an identifier to allow targeted searching. Thus links can be automatically established to display a typescript image page and a questionnaire image page for any target word.

The JPEG files of typescripts were sent to an agency for keyboarding. The XML was subsequently enriched as seen in the snippet in Fig.1.

```
<listPerson>
 <person>
  <persName role="speaker">
   Kulaiji
  </persName>
 </person>
 <person>
  <persName role="speaker">
   Ijala
  </persName>
 </person>
</listPerson>
<listOrg>
 <org>
  <orgName type="tribe">
   Barduwonga
  </orgName>
 </org>
 <org>
  <orgName type="tribe">
   Burdurad,a
  </orgName>
 </org>
</listOrg>
```

Figure 1. Template XML used for keyboarding the vocabularies

This template further references pages in the typescript, thus allowing any term to resolve to the image of its source page. All files are stored in a bitbucket[3] repository allowing us to work on them collaboratively at a distance and to track file versions.

At the end of the first stage of work we are able to visualise the wordlists in various ways, including a geographic map (Fig. 3), a list of all words and their frequencies, and a list of wordlists and the number of items they contain, in addition to being able to search the whole work for first time. Sorting and arranging the words helps in the correction of errors that inevitably

occur in the process of dealing with large numbers of vocabularies and exporting the lists in an RDF format allows us to generate the statistics about frequency of terms, and to identify the coverage of particular lists.

3 Design decisions for encoding the dataset

The scale of the Bates dataset requires outsourced transcription, but it is difficult to outsource the full (lexicographic) semantics, that is, capturing the meaning of added entries and examples. This is even more the case as the documents include a great deal of variation, both in their spellings and in their contents, so it is not necessarily easy to interpret them semantically. We focused the outsourced transcription task on a superficial (typographic) encoding of the documents. The encoding captured the tabular layout (i.e. the text is divided into rows and cells), local revisions (i.e. rows added to the table), and pagination. The right-hand column of these tables, generally containing a comma-separated list of indigenous words, was then marked up by an automated process (an XSLT transformation). To explicitly encode the lexicographic data in the forms, we needed to tag each of the words, classify it as either English or indigenous, and hyperlink each indigenous word or phrase to the English words or phrases to which it corresponds.

Given the size of the encoding task, it was essential to minimise the amount of manual work, and reduce the scope for human error, by automating the markup process as much as possible.

The typing did not include identification of the relationships between the words in the lexicon, recognising that it is preferable to use transcribers to capture source texts with a high level of accuracy, but conceptually at a superficial level, and then to add those semantics later, automatically, or using domain experts. We provided our keyboarders with document layout (i.e. pages and tables), rather than linguistic categories (terms and translations).

As an example of the automatic addition of semantic information, we decided to recover the lexicographic semantics implicit in the text by programmatic means, inserting explicit metadata (markup) in the text to record these inferred semantics. This had the additional advantage that the automated interpretation could be revised and re-run multiple times, and the output checked each time. We see the visualisation of the results

---

[3]   http://bitbucket.org/

that is permitted by this work as contributing to the repeated process of correction of the data.

The tabular layout itself implies a relationship between a prompt term (in the left hand column of the questionnaire), and one or more terms in the right hand column. The right hand column contains one or more terms in an indigenous language, but in addition it may contain other English words, typically in brackets, or separated from the indigenous words by an "=" sign. (e.g. Sister joo'da, nar'anba = elder (57-033T[4])).

```
<row>
   <cell>Snake</cell>
   <cell>
     Burling, jundi (carpet),
     binma, yalun
   </cell>
</row>
```

Figure 2. A sample row of content

The left-hand column of the questionnaire form was pre-printed by Bates, for example, in Fig. 2 the printed word was "Snake". The right hand column was to be filled in with the local language term. In this case the recorder wrote *Burling, jundi (carpet), binma, yalun.* Our aim is to identify which of the words are intended to represent indigenous words, and which (like "carpet") are actually additional English words which specify a refinement of the original term. In this case, the word *jundi* is specifically for "carpet snake", whereas the other words may refer to snakes more generically.

The next step is to pass these XML documents through a series of small transformation programs, each of which makes some interpretation of the text and enhances the XML markup in one way or another. The cumulative effect of the transformations is to produce a final output document in which the English and indigenous words and their lexicographical relationships are marked up explicitly using hyperlinks.

For example, a few steps along in the transformation pipeline the same row will have been enhanced with punctuation characters parsed into <pc> markup:

```
<cell>Snake</cell>
<cell>Burling<pc>,  </pc>
jundi <pc>(</pc>carpet
<pc>)</pc><pc>,</pc> binma
<pc>,</pc> yalun</cell>
```

Once the punctuation characters "(", ")", "=", and ";" are picked out, a subsequent transformation classifies the residual words into different types, based on the surrounding punctuation. The TEI element <seg> (segment) is used to assign a type, which is either item or parenthetical:

```
<seg type="item">
   Burling</seg><pc>,</pc>
<seg type="item">
   jundi</seg> <pc>(</pc>
<seg type="parenthetical">
   carpet</seg><pc>)</pc>
<pc>,</pc>
<seg type="item">binma</seg>
<pc>,</pc>
<seg type="item">yalun</seg>
```

These "lexical" and "grammatical" transformations set the stage for final transformations to make a guess as to what the text actually *means*; which of the words are English and which are indigenous, and how they interrelate:

```
<cell><gloss xml:id="snake"
xml:lang="en">Snake</gloss>
</cell>
<cell>
  <term ref="#snake"
  xml:lang="nys">
    Burling</term>,
  <term ref="#snake-carpet
  #snake" xml:lang="nys">
    jundi</term>
  (<gloss type="narrow"
  xml:id= "snake-carpet"
  xml:lang="en">carpet
  </gloss>),
  <term xml:lang="nys"
  ref="#snake" >binma</term>,
  <term ref="#snake"
  xml:lang="nys">yalun</term>
</cell>
```

Note how the term *jundi* is linked to both the "Snake" and the "(carpet)" glosses, whereas the other terms are linked only to "Snake". Note also that the words "Snake" and "carpet" are both now explicitly identified as English and the language words are identified as being in a particular Australian language.

The intermediate TEI documents (containing automatically-inferred term/gloss markup) will contain errors in many places, due to inconsistency and ambiguity in the source documents.

---

[4] http://bates.org.au/images/57/57-033T.jpg

Those errors became most apparent in the word lists and maps generated in the first phase outputs of the project, as shown in Fig. 3.

4 Markup: automation and "markup by exception"

The transformation of the base XML files is via an XSLT script that parses the lists into distinct words, and inserts the appropriate hyperlinks to relate each indigenous word to the English word(s) to which it corresponds. Some indigenous words have multiple corresponding English words, separated by commas or sometimes semi-colons:

```
Ankle    Kan-ka, jinna
werree, balgu
```

Occasionally, the word "or" is used before the last item in a list:

```
Blood Ngooba or yalgoo
```

Sometimes the right hand column contains additional English language glosses, generally to indicate a narrower or otherwise related term. Most commonly, these additional English glosses were written in parentheses, following the corresponding indigenous word:

```
Kangaroo    Maloo (plains),
margaji (hill)
```

Sometimes an additional English gloss is written before the corresponding indigenous term, and separated with an equals sign (or occasionally a hyphen):

```
Woman, old    Wīdhu; old man
= winja
```

An XSLT script is easily able to handle all these cases, and rapidly produce markup which is semantically correct. However, as the forms were filled out by many different people, inevitably there are some inconsistencies in the text which can lead the XSLT script into error. Sometimes, for instance, the indigenous words are in brackets, rather than the English words. Sometimes the text is written in a style which is just not amenable to parsing with a simple script:

```
Bardari - like a bandicoot,
only with long ears and
nose.
```

```
Bira - also like a bandi-
coot, but short and thick
body, little yellow on back.
```

In these exceptional cases the easiest thing to do is apply some human intelligence and mark up the text by hand.

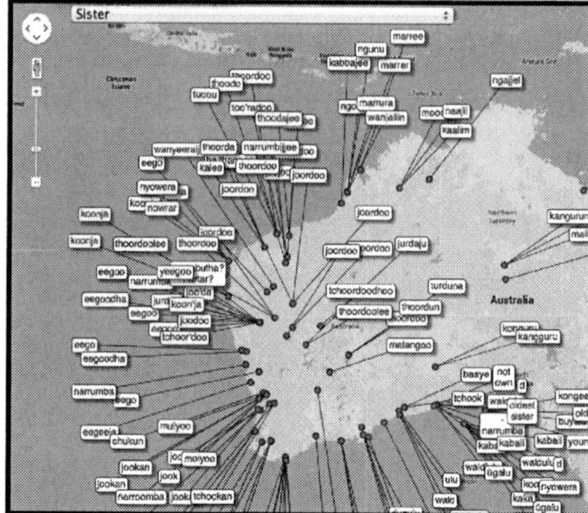

Figure 3 shows the range of equivalents for the word 'sister' mapped geographically

This naturally leads to an iterative data cleaning workflow in which a time-consuming batch process crunches through the documents, gradually enhancing them, performing automated validation checking, and finally generating visualisations for humans to review. We found the data visualisations to be a potent force for quality assurance. It is often very easy to spot interpretive errors made by the automated parser, and that correction can feed back, either as a refinement of the automated process, or as a manual correction of the document markup, leading to a gradual improvement in the data quality.

5 Conversion to Linked Data

The TEI XML contains a great deal of detail about the questionnaires as texts, such as how the word lists were formatted, punctuated, and paginated, and although this is essential in order to be able to read the questionnaires as texts, for proofing, it is also helpful to be able to abstract away from that contingent information and deal only with the vocabularies as linguistic data. For this purpose, once the TEI XML has been automatically enhanced to include the explicit lexicographic semantics, a final XSLT extracts information from each of the TEI documents and re-expresses it as an RDF graph encoded in

RDF/XML, using the SKOS[5] vocabulary for the lexicographical information, and the Basic Geo (WGS84 lat/long)[6] vocabulary for the geospatial location of each vocabulary. The distinct RDF graphs are then merged to form a union graph, by saving them into a SPARQL Graph Store.

Each vocabulary is represented as a SKOS:ConceptScheme, which in turn contains a SKOS:Concept for each distinct concept; either a concept identified by Bates in her original questionnaire, or a concept added during the original interviews. In addition, a special SKOS:ConceptScheme (called "bates") represents the original blank questionnaire, and functions as a hub in the network of concepts. Each concept in the "bates" vocabulary is explicitly linked (as a SKOS:exactMatch) to the corresponding concept in every one of the indigenous vocabularies.

The concepts in the "bates" vocabulary have labels in English, whereas the corresponding concepts in the other vocabularies are labelled with indigenous words. Many of the concepts in the indigenous vocabularies have multiple labels attached, representing the synonyms recorded in the questionnaires.

Once the RDF graphs are loaded into the SPARQL Store, the union graph can be easily queried using SPARQL. We use SPARQL queries to produce a map of each word, histograms of the frequency of vocabularies containing a given concept, and of the varying conceptual coverage of the different vocabularies. We can also extract the indigenous words in a form convenient for further processing, including computing Levenshtein Distance between vocabularies, to support automated clustering of the vocabularies.

6   Next steps

Once all the typescripts have been keyboarded we will be in a position to edit the whole collection for consistency. As noted, each wordlist was compiled by different people, and was then typed under Bates's supervision, so having access to both the manuscript and typescript will enable an edition that captures the content more accurately than is currently the case. In phase two, we will implement a framework that allows these images and text to be presented together, and then ex-

tend the model into other parts of the Bates collection that also includes words and sentences in Aboriginal languages with the potential that we can attract volunteers (crowdsourcing) to work on transcribing and correcting the content. We will also be in a position to generate similarity measures between vocabularies and from them a multidimensional scaling view of the distance between the vocabularies as in [2], and more recently [1].

7   Conclusion

With the work undertaken so far it is clear that the process of encoding has led to a deeper understanding of the target material. It has provided novel visualisations and helped us to appreciate the context of the original material. While the more usual approach to archival lexical material has been to extract lexical items into a relational database or spreadsheet, the data could not be coerced into such a form now without a significant amount of interpretation and loss of contextual information.

It would be a mistake to focus immediately on the lexicographic data embedded in the forms, and neglect other aspects of the forms. We have no access to the original language speakers; for us the questionnaires are themselves the data, and we should therefore record the questionnaires, not just the data "contained in" the questionnaires. Further, by maintaining the links back to the primary records we allow users to situate the encoded material in its source. Premature data reduction to cells in a database risks ignoring useful information. The data modelling task aims to capture the data along with all possible context. The use of TEI, rather than, say, a relational database enables that conceptually openended, exploratory and iterative data modelling.

References

[1] Embleton, Sheila, Dorin Uritescu and Eric S. Wheeler. 2013. Defining dialect regions with interpretations: Advancing the multidimensional scaling approach *Lit Linguist Computing* 28: 1 13-22.

[2] Nash, David. 2002. Historical linguistic geography of south-east Western Australia, pp. 205-30 in *Language in Native Title*, ed. by John Henderson & David Nash. Canberra: AIATSIS Native Title Research Unit, Aboriginal Studies Press.

[3] Thieberger, Nick. fc. Daisy Bates in the digital world. In Peter Austin, Harold Koch, & Jane Simpson (eds) *Language, Land and Story in Australia*. London: EL Publishing.

---

5 Alistair Miles, Sean Bechhofer, eds. 2009. SKOS Simple Knowledge Organization System Reference. https://www.w3.org/TR/skos-reference/
6 Dan Brickley, ed. 2004. Basic Geo (WGS84 lat/long) Vocabulary. https://www.w3.org/2003/01/geo/

Issues in digital text representation, online dissemination, sharing and reuse for African tone languages

Emmanuel Ngué Um
University of Yaoundé I – Cameroon
ngueum@gmail.com

Abstract

In tone languages of Africa, tones may encode meaning either as separate linguistic units or in association with segmental morphemes. In mainstream text representation models, however, the linguistic autonomy of tones is often overridden by the graphical layout of characters. In these models, accents which mark tones cannot be easily parsed for their linguistic information apart from the segments which bear them. This paper suggests a model or representation based on TEI-XML where both tones and segments can be represented as a unique string of characters, therefore making text information easily parsable.

1   Introduction

Language Documentation (LD) and description have generated textual resources for minority tone languages of Africa. With the event of computers, text resources are being created mostly in the form of digital-born texts. But visual layout of texts in these languages follows a variety of representation models, even within the same writing system. Some of the issues at stake are IPA vs Latin characters; omission vs surface representation of tones as accents; surface vs deep representation of tones, one tier vs multiple tier representation of linguistic analysis.

Even when widely shared standards exist, implementation of these standards from one project to another, or from one software to another is not consistent. This raises the issue of which technology is best suited for optimal graphical rendering of the linguistic information encoded through texts in tone languages of Africa. The question to know how to better reach a compromise between end-user-friendly orthographies of previously unwritten languages on the one hand, text-to-human transparency of linguistic information conveyed through texts, and computability of derived text corpora on the other hand is left unanswered.

The objectives for which text corpora are produced also dictate models of text representation. Lehman (2001) suggests that textual resources stemming from LD should be designed in such a way that they "represent the language for those who do not have access to the language itself". In the case of African tone languages, this entails representation of tone sequences as anchored in the melody pattern of speech production. The reason for representing tones in writing is that they form independent prosodic units of meaning which deserve appropriate analytical attention.

Taken from the point of view of a theory of text representation, this approach is undoubtedly more analytic than early missionary orthography models which are devoid of tone markers. However from the point of view of the text layout model and digital processability, tone representation as it has been implemented so far, tend to create fuzzy boundaries and associations between the text structure and the linguistic information. This is so because current models of tone representation in text production have built up from the Latin scripting framework where the linguistic information is encoded in a one-grid string of characters.

Sometimes tone markers represented as accents and associated with letter characters form pre-composed or ad hoc binary or ternary graphical unites. This actually adds an additional and somehow artificial layer of information.

The purpose of this paper is to bring out the limitations of tone representation and analysis as an upper layer of character strings, and to suggest an alternative model based on the TEI-XML markup language. Section 2 will review some theoretical and technical issues involving tones

Proceedings of the 2nd Workshop on the Use of Computational Methods in the Study of Endangered Languages, pages 24–32,
Honolulu, Hawai'i, USA, March 6–7, 2017. ©2017 Association for Computational Linguistics

in African languages, and the implication of a tone model of representation for the linguistic analysis. Section 3 will deal with the limitations of existing models of tone representation with regard to granularity in linguistic analysis, fuzziness in text and linguistic information mapping, and parsability of textual information. In section 4 I will propose a prototypical model for enhanced representation of tone in African tone languages texts. This model is meant to address the limitations pointed out in existing models.

2 Theoretical and technical issues in graphical representation of tones in African languages

2.1 Theoretical issues

When tones are represented in texts, they may either surface as accents on syllable nuclei (1), or as alphabetical labels standing on a separate tier and linking to syllable nuclei by means of association lines (2). In (2), labels 'H' and 'L' respectively stand for 'high' and 'low' tones.

(1) màlép má ńsóbì[1]
    "water is poured"

(2) màlép má ńsóbì
    | | | | | |
    L H   H H H L

In (1), tones may either be interpreted as supra-segments, or as auto-segments. A supra-segmental approach to tone is one which poses tones and their Tone Bearing Units (TBU) as inherently bound linguistic units. In this approach, tones are not separated from or interpreted without their corresponding TBUs. An illustration of a supra-segmental analysis of tones is provided in (3).

(3) mà-lép má ń-sóbì
    CL6-water SM.CL6 PRES-PERF.pour
    "water is poured"

The nasal prefix [n] along with its associated high tone may be interpreted as a unique aspectual marker for the perfective. The same interpretive stance applies to other remaining building blocks, namely: class 6 noun préfix [ma] which

is associated with a low tone[2]; class 6 subject marker [ma] which is associated with a high tone; both roots [lep] and [sobi], where [lep] is assumed to inherently bear a high tone, whereas [sobi] is assumed to bear a sequence of two level tones H-L.

The supra-segmental approach to tone analysis, though still prevailing in some scholarly circles in Africa, is unable to account, for example, for why a word may bear a low tone in some situations, and a high tone in other situations. This is indeed the case with the root [sobi]. When standing alone, the verb *sobi* "to be poured" surfaces with a different tone melody, namely L-L[3], as in (4).

(4) /sòb-ì/ "to be poured"

Only if we consider tone to be an independent linguistic unit from its associated segment, can we consistently account for pitch variation in tone melody across word forms in a text. The strength of auto-segmental phonology (Goldsmith, 1990) lies in the fact that it views tone and it associated syllable as two distinct linguistics units, as in (2). Because at the abstract level of analysis tones exist independently from their TBUs, changes affecting one of the two associated units may not necessarily affect the other, as can be seen in the alternation between [sòbì] and [sóbì].

In spite of its theoretical robustness and validity, auto-segmental phonology has not significantly impacted traditional models of text representation and analysis in tone languages of Africa. Given that linear analysis of textual information relies on the text layout, it follows that much of the linguistic information encoded through texts in African tone languages is sometimes overridden by the constraints and limitations of a one-grid and linear representation of the linguistic information. This does not favor automatic processing of textual information; a situation which is further hampered by technical issues such as character encoding and typesetting technologies.

---

[1] Most examples provided in this paper are taken from Basaa, a Bantu language spoken in the Center and Coastal regions or Cameroon.

[2] In spite of the fact that noun class prefixes are generally represented as toneless morphemes in Bantu languages.

[3] Another possible reading of the tone melody associated with /sòb-ì/ is /L-ø/ where the final syllable nucleus is assumed to be toneless.

2.2 Technical issues in digital text representation of African tone languages

Within both the scholarly community and the speech groups of minority tone languages of Africa, there is currently much emphasis on developing typesetting technologies such as virtual keyboards and extension of Unicode character sets. The focus here is on facilitating end-user creation and editing of texts, and less so on ensuring digital exploration, automatic processing, software-independence, and universal sharing of these texts.

In the first place, surface representation of tones as accents is a thorny issue. This may be a convenient graphical method with regard to human cognitive ability to process visual information, but much less convenient from a computational perspective. This is so for many reasons.

(1) Graphical clustering of tone markers with letters (a, e, n, o, i, etc.) is perceived as a binary unit of writing by humans, but as two separate digital objects by the computer, given that Latin characters and accents bear distinct digital codes[4].

(2) When accented letters such as [é], [è] or [ê] are available as pre-composed characters and therefore assigned unique unicode code points, stability and consistency of character sets is achieved at the expense of parsability of textual information. For example, a search algorithm could be meant to determine the frequency of high tones in a text, as compared to low tones. If high tones are only counted as acute accents, the algorithm would only parse those characters with an acute accent. This would be misleading because in an auto-segmental approach to tone analysis, a contour high-low tone shape must be interpreted as a sequence of independent 'high' + independent 'low'. A workaround solution could be to count contour tones as representing tokens of both high and low tones. However this workaround solution would not hold if, in addition to looking for high tone frequency, the search algorithm also encompassed retrieving specific meaning associated with high tones.

(3) Deciphering of pitch associated with a given accent, whether acute, grave, circumflex or caron by humans does not require neither intrinsic knowledge of the linguistic information encoded by the tone marker or the digital code point associated with it. In (3) for example, acute accent on the syllable [so] in [ńsóbì] signals both high tone and perfective aspect; however, this grammatical knowledge is not a prerequisite for proper pronunciation and semantic interpretation of the root morpheme [sob] by a human. For the computer, however the grammatical information encoded through the high tone on the syllable [so] in [ńsóbì] has to be labelled differently from the lexical information associated with the same syllable in the lexical form of the word in (4). If applied to text-to-machine modeling, it might be necessary to assign persistent digital codes for each tone level. This calls for explicit and unambiguous markup of the linguistic information associated with each single tone in a text, as opposed to merely representing tones as iconic pitch signals on syllables.

(4) Graphical representation of tones as accents does not facilitate linear glossing and markup of tone morphemes in a one-to-one relationship with their corresponding meanings, as is the case with 'ordinary' morphemes made up of 'conventional' Latin character strings.

Efforts to make it possible to parse tones automatically in text resources of African tone languages have been attempted with *TOOLBOX*, one of SIL's fieldwork software for text creation, editing, and analysis. This functionality is achieved thanks to a specific data input method designed by Buseman, as cited in McGill (2009). Buseman's method has been chiefly motivated by the need to overcome the software's understanding of tones as intrinsic parts of the string of characters. Overall, Buseman's method consists in separating tone marking and the corresponding segmental string of characters triggering TBUs, and then glossing them each on their own, as in (5)[5], which I have borrowed from McGill (2009: 244).

```
(5) \tx     dùkwá
    \mb     dukwa  -L      -H
    \ge     go     IMP
    \ft     'go'
```

---

[4] See the most current Unicode character map at: http://www.unicode.org/Public/UCD/latest/charts/CodeCharts.pdf

[5] Data in this example come from Cicipu, a Niger-Congo language spoken in Northwest Nigeria. Backslash is standard markup signaling the Toolbox input field; '\tx' is the transcription field; '\mb' is the morpheme-by-morpheme field; '\ge' is the English gloss field; and '\ft' is the free translation field. Each field stands on a separate tier.

Enhancement and enrichment of Buseman's method has been suggested by McGill (2009) in view of further development of *TOOLBOX* as well as development of new software. Among other suggestions, McGill advocates the implementation of SIL's *TonePars* program (Black 1997) into future software development for corpora creation for endangered languages. "The TonePars program [...] allows for modeling an auto-segmental approach to tone"[6].

It is desirable that further refinement of *Toolbox* and/or its offspring *Fieldwork's Language Explorer (FLEx)* should include auto-segmental modeling of tone. This could be achieved through multiple-tier mapping where both character strings and tone markers could be separately analyzed for the linguistic information they encode. The resulting text file could then be transformed into parsable *XML* files. However, even if such software development could be implemented in *TOOLBOX* or similar linguistic analysis tools, many issues would still be left unresolved.

(1) Text representation and processing of tone languages with *TOOLBOX* is usually biased towards an exclusively scholarly stance, over other possible language usage frameworks, where surface representation of tones might be optional or even unecessary. As a matter of evidence, it should be noted that non-marking of tones in orthography in tone language communities is the norm rather than the exception. An edifying illustration is the case of *Google Translate*, where none of the five African tone languages which are available for online translation[7] (namely Hausa, Igbo, Shona, Xhosa and Yoruba) uses tone marking in their writing system. Plain Latin scripts devoid of tone markers are preferred over the IPA-based writing systems mostly advocated by linguists, which marks tones.

(2) Assuming *TonePars* algorithms are incorporated into *TOOLBOX*, the issue of character encoding is left unresolved. *TonePars* interprets the content value associated with a given tone, whether high or low, on the basis of its graphical shape, namely acute or grave. However, there may exist multiple character input possibilities for representing the same toned-segment graphically. For example <é> (the character <e> bear-

ing and acute accent), may have as possible typesetting inputs:

(a)   The unique pre-composed character **<é>** (*Unicode C1 Controls and Latin-1 Supplement*, code point 00E9);

(b)   **<e>** (*Unicode C0 Controls and Basic Latin*, code point 0065) and acute accent < ´> (*Unicode C1 Controls and Latin-1 Supplement*, code point 00B4);

(c)   **<e>** (*Unicode C0 Controls and Basic Latin*, code point 0065) and acute accent < ´> (*Unicode Spacing Modifier Letters*, code point 02CA);

(d)   **<e>** (*Unicode C0 Controls and Basic Latin*, code point 0065) and acute accent < ´> (*Unicode Combining Diacritical Marks*, code point 0301);

(e)   etc.

In other words, the existence of multiple graphical representations of the same prosodic reality creates the possibility of arbitrary digital encoding of tones in a program such as TOOLBOX. This is definitely not good practice with regards to current standards in data sharing and dissemination as advocated by such data consortia as the Text Encoding Initiative (TEI), the Data Research Alliance (RDA), Component MetaData Infrastructure (CMDI), etc.

(3) As a consequence of the above two issues, text corpora created with tools such as TOOLBOX and FLEx cannot lend themselves appropriately to open data sharing and re-use, in a global text 'industry' where sustainability of data infrastructures rely heavily on interoperability. It should be noted, in addition, that mainstream linguistic analysis methods implemented in these software, namely standard morpheme-by-morpheme glossing of text information, does not provide a scheme for rich metadata input for linguistic information.

3   Limitations of existing models of tone analysis

Coming back to example (3) which is repeated in (6) for convenience, it appears that linguistic information is mapped in a one-to-one correspondence with the text building blocks.

(6)   mà-lép má ń-sóbì
      CL6-water SM.CL6 PRES-PERF.pour
      "water is poured"

---

⁶Weblink: http://www-01.sil.org/silewp/1997/007/silewp1997-007.html, accessed on 14 October 2016.

⁷ As of the date of writing completion of this paper (2017-02-12).

This mode of text representation is common practice in linguistics scholarship, and there exists a set of standards for glossing linguistic information. The Leipzig Glossing Rules are one such standards. "They consist of ten rules for the 'syntax' and 'semantics' of interlinear glosses, and an appendix with a proposed 'lexicon' of abbreviated category labels" (Comrie, Haspelmath & Bickel 2015: 1). Rule 2 of the Leipzig Glossing Rules states that "there must be exactly the same number of hyphens in the example and in the gloss" (Comrie, Haspelmath & Bickel 2015: 2). Rule 4 further stipulates that "when a single object-language element is rendered by several metalanguage elements (words or abbreviations), these are separated by periods" (Comrie, Haspelmath & Bickel 2015: 3). This last rule justifies why 'SM' and 'CL6', then 'PERF' label and the lexical meaning 'pour' are clustered into two binary glosses in (3). This clustering indicates that the two labels making up a binary gloss are encoded by the same morpheme.

Single morphemes which encode more than one meaning are commonplace across the world's languages. What is problematic in clustering for example the 'PERF' label and the lexical meaning of the root 'pour' in (3) and (6) is that, these two meanings are indeed separately encoded by two linguistic units: 'PERF' is encoded by the high tone on the first syllable of the root, while 'pour' (the lexical meaning) is encoded by deep lexical structure of the verb root [sobi]. However, simply graphically mapping a piece of complex linguistic information such as 'PERF.pour' with textually 'unparsed' structural bundle such as [sòbì] without explicit and unambiguous assignment of this information is fuzzy.

Because morpheme-by-morpheme glossing tends to prioritize synchronization of analysis with on-line stretching of text for the sake of grammatical information tracking, only information needed for ad hoc understanding of the grammatical sequenciation of the test is deemed relevant. It is questionable, for example, why tones in African tone languages are only provided with glosses (analytical labels such as 'PERF', 'PRES', etc.) when they appear to trigger variation in the tone shape of a given root as in the [sòbì] ~ [sóbì], or in grammatical morphemes such as the nasal prefix [ń]. To put it in simple terms, there is structural inconsistency in glossing some tones, and not others. After all, if the high tone signals grammatical meaning in situations such as [sóbì], there are good reasons to believe that the low tone which occupies the same position in [sòbì] also signals some form of linguistic information. However, the primitive information associated with this low tone is overridden in standard linguistic glossing. To further demonstrate why glossing every single tone in a text is a pre-requisite to systematic and accurate parsing of the linguistic information associated with tones, lets take this other example (7).

(7) ndʒɔ̀ŋ   ì
CL9.palm.oil.residue SM.CL9
ǹ-sóbì
PRES-PERF.pour
"palm oil residue is poured"

In (7) the nasal prefix in [ǹsóbì] is now associated with a low tone, as opposed to a high tone in (3) and (6). This variation is linked with the noun class of the subject word [ndʒɔ̀ŋ], namely class 9. If we take a third (8) and fourth (9) example where the subject nouns both belong to class 10 while surfacing with different tone shapes, this becomes even more glaring.

(8) ɓàs   í
CL10.salt SM.CL9
ń-sóbì
PRES-PERF.pour
"salt is poured"

(9) láŋ   í
CL10.palmist oil SM.CL9
ń-sóbì
PRES-PERF.pour
"palmist oil is poured"

These examples clearly show that some critical linguistic information is overridden in the glossing of the nasal prefix which attaches to the verb root, whether it surfaces with a high tone as in (3), (6), (8) and (9), or with a low tone as in (7). Therefore a rigorous model for linguistic information analysis and retrieval would be one which systematically accounts for every bit of linguistic information encoded by every tone, in conjunction with the linguistic information encoded by segmental morphemes. The syllabic nasal prefix in the examples which precede should be glossed distinctively for both its segmental component which encodes tense, and its tonal component which encodes noun class. Likewise, tones surfacing on the subject noun roots, the subject concord markers, and the verb roots should each be glossed for the linguistic information they encode.

If this assumption is valid - and there is robust evidence that it is -, then it becomes inescapable that existing models of tone analysis in African tone languages are flawed by inadequate analysis matrices.

The issue discussed here is just one of the many inconsistencies which may be observed in the analysis of tones in African languages using standard analysis tools and glossing models. Other issues are: proper deep representation of contour tones as in (10), (11), and (12)[8]; floating tones; tone spreading; tone shift; upstep; downstep, low tone rising, etc; all of which will not receive attention in this paper due to space constraint.

(10) m-ùt   à
      CL1.person   SM.CL1
      bí-lɔ̂
      PST-come
      "somebody has come"

(11) m-ùt   à
      CL1.person   SM.CL1   ǹ-lɔ̂
      PRES-PERF.come
      "somebody has come"

(12) mɛ̀   ǹ-tɛ́hɛ́
      I   PREST-see
      m-ût
      CL1-person
      "I have seen somebody"

Examples (10) and (11) show how tone shape changes on the verb root [lɔ]. It should be reminded that this verb root is associated with a low tone lexically. Tone shape in (10) is therefore a 'normal' one, yet it deserves proper glossing. It is relevant for automatic analysis of tone-induced linguistic information, to identify the low tone on the root of the verb form [bílɔ̂] as a lexical tone, in order to make consistent parsing possible. As for the contour high-low shape in (11) namely [lɔ̂], it quite a simple logical explanation. This is the result of the association of the high tone marking perfective aspect in (3), (6), (7), (8), and (9), with the underlying lexical low tone. If every tone were glossed consistently, then changes affecting tone shapes in and across words in a text could be modeled with more ac-

curacy, and anticipation of these changes would me made much easier for a computer program.

Another illustration of change in tone melody across words is seen in (10), (11) and (12), where the noun form [mùt] surfaces with a lexical low tone in (10) and (11), then with a contour falling tone in (12). The contour tone melody here is the result of a process known in Bantu languages as metatony (Nurse 2006, Hyman and Linnet 2011, Makasso 2012). This process triggers a high tone at post-verbal positions to signal prosodic conjunction between the verb and the object (Makasso 2012: 15). While metatony signals prosodic relationship across words in a verb phrase, this phenomenon also encodes syntactic information worth being accounted for in an optimal analysis scheme.

4 A prototype of the TEI-based Model for Enhanced Linguistic Annotation for African Tone Languages

TEI (the Text Encoding Initiative) provides comprehensive guidelines for the development of text encoding standards and schemes for virtually any text encoding project. Chapter 15 of the Guidelines (TEI consortium, 2016: 504-517) deals with annotation of language corpora. Section 17 (TEI consortium, 2016: 570-587) deals with 'Linguistic Segments Categories' and 'Linguistic Annotation', among other issues. Section 18 (TEI consortium, 2016: 588-620) is about annotation of 'Feature Structures' and 'Atomic Feature Values', among other issues. Specific structural phenomena such as tones, which are pervasive in Bantu languages are not yet addressed in the Guidelines.

TEI is a community-driven initiative and maintained by dynamic contributing members who share experiences and shape its further development. The Model for Enhanced Linguistic Annotation for African Tone Languages which I propose here is destined to be submitted to the Technical Council of the TEI consortium for review, enrichment and standardization. As in other TEI-related annotation schemes, the current model is not intended to address every specific aspect having to do with tone annotation in African languages. On the contrary, the model is a starting point, and therefore aims to stimulate discussions and contributions that could help build up a standard, digitally processable, interoperable and sustainable framework for the development of text corpora and text resources in African tone languages. Each individual lan-

---

[8] Glossing in these examples follow standard glossing models, namely the Leipzig Glossing Rules

guage encoding project for African tone languages could draw from this general scheme to tailor the model to their specific needs. The model is expected to be refined and adjusted as more stake-holders join in, either linguists, TEI experts, developers, projects managers, etc.

TEI being based on the XML encoding language, I will not deal here with modules such as Data Type Definition (DTD), XML schemas and name spaces. The model complies with the overall TEI XML infrastructure, namely as concerns validation protocols and standards. For the sake of brevity, I will limit the presentation to tone encoding at the @word element. However, the model also encompasses issues such as optional non ASCII character encoding as well as phonological features, lexical, morphological, syntactic and discourse encoding.

I have adopted ad hoc vocabulary[9] for naming the following attributes:

a. @type describes a word or morpheme type; word types can be "nouns", "verbs", "adjectives", etc.; morpheme types can be "prefixes", "roots", "suffixes", "segmental", "tonal", etc.

b. @gloss describes the semantic value of a morpheme; this may apply to tense, aspects, plural, noun class markers, etc; gloss values are labels of linguistic information which conform to a standard glossing scheme such as the Leizig Glossing Rules.

c. @category describes a linguistic class to which a specific morpheme relates; a morpheme may fit into the "lexical", "grammatical", "syntactic", or "prosodic" classes.

d. @nounClass describes an integer for the noun class of a noun prefix, following standard Bantu grammatical reconstructions for noun classes (Meeussen 1967, etc.)

e. @segmental describes segmental morphemes, that is a word's building blocks devoid of their tone associates.

f. @tonal describes tone morphemes. The content of a tone element is represented by the unicode code point for the accent whose shape depicts the pitch level of the tone. Thus, the acute accent standing for high tone is represented in the model by the Unicode code point 02CA, while the grave accent is encoded by the Unicode code point 02CB. However, for the sake of economy and consistency, the content of tone elements is assumed to have earlier been described in the XML schema or DTD file as @high and @low entities with the value of each corresponding to its Unicode codepoint.

The model provides a comprehensive and linear analysis of every bit of linguistic unit which contributes to the meaning of the utterance. The analysis can be extended to more granular units such as consonant or vowel features for specific characters, depending on the needs of the encoder, without having to call multiple tier analysis into play (see Table 1).

---

[9] The vocabulary used in the model for attributes names, attributes values, and entity names is NOT yet standardized. It is expected that the TEI community along with linguistics will come together, perhaps within the framework of existing TEI Expert Groups, and work towards standardizing the model and its related vocabulary and other structural aspects.

Table 1   Implementation of the model for source utterance : [mùt à ǹlɔ̂]

```
<w type = "noun">
  <m type = "prefix" nounClass ="1">m<\m>
        <m type = "root">
                <m type = "segmental">ut<\m>
                <m type = "tone" category = "lexical">&low<\m>
  <\m>
<\w>
<w type = "nounParticle">
  <m type = "subjectMarker">
        <m type = "segmental" nounClass = "1">a<\m>
        <m type = "tone" category = "grammatical" nounClass = "1">&low<\m>
  <\m>
<\w>
<w type = "verb">
  <m type = "prefix">
        <m type = "segmental" gloss = "PRES">n<\m>
        <m type = "tone" nounClass = "1">&low<\m>
  <\m>
  <m> type= "root">
        <m type = "segmental">lɔ<\m>
        <m type = "tone" category = "grammatical" gloss = "PERF">&high<\m>
        <m type = "tone" category = "lexical">&low<\m>
  <\m>
<\w>
```

5   Conclusion

The above model of text representation solves the following problems otherwise not addressed in any existing annotation scheme:

(1) It brings out every unit of meaning distinctively, whether segmental or tonal. In the present model, linguistic information is analyzed unambiguously and consistently; whereas in mainstream linguistic glossing models the contour H-L tone in [lɔ̂] would have been represented as a complex gloss 'PERF.pour' without explicit specification as to which linguistic element encodes aspect and which other encodes lexical meaning;

(2) the XML encoding framework which the model builds on allows extensibility of the linguistic analysis; in this respect, a given encoding project may be reusable;

(3) it assigns persistent unicode code points[10] to each level tone, therefore making it easier for conversion, transliteration, compression and parsing of characters from one orthography scheme to another;

(4) the model equality reduces multiple representation of segments and tones into one linear string of text, making the text more conducive to interoperability across APIs[11];

(5) it forces granularity in linguistic analysis; in traditional grammatical analysis, the contour tone in the root 'lɔ' would not have been subject to binary glossing partly because of shortage of glossing space; in the present annotation model however, glossing of tones may apply to level and melody, toneless units, as well as in monosyllabic or polysyllabic words.

(6) Inasmuch as the model forces granularity upon units of meaning in a text, it triggers fine-grained description of tone phenomena, and therefore is likely to stir up further in-depth research in the prosody of African tone languages.

(7) Because the model makes the text more easily parsable, it may not only be implemented in text to to-text applications, but only in text-to-speech modeling.

10

http://www.unicode.org/versions/Unicode9.0.0/UnicodeStandard-9.0.pdf

[11] Application Programming Interface such as programming languages.

References

Black, H. Andrew. 1997. TonePars: A computational tool for exploring autosegmental tonology. SIL Electronic Working Papers 1997-007. http://www.sil.org/silewp/1997/007/SILEWP1997-007.html.

Comrie, B., Haspelmath, M. and Bickel, B. 2015. The Leipzig Glossing Rules. Conventions for Interlinear morpheme-by-morpheme glosses. Weblink: http://www.eva.mpg.de/lingua/resources/glossing-rules.php

Goldsmith, John. 1990. *Autosegmental and metrical phonology.* Oxford: Blackwell.

Hyman, Larry, and Florian Lyonnet. 2011. Metatony in Abo (Bankon), A42. *UC Berkeley Phonology Lan Annual Report (2011),* 168-182.

Leben, William. 1973. *Suprasegmental phonology.* Ph.D. thesis, MIT, Cambridge, MA.

Lehmann, Christian. 2001. Language documentation: a program. In Walter Bisang (ed.) *Aspects of typology and universals,* 83-97. Berlin: Akademie Verlag.

Makasso, Emmanuel-Moselly. 2012. Metatony in Basaa. In *Selected Proceedings of the 42nd Annual Conference on African Linguistics,* ed. Michael R. Marlo et al., 15-22. Somerville, MA: Cascadilla Proceedings Project. www.lingref.com, document #2754.

Meeussen, A. E. 1967. Bantu grammatical reconstruction. *Africana Linguistica,* (3), 79–121. Nurse, Dereck. 2006. Focus in Bantu: verbal morphology and function. *ZAS Papers in Linguistics* 43, 189-207.

Stuart McGill (2009). Documenting grammatical tone using Toolbox: an evaluation of Buseman's interlinearisation technique. In Peter K. Austin (ed.) Language Documentation and Description, vol 6. London: SOAS. pp. 236 – 250.

TEI Guidelines. Weblink: http://www.tei-c.org/release/doc/tei-p5-doc/en/Guidelines.pdf.

Developing collection management tools to create more robust and reliable linguistic data

Gary Holton
Department of Linguistics
University of Hawai'i
holton@hawaii.edu

Kavon Hooshiar
Department of Linguistics
University of Hawai'i
kavon@hawaii.edu

Nicholas Thieberger
Department of Linguistics
University of Melbourne
thien@unimelb.edu.au

Abstract

Lack of adequate descriptive metadata remains a major barrier to accessing and reusing language documentation. A collection management tool could facilitate management of linguistic data from the point of creation to the archive deposit, greatly reducing the archiving backlog and ensuring more robust and reliable data.

1 Introduction

One of the greatest barriers to accessing language documentation materials is not the lack of standard data formats or archive infrastructure, but rather the lack of descriptive metadata. The 2016 *Language Documentation Tools and Methods Summit* identified a collection management tool as a priority need for documentary linguistics.[1] In response we outline a vision for a collection management tool which will enable linguists to create and manage descriptive metadata from the point of data collection to the point of archive deposit.

The purpose of language documentation is to create and maintain a record of the world's languages and their use (Woodbury 2003). This record is not intended to be locked away on a shelf or a hard drive but rather to be used for further research by future generations of scholars and community members. The record of language documentation should thus be "multipurpose," able to be used for a variety of possibly unanticipated purposes (Himmelmann 2006). Thus, the concept of reuse is a foundational principle of language documentation and arguably one which

lies at the heart of linguistics more broadly. To the extent that linguistics is a data driven science, the field relies crucially on access to primary language data.

However, while linguists have always relied on language data, they have not always facilitated access to those data. Linguistic publications typically only include short excerpts from data sets, often without citation (Gawne et al. 2015). There is no single explanation for the slow uptake of archiving and open science among linguists, but three types of barriers stand out, namely:

- lack of archiving infrastructure

- lack of data citation standards and best practices

- lack of appropriate tools

Lack of archiving infrastructure impedes access, since each repository has its own protocols and access restrictions. Lack of citation standards impedes access since researchers have little incentive to share data if they have no guarantee of receiving appropriate attribution. And the lack of tools impedes access by making it difficult to collect, organize, and search language data.

Over the past decade enormous progress has been made to address the first two of these barriers. Yet in spite of these advances in archiving infrastructure and citation practices, the upsurge in data sharing within linguistics has been relatively low. Even among those who are philosophically supportive of open data, there remain significant bottlenecks to actually getting those data into an appropriate archive. We believe the most serious bottleneck concerns the lack of appropriate tools for managing linguistic data. While no two linguistic documentation projects are alike in all aspects, the tools for analyzing field data have become fairly standardized over

---

[1] https://sites.google.com/site/ldtoolssummit/

Proceedings of the 2nd Workshop on the Use of Computational Methods in the Study of Endangered Languages, pages 33–38,
Honolulu, Hawai'i, USA, March 6–7, 2017. ©2017 Association for Computational Linguistics

the past few decades. The details of the workflows may differ, but the basic approach is common to most documentation projects. However, the management of digital files varies significantly across different projects and across different stages of the same project.

File systems and naming conventions are often developed on an ad-hoc basis and may go through several stages of evolution throughout the course of a documentation project. Metadata may be recorded in a variety of different ways, e.g., in a spreadsheet, a dedicated metadata editor, a text document, a field notebook, or a custom database. Depositing these data into an archive thus requires the linguist to reorganize data, file names, and descriptive metadata in order to satisfy the requirements of the receiving archive. And because different archives require different deposit formats, the linguist must in some cases repeat this process multiple times. For example, a researcher receiving funding from multiple sources may have to satisfy multiple archiving requirements. As a result even well-intentioned researchers may postpone or even forgo archiving altogether. What these researchers lack is a tool to assist with the organization of their collections of data and metadata. While some useful tools have been developed, such as SayMore and CMDI Maker, the lack of uptake among the community of documentary linguists suggests that more development work is needed.

By improving the dialogue between language documenters, language archivists, and developers, this project will serve as a model for the development of linguistic software. The collection management tools in particular will lead to greater uptake of linguistic archives and thus greater availability of language documentation. Most crucially, the collection management tools will lead to better metadata description, as field linguists will be able to enter metadata at the time of file creation rather than after the fact. This improved metadata will in turn lead to greater accessibility and discoverability of language data. This greater availability of primary language resources will transform not only various subfield of linguistics, but also related fields such as anthropology and social psychology, which rely on careful management of field data

2 Version control

Language documentation is an ongoing process, often consuming decades or lifetimes. Tradition-ally, archiving took place only at the end of a researchers career or following their passing. The obvious advantage to waiting to archive is that one can be certain that all work has been completed. No future versions of materials will be created by the researcher. But the disadvantages are equally obvious and are of two primary sorts.

First, waiting to archive makes the material inaccessible to other researchers for a long period of time. This decreases the efficiency of language documentation since other researchers cannot easily discover what documentation exists for a particular language. Moreover, since linguistic research typically generates vastly more data than can be compiled and analyzed by a single researcher, waiting to archive fails to take advantage of existing expertise. For example, a researcher interested in discourse phenomena may collect vast amounts of recordings which could be relevant to phonetic research but which will not be available to phoneticians until the material is archived. Waiting to archive thus greatly delays the repurposing of linguistic data. This delay is especially salient in cases where the materials may be of use to language maintenance efforts.

A second problem with delaying archiving is that it can be extremely difficult to create descriptive metadata decades after the initial research was done. This problem is particularly difficult when the researcher is deceased and not available to assist in the creation of metadata. In such cases the process of archiving becomes a research activity itself, requiring significant philological work to uncover the intent of the original research effort. Immediate and continuous archiving ensures that descriptive metadata are created in a timely fashion, with minimal additional effort.

Recognizing the problems inherent in delaying archiving, documentary linguists have overwhelmingly endorsed archiving as an essential part of the language documentation process (cf. Gippert et al. 2006). However, there remain significant barriers to archiving language data in practice. Much of the problem stems from the mismatch between current notions of archiving and the established practices of language documentation. Most language archives have been built from the top-down, with pre-defined assumptions about how depositors and other users should interact with the archive. But there is great need to understand the ways in which linguists actually interact with archives. As part of the development process for the Computational

Resource for South Asian Languages (CoRSAL), a new language archive under construction, students at the University of North Texas studied the needs of potential archive users and discovered that depositors may not be well served by traditional archives. Their report states:

> "The concept of an 'archive' and its associated practices are a poor fit with the work practices of linguist depositors. While the logic of archiving requires the deposit of a completed, unchanging artifact, linguists engage in a never-ending process of updating and revising their transcriptions and annotations." (Wasson et al. 2017)

This statement speaks to the need for some kind of version control which allows depositors to archive materials but continue to interact with and engage with those materials as their research continues.

3 Software design issues

3.1 Data model

Although linguistic documentation projects share numerous features, the need to accommodate specific project-based requirements has resulted in a plethora of ad-hoc, proprietary solutions to linguistic data management (cf. Dima et al. 2012). For this reason data models must be extensible in order to accommodate the needs of individual projects. Nonetheless, there are several core aspects which should be a part of any data model, even though they provide challenges. A fundamental requirement is the need to model the interrelationship of recording sessions, media files, and associated secondary data such as transcripts (Hughes et al. 2004). The data model must also robustly handle incomplete information, such as approximation of birth dates. Finally, the data model must employ an ontology to handle the use of non-standard categories and terminology.

3.2 User interface

One of the failures of much linguistic software is to be found in user interface design. It is tempting to think of the user interface as something "extra" which is added onto the core functionality of the software, but if we are to encourage widespread adoption of software it is critical that we design software that people want to use. Currently, most linguistic software is designed to accomplish a specific task. In contrast, most modern software outside the world of linguistics (i.e., "real" software) is designed to attract users. In other words, in the world of real software the focus is on the user rather than the task. Unfortunately, the task-based approach to software is often encouraged by the discipline and its funding regimes. The task is viewed as the intellectual content and hence the object of focus for academic linguists. In contrast, the user interface is seen as an ancillary or decorative -- not part of the core functionality. We argue that good UI design attracts users and is thus critical to the ultimate success of the software. If you want people to do something, you can enable that with your software, but you have to convince them to actually use your software by making it sufficiently user friendly.

Much linguistic software is particularly clunky when compared to modern commercial products. For example, the Arbil metadata editor requires users to enter dates in a very specific YYYY-MM-DD format, though it provides little guidance as to how the date should be entered (Defina 2014). In contrast, most modern software allows dates to be entered in any format which makes sense to the user. The actual date is then inferred. If a user enters "yesterday" in the date field this can readily be interpreted by checking the current date. If a user enters "22 May" in the date field the software assumes that the current year is intended. If a user enters "May 2012" the software infers that the actual day of the month is unknown or irrelevant and thus stores the date as 2012-05.

There are many precedents for good data management software outside the field of linguistics. One familiar example can be found in Apple's iTunes software, which facilitates management of large collections of music files. iTunes facilitates metadata management without requiring that users be aware of collection management best practices. Users make use of iTunes not because they want to manage metadata for their music files but because they want to listen to music. In fact, the user-friendly nature of the iTunes interface has even inspired the repurposing of iTunes as a collection management tool for linguistics and ethnomusicology (Barwick et al. 2005). Another example of good data management software can be found in image organization tools such as Adobe Lightroom. These tools add an additional level of functionality beyond file and metadata management by allowing users to process files directly in associated tools such as image processing software. It is easy to envision this sort of functionality being added to a linguistic data management tool, facilitating interchange with annotation tools and audio/video editors.

By attracting users, good user interface design can also force and facilitate good practice. An example of this in commercial software can be found in the suite of Google web apps. Google Gmail popularized a number of novel features such as tagging email messages instead of sorting them into folders. But Gmail also subtly forces users to adopt certain practices, such as organizing messages into threads. Moreover, by explicitly avoiding the creation of a stand-alone client, Gmail forced users to access their email in a web-based environment, thus paving the way for adoption of various related web-based applications that are now ubiquitous. As an example of how this force-and-facilitate concept could be applied to linguistic software can be found in automating the creation of certain metadata. For example, the date of a session can be inferred from the timestamp on the associated media files, and graphical cues such as different font colors can be used to prompt that this date needs to be checked by a human. Users can be prompted to enter missing metadata fields, and consistency checks can identify potential errors. Automation can be further facilitated through machine learning algorithms.

3.3 Open source and open development

Ideally, the development of a collection management tool should be accomplished via a collaborative open source effort. Here we use the term open source in the broadest sense which also includes open development. Many linguistic software projects are open source only in the narrower sense. They share their source code, but they do not provide any mechanisms for other users to contribute to the development. That is, they do not facilitate the development of a user community. In more concrete terms such projects may allow users to fork code from a repository and make changes to that code, but they do not permit the code to be pushed back to the repository. As a result the number of contributors to the development of any particular linguistic software tool remains small, and intellectual efforts remain siloed. Given the limited resources available for linguistic software development, the inefficiencies inherent to this approach are a substantial drawback. In contrast, an open development process will take advantage of an untapped pool of coding abilities among practicing linguists and linguistics students.

3.4 Modern software

Modern software should be built using modern best practices. In part this includes the three features discussed above: implementation of a robust and extensible data model; a user-interface which forces and facilitates good practice; and a reliance on open development processes. Modern software should also be cross-platform, not relying on the use of any particular operating system or hardware. Today such software is often built as a web application. Web applications have many advantages that are specifically relevant to language documentation. Not only do they eliminate reliance on a particular platform or device, they also remove the installation process. They can be designed to be used offline, which is essential for much of fieldwork, but they also facilitate sharing information across networks, which fits the goals of archiving and best practice.

4 Building on existing tools

Existing metadata editors provide a good starting point for development of a collection management tool. Early iterations of linguistic metadata editors were closely tied to specific projects and specific metadata standards. Tools such as Arbil (Withers 2012) serve the needs of those required to use IMDI users but do not extend easily to other metadata formats and have a non-intuitive user interface (Defina 2014).

CMDI Maker is a relatively new tool which attempts to overcome these difficulties by making use of HTML browser-based technology and employing an extensible metadata format (Rau 2016).[2] At present metadata can be created in two formats, CMDI and ELAR, reflecting the metadata standards for The Language Archive and the Endangered Languages Archive, respectively. Since the CMDI standard is extensible, additional schema can ostensibly be created. However, the major drawback of CMDI Maker is that it is limited to metadata creation. The workflow assumes that the researcher has already been maintaining metadata in some other format (spreadsheet, field notebook, etc.); the CMDI Maker tool is then used essentially to translate this metadata into the format required for the archive deposit. It is this extra step of metadata translation which becomes a barrier to the archiving process. More significantly, CMDI Maker focuses too narrowly on metadata rather than on the management of a collection of files, in-

---

[2] http://cmdi-maker.uni-koeln.de

cluding media, analysis, and metadata. Field workers need to begin managing files from the moment a digital recordings is created on their computer; through to the assigning of descriptive metadata; and on to the addition of analyses such as transcription and other annotation. Ideally this entire ecosystem surrounding the management of the collection would be managed by one tool. The drawback of tools such as CMDI Maker is that they focus too narrowly on metadata entry rather than collection management more broadly.

One existing tool which takes a holistic approach to linguistic data management is SayMore (Hatton 2013).[3] SayMore organizes files directly on the users computer, using a human readable and intuitive directory structure (Moeller 2014). Information about participants is stored in directories named with the participants' names. Information about individual recording sessions is stored similarly according to session name. Metadata is stored in simple human-readable XML files consisting of attribute-value pairs, and these XML files are stored within the relevant directories.

While SayMore does not adhere to any particular metadata schema, the ad-hoc format employed could in theory be ported to any of the commonly used formats. Moreover, because SayMore stores metadata within relevant directories, the entire directory structure could in theory be dumped into an archive as a single deposit while retaining all relevant information. In this way SayMore achieves a crucial disaster-recovery function. Namely, should a researcher become incapacitated or pass away prior to completing an archival deposit, the entire project including media files, analysis files and metadata could be recovered and uploaded without difficulty. This crucial feature is lacking in most other approaches to metadata management.

One drawback to SayMore is that it was designed to run on Windows and cannot be easily ported to other platforms. Moreover, as with much linguistic software SayMore attempts to do too much, including both an annotation tool and a limited respeaking facility. This added functionality is not sufficient to replace dedicated tools such as ELAN and Aikuma, respectively, so it tends to bloat the software and detract from its primary management function. In future it may be possible to more fully integrate a collection management tool like SayMore with other tools, following the Lightroom model

discussed above. In the meantime, while SayMore can be considered to be the premier extant tool for collection management, it has yet to be adopted by more than a small percentage for field linguists. Instead most field workers continue to use ad-hoc idiosyncratic methods for managing the collections. Indeed, linguists may not even conceive of their materials as "collections," since they appear more as a conglomeration of disconnected computer files.

5 Conclusion

Management of linguistic data remains a major bottleneck in the language documentation process. Providing better tools for collection management will ease the burden on field linguists and increase the rate of uptake of archiving. As noted by Thieberger & Berez, "our foundations need to be built today in a manner that makes our data perpetually extensible" (2012: 91). A collection management tool will help to strengthen those foundations.

In this short paper we have outlined some desiderata for a collection management tool and suggested ways in which such a tool could be built upon existing foundations. Moving forward, it may well be that that a single solution does not fit all users. However, this is difficult to determine without a better understanding of current practices. In the near future we plan to conduct a collection management survey to assess the range of practices currently employed by linguists. We also envision a series of workshops to bring stakeholders into dialogue regarding the development of a collection management tool.

Acknowledgements

Funding for the June 2016 *Language Documentation Tools and Methods Summit* was provided by the ARC Centre for Excellence in the Dynamics of Language. We are grateful to the participants in the summit for helping to establish the trajectory of this research. We are also grateful to participants in an informal planning workshop held following the Workshop on Open Access at the University of Cologne in October 2016. Current work in progress by the authors to map out desiderata for a collection management tool is support by the US National Science Foundation under grant 1648984.

---

[3] http://saymore.palaso.org

References

Linda Barwick, Allan Marett, Michael Walsh, Nicholas Reid and Lysbeth Ford. 2005. Communities of interest: Issues in establishing a digital resource on Murrinhpatha song at Wadeye (Port Keats), NT *Literary and Linguistic Computing,* 20, 383-397.

Rebecca Defina. 2014. Arbil: Free tool for creating, editing, and searching metadata. *Language Documentation & Conservation,* 8, 307-314.

Emanuel Dima, Erhard Hinrichs, Christina Hoppermann, Thorsten Trippel and Claus Zinn 2012. A metadata editor to support the description of linguistic resources. *In:* N. Calzolari, K. Choukri, T. Declerck, M. U. Doğan, B. Maegaard, J. Mariani, A. Moreno, J. Odijk and S. Piperidis, editors, *Proceedings of the Eighth International Conference on Language Resources and Evaluation (LREC'12).* Istanbul: European Language Resources Association, pages 1061-1066.

Lauren Gawne, Barbara Kelly, Andrea Berez and Tyler Heston. Putting practice into words: Fieldwork methodology in grammatical descriptions. *International Conference on Language Documentation and Conservation,* Honolulu, February 28. http://hdl.handle.net/10125/25256.

J. Gippert, Nikolas P. Himmelmann and Ulrike Mosel, editors. 2006. *Essentials of Language Documentation,* The Hague: Mouton de Gruyter.

John Hatton. SayMore: Language documentation productivity. *International Conference on Language Documentation and Conservation,* Honolulu, February 28. http://hdl.handle.net/10125/26153.

Nikolas P. Himmelmann 2006. Language documentation: What is it and what is it good for? *In:* J. Gippert, N. P. Himmelmann and U. Mosel, editors, *Trends in Linguistics: Studies and Monographs 178.* The Hague: Mouton de Gruyter, pages 1-30.

Baden Hughes, David Penton, Steven Bird, Catherine Bow, Gillian Wigglesworth, Patrick McConvell and Jane Simpson 2004. Management of Metadata in Linguistic Fieldwork: Experience from the ACLA Project. *On Language Resources and Evaluation.* European Language Resource Association, pages 193-196.

Sarah Ruth Moeller. 2014. SayMore, a tool for Language Documentation Productivity. *Language Documentation and Conservation,* 8, 66-74.

Felix Rau. CMDI Maker – the state and prospects of a HTML5 Web app. *Language Documentation Tools and Methods Summit,* Melbourne, June 1-3.

Nicholas Thieberger and Andrea L. Berez 2012. Linguistic data management. *In:* N. Thieberger, editor *The Oxford Handbook of Linguistic Fieldwork.* Oxford: Oxford University Press, pages 90-118.

Christina Wasson, Gary Holton and Heather Roth. 2017. Bringing user-centered design to the field of language archives. *Language Documentation & Conservation,* 11.

Peter Withers 2012. Metadata management with Arbil. *In:* N. Calzolari, K. Choukri, T. Declerck, M. U. Doğan, B. Maegaard, J. Mariani, A. Moreno, J. Odijk and S. Piperidis, editors, *Proceedings of the Eighth International Conference on Language Resources and Evaluation (LREC'12).* Istanbul: European Language Resources Association, pages 79-82.

Anthony C. Woodbury 2003. Defining documentary linguistics. *In:* P. Austin, editor *Language Documentation and Description, Volume 1.* London: Hans Rausing Endangered Language Project, pages 33-51.

STREAMLInED Challenges:
Aligning Research Interests with Shared Tasks

**Gina-Anne Levow[1], Emily M. Bender[1], Patrick Littell[2], Kristen Howell[1],
Shobhana Chelliah[3], Joshua Crowgey[1], Dan Garrette[1], Jeff Good[4]
Sharon Hargus[1], David Inman[1], Michael Maxwell[5], Michael Tjalve[1], Fei Xia[1]**

[1] University of Washington, [2] Carnegie Mellon University,
[3] University of North Texas, [4] University at Buffalo, [5] University of Maryland

`levow,ebender,kphowell,jcrowgey,garrette,sharon,davinman,mtjalve,fxia@uw.edu`
`littell@alumni.ubc.ca, Shobhana.Chelliah@unt.edu, maxwell@umiacs.umd.edu`

Abstract

While there have been significant improvements in speech and language processing, it remains difficult to bring these new tools to bear on challenges in endangered language documentation. We describe an effort to bridge this gap through Shared Task Evaluation Campaigns (STECs) by designing tasks that are compelling to speech and natural language processing researchers while addressing technical challenges in language documentation and exploiting growing archives of endangered language data. Based on discussions at a recent NSF-funded workshop, we present overarching design principles for these tasks: including realistic settings, diversity of data, accessibility of data and systems, and extensibility, that aim to ensure the utility of the resulting systems. Three planned tasks embodying these principles are highlighted: spanning audio processing, orthographic regularization, and automatic production of interlinear glossed text. The planned data and evaluation methodologies are also presented, motivating each task by its potential to accelerate the work of researchers and archivists working with endangered languages. Finally, we articulate the interest of the tasks to both speech and NLP researchers and speaker communities.

1 Introduction

It is a perennial observation at every workshop on computational methods (or digital tools) for endangered language documentation that we need to find a way to align the interests of the speech and language processing communities with those of endangered language documentation communities if we are to actually reap the potential benefits of current research in the former for the latter.

We propose that a particularly efficient and effective way to achieve this alignment of interest is through a set of "Shared Task Evaluation Challenges" (STECs) for the speech and language processing communities based on data already collected and annotated in language documentation efforts. STECs have been a primary driver of progress in natural language processing (NLP) and speech technology over several decades (Belz and Kilgarriff, 2006). A STEC involves standardized data for training (or otherwise developing) NLP/speech systems and then a held-out, also standardized, set of test data as well as implemented evaluation metrics for evaluating the systems submitted by the participating groups. This system is productive because the groups developing the algorithms benefit from independently curated data sets to test their systems on as well as independent evaluation of the systems, while the organizers of the shared task are able to focus effort on questions of interest to them without directly funding system development.

Organizing STECs based on endangered language data would take advantage of existing confluences of interest: The language documentation community has already produced large quantities of annotated data and would like to have reliable computational assistance in producing more; the NLP and speech communities are increasingly interested in low-resource languages. Currently, work on techniques for low-resource languages often involves simulating the low-resource state by working on resource-rich languages but restricting the available data. Providing tasks based on actual low-resource languages would allow the NLP and speech communities to test whether their techniques generalize beyond the now familiar small sample of languages that are typically studied (see Bender, 2011).

39

Proceedings of the 2nd Workshop on the Use of Computational Methods in the Study of Endangered Languages, pages 39–47,
Honolulu, Hawai'i, USA, March 6–7, 2017. ©2017 Association for Computational Linguistics

In this paper, we present the design of three possible shared tasks, which together go under the rubric of STREAMLInED Challenges: Shared Tasks for Rapid Efficient Analysis of Many Languages in Emerging Documentation. These proposed tasks are the result of an NSF "Documenting Endangered Languages" (DEL) funded workshop bringing together researchers from the fields of language documentation and description, speech technology, and natural language processing. Our goals in describing these proposed shared tasks are to illustrate the general notion as a way forward in creating useful and usable technology, to connect with other members of the community who may be interested in contributing their data to the shared tasks when they are run, and finally to provide some information to working field linguists as well as language archivists about the size of data sets, type of annotations, and format of data and annotations that would be required to be able to take advantage of any systems that are published as the result of these shared tasks. In the following section (§2), we lay out the design principles we set forth for our shared tasks. In §3, we describe three shared tasks, relating to three different kinds of input data: audio data, data transcribed in varying orthographies, and interlinear glossed text (IGT). §4 briefly motivates the interest of the tasks to the speech and NLP research communities. Finally, in §5 we describe how the software systems created in response to these shared tasks, beyond their potential to benefit working field linguists, can also be of interest to the speaker communities whose languages are being studied.

2 Design Principles

A key goal of the EL-STEC workshop was to identify STECs that would actually align the interests of the communities involved. In discussing specific instances (including those developed in §3), we identified several design principles for our shared tasks:

Realism Whereas shared tasks in speech and NLP are often somewhat artificial, it is critical to our goals that our shared tasks closely model the actual computational needs of working linguists. It directly follows from this design principle that the software contributed by shared task participants should work off-the-shelf for stakeholders in documentary materials who are interested in using it later (e.g., linguists, speaker

community members, archivists, etc.). This is ensured in our shared tasks by choosing a virtual environment for the evaluation, such as the Speech Recognition Virtual Kitchen (`http://speechkitchen.org/` Plummer et al., 2014), described in §3.1. Similarly, while some shared tasks artificially limit the data that participants can use to develop (or train) their systems, our shared tasks have a "use whatever you can get your hands on" approach, and we will explicitly point participants to resources that may be useful, such as ODIN (Lewis and Xia, 2010) or WALS (Haspelmath et al., 2008). Furthermore, in contrast to previous NLP and speech research which simulates low-resource languages by using only a small amount of data from actually well-resourced languages,[1] our STECs will be true low-resource environments, bringing in, we expect, complications not anticipated in work on familiar languages.

Typological diversity In order to facilitate the development of truly cross-linguistically useful technology, we will insist on typological diversity in the the languages used for the shared tasks. Specifically, we envision each shared task involving multiple development languages from different language families and instantiating different typological categories. These languages will be represented by data sets split into *training* and *development* data. Teams participating in the shared task will use the training data to train their systems and the development data to test the trained systems. By working with multiple languages from the start in developing their systems, shared task participants are more likely to create systems that work well across languages. To really test whether this is the case, however, each shared task will feature one or more *hidden* test languages, from yet other language families and typological classes. Of course, the shared task organizers will also provide training data for these hidden test languages (of the same general format and quantity as for the development languages), but no further system development will be allowed once that data is released.

Accessibility of the shared task The shared tasks must have relatively low barriers to entry, in

---

[1]There are some notable exceptions, including Xia et al's (2009) work on language identification in IGT harvested from linguistics papers on the web (Xia et al., 2009), the Zero Resource Speech Challenge (Versteegh et al., 2015), and the recent BABEL (Harper, 2014) program.

order to encourage broad participation. This can be ensured by having the shared task organizers provide baseline systems which provide working, if not necessarily high-performing, solutions to the task. The baseline systems not only establish the basic feasibility of the tasks, but also provide a starting point for teams (e.g. of students) who have ideas about how to improve performance on the task but lack the resources to create end-to-end solutions.

Accessibility of the resulting software We wish to ensure that the research advances achieved during the shared tasks are accessible to all of the constituencies we have identified: NLP and/or speech researchers, linguists working on language documentation, and speaker communities. This in turn means that the software systems submitted for evaluation should be available at a reasonable cost (ideally free) to third parties and reasonably easy to run. Furthermore, the systems should be well documented in papers published in the shared task proceedings, such that future researchers could re-implement the algorithms described and verify their performance against published numerical evaluation results on the development languages.

Extensibility From the point of view of the speech/NLP research communities, one of the merits of shared tasks is the establishment of standard data sets and published state of the art results on those data sets against which future research can be compared. There is a paucity of typologically diverse multilingual data sets. The initial data sets (including both development and test languages) for our shared tasks will immediately become a resource that addresses this need, but we would like these resources to grow over time. Accordingly, each shared task will include documentation of what is required for a new data set to be added and welcome submission of such data sets. On in-take, the existing available systems can be run on the data sets to establish baseline numbers for comparison in future work.

Nuanced Evaluation Rather than having one single metric (such as might be required to anoint a single "winner" of each shared task), the shared tasks will have multiple metrics to allow for nuanced evaluations of the relative strengths and weaknesses of each submitted system.

Having articulated these design principles, we now turn to the explanation of our three proposed shared tasks.

3 Proposed Shared Tasks

In this section, we briefly outline three proposed (families of) shared tasks which we believe to meet the design principles described in §2 above. For each shared task, we describe the input data and output annotation (or other information), the proposed evaluation metrics, and information about required data formats.

3.1 Grandma's Hatbox

The process of documenting an endangered language often begins with recordings of elicitations between the linguist and their consultant. Work continues through transcription, alignment, analysis, and glossing. Each of these steps is time-consuming. As a result, a kind of funneling occurs where less data can be analyzed in as great of a level of detail at each stage in the pipeline. Some recordings may never be transcribed or aligned by the linguist due to insufficient time or resource or even a shift in research priorities. We have defined a cascade of shared tasks focused on processing audio recordings to facilitate the transcription and alignment process, to widen and speed up this pipeline. The tasks further aim to develop technology that would make a backlog of unanalyzed recordings more accessible to other linguists, to archivists, and to members of the community through automatic extraction of information about the languages, participants, genre, and content of the recordings.

We name our cascade of shared tasks "Grandma's hatbox" to describe the sequence of steps to follow when a collection of field recordings is found with little associated information: imagine a box of telegraphically labeled tapes and field notebooks. The specific subtasks are defined below.

1. Language Identification

   High-resource (HRL) versus Low-resource language (LRL): Given the identities of the high-resource language, such as English, and the low-resource language used in the recordings, participants should produce a segmentation of the speech in the recordings, identifying the points at which transitions to and from the HRL occur.

All languages: Given a recording with a known HRL and an unspecified number of unknown LRLs, identify the number of distinct languages being spoken, the time points of transitions between languages, and which of the unknown languages is being spoken in each interval.

Training and test data will include audio files in .wav format with fine-grained language segmentation consistent with the subtasks above for: a) one HRL and one LRL, and b) a single HRL and at least two LRLs. In the case of overlapped speech, both (all) languages should be labeled. To score the results, we will use a language-averaged time-percentage F1-score (a standard measure that balances between precision and sensitivity of classification). This metric overcomes the weakness of a simple accuracy measure, which could perform well simply by always selecting the majority language.

2. Speaker identification

Speaker clustering and segmentation: Given a collection of audio files with multiple speakers and multiple languages, assign a unique speaker code to each speaker and label all times when each speaker is talking.

Known speaker segmentation: Given spans of speech labeled with speaker identity for one or more speakers, identify all other spans where each of the known speakers talks.

Training and test data will be provided with speaker labeling and segmentation. To allow focus on both frequent and infrequent speakers, we will employ two evaluation metrics: F1 scores averaged across all time segments in the corpus and all speakers in the corpus, respectively. As above, in the case of overlapped speech, both (all) speakers should be labeled.

3. Genre classification
For a span of audio, identify which of a fixed inventory of genres, e.g., elicitation, monolog, LRL dialog, reading, or chanting, is present. This inventory will be provided by the organizers along with the training data. Training and test samples will be provided for the range of genres and scored using F1 score.

4. Automatic metadata extraction by HRL Automatic Speech Recognition (ASR)
Given a recorded preamble to an interview in an HRL, identify key metadata for the recording, including: date, researcher name, consultant name, and location. Task participants will only have access to the audio itself, with no further metadata. Training and evaluation data will comprise at least 500 examples each per HRL along with corresponding metadata templates, specifying slots and fillers. Evaluation will be based on slot filling accuracy: #(correctly filled slots)/#(total slots).

5. Transcription alignment
Given noisy, partial text transcripts of 2-3 sentences in length, find the time alignment of the text to the recorded speech. Transcripts may include a mix of HRL and LRL-specific orthography. Training and evaluation data will include transcribed spans across a representative range of orthographic conventions with corresponding time alignments to audio files. This task will be evaluated based on absolute time difference between hypothesized and true boundary times.

For each of these tasks, the organizers will create a baseline system, from input to evaluation, to be distributed to the participants. These baseline systems and participants' submitted systems will all be provided as "virtual machines", encapsulated computing environments containing all the required components to run the systems, which can then be deployed in most common operating system environments. Using this framework for speech systems has been promoted by the Speech Recognition Virtual Kitchen team (Plummer et al., 2014) to deploy speech recognition components and systems in educational settings. This will allow ready system comparison and a natural path to deployment on multiple platforms.

The results of each of these cascading tasks can feed into subsequent stages and into the enrichment of the audio archive. General metadata will be stored in a template, including language type and quantity information, speaker number and quantity information, as well as genre, speaker names, recording dates, and so on. Time span information for language and speaker segmentation as well as alignment can readily be encoded in formats readable by tools such as ELAN[2] (Brugman and Russel, 2004), which has seen increasing adoption for endangered language research and which provides an easy visual interface to time-aligned speech and language annotations.

The techniques developed through the "Grandma's hatbox" ensemble of shared tasks have potential benefit for field linguists, researchers in endangered languages, and language archivists. For those collecting data, these techniques can accelerate the process of transcription and alignment of speech data. They can also facilitate consistent metadata extraction from recordings, including language and speaker information, recording dates and locations, as well as genre. These techniques can likewise be applied to existing archive data or ingestion of new materials, for which detailed metadata or time-aligned transcription were unavailable or as a means of testing the quality of existing metadata and transcriptions. This information can be provided in standard formats consistent with best practices established by the community.

3.2 Orthographic Regularization

One of the central problems facing endangered-language technology is the lack of substantial and consistent text corpora; what texts exist are often written in a variety of orthographies (ranging from the scientific to the naïve), written by transcribers of a wide range of expertise, and frequently written by speakers of significantly different dialects. Only a few endangered languages have a sufficient corpus of expert-transcribed text to enable conventional high-resource text technologies; more often, the number of writers trained in a regular orthography is quite small. Similarly, for any such technology that takes text input, there are often only a small pool of potential users who can form inputs in the particular orthography the system expects.

Any text technology for an endangered language must, therefore, be prepared to work with inexpert and approximate transcriptions, transcriptions using variant orthographies, and even transcriptions in which there is no systematic orthography at all.

We therefore propose an orthographic regularization shared task in which systems are provided

a set of text passages in a single endangered language, including both expert transcriptions in a systematic orthography and a variety of inexpert transcriptions. These variant transcriptions can range from attempts at formal orthography from inexpert transcribers (e.g., student work), to historical transcriptions, to dialectal variants, to renderings by writers without any background in a formal orthography (what is sometimes called "naïve transcription"). The task of the system is to normalize the variant transcriptions into their correct orthographic forms, and the results will be judged on a held-out set of text passages for which both expert and inexpert transcriptions are available.

The Orthographic Regularization shared task will have three evaluation conditions, which differ with respect to the presence or absence of parallel transliterations, metadata, and audio.

T1. Only mono-orthographic material is available; no parallel data or metadata can be used.

T2. Parallel data (although likely in small amounts) is available.

T3. Metadata (author ID, date of composition, etc.) and/or audio recordings are available.

The division into three conditions is to stimulate the development of systems that train on a comparatively bare minimum of material, while not discouraging the development of systems that make use of wider (although still commonly available) resources.

Text data will be provided in UTF-8 text format, metadata in JSON format, and audio recordings in WAV format. Data will further be organized based on the task conditions they are permissible in.

The system is tasked with producing a normalization of each test text into each regular, named orthography. That is, given a file in an irregular orthography and one (or more[3]) regular, named orthographies appropriate for the language, the system should produce an output file for each regular, named orthography. System output files will be compared to gold-standard, held-out texts in the desired orthographies, corresponding to the test passages. The evaluation metric will be character

---

[3]Some endangered language communities have several competing "official" orthographies. When multiple such orthographies exist and text is available in each, the goal will be to normalize into each orthography, to avoid the appearance of judging one orthography as "correct" and the other as non-standard.

error rate, based on the number of insertion, deletion, and substitution errors at the character level in the system output relative to the gold-standard texts. Only a subset of generated documents may be evaluated, depending on the availability of parallel gold-standard texts in each of the regular, named orthographies.

Systems will be submitted as containers (such as a Docker container or a similar service), and will be immediately available for use by community members via a web interface.

3.3 First-pass IGT Production

Our final proposed shared task concerns the production of interlinear glossed text (IGT) on the basis of transcribed, translated text. That is, we assume a workflow by which linguists collect spoken texts, transcribe them, elicit translations from the speakers they are consulting, and then work on producing IGT, including segmenting the words into morphemes and glossing each morpheme. Given this workflow, it is typical for a given field project to produce more transcribed texts than translated texts and more translated texts than glossed texts. The goal of this task is to even out the last two categories–that is, to create more glossed texts from translated texts.

For this shared task, we will provide for each development language a collection of at least 500 fully glossed IGT instances (typically sentence-like units, as segmented by the transcriber), plus whatever other materials are available for the language. In addition, there will be another 500 IGT instances designated for evaluation. In this shared task, we are assuming that the goal is to produce five-line IGT, where the first line represents the instance in some standard orthography or broad IPA transcription, the second segments the line into morphemes[4], the third glosses each morpheme, and the fifth provides a translation to a language of broader communication. In addition to these relatively standard lines, we also anticipate a fourth line which gives "word glosses". These are phrasal representations of the grammatical and lexical information provided in each source language word that are sometimes produced by linguists as a shorthand and are valued by speaker

communities engaged in language revitalization, as they are far more approachable than linguist-oriented glosses. An example for Nuuchahnulth (nuk) is given in (1).

(1)   hayimḥ   qʷicič̓x̌ii
           hayimḥa qʷi-ci-čix̌-ii
           not.know what-go-MO-WEAK.3
           not know where she went

           'They did not know where she had gone'

The participating teams will develop systems that can be "trained" on the data for a given language, and then produce first-pass segmentation and glossing (both standard glossing and "word glossing") on further data, given as input transcription and translation. The expectation is not that such automatically produced glosses would be perfect, but rather that the first pass glossing, even if somewhat incorrect, will still be useful. For example, it could be good enough that correcting the glosses is faster than doing them by hand or that the automatically produced glosses facilitate searching the relatively unanalyzed portion of the corpus for examples of phenomena of interest.

For each development language, the shared task organizers will provide 500 more instances of IGT designated as "development test" data. System developers can use this data to check system performance, by passing in the transcription and translation lines, and comparing the output segmentation and gloss lines to the "gold standard" to gauge system performance, perform error analysis, and determine how to improve their systems.

The final shared task evaluation will involve one or more hidden test languages. Each participating system will be trained on the data (at least 500 instances of IGT, plus whatever else is available) from the hidden test language(s) and tested against linguist-provided annotations for 500 test instances of IGT per language. Both development and test language data will be formatted in Xigt (Goodman et al., 2015), and the shared task organizers will provide converters between Xigt and formats such as Toolbox[5], FLEx[6], or Elan (Brugman and Russel, 2004) so that linguists can use the resulting systems with their own data.

In selecting development and test languages for this task, we will look for morphologically

---

[4]Depending on the analytical style of the linguists producing the data and the traditions for that language area, this line might have one canonical 'underlying' form for each morpheme, or it might allow different allomorphs. Participating systems will be expected to reproduce the style of the input data.

[5]http://www.sil.org/resources/
software_fonts/toolbox
[6]http://www.sil.org/resources/
software_fonts/flex

complex languages, but attempt to find typological diversity along dimensions such as prefixing/suffixing and agglutinating/fusional, as well as language family and areal diversity. To serve as a development of test language for this shared task, a project would need at least 1000 fully glossed instances of IGT for that language. For the resulting software to produce useful output to the linguist, the glossed IGT should be representative of what else is in the text (e.g., if the text is mostly transcribed narratives, it is important for the training IGT to include a good sample from narratives).

This task differs from what is already accomplished by the glossing assist function in FLEx (Baines, 2009) in several ways. First, where FLEx produces all possible analyses, the systems participating in this shared task will be asked to choose from among possible outputs the one deemed most likely (on the basis of the training data). Second, where FLEx typically assumes "surface-true" segmentation for the morpheme-segmented line, systems participating in this shared task will be expected to produce underlying forms if that is what is provided in the training data. Finally, where FLEx requires direct input from the linguist if it is to have information about constraints such as affixes only attaching to particular parts of speech, it is anticipated that participating systems will pick this information up from the training data.

4 Intellectual Merit: Research Interest in Speech/NLP

All three of our proposed shared tasks not only solve problems of relevance to field linguists, they also carry inherent research interests for speech and NLP researchers. All three tasks share the properties that they produce data sets and benchmarks to allow researchers to test whether their proposed language-independent solutions work across a broad range of language types. Furthermore, they allow researchers to explore truly low-resource scenarios. These contrast with the typical simulated low-resource scenarios in that the latter involve decisions about which data to keep, and this might not be representative of what an actual low-resource situation might be like. Each task has additional inherent research interest of its own, as detailed below.

The "Grandma's hatbox" shared task suite spans a range of speech processing technologies, including language identification, speaker identification, slot filling, and alignment. Shared task regimes exist for some of these broad areas, such as the NIST speaker (NIST, 2016) and language recognition (NIST, 2015) tasks. The slot filling task also bears some similarities to spoken dialog system tasks, such as the Air Travel Information System (Mesnil et al., 2013) task and components of the Dialog State Tracking Challenge tasks (Williams et al., 2016). However, the setting of endangered language field recordings poses new and exciting challenges, while leveraging techniques developed for other languages in high resource settings. In addition to using languages and language families not typically used in the classic tasks, the recording conditions and audio quality differ from those in typical controlled settings. Both language and speaker segmentation must operate over short, possibly single-word spans, a finer granularity than even 2 second train/test conditions in some tasks (NIST, 2016). Furthermore, these recordings can contain substantial fine-grained code-mixing, with individual speakers talking different languages, and may attract interest from a growing community interested in code-switching in text and speech. The slot filling task will operate over less-structured human-directed speech, rather than the computer-directed speech prevalent in dialog systems tasks listed above. Finally, the alignment task requires not only noisy, partial, multilingual alignment, but alignment over non-standard orthographies. These new challenges will push the state of the art in these speech processing tasks.

The orthographic regularization shared task builds on other work on orthographic regularization in widely spoken languages (see, for example (Mohit et al., 2014; Rozovskaya et al., 2015; Baldwin et al., 2015) on social media text and Dale and Kilgariff (2011) on text produced by language learners), but pushes the frontiers of work in this area in several ways: While this proposed shared task has much in common with these previous shared tasks, endangered language text normalization poses additional interesting problems. In languages like English or Arabic, there is usually a single, established orthography in which almost all users have formal schooling and extensive digital corpora in this orthography that establish "correct" practices. Endangered languages often only have small amounts of material available, often non-normalized and/or in conflicting orthographies; there may be more material available in need of normalization than there is material that establishes correct practices. On the other hand, there are fewer individual authors, meaning that author identification can potentially lead to greater gains, and supplementary material like audio is likely to be available for at least some of the texts (because much endangered language text is transcribed from audio recordings).

The first-pass IGT production shared task resembles earlier shared tasks on morphological analysis, most notably the Morpho Challenge series (Kurimo et al., 2010). It differs, however, in working with words in context (rather than word lists), and in going beyond segmentation of words into morphemes to associating morphemes with particular glosses. The presence of the translation line also provides a new source of information in producing the glosses, not available in previous shared tasks. Finally, the task of producing word-glosses is a novel one, with connections to low-resource machine translation.

5   Broader Impacts: Benefits to Speaker Communities

Beyond helping with the project of endangered language documentation, the shared tasks described here all also hold potential interest for speaker communities, especially those interested in language revitalization.

The techniques developed through the "Grandma's hatbox" ensemble of shared tasks will allow more rapid and automatic extraction of information describing the content of recordings. By providing easy access to information about the languages, speakers, and types of recorded materials, they will make such recordings more accessible to speaker communities. This automatically extracted information will allow simple search and navigation within and across recordings based on language, speaker, genre, and even content, through aligned transcriptions, allowing speaker communities to more easily engage with recorded materials.

The orthographic regularization shared task will produce technology which, in our experience, is among the most requested and most used among endangered-language communities. Many communities have collections of texts in heterogeneous orthographies, and writers have often been trained in different orthographies (and trained to varying degrees), so the possibility of normalizing texts (both old and new) to a consistent format can solve many practical problems communities face.

At best, such technologies can even help to diffuse "orthography conflicts" between dialects, regions, schools, or generations. For example, as several students of the SENĆOŦEN language told one of the authors, their parents' generation (the last generation of fully fluent speakers) had been taught a particular orthographic tradition, and since that time their schools have adopted a different orthography, developed within (and preferred by) the community. The two orthographies are visually quite different, and students and parents therefore have difficulty writing to each other in their language. Technology that could render the students' writing into their parents' orthography (and meanwhile correct some student errors), or render their parents' writing into the students' orthography, would better enable the kind of intergenerational collaboration that the students need to learn and preserve their language.

Of the outputs provided by the first-pass IGT production shared task, the word glosses are anticipated to be the most interesting to speaker communities. This style of information presentation is much more accessible to language learners than glosses produced for linguists, and the ability to produce it automatically for additional texts will facilitate the development of language learning materials as well as making otherwise inaccessible texts into objects of interest for language learners.

6   Conclusion: Next Steps

We have described how shared task evaluation challenges can be used to align the research interests of the speech and natural language processing communities with those of the language documentation and description community and articulated design principles for creating shared tasks that achieve this goal. In addition, we have described three particular shared tasks which we believe to meet those design principles. The next steps are to secure funding to actually run one or more of these shared tasks as well as getting them accepted to appropriate venues and to solicit data collections, either from active language documentation projects or from language archives to use as development and test data sets in these tasks.

Acknowledgments

We are also grateful for the contributions of Mark Hasegawa-Johnson, Russ Hugo, Jeremy Kahn, Lori Levin, Alexis Palmer, and Laura Welcher, during the EL-STEC workshop. This work has been supported by NSF #: 1500157. Any opinions expressed in this material are those of the author(s) and do not necessarily reflect the views of the National Science Foundation.

References

David Baines. 2009. Fieldworks language explorer (FLEx). *eLEX2009*, page 27.

Timothy Baldwin, Young-Bum Kim, Marie Catherine de Marneffe, Alan Ritter, Bo Han, and Wei Xu. 2015. Shared tasks of the 2015 workshop on noisy user-generated text: Twitter lexical normalization and named entity recognition. *ACL-IJCNLP*, 126:2015.

Anja Belz and Adam Kilgarriff. 2006. Shared-task evaluations in HLT: Lessons for NLG. In *Proceedings of the Fourth International Natural Language Generation Conference*, pages 133–135, Sydney, Australia. Association for Computational Linguistics.

Emily M. Bender. 2011. On achieving and evaluating language independence in NLP. *Linguistic Issues in Language Technology*, 6:1–26.

H. Brugman and A. Russel. 2004. Annotating multimedia/ multi-modal resources with ELAN. In *Proceedings of LREC 2004, Fourth International Conference on Language Resources and Evaluation*.

Robert Dale and Adam Kilgarriff. 2011. Helping our own: The HOO 2011 pilot shared task. In *Proceedings of the 13th European Workshop on Natural Language Generation*, ENLG '11, pages 242–249, Stroudsburg, PA, USA. Association for Computational Linguistics.

Michael Wayne Goodman, Joshua Crowgey, Fei Xia, and Emily M. Bender. 2015. Xigt: Extensible interlinear glossed text. *Language Resources and Evaluation*, 2:455–485.

M. Harper. 2014. IARPA BABEL Program. http://www.iarpa.gov/Programs/ia/Babel/babel.html. Accessed September 2014.

Martin Haspelmath, Matthew S. Dryer, David Gil, and Bernard Comrie, editors. 2008. *The World Atlas of Language Structures Online*. Max Planck Digital Library, Munich. http://wals.info.

Mikko Kurimo, Sami Virpioja, Ville Turunen, and Krista Lagus. 2010. Morpho Challenge competition 2005–2010: Evaluations and results. In *Proceedings of the 11th Meeting of the ACL Special Interest Group on Computational Morphology and Phonology*, pages 87–95. Association for Computational Linguistics.

William D. Lewis and Fei Xia. 2010. Developing ODIN: A multilingual repository of annotated language data for hundreds of the world's languages. *Journal of Literary and Linguistic Computing*, 25:303–319.

Gregoire Mesnil, Xiaodong He, Li Deng, and Yoshua Bengio. 2013. Investigation of recurrent-neural-network architectures and learning methods for spoken language understanding. In *Interspeech 2013*.

Behrang Mohit, Alla Rozovskaya, Nizar Habash, Wajdi Zaghouani, and Ossama Obeid. 2014. The first QALB shared task on automatic text correction for Arabic. In *Proceedings of the EMNLP 2014 Workshop on Arabic Natural Language Processing (ANLP)*, pages 39–47.

NIST. 2015. 2015 Language Recognition Evaluation Plan. https://www.nist.gov/file/325251. Downloaded October 8, 2016.

NIST. 2016. 2016 NIST Speaker Recognition Evaluation Plan. https://www.nist.gov/file/325336. Downloaded October 8, 2016.

Andrew Plummer, Eric Riebling, Anuj Kumar, Florian Metze, Eric Fosler-Lussier, and Rebecca Bates. 2014. The Speech Recognition Virtual Kitchen: Launch party. In *Proceedings of Interspeech 2014*.

Alla Rozovskaya, Houda Bouamor, Nizar Habash, Wajdi Zaghouani, Ossama Obeid, and Behrang Mohit. 2015. The second QALB shared task on automatic text correction for Arabic. In *ANLP Workshop 2015*, page 26.

Maarten Versteegh, Roland Thiolliere, Thomas Schat, Xuan Nga Cao, Xavier Anguera, Aren Jansen, and Emmanuel Dupoux. 2015. The zero resource speech challenge 2015. In *Proceedings of Interspeech 2015*, pages 3169–3173.

Jason D. Williams, Antoine Raux, and Matthew Henderson. 2016. The dialog state tracking challenge series: A review. *Dialogue & Discourse*, 7(3):4–33.

Fei Xia, William Lewis, and Hoifung Poon. 2009. Language ID in the context of harvesting language data off the web. In *Proceedings of the 12th Conference of the European Chapter of the ACL (EACL 2009)*, pages 870–878, Athens, Greece, March. Association for Computational Linguistics.

Work With What You've Got

Lucy Bell
Xaad Kihlgaa Hl Suu.u Society
Box 543
Old Massett, Haida Gwaii, BC
V0T 1M0
lucybell@uvic.ca

Lawrence Bell
Lawrence Bell
C\O Simon Fraser University
First Nations Language Dept.
Burnaby, BC
V5A 1S6

Abstract

It is a race against time when revitalizing an endangered language isolate. We learned an important lesson over the years: we learned to work with what we've got. We do not have time to reinvent the wheel or be indecisive in our language revitalization. With our fluent elders passing away at such a fast rate and new learners scrambling to learn Xaad Kil, we have to be efficient. We have to share resources between the dialects and value and learn from the precious resources we have each created. By sharing across the dialects, we have been able to quickly create new resources like a digital Haida phrasebook.

The Haida language is dangerously close to extinction. With only a couple handfuls of fluent speakers from Haida Gwaii, British Columbia and Southeast Alaska, it is a race against time to pass Xaad Kil, the Haida language isolate to the next generation. As with many endangered languages, it is a struggle to create resources, interest and fluency on limited budgets. The Haida language is no exception.

Sharing resources is such an important part of indigenous language revitalization. Aboriginal languages are not like English, French, Spanish or German. There are not a ton of resources or a ton of speakers in the world.

Grassroots language revitalization was happening in southeast Alaska and on Haida Gwaii. There have been strong and very different efforts in all communities. For instance, in Skidegate, the Skidegate Haida Immersion Program focused on recording elders. In Massett, we developed a strong cohort of immediate language learners through accredited courses. In Alaska there were courses and publications happening. The International Haida Language conferences became a way to share resources, plan and work together on new projects. This became a valuable part of Xaad Kil revitalization. There was some sporadic communication between the communities but it wasn't until the International Haida language conferences that the sharing of resources and working towards a common orthography began. Once we began sharing dictionaries, glossaries, recordings and lessons our library of resources blossomed.

One of our successful cross-dialect initiatives was an adult accredited class offered to a cohort of 30+ students in Old Massett and in Ketchikan Alaska. The students in Alaska gathered with linguist Dr. Jordan Lachler. The Old Massett students gathered with elder Claude Jones. We worked from the *Dii Tawlang* lessons done by Dr. Lachler in the Alaskan dialect and orthography. We used the Haida health centre's video technology to connect to the Alaskans three evenings per week. The system was great when the technology worked. Having an elder in Massett present helped us tweak the lesson plans and all of the students were able to learn the subtleties between the two dialects. Not only did the students' language improve greatly, but our understanding of the dialect similarities and differences improved as well. This course was a good lesson in the importance of cross-communication between dialects.

Proceedings of the 2nd Workshop on the Use of Computational Methods in the Study of Endangered Languages, pages 48–51,
Honolulu, Hawai'i, USA, March 6–7, 2017. ©2017 Association for Computational Linguistics

Jordan Lachler and Erma Lawrence. Photo by Farah Nosh.

We began a partnership with the Simon Fraser University with a 7-year grant from SSHRC called *First Nations Languages in the 21st Century: Looking Back, Looking Forward*. The First Nations Language Centre at SFU coordinates many grassroots community projects across BC and academic linguists from SFU, UBC, UNBC, and many other universities to document, analyze, and revitalize Aboriginal languages.

We decided to develop language lessons in an App, focusing on the Skidegate and Northern (combined Alaskan and Massett) Haida dialects. We also decided to work with what we had and we focused on already-developed lessons. This saved valuable time and resources. The lessons were further developed, recorded with fluent elders and learners and put into the App. The *Dii Tawlang* App is a great introductory to the Haida language. This wasn't without challenges. There is great physical distance between the partners and the elders. This made it a timely process. With an aging population of fluent speakers, over time we lost valuable speakers who originally contributed to the project. The App has been tested by language learners on a small scale. The students agreed that the 40+ online lessons were a valuable tool. We started to receive requests from schools, especially urban schools who want to offer their aboriginal students a second language other than French or Spanish. We realized that we needed to make the App more accessible and form relationships with educators to offer the *Dii Tawlang* App to a broader audience.

Book that we worked from to create the digital phrasebook.

In 2017, we began working on a digital phrasebook to add to our App. Following our *use what you got* philosophy, we decided to take an existing book and digitize it. We worked from the 240-page <u>Xaat Kil hl Sk'at'aa! Haida Phrasebook</u> created by elder Erma Lawrence and Dr. Lachler in the Alaskan dialect (Lawrence, 2010). We chose this book to work from for a couple of reasons. First of all, the book is widely used by Massett learners. Most of the beginner and intermediate learners have an understanding of how to read the language and know how some of the subtle differences between the two dialects. It has been a valuable resource. We chose to digitize this book because students requested to hear the phrases. Dr. Lachler compiled the phrasebook with Erma Lawrence and informed us that he did not make a digital recording of the phrases but he thought it would be a useful tool to create. We also heard from northern Haidas that they enjoy accessing the Skidegate app but would prefer to have an App in the dialect of their ancestors.

This work brought us together in Lawrence's hometown of Vancouver. We worked on the project together for four months. We translated the phrases in to our orthography, making slight adjustments to the spelling, added to the phrases and most importantly, recording the phrases in our northern Haida dialect. It was important for us to document and record the 200+pages of everyday phrases. We used the easy-to-use Amadeus Lite to make the recordings. For $35, Amadeus Lite was a simple but effective program. We systematically went through the phrasebook, recording 12 pages per day and making notes and changes to the spelling and pronunciation along the way. Luckily, with our partnership with SFU, we were provided a classroom at the downtown campus to record in. To have our own soundproofed studio would have been ideal but we had to work with what we had. Some days were noisier than others, and we ended up having to re-record some of our work or I had to do extra editing.

After two months, we went back to Massett and showed a sample of the work to the beginner adult learners. They gave some valuable feedback. Some valuable advice they had included asking for a simple recording of the sounds of _Xaad Kil_ and the dictionary. We have since compiled this. The students liked the format of the App since it follows the same format as the hardcover phrasebook that they have been using. It was also important for us to hear from learners how they would be using the digital phrasebook. All of them said they would prefer to use it on their phones or other devices while in a classroom situation and on their own. Students want to The App is being developed for smartphones.

We recorded the phrasebook for a total of 4 months. Then I began editing the 3000 raw sound-files. This was a tedious process and I recruited the help of my family, including my 7-year-old niece Nora-Jane who became quite efficient at sound-file editing. From there, we compiled these into the App with the help of the SFU team after receiving a crash-course in in-putting our data. I also recruited someone to input the written phrasebook to the App once I realized how much more work this would be.

The digital phrasebook could be used in a number of ways. First of all, language learners can put the App on their phones to learn from. Secondly, school programs can use the phrasebook alongside the recordings in their classrooms to teach students how to write the Haida language. The phrasebook could also be used by the many people who just want to learn a few phrases related to a specific topic. For instance, the fisheries department may use the phrases in their publications and around the office just as people can learn potlatch phrases when they are planning a potlatch.

We will store the sound files at SFU for future uses. The phrases are a good start towards a digital dictionary. By saving them at SFU, we can guarantee secure access to the files and we can work with SFU to ensure they are saved and distributed appropriately to the Haida community and partners in language revitalization.

The digital phrasebook work was good lesson for us. We learned that being a small team was more time efficient than having a big team. We also realized how important it is for the team to be in the same town! In the past, we relied on Lawrence coming to Massett once a month and squeezing in recording time with Dr. Ignace after they taught classes all day. With Lawrence being the only fluent male speaker of the Massett dialect, this has been such a valuable resource to create and it would not have happened if I did not move to Vancouver to work 1-on-1 with him on this project. Lawrence brought his language fluency and I brought my limited computer skills and Haida language reading and writing skills. Lastly, it was beneficial for us to learn how to input the data and create the App ourselves with the help of the SFU technical team.

On a personal level, the process of creating a digital phrasebook was beneficial for us both. It gave us valuable 1-on-1 time to pass the Haida language from a fluent speaker to a learner. This was quality mentoring time. The process was good for Lawrence because it greatly improved his _Xaad Kil_ reading skills. By the end of the four months, he was reading the Haida phrasebook like a pro. This process improved my speaking ability. The recording time with Lawrence as well as the editing time I put in to the project added to my fluency. I often refer to Lawrence as a walking Haida encyclopedia so the opportunity to sit with him for four months gave me the time to learn not only the Haida language but Haida genealogy and Haida history as well.

The lesson for us is that we have to use the resources we already have. We have to think creatively of the best way to quickly make resources and get them to learners. We have to think of our audience. We already had the phrasebook in another dialect. We already had a good working relationship with a University to create the App. We were also already willing and capable of recording, writing and inputting the data into the app. By working with our already existing resources and working with our existing relationships, we were able to create a valuable everyday digital phrasebook.

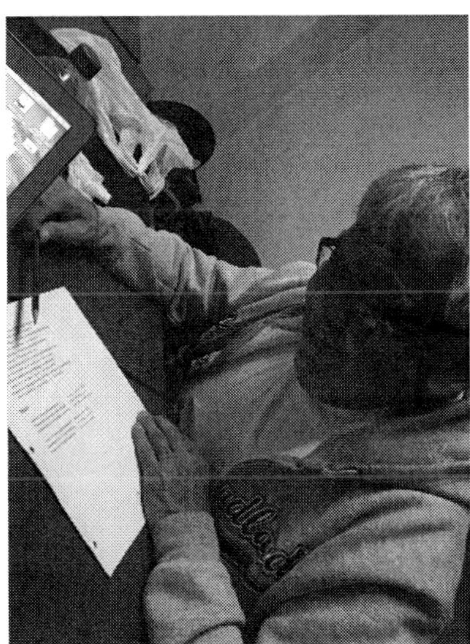

Lawrence Bell. A typical day at work. Photo by Lucy Bell.

Acknowledgements

We are grateful for the work of Erma Lawrence and Jordan Lachler who created the Alaskan Haida Phrasebook, <u>Xaat Kil hl Sk'at'aa</u>. Your valuable work has guided us to create the digital version of the book. Haw.aa.

We are also so grateful for SFU and the SSHRC partnership grant that allowed us the time, space and funding to create this resource.

References

Lachler, Jordan. 2010. <u>Dictionary of Alaskan Haida.</u> Sealaska Heritage Institution, Juneau, AK.

Lawrence, Erma. 2010. <u>Xaat Kil hl Sk'at'aa!</u> Haida Phrasebook. Sealaska Heritage Institute, Juneau, AK.

Converting a comprehensive lexical database into a computational model: The case of East Cree verb inflection

Antti Arppe
Department of
Linguistics
University of Alberta
arppe@ualberta.ca

Marie-Odile Junker
School of Linguistics and
Language Studies
Carleton University
marieodile.junker
@carleton.ca

Delasie Torkornoo
School of Linguistics and
Language Studies
Carleton University
Delasie.Torkornoo
@carleton.ca

1 Introduction

In this paper we present a case study of how comprehensive, well-structured, and consistent lexical databases, one indicating the exact inflectional subtype of each word and another exhaustively listing the full paradigm for each inflectional subtype, can be quickly and reliably converted into a computational model of the finite-state transducer (FST) kind. As our example language, we will use (Northern) East Cree (Algonquian, ISO 639-3: crl), a morphologically complex Indigenous language. We will focus on modeling (Northern) East Cree verbs, as their paradigms represent the most richly inflected forms in this language.

2 Background on East Cree

East Cree is a Canadian Indigenous language spoken by over 12,000 people in nine communities situated in the James Bay region of Northern Quebec. It is still learned by children as their first language and fluently spoken in schools and in the communities overall, involved in most spheres of life as an oral language. Speakers have basic literacy in East Cree, but written communication tends to be in English or, to a lesser extent, French. The language is fairly well documented, with main resources available on a web site (www.eastcree.org) that includes multilingual dictionaries of two dialects (English, French, East Cree Northern and Southern dialects), thematic dictionaries, an interactive grammar, verb conjugation applets, oral stories, interactive lessons and exercises, a book catalogue, and other various resources like typing tools for the syllabics used, tutorials, spelling manuals, and so forth.

3 Verb structure

The verb in Northern East Cree follows the general Algonquian structure. Verbs fall into four major types according to transitivity and the animacy of the participants (intransitive with inanimate, or no, subject: II; intransitive with animate subject: AI; transitive with animate subject and inanimate object: TI; and transitive with animate subject and animate object: TA). Verbs are inflected for the person of the subject and/or object, and for modality. There are three major types of inflections, with their specific properties, known as orders: *independent*, *conjunct*, and *imperative*. As can be seen in the examples below, only the independent forms have person prefixes, while for conjunct and imperative forms person is only marked in the suffixes.

The orders can be divided into sub-paradigms according to how modality is marked in the post-verbal suffix complex. For Northern East Cree, a total of 15 distinct sub-paradigms have been identified, 7 for independent, 6 for conjunct, and 2 for imperative (Junker & MacKenzie, 2015), taking a classical *Word-and-Paradigm* approach (Blevins, 2011). In addition, verb stems can be combined with several pre-stem elements, known as preverbs, which can be divided into grammatical and lexical ones and which functionally correspond to auxiliary verbs or adverbials in English. For example, the preverb *chî(h)* indicates 'past' tense, *wî* 'want', and *nitû* 'go and V'. These are illustrated in examples (1a-c) below.

(1a) INDEPENDENT INDIRECT
   chichî wî nitû mîchisunâtik
   chi-chî wî nitû mîchisu-n-âtik
   2-PAST WANT GO eat.AI-1/2SG-INDIRECT
   'You wanted to go eating (so I was told)'

Proceedings of the 2nd Workshop on the Use of Computational Methods in the Study of Endangered Languages, pages 52–56,
Honolulu, Hawai'i, USA, March 6–7, 2017. ©2017 Association for Computational Linguistics

(1b) CONJUNCT DUBITATIVE PRETERITE
châ sâchihîtiwâhchipinâ
châ sâchih-îti-w-âhch-ipin-â
FUT love.TA-INV-DUB-1PL→2(PL)-PRET-DUB
'If only we could love you'

(1c) IMPERATIVE IMMEDIATE
sâchihînân
sâchih-înân
love.TA-2(PL)→1PL
'(You [sg. or pl.]) love us!'

As for orthographical conventions, grammatical and lexical preverbs are separated from the rest of the verb construction by spaces, (though this is not followed consistently for lexical preverbs, sometimes written attached to the stem). Personal prefixes (in the case of independent order forms) are attached onto the first preverb or the verb stem, as can be seen in (1a) and (3a-b). Moreover, long vowels may be indicated with a circumflex, such as <â>, used throughout the examples in this paper, or by doubling the vowel graphemes, i.e. <â> could alternatively be written as <aa>. The double-vowel notation is used for long-vowels in the computational model to be discussed below.

Morphophonology: While Northern East Cree (NEC) is fairly regularly agglutinative in its structure, there are some morphophonological phenomena occurring at the stem-suffix juncture, at the prefix-preverb/verb stem initial morpheme juncture, as well as within the suffix complex. For instance, a template morphology approach such as Collette (2014) presents 10 different suffix positions for the NEC verb. Furthermore, in the case of conjunct verb forms, the first syllable of the verbal complex, whether that of the first preverb or the stem, can undergo *ablaut*, known as *Initial Change* (IC), and resulting in a *changed conjunct* form. For example, the vowel -â- of the first syllable of the verb *mâtû* below (2a-c) changes to -iyâ- in the conjunct neutral form used in partial questions. Initial change of the verb stem only happens when there is no preverb before the verb stem, as preverbs can undergo initial change as well (cf. Junker, Salt & MacKenzie, 2015a).

(2a) m**a̱**tu-u
cry.AI-3(INDEPENDENT)
'S/he is crying'

(2b) âh m**a̱**tu-t
when cry.AI-3(CONJUNCT)
'When s/he is crying'

(2c) awân m**iyâ**tu-t
who IC.cry-3(CONJUNCT)
'Who is crying?'

To account for stem-suffix juncture morphophonological phenomena, Junker, Salt and MacKenzie (2015b) identify up to 19 stem types[1]. For example, *t-/sh*-stems alternate depending on person marking (3a-b), and *h*-stems trigger vowel *i*- lengthening (4).

(3a) t/sh-stem: *nâtâu*
chinâshin
chi-nâ**sh**-in
2-come.to.TA- DIR.2SG(SUBJ)→1SG(OBJ)
'you [sg.] come to me'

(3b) t/sh-stem: *nâtâu*
chinâtitin
chi-nâ**t**-itin
2-come.to.TA-INV.1SG(SUBJ)→2SG(OBJ)
'I come to you [sg.]'

(4) *h*-stem: *sâchihâu*
chisâchihîtin
chi-sâchih-îtin
2-love.TA- INV.1SG(SUBJ)→2SG(OBJ)
'I love you [sg.]'

All the inflectional information above is encoded into two databases, (1) a verb paradigm database and (2) a dictionary database. The verb paradigm database, consisting of 9,457 entries, lists exhaustive paradigms for each inflectional subtype (19 in all), plus some partial paradigms as well. That is, all basic prefix and suffix sequence combinations, indicating the person and number of subject (for all verb classes) and object (for TA verbs) as well as the various possible types of modality, are identified for each inflectional paradigm subtype and verb class (II, AI, TI, TA). Each entry in the verb paradigm database is a fully inflected verb form, which is associated with the relevant set of morphological features (Table 1). Importantly, each entry is provided with several different orthographical representations and structural partitions for different usage purposes. In particular, in a field named 'Search engine chunks', not only are all the suffixes lumped together, but this word-final segment/chunk, which we can call the *technical suffix*, also includes the stem final vowel or consonant (*h*- here), leaving behind what we call

---

[1] These are divided into 7 subtypes for TA verbs, 3 for II verbs, 6 for AI verbs, 1 for AI+O-verbs, and 2 for TI verbs.

a *technical stem* (*sâchi-* here), which remains invariant throughout the entire paradigm.

Table 1. ECN verb paradigm database entry representing one inflected form (selected fields)

ᒋᓵᒋᐦᐃᑎᐣ	Word form in standard ECN syllabic spelling
chisâchihîtin	Word form in standard ECN roman spelling
chi-sâchi-hîtin	**Search Engine chunks**
chi-sâchih-îtin	Morpheme cuts for display
chi-sâchih-it-in	Morpheme breaks with underlying forms
1→2	Person (Subject→Object)
h	**Stem type**
VTA	Grammatical class
sâchihâu	Dictionary entry
01	Paradigm number

Table 2. ECN Dictionary database entry (selected fields)

ᓵᒋᐦᐋᐤ	Word form in standard ECN syllabic spelling
sâchihâu	Word form in standard ECN roman spelling
h	**Stem type**
VTA	Grammatical class
sâchi	**Technical stem (regular)**
siyâ-chi-hât	changed conjunct (first syllable + rest of technical stem + endings for conjunct indicative neutral, *h* stem)
s/he loves someone	English translation

The dictionary database (15,614 entries) (Junker et al. 2012) determines the inflectional subtype for each verb. This allows for linking each verb with its entire paradigm according to a model verb for each inflectional subtype, as enumerated in the verb paradigm database. In addition, the aforementioned technical stem, in both its regular and changed (conjunct) form, is explicitly stored directly for each verb in the dictionary database. Using these technical stems and the corresponding word-final (and word-initial) technical suffix chunks from the verb paradigm database, one can generate all the inflected forms by simple concatenation, without needing any morphophonological rules. Nevertheless, one needs to bear in mind that these technical stems and word-final technical suffix chunks have no morphological reality, but are simply representations of convenience (see Junker & Stewart, 2008). Furthermore, all grammatical and lexical preverbs are also included as their own entries in the dictionary database, and we are treating initial-changed forms of preverbs as separate entries labelled as conjunct preverbs.

4 Computational modeling of the Northern East Cree verb

As our computational modeling technology, we are using Finite-State Transducers (FST) (e.g. Beesley & Karttunen 2003), well-known computational data structures that are optimized for word form analysis and generation, with a calculus for powerful manipulations. FSTs are easily portable to different operating systems and platforms, and thus can be packaged and integrated with other software applications, like providing a spell-checking functionality within a word-processor. In designing a finite-state computational model, with a fairly regularly agglutinative language such as East Cree, one has to decide whether one models morphophonological alternations at stem+affix junctures by (1) dividing stems into subtypes which are each associated with their own inflectional affix sets that can simply be glued onto the stem, or whether (2) one models such morphophonological alternations using context-based rewrite rules. Furthermore, one has to decide the extent to which one treats affix sequences by splitting these into their constituent morphemes, each associated with one morphosyntactic feature, or rather treats affixes as chunks which are associated with multiple morphosyntactic features (Arppe et al., in press). The more one splits affix sequences, the more one may need to develop and test rules for dealing with morphophonological alternations at these morpheme junctures, whereas in the case of chunking such alternations are precomposed within the chunk. In contrast, the more one uses chunks, the more one has to enumerate chunks based on the number of relevant inflectional subtypes.

While the chunking strategy is not parsimonious and compact, in our experience it results in FST source code which is nevertheless structurally quite flat and easily comprehensible for scholars who are not specialists for the language in question. Importantly, current finite-state compilers, e.g. XFST, HFST, or FOMA (Beesley and Karttunen 2003; Lindén et al. 2011; Hulden 2009), implement a minimization procedure on the finite-state model, so that recurring realizations of string-final character sequences and associated morphological features are systematically identified and merged, resulting in the end in a relatively compact model (that in practice might not be much larger, nor structurally substantially different, than a model compiled from source code implementing maximal splitting). On the other hand, if some aspect of the chunked morpheme sequences needs to be changed, with the chunking strategy these have to be implemented in potentially quite a large number of locations.

For the Northern East Cree model, we decided to (1) split the pre-stem morphemes (personal prefixes for the independent order forms, and the regular and initial-changed forms of the grammatical and lexical preverbs), as there are very few morphophonological phenomena (initial change, epenthesis), and these are very regular. We deal with initial change by exhaustively listing the two alternative preverbs or stems (regular vs. changed); (2) entirely chunk the post-stem suffix morphemes, associating the chunks with multiple morphological feature tags; and (3) make maximal use of inflectional subtypes through using the aforementioned technical stems and post-stem word-final technical suffix chunks. Thus we will require no morphophonological rules for the stem-suffix morpheme juncture, and only two regular morphophonological rules in the pre-stem part.[2] These morphophonological rules are implemented using the TWOLC formalism within the FST framework. As to the rest, the LEXC formalism in the FST framework is used to define the concatenation of the morpheme sequences as treated above. For Independent order forms with subject (and object) person and number marked with a combination of a prefix and suffix (which can be understood to constitute a circumfix), agreement constraints between these affixes are implemented with the flag diacritic notation within the LEXC formalism.

5 Model statistics and details

The computational model currently includes stems and suffixes for AI, TI, and TA, but not for II verbs (which have the simplest paradigms). The LEXC source code for verb affixal morphology in its current form consists of 16,590 lines, of which 68 concern the pre-stem

component and 16,514 the post-stem technical suffix chunks.[3] With minimization, its compilation with XFST takes 5.462 seconds with a 2 GHz Intel Core i7 processor and 8MB of RAM, resulting in a 108 kB XFST model (1,084kB with HFST).[4]

While this full enumeration of suffix chunks per each inflectional paradigm type results in a large number lines in the LEXC code, in comparison to a decompositional approach, the structure of the source code is quite flat and easy to grasp. As can be seen in Table 3 presenting the source code for the Independent Neutral Indicative suffix chunks for Animate Intransitive verbs of the *-aa* paradigm type, the suffix chunk *-aan*, which requires a first person prefix *ni-* to have been observed at the very beginning of the verb construction, indicated by the flag-diacritic `@U.person.NI@`, is associated with three morphological tags `+Indic`, `+Neu` and `+1Sg`, corresponding to the morphological features INDICATIVE, NEUTRAL and FIRST PERSON SINGULAR actor, respectively. In addition, the numeric code `+[01]` is provided, indicating the paradigm subset for Regular (Non-Relational) Independent Neutral Indicative verb forms.

Table 3. LEXC description of suffix chunk set for the Regular (Non-Relational) Independent Neutral Indicative forms for Animate Intransitive verbs of the *-aa* paradigm subtype.

```
LEXICON VAI_SUFFIX_aa_IND01
@U.person.NI@+[01]+Indic+Neu+1Sg:@U.person.NI@aan # ;
@U.person.NI@+[01]+Indic+Neu+1Pl:@U.person.NI@aanaan # ;
@U.person.KI@+[01]+Indic+Neu+2Sg:@U.person.KI@aan # ;
@U.person.KI@+[01]+Indic+Neu+21Pl:@U.person.KI@aanaaniu # ;
@U.person.KI@+[01]+Indic+Neu+2Pl:@U.person.KI@aanaawaau # ;
@U.person.NULL@+[01]+Indic+Neu+3Sg:@U.person.NULL@aau # ;
@U.person.NULL@+[01]+Indic+Neu+3Pl:@U.person.NULL@aawich # ;
@U.person.NULL@+[01]+Indic+Neu+4Sg/Pl:@U.person.NULL@aayiuh
# ;
@U.person.NULL@+[01]+Indic+Neu+XSg:@U.person.NULL@aaniuu # ;
@U.person.NULL@+[01]+Indic+Neu+XSgObv:@U.person.NULL@aanaani
wiyiu # ;
```

Example analyses provided by the FST analyzer for the forms (1a-c) are presented below in (5a-c). Grammatical and lexical preverbs are indicated with the notation `PV/…+`, and the subset of the paradigm using a notation with bracketed

---

[2] (i) insertion of an epenthetic *-t-* between the personal prefix and a vowel-initial stem or preverb; and (ii) assimilation of *i-* before a stem-initial *u-*.

[3] The entire source code for the (Northern) East Cree computational model presented here can be found at: `https://victorio.uit.no/langtech/trunk/startup-langs/crl/src/`

[4] This compares well with HFST models for other Algonquian languages the first author has experience of, e.g. 1,728kB for Odawa (otw) and 5,320kB for Plains Cree (crk), though on must note these two models cover also noun morphology not yet implemented in our East Cree model.

numbers, e.g. +[05] for Independent Indirect Neutral verb forms, +[15] for Conjunct Dubitative Preterite verb forms, and +[17a] for Immediate Imperative forms.

```
(5a) chichii wii nituumiichisunaatik
PV/chi+PV/wii+PV/nituu+miichisuu+V+AI+Ind+[05]+Indir+Neu+2Sg

(5b) chaa saachihiitiwaahchipinaa
     PV/chaa+saachihaau+V+TA+Cnj1+[15]+Dub+Prt+1Pl+2(P)1O

(5c) saachihiinaan
     saachihaau+V+TA+Imp+[17a]+Imm+2(P)1+1P1O
```

This almost entirely concatenative modeling strategy described above is made possible thanks to the exhaustive listing of the technical stems (both regular and changed) for each verb in the dictionary database, and the likewise comprehensive enumeration of all inflected forms for each subtype in the verb paradigm database, with one of the representations of each inflected form providing a partitioning into the technical stem and a technical suffix chunk. All the forms in the verb paradigm database have been verified in countless sessions with fluent East Cree Elders over decades.

Importantly, though the creation of the two databases has taken a substantial amount of meticulous human work and scrutiny, and while FST source code for the (relatively straight-forward) pre-stem component has been written by hand, the FST source code for the suffix component is generated in its entirety from the underlying two lexical databases, minimizing the risk for human typing error (when the underlying databases are error-free). Equally importantly, the automatic generation allows for easy generation of revised versions, if changes need to be implemented.

In terms of time required to create this this general FST architecture, the manual coding of the basic pre-stem morphology, and developing the scripts for automatically generating the post-stem FST source code has taken altogether 2 weeks of 3 people's work.

6   Conclusion

Having comprehensive, well-structured resources such as those described above, and people with appropriate programming and linguistic skills, the brute-force listing strategy presented in this paper is a surprisingly fast and efficient way of creating a finite-state computational model, to form a basis for subsequent development of practical end-user applications.

Acknowledgements

This work has been supported by funding from the Social Sciences and Humanities Research Council of Canada Partnership Development (890-2013-0047) and Insight (435-2014-1199) grants, a Carleton University FAAS research award, and Kule Institute for Advanced Study, University of Alberta, Research Cluster Grant.

References

Arppe, A., Junker M.-O. Harvey, C., and J. R. Valentine (in press). Algonquian verb paradigms. a case for systematicity and consistency. *Papers of the Algonquian Conference 47*.

Beesley, K. R. and L. Karttunen (2003). *Finite State Morphology*. CSLI Publications.

Blevins, James P. (2006) Word-based morphology. *Journal of Linguistics* 42: 531-573.

Collette, V. (2014) Description de la morphologie grammaticale du cri de l'Est (dialecte du Nord, Whapmagoostui) (unpublished doctoral thesis). Québec: Université Laval.

Hulden, M. (2009). Foma: A finite state toolkit and library. In *Proceedings of the 12th Conference of the European Chapter of the Association for Computational Linguistics*, 29–32.

Junker, M.-O., MacKenzie, M., Bobbish-Salt, L., Duff, A., Salt, R., Blacksmith, A., Diamond, P., & Weistche, P. (Eds.). (2012). *The Eastern James Bay Cree Dictionary on the Web: English-Cree and Cree-English, French-Cree and Cree-French (Northern and Southern dialects)*. Retrieved from http://dictionary.eastcree.org/

Junker, M.-O. & MacKenzie, M. (2010-2015). *East Cree (Northern Dialect) Verb Conjugation* (4th ed.). Available at: http://verbn.eastcree.org/.

Junker, M.-O., Salt, L., & MacKenzie, M. (2015). *East Cree Verbs (Northern Dialect)*. [Revised and expanded from 2006 original edition] In *The Interactive East Cree Reference Grammar*. Retrieved from:
   (a) [http://www.eastcree.org/cree/en/grammar/northern-dialect/verbs/cree-verb-inflection/initial-change/]
   (b) [http://www.eastcree.org/cree/en/grammar/northern-dialect/verbs/cree-verb-stems/]

Junker, M-O. & Stewart, T. (2008). Building Search Engines for Algonquian Languages. In Karl S. Hele and Regna Darnell (eds). *Papers of the 39th Algonquian Conference*. London: University of Western Ontario Press, 378-411.

Lindén, K., E. Axelson, S. Hardwick, M. Silfverberg, and T. Pirinen (2011). HFST - Framework for Compiling and Applying Morphologies. Proceedings of *Second International Workshop on Systems and Frameworks for Computational Morphology (SFCM)*, 67-85.

Instant annotations in ELAN corpora of spoken and written Komi, an endangered language of the Barents Sea region

Ciprian Gerstenberger[*]
UiT The Arctic University of Norway
Giellatekno – Saami Language Technology
`ciprian.gerstenberger@uit.no`

Niko Partanen
University of Hamburg
Department of Uralic Studies
`niko.partanen@uni-hamburg.de`

Michael Rießler
University of Freiburg
Freiburg Institute for Advanced Studies
`michael.riessler@frias.uni-freiburg.de`

Abstract

The paper describes work-in-progress by the Izhva Komi language documentation project, which records new spoken language data, digitizes available recordings and annotate these multimedia data in order to provide a comprehensive language corpus as a databases for future research *on* and *for* this endangered – and under-described – Uralic speech community. While working with a spoken variety and in the framework of *documentary linguistics*, we apply *language technology* methods and tools, which have been applied so far only to normalized written languages. Specifically, we describe a script providing interactivity between ELAN, a Graphical User Interface tool for annotating and presenting multimodal corpora, and different morphosyntactic analysis modules implemented as Finite State Transducers and Constraint Grammar for rule-based morphosyntactic tagging and disambiguation. Our aim is to challenge current manual approaches in the annotation of language documentation corpora.

1 Introduction

Endangered language documentation (aka *documentary linguistics*) has made huge technological progress in regard to collaborative tools and user interfaces for transcribing, searching, and archiving multimedia recordings. However, paradoxically, the field has only rarely considered applying NLP methods to more efficiently annotate qualitatively and quantitatively language data for endangered languages, and this, despite the fact that the relevant computational methods and tools are well-known from corpus-driven linguistic research on larger written languages. With respect to the data types involved, endangered language documentation generally seems similar to corpus linguistics (i.e. "corpus building") of non-endangered languages. Both provide primary data for secondary (synchronic or diachronic) data derivations and analyses (for data types in language documentation, cf. Himmelmann 2012; for a comparison between corpus linguistics and language documentation, cf. Cox 2011).

The main difference is that traditional corpus (and computational) linguistics deals predominantly with larger non-endangered languages, for which huge amounts of mainly written corpus data are available. The documentation of endangered languages, on the other hand, typically results in rather small corpora of spoken genres.

Although relatively small endangered languages are also increasingly gaining attention by the computational linguistic research (as an example for Northern Saami, see Trosterud 2006a; and for Plains Cree, see Snoek et al. 2014), these projects work predominantly with *written* language varieties. Current computational linguistic projects on endangered languages seem to have simply copied their approach from already established research on the major languages, including the focus on written language. The resulting corpora are impressively large and include higher-level morphosyntactic annotations. However, they represent a rather limited range of text genres and include predominantly translations from the relevant

---

The order of the authors' names is alphabetical.

57

Proceedings of the 2nd Workshop on the Use of Computational Methods in the Study of Endangered Languages, pages 57–66,
Honolulu, Hawai'i, USA, March 6–7, 2017. ©2017 Association for Computational Linguistics

majority languages.

In turn, researchers working within the framework of endangered language documentation, i.e. fieldwork-based documentation, preservation, and description of endangered languages, often collect and annotate natural texts from a broad variety of genres. Commonly, the resulting spoken language corpora have phonemic transcriptions as well as several morphosyntactic annotation layers produced either manually or semi-manually with the help of software like Field Linguist's Toolbox (or Toolbox, for short),[1] FieldWorks Language Explorer (or FLEx, for short),[2] or similar tools. Common morphosyntactic annotations include glossed text with morpheme-by-morpheme interlinearization. Whereas these annotations are qualitatively rich, including the time alignment of annotation layers to the original audio or video recordings, the resulting corpora are relatively small and rarely reach 150,000 word tokens. Typically, they are considerably smaller. The main reason for the limited size of such annotated language documentation corpora is that manual glossing is an extremely time consuming task and even semi-manual glossing using FLEx or similar tools is a bottleneck because disambiguation of homonyms has to be solved manually.

Another problem we identified especially in the documentation of endangered languages in Northern Eurasia is that sometimes the existence of orthographies is ignored, and instead, phonemic or even detailed phonetic transcription is employed. It is a matter of fact that as a result of institutionalized and/or community-driven language planning and revitalization efforts many endangered languages in Russia have established written standards and do regularly use their languages in writing. Russia seems to provide a special case compared to many other small endangered languages in the world, but for some of these languages, not only Komi-Zyrian, but also for instance Northern Khanty, Northern Selkup, or Tundra Nenets (which are all object to documentation at present), a significant amount of printed texts can be found in books and newspapers printed during different periods, and several of these languages are also used digitally on the Internet today.[3] Compared to common practice in corpus building for non-

endangered languages or dialects (for Russian dialects, cf. Waldenfels et al. 2014), the use of phonemic transcriptions in the mentioned language documentation projects seems highly anachronistic if orthographic systems are available and in use. Note also, that many contemporary and historical printed texts written in these languages are also already digitized,[4] which would make it easily possible in principle to combine spoken and written data in one and the same corpus later. The use of an orthography-based transcription system not only ease, and hence, speeds up the transcription process, but it enables a straightforward integration of all available (digitized) printed texts into our corpus in a uniform way, too. Note also, that combining all available spoken and written data into one corpus would not only make the corpora larger token-wise, but such corpora will also be ideal for future corpus-based variational sociolinguistic investigations. Falling back to orthographic transcriptions of our spoken language documentation corpora seems therefore most sensible. Last but not least, if research in language documentation is intended to be useful for the communities as well, the representation of transcribed texts in orthography is the most logical choice.

In our own language documentation projects, we question especially the special value given to time consuming phonemic transcriptions and (semi-)manual morpheme-by-morpheme interlinearizations when basic phonological and morphological descriptions are already available (which is arguably true for the majority of languages in Northern Eurasia), as such descriptions serve as a resource to accessing phonological and morphological structures. Instead, we propose a step-by-step approach to reach higher-level morphosyntactic annotations by using and incrementally improving genuine computational methods. This procedure encompasses a systematic integration of all available resources into the language documentation endeavor: textual, lexicographic, and grammatical.

The language documentation projects we work with (cf. Blokland, Gerstenberger, et al. 2015; Gerstenberger et al. 2017b; Gerstenberger et al. 2017a) are concerned with the building of mul-

---

[1] http://www-01.sil.org/computing/toolbox

[2] http://fieldworks.sil.org/flex

[3] See, for instance, The Finno-Ugric Languages and The Internet Project (Jauhiainen et al. 2015).

[4] For printed sources from the Soviet Union and earlier, the Fenno-Ugrica Collection is especially relevant: http://fennougrica.kansalliskirjasto.fi; contemporary printed sources are also systematically digitized, e.g. for both Komi languages, cf. http://komikyv.ru.

timodal language corpora, including at least spoken and written (i.e. transcribed spoken) data and applying innovative methodology at the interface between endangered language documentation and endangered language technology. We understand language technology as the functional application of computational linguistics as it is aimed at analyzing and generating natural language in various ways and for a variety of purposes. Language technology can create tools which analyze spoken language corpora in a much more effective way, and thus allow one to create better linguistic annotations for and descriptions of the endangered languages in question. A morphosyntactic tagger applied in corpus building is but one example of such a practical application. Using automated tagging, rather than the non-automated methods described in the previous section, allows for directing more resources towards transcription and for working with larger data sets because slow manual annotation no longer necessarily forms a bottleneck in a project's data management workflow.

The examples in our paper are taken specifically from Komi-Zyrian, although we work with several endangered Uralic languages spoken in the Barents Sea Area. We are developing a common framework for these different language projects in order to systematically apply methods from Natural Language Processing (NLP) to enrich the respective corpora with linguistic annotations. In order to do so, we rely on the following two main principles, which we have begun implementing consistently in our own documentation projects:

1. the use an *orthography-based transcription* system, and

2. the application of *computer-based methods* as much as possible in *creating higher-level annotations* of the compiled corpus data.

2 Available Data and Tools for Dialectal and Standard Komi

Izhva Komi is a dialect of Komi-Zyrian, henceforth Komi, spoken in the Komi Republic as well as outside the republic in several language islands in Northeastern Europe and Western Siberia. Beside Izhva dialect data we have also a smaller amount of data from the Udora dialect, spoken in the West of the Komi Republic. Komi belongs to the Permic branch of the Uralic language family

and is spoken by approximately 160,000 people who live predominantly in the Komi Republic of the Russian Federation. Although formally recognized as the second official language of the Republic, the language is endangered as the result of rapid language shift to Russian.

Komi is a morphologically rich and agglutinating language with primarily suffixing morphology and predominantly head-final constituent order, differential object marking, and accusative-nominative alignment. The linguistic structure of Komi and its dialects is relatively well described (for an English language overview, cf. Hausenberg 1998). However, the existing descriptions focus on phonology and morphology and are not written in modern descriptive frameworks.

The most important official actor for (corpus and status) language planning for standard written Komi is the Centre for Innovative Language Technology at the Komi Republican Academy of State Service and Administration in Syktyvkar, which is currently creating the Komi National Corpus, a corpus that already now contains over 30M words. The spoken data we work with come from our own "Iźva-Komi Documentation Project" (2014–2016) and include fully transcribed and translated dialect recordings on audio and (partly) video. These recordings were mostly collected during fieldwork or origin from legacy data. The Udora data are similar in structure and origin from the project "Down River Vashka" (2013). An overview of the Komi data we have at our disposal is shown in Table 1.

Our language documentations are archived at The Language Archive (TLA, for short) at the Max Planck Institute for Psycholinguistics in Nijmegen/Netherlands (cf. Partanen et al. 2013; Blokland, Fedina, et al. 2009–2017). For the written Komi data, see Fedina et al. (2016–2017) and the online portal to the above mentioned Centre's data and tools, which is called "The Finno-Ugric Laboratory for Support of the Electronic Representation of Regional Languages".[5] The Centre has also made free electronic dictionaries and a Hunspell checker (including morpheme lists) available, but research towards a higher-level grammar parser has not been carried out in Syktyvkar so far.

Another important open-source language technology infrastructure for Komi is under development by Jack Rueter (Helsinki) at *Giella-*

---

[5]`http://fu-lab.ru`

Table 1: Overview on the amount of Komi spoken and written data in our projects at present; the category Tokens refers to the number of transcribed tokens in both audio/video recordings and digitized transcribed spoken texts lacking a recording; note that these numbers are only very rough estimates; note also that typically, our data include translations into at least one majority language too.

Language		Modality	Recorded speakers/writers	Time span of texts	Tokens in corpus
Komi-Zyrian	(Standard)	written	~2,500	1920–2017	30,000,000
Komi-Zyrian	(Izhva dialect)	spoken	~150	1844–2016	200,000
Komi-Zyrian	(Udora dialect)	spoken	~50	1902–2013	40,000

tekno/Divvun – Saami Language Technology at UiT The Arctic University of Norway.[6] The Giellatekno group works with computational linguistic research into the analysis of Saamic and other languages of the circumpolar area. Giellatekno has the know-how and the infrastructure necessary to deal with all aspects of corpus and computational linguistics and has fully implemented this for Northern Saami (cf. Moshagen et al. 2013; Johnson et al. 2013; Trosterud 2006b).

The project described in this paper makes use of the infrastructure and tools already available in Syktyvkar and Tromsø, but works specifically with corpus construction and corpus annotation of spoken data, which have not been in focus of computational linguistic research so far.

3 Data Annotation Process

Nowadays, there is a multitude of approaches for Natural Language Processing (NLP) with 'pure' statistic-based on one end of a scale, 'pure' rule-based on the other end, and a wide range of hybridization in between (cf. also a recent "hybrid" approach using a manually interlinearized/glossed language documentation corpus from Ingush as training data for a tagger, Tiedemann et al. 2016).

For major languages such as English, Spanish, or Russian, the dominating paradigm within computational linguistics is based on statistical methods: computer programs are trained to understand the behavior of natural language by means of presenting them with vast amounts of either unanalyzed or manually analyzed data. However, for the majority of the world's languages, and especially for low-resourced endangered languages, this approach is not a viable option because the amounts of texts that would be required – analyzed or not – are often not available. In many cases the language

documentation work is the first source of any texts ever, although the increasing written use of many minority languages cannot be underestimated either. There have been successful projects which have built online corpora for a large of variety of these languages,[7] and it remains to be seen how they can be integrated to language documentation materials on these and related languages.

The older paradigm of language data analysis is the rule-based or grammar-based approach: the linguist writes a grammar rules in a specific format that is machine-readable, the formal grammar is then compiled into a program capable of analyzing (and eventually also generating) text input. There are several schools within the rule-based paradigm; the approach chosen by our projects is a combination of Finite-State Transducer (FST) technology for the morphological analysis, and Constraint Grammar (CG) for the syntactic analysis.

This approach has been tested with several written languages, for which it routinely provides highly robust analyses for unconstrained text input. We adapt the open preprocessing and analysis toolkit provided by Giellatekno (cf. Moshagen et al. 2013) for both written and spoken, transcribed language data. Since the chosen infrastructure is built for standard written languages, we have developed a set of conventions to convert our spoken language data into a "written-like" format, which is thus more easily portable into the Giellatekno infrastructure. First, we represent our spoken recordings in standardized orthography (with adaptations for dialectal and other sub-standard forms if needed). Second, we mark clause boundaries and use other punctuation marks as in written language, although surface text structuring in spoken texts is prosodic rather than syntactic and the alignment of our texts to the original record-

---

[6]http://giellatekno.uit.no, http://divvun.no

[7]http://web-corpora.net/wsgi3/minorlangs/

ing is utterance-based, rather than sentence-based. For specific spoken language phenomena, such as false starts, hesitations or self-corrections as well as for marking incomprehensible sections in our transcription, we use a simple (and orthography-compatible) markup adapted from annotation conventions commonly used in spoken language corpora.

Our transcribed spoken text data (using standard orthography) as well as any written text data are stored in the XML format provided by the multimedia language annotation program EUDICO Linguistic Annotator (ELAN, for short)[8] which allows audio and video recordings to be time-aligned with detailed, hierarchically organized tiers for transcriptions, translations and further annotations.

The annotation process contains the following steps:

1. **preprocessing**: a Perl script configured with a list of language-specific abbreviations that takes care of tokenization;

2. **morphosyntactic analysis**: an FST that models free and bound morpheme by means of linear (`lexc`) and non-linear rules (`twolc`) needed for word formation and inflection;

3. **disambiguation**: a formal grammar written in the CG framework.

The process of annotation enrichment in ELAN follows the usual analysis pipeline of the Giellatekno infrastructure. The string of each utterance is extracted from the `orthography`-tier, tokenized, then sent to the morphosyntactic analyzer, and finally to the disambiguation module. The analysis output is then parsed and the bits of information are structured and put back into the ELAN file.

Yet, as simple as it looks, the implementation required a careful analysis of item indexing in ELAN. On the one hand, all new annotation items have to land in the correct place in the structure, which involves keeping track of the respective indices for speaker and utterance. On the other hand, new XML element indices have to be generated in such a way that they should not conflict with the extant indices assigned when an ELAN file is created. Since ELAN data can include the transcribed overlapping speech of several recorded speakers, it is not only four new tiers for `word`, `lemma`, `part-of-speech`, and

———
[8]`https://tla.mpi.nl/tools/tla-tools/elan`.

`morphosyntactic description` that need to be generated and added to the initial structure, but 4xN, with N being the total number of speakers recorded in the ELAN file. If the new tiers were not generated and placed in the correct place, the ELAN XML structure would be spoiled, thus blocking the enriched ELAN file from showing up in the ELAN GUI as desired.

Since the ELAN files are in XML format, they can be both read and edited by humans with any text editor and accessed automatically by virtually any programming language. For the implementation of the script that links the ELAN data and the FST/CG, we decided to use Python because:

1. it is a flexible, interpreted programming language with support for multiple systems and platforms;

2. it is easy to read and to learn for even a novice programmer, which is perhaps the reason why it is often used for linguistic applications;

3. and finally, it offers XML processing support by means of XML packages such as ElementTree and lxml.

The input file for the whole process is an ELAN file lacking `word`, `lemma`, `part-of-speech`, and `morphological description` tiers. Thus, all tiers dependent on the `word`-tier are inserted dynamically (cf. Figure 1). For each speaker recorded in the ELAN file, the values of each utterance string from each individual `orth`-tier are extracted by the Python script and sent to the appropriate morphosyntactic analyzer.

After the FST has analyzed the word forms, has output the analyses, and the analyses are sent to disambiguation, the Python script parses the final output of the pipeline and restructures it when multiple analyses in a cohort are possible, that means when the disambiguation module could not disambiguate the output totally. A cohort is a word form along with all its possible analyses from the FST. Each individual lemma depends on the word form sent to the FST, each part-of-speech depends on a specific lemma, and finally each morphosyntactic description depends on a specific part-of-speech. With these constraints, new ELAN tiers for the analysis are built by factoring the different item types accordingly.

Ambiguities in language analyses are quite common, but with FSTs in development for minority languages, they are even more frequent. Our

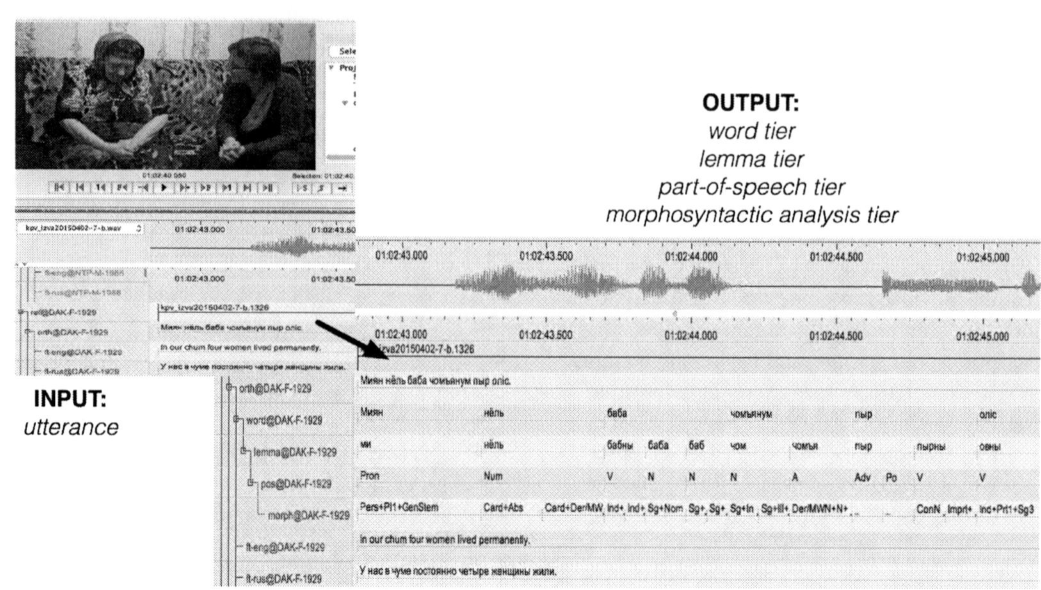

Figure 1: The result of the first two processing steps – tokenization and morphosyntactic analysis for the Komi sentence *Миян нёль баба чомъянум пыр оліс.* 'In our chum (tent) four women lived permanently.'

Figure 2: The result of the last processing step – (partial) disambiguation of morphosyntactic ambiguous analyses for the same Komi sentence as in Figure 1: for instance, for the word form *чомъянум* the contextually appropriate noun reading with lemma *чом* is chosen while the adjective reading with lemma *чомъя* is discarded.

plan is to further develop the extant disambiguation module in a similar way as for Northern Saami (cf. Antonsen, Huhmarniemi, et al. 2009).

Note that the lack of a higher-level analysis often leads to cases of ambiguity concerning the morphological analysis, i.e., multiple analyses for one and the same word form. As already mentioned, for the disambiguation of these homonyms, we use CG, which takes the morphologically analyzed text as its input, and ideally only returns the appropriate reading, based on the immediate context of a specific word form–analysis pair. CG is a language-independent formalism for morphological disambiguation and syntactic analysis of text corpora developed by Karlsson (1990) and Karlsson et al. (1995). Since we use the standard analysis pipeline offered by the Giellatekno's infrastructure, we use the CG implementation vislcg3,[9] which is freely available.

The CG analysis can be enriched with syntactic functions and dependency relations if all underlying grammatical rules are described sufficiently. Since the output of a CG analysis is a dependency structure for a particular sentence, the output may also be converted into phrase structure representations.

Our work with the CG description of Komi is only at the beginning stage. To be completed, it would likely need to include several thousand rules. However, the experience of other Giellatekno projects working with CG shows that some months of concentrated work can result in a CG description that can already be implemented in a preliminary tagger useful for lexicographic work as well as for several other purposes. For instance, the rather shallow grammar parser for Southern Saami described by Antonsen and Trosterud (2011) includes only somewhat more than 100 CG rules, but already results in reasonably good lemmatization accuracy for open class parts-of-speech. This means that the approach is readily adjustable to language documentation projects with limited resources. Furthermore, CG rules can potentially be ported from one language to another, e.g. the rule for disambiguating the connegative verb in Komi would also work in several other Uralic languages.

Komi is an agglutinative language, so with morphologically more complex forms the homonymy is rare. However, there are specific forms which tend to collide with one another, especially with some verb and noun stems which happen to be identical. The monosyllabic stems have canonical shape CV(C), and this simple structure is one reason that makes morphologically unmarked forms to be homonymous: nominative singular nouns, and some of the imperative and connegative forms in the verbal paradigm.

4 Post-Processing of Corpus Data in ELAN

Note that so far, our work with the script has resulted in a rather insular solution which is directly applicable to our own projects only. In order to make our workflow usable for other projects we have to find a more generic solution. Potentially, our script could be integrated into the ELAN program using a web service. On the other hand, modifying the Python script to work with somewhat different ELAN input files would not be very difficult.

However, since our approach aims at separating the annotation tool (i.e. the FST/CG-based tagger) from the non-annotated corpus data (i.e. the transcription), we are relying on the ELAN GUI only until the transcription (and translation) of the original recordings is done in this program. The ELAN-FST/CG interaction does not depend on the ELAN tool, but only on the data in ELAN XML. Once the corpus is extended by new transcripts (or existing transcripts are corrected) or the FST/CG rules are refined, the whole corpus will be analyzed anew. This will simply overwrite the previous data in the relevant ELAN tiers.

In this way, we will release new annotated corpus in regular intervals and make them available at TLA in Nijmegen, where we archive and make available our project data. One significant advantage of working with ELAN XML is that it can be accessed through the online tools Annotation Explorer (ANNEX, for short)[10] and TROVA[11], which are basically online GUIs of the same search engines built into the ELAN tool. ANNEX is an interface that links annotations and media files from the archive online (just as ELAN does on a local computer). The TROVA tool can be used to perform complex searches on multiple layers of the corpus and across multiple files in basically the

---

[9]https://visl.sdu.dk/cg.html

[10]https://tla.mpi.nl/tools/tla-tools/annex

[11]Search engine for annotation content archived at TLA, https://tla.mpi.nl/tools/tla-tools/trova

same was as within ELAN itself. As a practical benefit, the integration of TROVA and the whole infrastructure at TLA makes it easy to control corpus access, something that regularly demands significant consideration when sensitive language documentation materials are concerned. At the same time this infrastructure also allows examples to be disseminated more widely because it is easy to provide links for specific utterances in the data. Ultimately of course, the access rights of a specific file in the archive determine whether this works or not.

5 Summary

In this paper, we describe a project at the interface between language technology and language documentation. Our aim is to overcome manual annotation of our language documentation corpora. We achieve this by implementing Finite State Transducers and Constraint Grammar for rule-based morphosyntactic tagging and disambiguation. The different modules in our annotation tool interact directly with our corpus data, which is consistently structured in ELAN XML.

Since Constraint Grammar can be simply chained, we plan not only to extend and improve the current disambiguation module but also to implement Constraint Grammar for further, syntactic analysis, to achieve fully disambiguated dependency treebanks. The relevant work will be carried out as part of the project "Language Documentation meets Language Technology: The Next Step in the Description of Komi" which already started in 2017.

While the rule-based morphosyntactic modeling is not state of the art in contemporary NLP, it does have significant advantages specifically in *endangered* language documentation:

1. the results of the automatic tagging are *exceptionally precise* and cannot normally be reached with statistical methods applied on the relatively small corpora endangered language documentation normally creates;

2. while incrementally formulating rules and testing them on the corpus data, we are not only creating a tool but producing a *full-fledged grammatical description based on broad empirical evidence* at the same time;

3. and last but not least, our work will eventually also help develop new (I)CALL technology, i.e. *(intelligent) computer-assisted language learning* systems for the languages we work on.

One relatively simple example for the latter is the direct implementation of our formalized morphosyntactic description in Voikko spell-checkers, which is a easily done with the Giellatekno/Divvun infrastructure setup and which is an highly important tool to support future writers of the endangered language.

Last but not least, since the official support and language planning activities are significant at present for Komi and some of the other languages we are working on, these languages are increasingly used in spoken and written form. Better adaptation of computational technology by language documenters will eventually be necessary in order to annotate and make efficient use of the ever increasing amount of available data.

Ultimately, our work will therefore also contribute to future language planning, language development, and language vitalization.

Acknowledgments

This paper describes on-going work by the Izhva Komi Documentation Project, which is funded by the Kone Foundation between 2014–2016 and 2017–2020 and embedded in a larger research group[12] working with the documentation and description of several endangered languages of the Barents Sea Area in Northeastern Europe. The present article builds on and continues our preliminary research published in Blokland, Gerstenberger, et al. 2015; Gerstenberger et al. 2017a; Gerstenberger et al. 2017b. We would like to thank the other co-authors of these papers, Rogier Blokland, Marina Fedina, and Joshua Wilbur for their ongoing collaboration. We also want to express our gratitude to Trond Trosterud and Jack Rueter for continuous valuable feedback. Last but not least, important ideas for our research were developed while writing the application for the long-term project INEL[13] by Beáta Wagner-Nagy together with Michael Rießler and The Hamburg Center for Language Corpora (University of Hamburg).

[12]http://saami.uni-freiburg.de
[13]https://inel.corpora.uni-hamburg.de

References

Antonsen, Lene, S. Huhmarniemi, and Trond Trosterud (2009). "Constraint Grammar in dialogue systems". In: *NEALT Proceedings Series 2009*. Vol. 8. Tartu: Tartu ülikool, pp. 13–21.

Antonsen, Lene and Trond Trosterud (2011). "Next to nothing. A cheap South Saami disambiguator". In: *Proceedings of the NODALIDA 2011 Workshop Constraint Grammar Applications, May 11, 2011 Riga, Latvia*. Ed. by Eckhard Bick, Kristin Hagen, Kaili Müürisep, and Trond Trosterud. NEALT Proceedings Series 14. Tartu: Tartu University Library, pp. 1–7. url: http://hdl.handle.net/10062/19296.

Blokland, Rogier, Marina Fedina, Niko Partanen, and Michael Rießler (2009–2017). "Izhva Kyy". In: *The Language Archive (TLA). Donated Corpora*. In collab. with Vasilij Čuprov, Marija Fedina, Dorit Jackermeier, Elena Karvovskaya, Dmitrij Levčenko, and Kateryna Olyzko. Nijmegen: Max Planck Institute for Psycholinguistics. url: https://corpus1.mpi.nl/ds/asv/?5&openhandle=hdl:1839/00-0000-0000-000C-1CF6-F.

Blokland, Rogier, Ciprian Gerstenberger, Marina Fedina, Niko Partanen, Michael Rießler, and Joshua Wilbur (2015). "Language documentation meets language technology". In: *First International Workshop on Computational Linguistics for Uralic Languages, 16th January, 2015, Tromsø, Norway. Proceedings of the workshop*. Ed. by Tommi A. Pirinen, Francis M. Tyers, and Trond Trosterud. Septentrio Conference Series 2015:2. Tromsø: The University Library of Tromsø, pp. 8–18. doi: 10.7557/scs.2015.2.

Cox, Christopher (2011). "Corpus linguistics and language documentation. Challenges for collaboration". In: *Corpus-based Studies in Language Use, Language Learning, and Language Documentation*. Ed. by John Newman, Harald Baayen, and Sally Rice. Amsterdam: Rodopi, pp. 239–264.

Fedina, Marina, Enye Lav, Dmitri Levchenko, Ekaterina Koval, and Inna Nekhorosheva (2016–2017). *Nacional'nyj korpus komi jazyka*. Syktyvkar: FU-Lab. url: http://komicorpora.ru.

Gerstenberger, Ciprian, Niko Partanen, Michael Rießler, and Joshua Wilbur (2017a). "Instant annotations. Applying NLP methods to the annotation of spoken language documentation corpora". In: *Proceedings of the 3rd International Workshop on Computational Linguistics for Uralic languages. Proceedings of the workshop*. Ed. by Tommi A. Pirinen, Michael Rießler, Trond Trosterud, and Francis M. Tyers. ACL anthology. Baltimore, Maryland, USA: Association for Computational Linguistics (ACL). url: http://aclweb.org/anthology/. In press.

– (2017b). "Utilizing language technology in the documentation of endangered Uralic languages". In: *Northern European Journal of Language Technology: Special Issue on Uralic Language Technology*. Ed. by Tommi A. Pirinen, Trond Trosterud, and Francis M. Tyers. url: http://www.nejlt.ep.liu.se/. In press.

Hausenberg, Anu-Reet (1998). "Komi". In: ed. by Daniel Abondolo. Routledge Language Family Descriptions. London: Routledge, pp. 305–326.

Himmelmann, Nikolaus (2012). "Linguistic data types and the interface between language documentation and description". In: *Language Documentation & Conservation* 6, pp. 187–207. url: http://hdl.handle.net/10125/4503.

Jauhiainen, Heidi, Tommi Jauhiainen, and Krister Lindén (2015). "The Finno-Ugric Languages and The Internet Project". In: *First International Workshop on Computational Linguistics for Uralic Languages, 16th January, 2015, Tromsø, Norway. Proceedings of the workshop*. Ed. by Tommi A. Pirinen, Francis M. Tyers, and Trond Trosterud. Septentrio Conference Series 2015:2. Tromsø: The University Library of Tromsø, pp. 87–98. doi: 10.7557/5.3471.

Johnson, Ryan, Lene Antonsen, and Trond Trosterud (2013). "Using finite state transducers for making efficient reading comprehension dictionaries". In: *Proceedings of the 19th Nordic Conference of Computational Linguistics (NODALIDA 2013), May 22–24, 2013, Oslo*. Ed. by Stephan Oepen and Janne Bondi Johannessen. Linköping Electronic Conference Proceedings 85. Linköping: Linköping University, pp. 59–71. url: http://emmtee.net/oe/nodalida13/conference/45.pdf.

Karlsson, Fred (1990). "Constraint Grammar as a framework for parsing unrestricted text". In: *Proceedings of the 13th International Conference of Computational Linguistics*. Ed. by Hans Karlgren. Vol. 3. Helsinki, pp. 168–173.

Karlsson, Fred, Atro Voutilainen, Juha Heikkilä, and Arto Anttila, eds. (1995). *Constraint Grammar. A language-independent system for parsing unrestricted text*. Natural Language Processing 4. Berlin: Mouton de Gruyter.

Moshagen, Sjur, Tommi A. Pirinen, and Trond Trosterud (2013). "Building an open-source development infrastructure for language technology projects". In: *Proceedings of the 19th Nordic Conference of Computational Linguistics (NODALIDA 2013), May 22–24, 2013, Oslo*. Ed. by Stephan Oepen and Janne Bondi Johannessen. Linköping Electronic Conference Proceedings 85. Linköping: Linköping University, pp. 343–352. url: http://emmtee.net/oe/nodalida13/conference/43.pdf.

Partanen, Niko, Alexandra Kellner, Timo Rantakaulio, Galina Misharina, and Hamel Tristan (2013). "Down River Vashka. Corpus of the Udora dialect of Komi-Zyrian". In: *The Language Archive (TLA). Donated Corpora*. Nijmegen: Max Planck Institute for Psycholinguistics. url: https://hdl.handle.net/1839/00-0000-0000-001C-D649-8.

Snoek, Conor, Dorothy Thunder, Kaidi Lõo, Antti Arppe, Jordan Lachler, Sjur Moshagen, and Trond Trosterud (2014). "Modeling the noun morphology of Plains Cree". In: *Proceedings of the 2014 Workshop on the Use of Computational Methods in the Study of Endangered Languages*. Baltimore, Maryland, USA: Association for Computational Linguistics, pp. 34–42. url: http://www.aclweb.org/anthology/W/W14/W14-2205.

Tiedemann, Jörg, Johanna Nichols, and Ronald Sprouse (2016). "Tagging Ingush. Language technology for low-resource languages using resources from linguistic field work". In: *Proceedings of the Workshop on Language Technology Resources and Tools for Digital Humanities (LT4DH). Osaka, Japan, December 11–17 2016*, pp. 148–155. url: https://www.clarin-d.de/joomla/images/lt4dh/pdf/LT4DH20.pdf.

Trosterud, Trond (2006a). "Grammar-based language technology for the Sámi Languages". In: *Lesser used Languages & Computer Linguistics*. Bozen: Europäische Akademie, pp. 133–148.

– (2006b). "Grammatically based language technology for minority languages. Status and policies, casestudies and applications of information technology". In: *Lesser-known languages of South Asia*. Ed. by Anju Saxena and Lars Borin. Trends in Linguistics. Studies and Monographs 175. Berlin: Mouton de Gruyter, pp. 293–316.

Waldenfels, Ruprecht von, Michael Daniel, and Nina Dobrushina (2014). "Why standard orthography? Building the Ustya River Basin Corpus, an online corpus of a Russian dialect". In: *Computational linguistics and intellectual technologies. Proceedings of the Annual International Conference «Dialogue» (2014)*. Moskva: Izdatel'stvo RGGU, [720–729]. url: http://www.dialog-21.ru/digests/dialog2014/materials/pdf/WaldenfelsR.pdf.

Inferring Case Systems from IGT:
Impacts and Detection of Variable Glossing Practices

Kristen Howell[*], Emily M. Bender[*], Michael Lockwood[*], Fei Xia[*], and Olga Zamaraeva[*]

[*]Department of Linguistics, University of Washington, Seattle, WA, U.S.A.
{kphowell, ebender, lockwm, fxia, olzama}@uw.edu

Abstract

In this paper, we apply two methodologies of data enrichment to predict the case systems of languages from a diverse and complex data set. The methodologies are based on those of Bender et al. (2013), but we extend them to work with a new data format and apply them to a new dataset. In doing so, we explore the effects of noise and inconsistency on the proposed algorithms. Our analysis reveals assumptions in the previous work that do not hold up in less controlled data sets.

1 Introduction

This work is situated within the AGGREGATION Project whose aim is to facilitate analysis of data collected by field linguists by automatically creating computational grammars on the basis of interlinear glossed text (IGT) and the LinGO Grammar Matrix customization system (Bender et al., 2010). Previous work by the AGGREGATION Project has looked at answering specific, high-level typological questions for many different languages (Bender et al., 2013) as well as answering as much of the Grammar Matrix customization system's questionnaire as possible for one specific language (Bender et al., 2014). In this paper, we revisit the case-related experiments done by Bender et al. (2013) in light of new systems for standardizing and enriching IGT and using a broader data set. Specifically, where Bender et al. considered only data from small collections of IGT created by students in a grammar engineering class (Bender, 2014), we will work with the larger and more diverse data sets available from ODIN version 2.1 (Xia et al., 2016). These data sets contain a great deal of noise in terms of inconsistent glossing conventions, missing glosses and data set bias. However, while these data sets are noisier,

they do benefit from more sophisticated methods for enriching IGT (specifically projecting structure from the English translation line to the source language line; Georgi (2016)). Additionally, we explore cleaning up some noise in the glossing, using the Map Gloss methodology of Lockwood (2016).

In the following sections, we provide a description of the methodology and data sets we build on (§2), before laying out the methodology as developed for this paper (§3) and presenting the numerical results (§4). The primary contribution of our paper is in (§5), where we do an error analysis and relate our results to sources of bias.

2 Background

This section briefly overviews the previous work that we build on in this paper: methodology developed by the RiPLes and AGGREGATION projects to extract typological information from IGT (§2.1), the construction and enrichment of the ODIN data set (§2.2), and Map Gloss system for regularizing glosses in IGT (§2.3).

2.1 Inferring Case Systems from IGT

Bender et al. (2013) began work on automatically creating precision grammars on the basis of IGT by using the annotations in IGT to extract large-scale typological properties, specifically word order and case system. These typological properties were defined as expected by the Grammar Matrix customization system (Bender et al., 2010), with the goal of eventually providing enough information (both typological and lexical) that the system can automatically create useful implemented grammars. A proof of concept for this end-to-end system was conducted with data from Chintang in Bender et al. (2014).

In their case experiment, Bender et al. (2013) explored two methods for inferring case systems from IGT. The first, called GRAM, counted all of the case grams for a particular language and ap-

Proceedings of the 2nd Workshop on the Use of Computational Methods in the Study of Endangered Languages, pages 67–75,
Honolulu, Hawai'i, USA, March 6–7, 2017. ©2017 Association for Computational Linguistics

plied a heuristic to determine case system based on whether or not certain grams were present (NOM, ACC, ERG, ABS). The second method, called SAO, collected all of the grams on all intransitive subject (S), transitive subject (A) and transitive object (O) NPs, and then proceeded with the assumption that the most common gram in each role was a case gram. The grammatical role was determined by mapping parses of the English translation (using the Charniak parser (Charniak, 1997)) through the gloss line onto the source language line, according to the methodology set forth in the RiPLes project for resource-poor languages (Xia and Lewis, 2007). Because this method looks for the most frequent gram to identify the case marking gram, it is not essential that the gloss line follow a specific glossing convention, provided that the grams are consistent with each other. As a result, this method was expected to be suited to a wider range of data than GRAM.

The data for this experiment comprised 31 languages from 17 different language families. Data was developed in a class in which students use descriptive resources to create testsuites and Grammar Matrix choices files (files that specify characteristics of the language so the Grammar Matrix can output a starter grammar) and has now been curated by the LANGUAGE COLLAGE project (Bender, 2014). Because the testsuites were constructed for grammar engineering projects, data from the testsuites are not representative of typical language use nor of typical field data collections, but nonetheless illustrate grammatical patterns. In addition, the testsuites generated in this class conform to standard glossing procedures (specifically the Leipzig Glossing Rules (LGR; Bickel et al. (2008)) and are annotated for the phenomena they represent.

The results of Bender et al. (2013) are given in Table 1, where the baseline is a 'most frequent type' baseline, i.e. chosen according to the most frequent case system in a typological survey (here, this would be neutral aka no case).[1]

In this experiment, both GRAM and SAO performed better than the baseline. The GRAM method outperformed SAO, which was attributed to the small size and LGR-compliant nature of the testsuites.

---

[1] We take this heuristic from Bender et al. (2013), although when we applied this heuristic to the 2013 data, our results did not quite match those in Table 1.

Data Set	Number of languages	GRAM	SAO	Baseline
DEV1	10	0.900	0.700	0.400
DEV2	10	0.900	0.500	0.500
TEST	11	0.545	0.545	0.455

Table 1: Accuracy of case-marking inference as reported in (Bender et al., 2013)

2.2 ODIN Data Set

The Online Database of Interlinear Text (Lewis and Xia, 2010; Xia et al., 2016) was developed by crawling linguistics papers and extracting IGT. In ODIN 2.1, this data is enriched with dependency parses by parsing the translation line with the MSTParser (McDonald et al., 2005), aligning the translation and language lines, and then projecting the syntactic structure of the English parse onto the language line, according to the methodology set forth by Georgi (2016). Dependency parses make explicit the grammatical role of items in a sentence. For our purposes, this means that identifying subjects, agents and objects is more straightforward than it was for Bender et al. (2013), who were working with projected constituency structures.

2.3 Map Gloss

One issue that arises when working with IGT, especially IGT taken from multiple different sources (as is found in the ODIN collection), is that the glossing cannot be assumed to be consistent. Different authors follow different glossing conventions, including different sets of grams; grams may be misspelled; and glossing may be carried out at different levels of granularity. Map Gloss (Lockwood, 2016) was developed to address the first two of these sources of variation, which are also found in the LANGUAGE COLLAGE data (though to a lesser extent). Map Gloss takes in a set of IGT for a language and outputs a standard set of grams for that language, as well as a mapping from glosses observed in the IGT to the standard set. Lockwood (2016) constructed a gold standard set of grams that follows the Leipzig Glossing Rules (Bickel et al., 2008) and the GOLD Ontology (Indiana University, 2010) conventions.

Map Gloss maps common misspelled glosses to their correct form, normalizes glosses such as IMP (for 'imperfective') to less ambiguous forms such as IPFV, adds grams where they were left out such as finding *he* in the gloss line instead of 3SG.M, and splits grams that were combined such as 3SGM to 3SG.M. Finally, Map Gloss allows for grams that are language specific (i.e. not known to the gold standard set but also not targets for correction). Though the gloss line in IGT will typically mix lemmas and grams, and may sometimes also contain part of speech tags, the final normalized set that Map Gloss outputs for a language will contain only the grams.

3   Methodology

In this experiment, we extend and adapt the methodology of Bender et al. (2013), designed to work with projected constituency structures, to use the dependency structures available for the enriched IGT in ODIN 2.1. To accomplish this, we first reimplemented the software from Bender et al. (2013) to work with the Xigt format (Goodman et al., 2015). Xigt, beyond being the format used in ODIN 2.1, has many advantages for this kind of work because it is set up to directly encode not only the base IGT but also further annotations (enrichments) over that IGT (in a stand-off fashion), such that one can easily query for items such as the subject in the projected dependency structure.

For better comparability with the results reported by Bender et al. (2013), ideally we would be working with the same languages. However, some of the languages used in the 2013 experiment have few or no instances of IGT in ODIN. These languages were not expected to yield useful results, so we added eight new languages which were available in both LANGUAGE COLLAGE and ODIN. Our final data set comprises 39 languages from 23 distinct language families, as shown in Table 3 below. The quantity of data varies widely across these languages, as do the number of authors contributing the data. The IGT for French [fra], for example comes from 4,787 separate documents, some of whom have overlapping authors. To account for the added languages, we re-ran the scripts from Bender et al. (2013) on their original data as well as the LANGUAGE COLLAGE testsuites for the newly added languages (shown in the LANGUAGE COLLAGE lin of Table 4).

We used Map Gloss (Lockwood, 2016) to standardize the glosses from the ODIN data. ODIN includes IGT from a wide range of authors with their own conventions for gloss naming. We hypothesized that mapping these glosses to a standard set

of grams is important in helping our inference procedure correctly assign case systems. Map Gloss features a default set of standard glosses and a generic training set, which we used, in lieu of annotating our own training set. For this experiment we were chiefly interested in the grams for case, which Map Gloss handles quite well off the shelf, using a list of commonly used case glosses that map to a standard set for each language. For example INS, INST, INSTR and INSTRUMENTAL all map to INS. Map Gloss was run on each of the ODIN language files individually to identify a standard set of grams. We then generated new Xigt files for each language, replacing the existing case glosses with the standardized case glosses from Map Gloss.

For case system extraction we adapt both the GRAM and SAO methodologies set forth in the 2013 experiment. The GRAM method loops through the IGT collecting glosses from a set of licensed grams (or tags) associated with case. We assign case systems according to the presence or absence of NOM, ACC, ERG and ABS, as in Table 2. This methodology assumes compliance with the Leipzig Glossing Rules, and therefore its performance relies on data being glossed according to these conventions with regards to case.

Case system	Case grams present	
	NOM ∨ ACC	ERG ∨ ABS
neutral		
nom-acc	✓	
erg-abs		✓
split-erg	✓	✓

Table 2: GRAM case system assignment rules (Adapted from Bender et al. (2013))

The second method, SAO, is intended to be less dependent on glossing choices. This method uses the dependency parses in ODIN to identify the subject of intransitive verbs (S), the agent of transitive verbs (A) and the patient of transitive verbs (O). We consider only clauses that appear to be simple transitive or intransitive clauses, based on the presence of an overt subject and/or object, and collect all grams for each argument type. We assume the most frequent gram for each argument type (S, A or O) to be the case marker. We then use the following rules to assign case system, where S_g, O_g and A_g denote the most frequent grams associated with these argument positions:

- Nominative-accusative: $S_g{=}A_g$, and $S_g{\neq}O_g$

- Ergative-absolutive: $S_g{=}O_g$, and $S_g{\neq}A_g$

- Neutral: $S_g{=}A_g{=}O_g$, or $S_g{\neq}A_g{\neq}O_g$ and S_g, A_g, O_g also present on each of the other argument types

- Tripartite: $S_g{\neq}A_g{\neq}O_g$, and S_g, A_g, O_g (virtually) absent from the other argument types

- Split-ergative: $S_g{\neq}A_g{\neq}O_g$, and A_g and O_g are both present in the list for the S argument type

(Bender et al., 2013)

The space of outputs of the two systems differ slightly. The GRAM method predicts four possible case systems: neutral, nominative-accusative, ergative-absolutive and split-ergative. The SAO method is a little more robust: in addition to the four case systems predicted by GRAM, it can also predict the tripartite case system. We compare the predicted case systems from each system to a gold standard, collected from the choices files and notes included with the LANGUAGE COLLAGE data. In the 2013 experiment, the gold standard for case systems was taken from the choices files produced by the grammar engineering students who produced the original testsuites. The Grammar Matrix customization system (Bender et al., 2010) allows users to choose from a list of possible case systems (as well as other linguistic phenomena) and records this information in a file named choices. However, in some cases, the student might not have used the customization system to establish their case system, so in the present experiment we reviewed their notes for clarification if no case system was specified in the choices file. Because our methodologies predict split-ergativity but are not so refined as to specify subtypes of split-ergativity which are available in the Grammar Matrix customization system, we have included both subtypes 'split-v' (a split based on properties of the verb) and 'split-s' (a split based on properties of the subject) as part of the super-type 'split-ergative' for evaluation.

4 Results

We re-ran the 2013 experiment on all of the data from the original experiment (DEV1, DEV2, and TEST) in addition to LANGUAGE COLLAGE testsuites for the eight new languages. Both GRAM

and SAO were run on ODIN data sets for each language both before and after running Map Gloss to standardize the case grams. In addition, we generated the baseline value in the same manner as Bender et al. (2013), using the 'most common type' heuristic. According to Comrie (2011) this is again 'neutral'. The results are given in Table 4.[2]

Our results for LANGUAGE COLLAGE are notably lower than the results reported in Bender et al. (2013), as shown in Table 1. This can be attributed to two changes from the 2013 experiment. First, we added 8 new languages which were not included in the 2013 results. Second, we updated the gold standard for some of the original languages, after mining through the grammar engineers' notes, rather than merely relying on the case system identified in the choices files. As a result, some languages now have specified case systems in the gold standard, which were assumed to be 'none' (or neutral) in the original experiment.

Although Map Gloss did standardize the case grams in our experiment, it had no measurable effect on the results of the experiment. Map Gloss changed 2.2% of case grams across data sets. The percentage of case grams changed per data set ranged from 0% for many to 50%. For example, in the Hausa data, 30% of case grams were changed, standardizing *sub* and *sbj* to *subject*. However, the most commonly found subject gram in the Hausa data was *abdu* and the most common object gram was *of*. This sort of data set bias is discussed in more detail in section 5.4 but it demonstrates the small impact that Map Gloss made on the results even when it made numerous changes to the data. For many other languages, no case grams were changed by Map Gloss because none were inconsistently spelled or misspelled, or those case grams that were inconsistently or misspelled were not in the subset relevant to either GRAM's or SAO's heuristics (NOM, ACC, ERG, ABS for GRAM or the most frequent gram for SAO).

The accuracy of SAO on ODIN data was just below baseline and GRAM preformed only slightly better with accuracy rates of 41.0% and 56.4% respectively. These results demonstrate that the ODIN data presents an even greater challenge than

---

[2]Code, data and instructions for reproducing the results in Table 4 can be found at `http://depts.washington.edu/uwcl/aggregation/ComputEL-2-Case.html`

[3]The baseline result is the same across the data sets, because the baseline compares the gold standard to the 'most common' case system, and is independent of the dataset.

Language Name	ISO	Language Family	# IGTs	# IGT with Dependency	Gold Standard Case System
French	fra	Indo-European	7412	1322	neutral
Japanese	jpn	Japanese	6665	2484	nom-acc
Korean*	kor	Korean	5383	2208	nom-acc
Icelandic	isl	Indo-European	4259	1100	neutral
Russian	rus	Indo-European	4164	1579	nom-acc
Hausa	hau	Afro-Asiatic	2504	1085	neutral
Indonesian*	ind	Austronesian	1699	1075	neutral
Georgian	kat	Kartvelian	1189	463	split-erg
Tagalog	tgl	Austronesian	1039	418	erg-abs
Thai	tha	Thai-Kadai	692	184	neutral
Czech	ces	Indo-European	664	257	nom-acc
Zulu	zul	Niger-Congo	604	86	neutral
Kannada*	kan	Dravidian	523	300	nom-acc
Chichewa*	nya	Niger-Congo	477	151	neutral
Old English	ang	Indo-European	431	136	nom-acc
Welsh	cym	Indo-European	404	191	neutral
Vietnamese	vie	Austro-Asiatic	352	176	neutral
Taiwanese	nan	Sino-Tibetan	275	148	neutral
Pashto	pbt	Indo-European	274	98	erg-abs
Tamil	tam	Dravidian	244	90	nom-acc
Malayalam	mal	Dravidian	172	91	nom-acc
Breton	bre	Indo-European	74	50	nom-acc
Lillooet*	lil	Salishan	72	16	neutral
Ojibwa	ojg	Algic	64	24	neutral
Hixkaryana	hix	Cariban	62	27	neutral
Lushootseed	lut	Salishan	52	16	neutral
Shona	sna	Niger-Congo	50	18	neutral
Huallaga	qub	Quechuan	46	27	nom-acc
Arabic (Chadian)*	shu	Afro-Asiatic	41	12	nom-acc
Ainu	ain	Ainu	40	21	nom-acc
Ingush	inh	Nakh-Daghestanian	23	13	erg-abs
Arabic (Moroccan)	ary	Afro-Asiatic	14	2	neutral
Haida*	hdn	Haida	7	1	split-erg
Mandinka	mnk	Mande	3	0	neutral
Hup	jup	Nadahup	2	1	nom-acc
Yughur*	uig	Altaic	2	0	nom-acc
Jamamadi	jaa	Arauan	1	1	neutral
Sri Lankan Creole Malay	sci	Malay	0	0	split-erg
Bosnian-Serbo-Croatian	hbs	Indo-European	0	0	nom-acc

Table 3: Languages used in our experiment and their IGT counts in ODIN 2.1. Language families are taken from Haspelmath et al. (2008). The asterisk indicates the 8 new languages that were added to the set of 31 languages from the 2013 experiment

Data	GRAM	SAO	BASELINE
LANGUAGE COLLAGE	0.743	0.589	0.462
ODIN	0.564	0.410	0.462
ODIN + MAP GLOSS	0.564	0.410	0.462

Table 4: Prediction accuracy for 39 languages.[3]

the LANGUAGE COLLAGE data for both methods. While these results are modest, they provide valuable insight into both the methodology and the data, which will be useful in future work to those developing inference systems and those who wish to benefit from them.

5 Error Analysis

In this section we report on the results of our error analysis, specifically looking into the likely causes of particular languages being misclassified by each system.

5.1 Little or no data in ODIN

Two of the languages, Sri Lankan Creole Malay [sci] and Bosnian-Serbo-Croatian [hbs], were not present in ODIN and therefore, the system had no data with which to predict the case and defaulted to 'neutral'. Furthermore, ten other languages had fewer than fifty IGTs in the ODIN collection. If we were to remove these twelve languages from the data, the adjusted results would improve marginally, as shown in Table 5.[4]

Data	GRAM	SAO	BASELINE
LANGUAGE COLLAGE	0.889	0.704	0.556
ODIN	0.593	0.481	0.556
ODIN + MAP GLOSS	0.593	0.481	0.556

Table 5: Prediction accuracy for the 27 languages with at least 50 IGTs

5.2 Availability of dependency parses

One of the anticipated benefits of using ODIN 2.1 data was the availability of dependency parses that could be used for the SAO method. These parses identified a subject and direct object, such that the corresponding noun could be extracted and broken into glosses. However, while the presence of these dependency parses is helpful for this type data, only a fraction of the IGTs had a subject and/or object that the dependency structure had successfully identified. However the reduced number of available IGT due to the lack of dependency parses had little affect on SAO. Filtering out data sets with fewer than 50 IGT with dependency parses, SAO's accuracy is 41.0%, which is no improvement over the results in Table 4.

5.3 Absence of Case Grams

Eight of the languages in ODIN (not counting the two for which there was no data) contained no case glosses at all. Of those eight, five had a neutral case system. The other three were Breton [bre] (nom-acc), Chadian Arabic [shu][5] (nom-acc) and Haida [hdn] (split-erg).[6] Twelve other languages had an average of < 1 case gram per IGT. Of these 20 languages, the only case systems which GRAM correctly predicted were those with neutral case systems. SAO preformed comparably on these languages, only correctly predicting those with neutral case systems and Breton [bre] (nom-acc), which was the result of IGT bias, discussed in more detail in section 5.4.

The under-glossing of case grams is symptomatic of linguistics papers that gloss only distinctions relevant to the argument at hand, rather than giving full IGT. We hope that the Guidelines for Supplementary Materials Appearing in LSA Publications will have an impact on the robustness of IGT glossing in future data collected by ODIN.[7]

5.4 IGT Bias

The vast majority of the predictions made by the SAO method were not based on case glosses at all. Due to a poverty of case glosses in the data, the most common subject, agent and object glosses in the data were usually root nouns. Our algorithm hinges on the hypothesis that case would be the most common gloss across the data if it were glossed on all nouns. We expected that in some languages, person, number or definiteness grams would out-number case grams; however, this was rarely the case in the ODIN data for the 39 languages we sampled. In French [fra] and Welsh [cym], the most common subject and agent gram was *I*, while in other languages it was *he* or 1SG. Breton's most common subject and agent was *children* and most common object was *books*. While in the case of Breton and others, this led to the correct prediction of nom-acc (because the subject and agent were the same as each other and different from the object) the prediction was made for the wrong reasons. Other most-frequent glosses were *dragon*, *jaguar*, *Maria* and *cows*, all of which were so frequently used in their respective data sets that they outnumbered inflectional morphemes that might be more informative for our purposes.

On the one hand, these results demonstrate that our assumption that case grams would be the most common among noun phrases is far too strong when applied to real world data. While the carefully constructed testsuites from LANGUAGE COLLAGE glossed grams throughly and took care to vary their vocabulary, data in linguistics papers may not be so diverse. Indeed in future work, our algorithm should exclude root glosses. Nevertheless, we consider the trend towards using the same noun as the subject across a dataset to be a form of 'IGT bias', as identified by Lewis and Xia (2008). Specifically, it is likely the result of the strategies used for elicitation or the way in which authors chose sentences to include in their

---

[4]We note that results also improve on the LANGUAGE COLLAGE data set when we restrict our attention to these languages.

[5]Chadian Arabic only expresses case-marking on pronouns.

[6]Haida only expresses overt case on pronouns and is generally considered to have a neutral case system.

[7]http://www.linguisticsociety.org/ sites/default/files/Supplemental% 20Materials%20Guide%20for%20LSA%20Pubs. pdf, accessed Feb 13, 2017.

papers. While keeping to a restricted range of vocabulary can perhaps be useful for systematic documentation or exposition of particular grammatical phenomena, it can also result in highly biased data sets. For our purposes, more varied sentences would produce more helpful data sets—and we believe that this is true for other research purposes as well. In addition to bias in the words themselves used for annotation, additional bias may be introduced if a linguist is collecting data for a specific phenomenon. For example, if a language includes an unrepresentatively large set of intransitive or unergative verbs, the system might not have data with which to identify a nominative-accusative system. This type of data set bias can be overcome by collecting a diverse set of data from a variety of sources that is large enough to overcome the biases of a particular set (Lewis and Xia, 2008).

5.5 Gold Standard

A final contributor to the accuracy measurements was the state of the gold standard itself. We do not consider this a source of error, but rather an inevitability of working with low-resource languages and the very reason a system such as this is useful. Some of the languages classified as having a neutral case system (corresponding to 'no-case' in the choices files we use as our gold standard) might be better analyzed as in fact having (non-neutral) case systems. The classification in the gold standard, rather than being an assertion on the part of the grammar engineer who created the choices file, might instead indicate that they did not have sufficient evidence to specify a case system. As noted in §4, we did adjust the gold standard away from 'no-case' for some languages, on the basis of the grammar engineers' notes. The cases described here, in contrast, did not have such evidence in the grammar engineers' notes. In some cases, the analyses made by the grammar engineering students that we used to develop our gold standard are not consistent with more common analyses. Icelandic for example was classified 'neutral' in our gold standard, but is widely considered nominative-accusative, as analyzed by Wunderlich Wunderlich (2003) in the ODIN data.

6 Discussion

We acknowledge that the primary result of this work is to show that this is a hard problem to approach automatically. Furthermore, given the fact that in the evaluation there is one data point per language, it is difficult for methods like Map Gloss, which work at the level of improving consistency of glossing of particular examples, to move the needle much. Nonetheless, we think that it is still interesting to pursue methods such as those described here. Aside from the big-picture goal of automatically creating precision grammars and using them to further the analysis of data collected by descriptive and documentary linguists, there is the fact that automated methods can provide interesting summaries of what is found in data sets.

For example, the results of the GRAM method on data collected from a variety of linguists brings to light varying analyses of the language's case system that can prompt a linguist to investigate further. GRAM predicted Lillooet [lil] and Indonesian [ind] to be split-erg. The Lillooet data contained nominative and ergative glosses, suggesting either a split-ergative analysis or authors of IGT-bearing documents choosing different analyses. In fact we find both nominative and ergative glosses in the data from Geurts (2010) and Wharram (2003), suggesting that they have either adopted a split-ergative analysis or that the case system demonstrated some complexity and was not the focus of their work. Indonesian had nominative, accusative and ergative glosses (some in the same IGT), suggesting a split-erg or tripartite analysis for this language as well. In fact the data came from a discussion of ergative-accusative mixed systems by Wunderlich (2006). Thus even in the capacity of mining the case grams used, the GRAM method is useful in shedding light on potential alternative analyses for a given language.

7 Conclusion

We have replicated and extended an experiment designed to automatically predict case system for languages using IGT as part of a larger goal to make inferences about a variety of linguistic characteristics. The results are mixed and in our analysis we identified a number of challenges in working with broad collections of data for low-resource languages. While IGT is a rich source of linguistic information, we find that the information that included in annotation may be incomplete or highly biased. While this is an inevitability in field data which is still in the process of being curated, we as linguists can strive to publish data whose annotation is as complete as possible, given the state of our analysis of the language at the time of publication. Referring again to the Guidelines for Supplementary Materials Appearing in LSA Publications,[8] we strongly encourage our fellow linguists to publish carefully annotated data.

Acknowledgments

This material is based upon work supported by the National Science Foundation under Grant No. BCS-1561833.

References

Emily M. Bender, Scott Drellishak, Antske Fokkens, Laurie Poulson, and Safiyyah Saleem. 2010. Grammar customization. *Research on Language & Computation*, pages 1–50. 10.1007/s11168-010-9070-1.

Emily M. Bender, Michael Wayne Goodman, Joshua Crowgey, and Fei Xia. 2013. Towards creating precision grammars from interlinear glossed text: Inferring large-scale typological properties. In *Proceedings of the 7th Workshop on Language Technology for Cultural Heritage, Social Sciences, and Humanities*, pages 74–83, Sofia, Bulgaria, August. Association for Computational Linguistics.

Emily M. Bender, Joshua Crowgey, Michael Wayne Goodman, and Fei Xia. 2014. Learning grammar specifications from IGT: A case study of Chintang. In *Proceedings of the 2014 Workshop on the Use of Computational Methods in the Study of Endangered Languages*, pages 43–53, Baltimore, Maryland, USA, June. Association for Computational Linguistics.

Emily M. Bender. 2014. Language CoLLAGE: Grammatical description with the LinGO grammar matrix. In Nicoletta Calzolari, Khalid Choukri, Thierry Declerck, Hrafn Loftsson, Bente Maegaard, Joseph Mariani, Asuncion Moreno, Jan Odijk, and Stelios Piperidis, editors, *Proceedings of the Ninth International Conference on Language Resources and Evaluation (LREC'14)*, pages 2447–2451, Reykjavik, Iceland, May. European Language Resources Association (ELRA). ACL Anthology Identifier: L14-1508.

Balthasar Bickel, Bernard Comrie, and Martin Haspelmath. 2008. The Leipzig glossing rules: Conventions for interlinear morpheme-by-morpheme glosses. Max Planck Institute for Evolutionary Anthropology and Department of Linguistics, University of Leipzig.

Eugene Charniak. 1997. Statistical parsing with a context-free grammar and word statistics. In *Proceedings of AAAI-1997*.

Bernard Comrie. 2011. Alignment of case marking of full noun phrases. In Matthew S. Dryer and Martin Haspelmath, editors, *The World Atlas of Language Structures Online*. Max Planck Digital Library, Munich.

Ryan Georgi. 2016. *From Aari to Zulu: Massively Multilingual Creation of Language Tools using Interlinear Glossed Text*. Ph.D. thesis, University of Washington.

Bart Geurts. 2010. Specific indefinites, presupposition and scope. *Presuppositions and Discourse: Essays Offered to Hans Kamp*, 21:125.

Michael Wayne Goodman, Joshua Crowgey, Fei Xia, and Emily M. Bender. 2015. Xigt: Extensible interlinear glossed text. *Language Resources and Evaluation*, 2:455–485.

Martin Haspelmath, Matthew S. Dryer, David Gil, and Bernard Comrie, editors. 2008. *The World Atlas of Language Structures Online*. Max Planck Digital Library, Munich. http://wals.info.

Department of Linguistics (The LINGUIST List) Indiana University. 2010. General ontology for linguistic description (gold). http://linguistics-ontology.org/gold/2010.

William D. Lewis and Fei Xia. 2008. Automatically identifying computationally relevant typological features. In *Proceedings of the Third International Joint Conference on Natural Language Processing*, pages 685–690, Hyderabad, India.

William Lewis and Fei Xia. 2010. Developing ODIN: A multilingual repository of annotated language data for hundreds of the world's languages. *Journal of Literary and Linguistic Computing (LLC)*, 25(3):303–319.

Michael Lockwood. 2016. Automated gloss mapping for inferring grammatical properties. Master's thesis, University of Washington.

Ryan McDonald, Fernando Pereira, Kiril Ribarov, and Jan Hajič. 2005. Non-projective dependency parsing using spanning tree algorithms. In *Proceedings of the conference on Human Language Technology and Empirical Methods in Natural Language Processing*, pages 523–530. Association for Computational Linguistics.

Douglas Wharram. 2003. *On the interpretation of (un)certain indefinites in Inuktitut and related languages*. Ph.D. thesis, University of Connecticut.

Dieter Wunderlich. 2003. Optimal case patterns: German and Icelandic compared. *New perspectives on case theory*, pages 331–367.

---

[8]See note 7.

Dieter Wunderlich. 2006. Towards a structural typology of verb classes. *Advances in the theory of the lexicon*, pages 58–166.

Fei Xia and William D. Lewis. 2007. Multilingual structural projection across interlinear text. In *Proc. of the Conference on Human Language Technologies (HLT/NAACL 2007)*, pages 452–459, Rochester, New York.

Fei Xia, William D. Lewis, Michael Wayne Goodman, Glenn Slayden, Ryan Georgi, Joshua Crowgey, and Emily M. Bender. 2016. Enriching a massively multilingual database of interlinear glossed text. *Language Resources and Evaluation*, 50:321–349.

The Automatic Characterization of Grammars from Small Wordlists

Jordan Kodner[1], Spencer Caplan[1], Hongzhi Xu[2], Mitchell P. Marcus[2], Charles Yang[1]

University of Pennsylvania

[1] Department of Linguistics

[2] Department of Computer and Information Science

{jkodner, spcaplan}@sas.upenn.edu

{xh, mitch}@cis.upenn.edu

charles.yang@ling.upenn.edu

Abstract

We present two novel examples of simple algorithms which characterize the grammars of low-resource languages: a tool for the characterization of vowel harmony, and a framework for unsupervised morphological segmentation which achieves state-of-the-art performance. Accurate characterization of grammars jump starts the process of description by a trained linguist. Furthermore, morphological segmentation provides gains in machine translation as well, a perennial challenge for low-resource undocumented and endangered languages.

1 Introduction

A persistent difficulty in describing a language's grammar is the time consuming and error prone task of pouring over collected data searching for patterns. While the idea of automation is appealing, existing natural language processing applications are often non-functional on the kind of data which may be collected in the field. They may rely on supervised algorithms which require labeled or annotated data, but that defeats the purpose here. A successful tool for characterizing an unknown grammar should not require the user to have described the grammar beforehand. So called unsupervised algorithms, which are are trained on unlabeled data, exist, but they tend to require very large digital corpora to perform well. This is not a problem for tools meant to run on English or French, but collecting enough material on an endangered or undocumented language is often extremely difficult or impossible.

Standard NLP applications are not up to the task. Useful tools in this field must run on unusually small corpora with high enough accuracy if they are to be a help rather than a hindrance to a trained linguist. So, what is needed is a class of tools designed specifically with small data in mind and which will work for a diverse variety of languages. We present two such tools that operate on different grammatical domains. The first is a method for automatically searching for, identifying, and characterizing vowel harmony. Designed with small raw wordlists in mind, it leverages basic typological and theoretical principles. Tested on families ranging from Turkic (Turkish, Uyghur) to Pama-Nyungan (Warlpiri), it accurately describes diverse harmony systems. Our approach is novel in that it does not require the researcher to specify what kind of harmony system, if any, to expect. The algorithm discovers the patterns on its own.

Additionally, we present an algorithm which achieves state-of-the-art results in unsupervised morphological segmentation. Prior work in unsupervised segmentation has taken advantage of very large corpora, on the order of billions of words (Goldwater et al., 2006; Narasimhan et al., 2015). Tested on English and Turkish, our algorithm produces superior results not on billions, but on only hundreds of thousands of words. An obvious issue here is the lack of languages to test on. While anyone can run the algorithm on any language, we can only test the quality of the segmentation on languages for which a gold-standard segmentation already exists. To remedy this, we are currently developing annotation standards for automatic morphological segmentation, with Korean and Faroese as test languages. We hope this will prove useful for other researchers working on their own languages of interest.

2 Discovering and Describing Vowel Harmony

We begin with an algorithm for discovering vowel harmony in unannotated wordlists. It is designed to produce some kind of useful output no matter

Proceedings of the 2nd Workshop on the Use of Computational Methods in the Study of Endangered Languages, pages 76–84,
Honolulu, Hawai'i, USA, March 6–7, 2017. ©2017 Association for Computational Linguistics

how small its input data, but the more that is provided to it, the more information it will extract. In all, it answers a number of important questions about a language's vowel harmony system beginning with the obvious: *does this language have vowel harmony?*. If so, then what are the harmonizing sets, and how do vowels map between them? Which vowels, if any, are neutral? Are neutral vowels transparent or opaque? Is secondary harmony present? And so on. These questions constitute the major part of what defines a harmony system. Answering them gives a trained linguist a leg up before working out the finer details, or serves to inform other NLP tools in a pipeline.

While prior work exists on the automatic discovery or analysis of vowel harmony systems, our method is, to our knowledge, the first end-to-end pipeline for describing both primary and secondary vowel harmony on arbitrary languages. The Vowel Harmony Calculator (Harrison et al., 2004) calculates metrics over a language given a specification of its harmony system. This is not useful for the present purpose because it requires a description of the system beforehand. Sanders and Harrison (2012) improves on this by not requiring a full description as input. Nevertheless, it only provides a metric for how "harmonic" languages are and not a description of the vowel harmony system (Sanders and Harrison, 2012). Baker (2009) describes a two-state Hidden Markov Model (HMM) which characterizes English and Italian, and may describe Turkish and Finnish correctly depending on random initial parameter settings (Baker, 2009). The model is restricting in that it requires the user to decide upfront how many levels of harmony to find. It only accounts for secondary harmony by setting up the HMM with four initial states at the outset. The paper also shows that a models using mutual information (MI) and Boltzmann fields can accurately identify vowel-to-vowel interactions but does not provide a means for describing vowel harmony given the results.

2.1 Algorithm Overview

In an approach broadly similar to (Baker, 2009)'s MI model, our algorithm leverages distributional patterns within the vowel system to extract information about vowel harmony. But due to clever transformations of the data and typologically motivated assumptions, it neatly extracts the detailed information about the system to produce a description.

The algorithm is flexible in its input. At a minimum, all it requires is a wordlist a few hundred words long. If the orthography corresponds more-or-less to a phonemic representation (like with Finnish, for example), no transcription is needed. This alone provides enough information for a basic rough analysis. A wordlist thousands long, with frequencies if possible, is better. For a complete analysis, the current version of the algorithm requires a short list of potentially relevant vowel features for each vowel. These basic features (e.g., ±rnd, ±hi, etc.) are not strongly tied to any particular phonological theory, and are customizable by the researcher.

The algorithm takes a wordlist (with frequencies if available) as input, a list of vowels in the same orthography as the input, and an optional table of proposed vowel features for each vowel. It outputs a partition of the vowel space into two primary harmonizing sets if present, and/or a neutral set. If provided with features, it outputs mappings between the two sets and a partition for secondary harmony if present.

Algorithm 1 describes the detection process. At a high level, it proceeds as follows. First, if frequencies are provided, the lowest frequency items are removed. These are more likely than high frequency items to contain names and loan words which fail to adhere to the harmony pattern. Then tier-adjacent vowel pairs are tabulated. For example, in the Finnish *Kalevala*, the tier-adjacent pairs are *a-e*, *e-a*, and *a-a*. These counts are converted to mutual information. The MI step is necessary to account for the uneven frequencies of individual vowels. For example, if *a* is very common in a language while *y* is rare, the counts for every vowel with *a* might be higher than with *y* in spite of harmony constraints. MI controls for these unconditioned frequency effects.

This process yields an MI co-occurrence vector for every vowel. In the absence of co-occurrence restrictions, each vector should correspond to a fairly level distribution. That is, each vowel is expected to co-occur with every other vowel at a more or less uniform rate if the frequencies of both vowels are accounted for. However, with vowel harmony restricting co-occurrence, the distributions should be skewed because vowels should rarely co-occur with members of the opposing harmony set. Any vowel with a sufficiently level distribution is probably neutral. If all or all but one of the language's vowels appears neutral, then the language does not have vowel harmony[1]. K-means clustering, a standard and simple unsupervised clustering algorithm, is used to find the optimal division of the non-neutral vowels into two harmonizing sets. If features are provided, they are used to match up which vowel maps to which between sets. Then the process is rerun with the harmonizing feature removed to find additional harmony patterns.

Algorithm 1 VH Characterization Algorithm

---

if frequencies provided **then**
    Trim tail off *wordlist*
while $True$ **do**
    Calculate tier-adjacent vowel-vowel co-occurrence matrix
    Calculate MI between each vowel pair
    Identify vowels whose MI distributions uniform within threshold.
    Assign these to the neutral vowel set and remove from consideration
    if number of non-neutral vowels ≤ 1 **then**
        return
    Run k-means ($k = 2$) clustering on the remaining vowels' MI vectors
    if no *features* provided **then**
        return
    else
        Map vowels between harmonizing sets by finding pairs that share the most features in common.
        vowel list ← Collapse vowels along the harmonizing feature
        rerun for secondary harmony
return

The algorithm requires that a list of vowels be provided as input. This might be a problem if the user chooses to include marginal vowels from loanwords as input, for example ⟨y⟩ in German or ⟨å⟩ in Finnish. So as a fail-safe, the algorithm has facilities for automatically detecting and removing such vowels from the analysis. Marginal vowels tend to have much higher self-MI than MI with any other vowel, allowing them to be identified. This follows intuitively from the assumption that marginal vowels tend to appear only in loanwords.

---

[1] Vowel harmony requires a partitioning of the vowel system into at least two sets. Therefore, there need to be at least two vowels with skewed distributions to propose harmony

2.2 Results

This simple algorithm performs very well on the languages tested. We choose languages with easily accessible corpora from Indo-European, Turkic, Uralic, and Pama-Nyungan, but we have good reason to believe that the results port to other families as well. We begin by testing Turkish, Finnish, Hungarian, Uyghur, and Warlpiri with corpora ranging in size from roughly 28,000 to 400,000. The model achieves perfect results out-of-the-box on three of five languages tested. This includes successfully capturing secondary harmony in Turkish.

The Warlpiri result is encouraging because it demonstrates that the algorithm may be expected to perform on wordlists in only the tens of thousands. It is worth noting that the Turkish results are despite upwards of 30% of lexical items containing at least one harmony violation (due mostly to a set of bound morphemes with refuse to participate in harmony). This underlines the algorithm's robustness. The algorithm also appropriately maps vowels between harmonizing sets in all cases when features are provided as input.

In both Hungarian and Uyghur, all errors were of the same type: they misclassified harmonizing vowels as neutral. It is encouraging that the algorithm never places a vowel in the wrong harmonizing set. In that way, it does not lead the researcher astray as to the nature of the specific language's harmony system. A second test was performed on Hungarian in which vowel length (as acute accents) was removed from the orthography. After this change, Hungarian achieved a perfect score as well.

English and German were chosen as control cases. Neither language exhibits vowel harmony, and vowel harmony was discovered in neither language.

Finally, two experiments were conducted to test the limits of the algorithm's power. First, the algorithm was run on Estonian (Finnic), which crucially once had, but has since lost productive harmony (Harms, 1962). We predicted that such a language would still show remnants of harmony's distributional fingerprint. This turns out to be the case. Run on 87,586 types with no frequency information (Eesti Kirjandusmuuseumi Folkloristika Osakond, 2005), we discover remnant front-back harmony. ⟨a⟩, ⟨e⟩, ⟨i⟩, and ⟨u⟩ are found to be neutral which is unsurprising since

Language	# Types	Primary H?	V correct	Secondary H?	V correct
Turkish	303,013	✓	8/8	✓	4/4
Finnish	396,770	✓	8/8	–	–
Hungarian	53,839	✓	11/15	–	–
Uyghur	392,403	✓	7/8	–	–
Warlpiri	28,885	✓	3/3	–	–
German	225,327	–	5/5	–	–
English	101,438	–	6/6	–	–

Table 1: Vowel co-occurrences are taken from corpus orthographies. Marginal vowels (e.g. Finnish *å* and German *y*) are automatically detected and removed. Corpora are from MorphoChallenge (Kurimo et al., 2010) when available. Uyghur and Hungarian were provided for the DARPA LORELEI project. Warlpiri is from (Swartz, 1997).

we expect some erosion in the distributional asymmetries. The remaining vowels divide into two classes along frontness: ⟨ä⟩, ⟨ö⟩, ⟨ü⟩ vs. ⟨o⟩, ⟨õ⟩ (/ɤ/). This is system is reminiscent of productive harmony in Finnish today and provides interesting insight into diachronic study of the language.

Second, we test the limits of the input data. A run on the most frequent 500 types for Turkish successfully discovers primary but not secondary harmony. This seems to represent the lower bound on the algorithm's performance window. A second test on Buryat (Mongolic) confirmed this lower bound. Only spurious harmony was detected on a wordlist of 235 stems without frequencies (Ladefoged and Blankenship, 2007). We expect that wordlists containing inflected forms to perform better than lists of stems because harmony alternations are frequently observed as allomorphy.

Overall, these results are highly encouraging. On all but the smallest of wordlists, the algorithm produces sufficiently accurate results to be of use to linguists. It is even useful for diachronic study, uncovering lost harmony in Estonian. Future work will leverage morphological segmentation to achieve mapping without the linguist having to provide vowel features to the algorithm. We also expect to test on a variety of poorly documented languages once we acquire more wordlists.

3 Morphological Segmentation for Small Data

We now turn to our algorithm for unsupervised morphological segmentation. As with the vowel harmony algorithm, this is designed specifically with small corpora in mind. Nevertheless, it has achieved state-of-the-art performance on standard test languages. This algorithm is unique in leveraging the concept of paradigms in discovering segmentation. While the notion of paradigms is common in traditional morphology literature (Stump, 2001), it has not often been used in automatic segmentation tasks.

Automatic segmentation should be contrasted with automatic feature analysis. Segmentation is the division of whole word strings into morpheme subunits. It is a function only of form. Well-equipped segmentation processes such as the one presented here, permit transformations as well. These account for orthographic rules (e.g., the doubling on <n> in *running* → *run +n ing*) or theoretical concerns, such as allomorphy or stem alternations (e.g., Latin *paludis* from *palus* as *palus +d-s is*). Feature analysis, on the other hand, is a function of meaning. Words are annotated by the semantic contribution of each of their component morphemes rather than split into substrings. Feature analysis is not well suited for unsupervised tasks because it requires that the meaning of each morpheme be provided beforehand. It is not possible, from a wordlist alone at least, to deduce them. The combination of segmental and featural analysis yields enough information for a standard Leipzig gloss.

Segmentation

```
nd aka chi teng es a
```

Features

```
buy CAUS FV 1SM CL7OM PAST
```

Gloss

```
nd  -aka -chi  -teng -es   -a
1SM -PAST -CL7OM -buy  -CAUS -FV
```

Figure 1: Gloss for the Shona (S-Bantu) verb *ndakachitengesa* 'I sold it' with accompanying segmental and featural analyses

While the paradigm approach is novel, other algorithms for morphological segmentation already exist. Probably the most famous is the Morfessor family of algorithms (Creutz and Lagus, 2005), which have come to be treated as a standard baseline. Also of note is the Morsel algorithm which achieved the best performance for English and Finnish at the most recent MorphoChallenge (Lignos, 2010).

The current published state-of-the-art, MorphoChain (Narasimhan et al., 2015) achieves top performance for English, Turkish, and Arabic. The algorithm gets its name from the way in which it conceives as words as derivational chains. Any word is composed of a stem plus some series of affixations and transformations. Then the probability of each step in a derivation is computed considering a number of features (in the machine learning sense, i.e., predictors). Most of these features are word-internal and can be computed directly from a wordlist. The would-be frequency of the proposed affix, whether or not the stem appears independently, correlations between affixes, and the scope of the required transformations are taken into account among other things.

Word-internal features alone push MorphoChain's performance above the competition. But to achieve its most impressive result, it falls back on word-external features as well. Cosine similarity between derivations in the chain is calculated via Word2Vec (Mikolov et al., 2013) feature vectors. The distributional similarities captures by Word2Vec approximate semantic and syntactic similarity. For example, *teach* and *teach-er* show high distributional similarity and are semantically related, while *corn* and *corn-er* are not distributionally similar and are not related. This information is useful for detecting spurious segmentations such as *corn-er* which would seem very plausible based on word-internal information alone. Word2Vec does not require labels and is thus unsupervised. However, corpora of *at least* hundreds of millions of words of running text are needed to calculate reliable vectors. Since these are on the order of a million times larger than the wordlists that we target, this subverts our goal.

The practical benefits of word segmentation models are more than simply theoretical. Our framework has been leveraged to improve the performance of the best systems for low-resource Uyghur machine translation as well as the auto-matic detection of named entities for the DARPA LORELEI project. Bridging the performance gap of NLP applications on languages without large annotated corpora, which is the vast majority, benefits the communities that speak them through greater accessibility of information.

3.1 Algorithm Overview

The morphological segmentation algorithm combines three processes: segmentation, paradigm construction, and pruning. An overview of each is provided. Iterative application of these three functions on an unannotated wordlist with frequencies yields segmentations as described in the introduction to this project.

Algorithm 2 Morphological Segmentation Algorithm Overview

---
  if pre-segmentation **then**
      Split compounds
      Calculate initial $P(r)$ on attested frequencies
  Perform initial segmentations
  while *iteration* **do**
      Create paradigms
      Prune paradigms
  return

3.1.1 Segmentation

Initial segmentation is achieved through a Bayesian model which estimates a probability $P(r, s, t)$ over candidate roots r, affixes s, and transformations t for each word. This process is itself iterative. 'Root' here refers to what remains after a single affix is removed from the word rather than its theoretically defined $\sqrt{ROOT}$. So after a single iteration, the Shona word *ndakachitengesa* with formal root $\sqrt{TENG}$ is segmented into root *ndakachitenges* and affix a. The algorithm acknowledges that affixation often triggers additional phonological (or at least orthographical) processes. These are captured through the transformations *deletion*, *substitution*, and *duplication* at segmentation boundaries. Only considering transformations at segmentation boundaries drastically reduces the search space but prevents us from considering Semitic templatic morphology, for example. We are working to incorporate this functionality into future versions of the algorithm.

The likelihood $P(r, s, t|w)$ of a segmentation (r, s, t) out of all possible candidate segmentations (r', s', t') given a word w is 0 if that segmentation

- **Deletion** (DEL) of the end letter x of root r. E.g., the word 'using' as (`use, ing, DEL-e`).

- **Substitution** (SUB) of the end letter x of root r with z. E.g., the word 'carries' as (`carry, es, SUB-y+i`).

- **Duplication** (DUP) of the end letter x of root r. E.g., the word 'stopped' as (`stop, ed, DUP+p`).

Figure 2: Description of transformations

cannot describe the word. Otherwise, it is defined as follows:

$$P(r, s, t|w) = \frac{P(r) \times P(s) \times P(t|f(r,s))}{\sum_{(r',s',t') \in w} P(r', s', t')}$$

This formula is based on the assumption that roots r and suffixes s are independent. Transformations, however, are conditioned on a function $f(r, s)$ defined over the entire corpus. For example, the *-ed* suffix in English deletes any immediately preceding e in the root. The f function allows these generalizations to be captured as morphological rules rather than individual cases.

Initially, each possible candidate segmentation is assumed to have equal probability $1/|(r, s, t) \in w|$. This generates spurious segmentations of atomic roots with high probability. Subsequent parameter estimation through paradigms and pruning removes spurious segmentations to yield a maximum likelihood segmentation.

$$(r, s, t|w) = \underset{(r',s',t')}{\mathrm{argmax}}\, P(r', s', t')$$

As an additional step, the algorithm has the option of pre-segmenting compound words. If a word w contains two individually attested words w_1 and w_2, the word is split and both of its components are evaluated separately. This process is found to improve overall recall. As a final optional step, initial $P(r)$ can be weighted by frequency. In languages which attest bare roots, more frequent roots are more likely to be valid.

3.1.2 Paradigm Construction

The segmentation step yields a triple (r, s, t) for each word. Grouping triples by their root yields a set of suffixes, a *paradigm* enumerating attested affixes on the root. For example, the root *walk*

surfaces with suffixes {*-s,-ing,-ed, -er*}. Note that many roots may share the same paradigm. For example, *stop*, and *bake* share a paradigm set with *walk*.

Paradigms are tabulated by the number of times each occurs in the proposed segmentations. We define a paradigm's *support* as its frequency in this calculation. We assume that more robustly supported paradigms are more likely to contain only valid affixes. Table 2 shows the most common paradigms discovered for English.

Paradigm	Support
(-ed, -ing, -s)	772
(-ed, -ing)	331
(-ed, -er, -ing, -s)	219
(-ly, -ness)	208
(-ed, -ing, -ion, -s)	154
(-ic, -s)	125

Table 2: Frequent English suffix paradigms contain valid affixes

Root	Paradigm
ticker	(-s, -tape)
piney	(-al, -apple, -a, -hill, -hurst, -ido, -iro, -wood)
corks	(-an, -screw, -well)
sidle	(-aw, -ed, -ee, -er, -ey, -in, -ine, -ing, -s)
lantz	(-anum, -ra, -ronix, -ry)
nadir	(-adze, -la, -ne, -s)
reith	(-a, -er, -ian)
bodin	(-ce, -es, -etz, -ford, -ly, -ne, -ng, -ngton)
musee	(-euw, -s, -um)
taiyo	(-iba, -uan)
bilge	(-er, -rami, -s)

Table 3: Ten suffix paradigms only supported by a single root. These contain many spurious affixes.

3.1.3 Paradigm Pruning

Not all proposed paradigms are real. Some are the result of segmentation errors. For example, if *closet* is segmented as (*close, t, NULL*), then it will yield a paradigm {*-er, -est, -ed, -ing, -s, -t*}. Identifying such spurious paradigms directs the algorithm towards potentially spurious affixes.

To avoid such spurious paradigms, we perform pruning. First, paradigms with support ≥ 3

and at least two members are retained as well-supported. All other paradigms are considered suspect. We identify which component affixes of these paradigms receive the most support from other paradigms. The score of a set of affixes S is described as follows. It is the combined frequency of each member affix across all paradigms.

$$score(S) = \sum_{s \in S} freq(s)$$

For example, the {*-er, -est, -ed, -ing, -s*} subset of the spurious *closet* paradigm has the highest possible score of all subsets, and is a well-supported paradigm in and of itself. Therefore we can discard *-t* with reasonable confidence.

The probability $P(s)$ of each suffix is re-estimated over its attestation all the remaining paradigms. We then rerun the initial segmentation step. This time, spurious affixes probabilities have been penalized, so errors along the lines of (*close, t, NULL*) are less likely to reoccur. This improves algorithm precision by eliminating spurious affixation.

3.2 Experiments and Results

3.2.1 Data and Evaluation

To facilitate comparison between our algorithm and currently used competitors, we adopt the same data set used by (Narasimhan et al., 2015) and (Kurimo et al., 2010), the MorphoChallenge 2010 set for training and the combined MorphoChallenge 2005-2010 for testing. We test against Morfessor, as well as AGMorph (Sirts and Goldwater, 2013), MorphoChain-C (with only word-internal information), and the full MorphoChain model which is trained on (word-external) word embeddings from English Wikipedia and the BOUN corpus (Sak et al., 2008). MorphoChain-C presents the best direct comparison to our model since we do not consider word-external data. Nevertheless, our model outperforms both implementations.

The output of each algorithm is scored according to the MorphoChain metric. Precision, recall, and F1 are calculated across segmentation points. For example, *walking* segmented as *wal king* contains one incorrect segmentation point after *wal* and is missing a correct segmentation point in *king*. However, *walk ing* contains a correct segmentation point and no incorrect ones.

First, we report the contribution from each of our algorithm's component processes. Table 4

shows the results. *Base* is only the initial Bayesian segmentation step. *Suff* extends the Bayesian model with a final re-estimation based on suffix frequencies. *Trans* implements the above plus segmentation. *Comp* extends *Trans* with compound splitting. *Prune* implements paradigm pruning as well, and *Freq* considers root frequencies in initial segmentation.

	English			Turkish		
	Prec	**Rec**	**F1**	**Prec**	**Rec**	**F1**
Base	0.414	0.725	0.527	0.525	0.666	0.587
Suff	0.490	0.648	0.558	0.617	0.621	0.619
Tran	0.524	0.757	0.619	0.589	0.726	**0.650**
Comp	0.504	0.843	0.631	0.581	0.727	0.646
Prun	0.709	0.784	0.744	0.652	0.518	0.577
Freq	0.804	0.764	**0.784**	0.715	0.467	0.565

Table 4: Contribution of each algorithm component

Segmentation on English performs the best when all optional processes are enforced in the model. This is not the case for Turkish however, which achieves its peak performance at *Trans*. This discrepancy has to do with the relative availability of bare roots in the languages. English has limited affixation, and it can be assumed that many bare roots will appear in any reasonable English dataset. This is not the case for Turkish, however, in which nearly all noun and verb tokens have at least one affix. Therefore, processes which rely on the presence of unaffixed bare roots in the corpus cannot function.

Lang.	Model	Prec.	Recall	F1
	Morfessor-Base	0.740	0.623	0.677
	AGMorph	0.696	0.604	0.647
English	MorphChain-C	0.555	0.792	0.653
	MorphChain-All	0.807	0.722	0.762
	Our model	0.804	0.764	**0.784**
	Morfessor-Base	0.827	0.362	0.504
	AGMorph	0.878	0.466	0.609
Turkish	MorphChain-C	0.516	0.652	0.576
	MorphChain-All	0.743	0.520	0.612
	Our model	0.589	0.726	**0.650**

Table 5: All numbers except for ours are reported in (Narasimhan et al., 2015). All scoring was performed using the MorphoChain metric. Best results are reported for English and Turkish.

3.3 Testing on Other Languages

While our segmentation algorithm is unsupervised, scoring its output requires human-segmented data to compare against. This presents a challenge when testing the process

Paradigm	Support
(-al)	54
(-ly)	43
(-idad)	32
(-ismo)	29
(-ing, -s)	25
(-er)	23
(-ed)	21
(-ista)	19
(-ly, -s)	15
(-ed, -s)	13
(-er, -ing, -s)	11
(-er, -s)	11
(-ed, -ing)	11

Table 6: Foreign influence among the top 30 most frequent Tagalog suffix paradigms

on under-documented languages for which segmented wordlists are hard to come by. The DARPA LORELEI project had originally planned to produce human-annotated segmentations for a wide range of languages, but this has not yet come to fruition. In response, we are developing simple annotation standards which linguists and knowledgeable native speakers may use to produce segmented wordlists of their own.

We have run segmentation on Navajo, Tagalog, and Yoruba in additional to the languages reported above. Unfortunately, because no gold standards are available, the algorithm's performance cannot be assessed quantitatively. Additionally, the DARPA LORELEI and Wikipedia data which we tested on contain substantial English (and Spanish for Tagalog) vocabulary. Table 6 shows the effect this has on paradigms.

4 Discussion and Conclusion

The success of these unsupervised algorithms attests to what can be accomplished by gleaning information from small corpora. The vowel harmony detector describes harmony systems with high accuracy at as few as 500 types. The segmentation performs very well, on languages for which its accuracy could be assessed quantitatively, with corpora orders of magnitude smaller than what can be successfully processed by the next best method. Nevertheless, both algorithms are incomplete.

An obvious next step is to combine the two into a single pipeline. This is projected to have benefits for both. One inconvenience with the current iteration of the harmony detector is that it requires a linguist to provide features for each of the language's vowels if a harmony mapping is desired. It would be nice for this process to happen automatically instead. And here it is useful to leverage morphology. A language with affixal morphology and harmony should present two or more sets of paradigms which differ according to harmony. For example, in Turkish, the plural *-lar* occurs in paradigms with other back vowel allomorphs while *-ler* occurs with other front vowel allomorphs. There should exist a mapping between morphemes like *-lar* and *-ler* which differ only in their vowels. Combining the evidence across all of the morphemes will allow us to create harmony mappings without explicit reference to features.

There are improvements to be made in the other direction as well. Vowel harmony information will improve segmentation accuracy. As it is, the segmentation algorithm has no way of knowing that two paradigms which differ only due to harmony constraints are in fact two sets of phonologically determined allomorphs. This forces it to spread sparse evidence over an unnecessarily large number of paradigms. Understanding harmony will allow the algorithm to collapse these sets, calculate more accurate support, and therefore improve overall performance.

Harmony aside, a vital resource for estimating and improving the performance of the segmentation algorithm is the presence of morphologically segmented gold standards in a variety of languages. We have taken up this task and are working towards annotation conventions for this kind of work. So far, we are still in the early phases of the process but have already begun annotation on Faroese and Korean as test languages. These are useful languages for testing because they exhibit a variety of affixes and alternations that need to be accounted for. With an effective annotation standard, we can also proceed to develop a new scoring metric for segmentation. It will address concerns raised by the existing MorphoChallenge metric (Kurimo et al., 2007) due to the lack of a unified annotation standard.

Finally, we plan to extend the distributional approach to vowel harmony to other typological patterns. We are developing models to detect whether a given language exhibits stem alternations, tends to be agglutinative, has common prefixes, infixes, and/or suffixes, shows reduplication, etc. As with vowel harmony, these will aid linguists seeking to describe the grammars of undocumented languages. Additionally, they will prove useful as inputs to the segmentation algorithm.

Acknowledgments

We thank the rest of the University of Pennsylvania's LORELEI summer research team for their helpful insights. We also thank audiences at the 10th Northeast Computational Phonology Circle (NECPhon) and Penn's Computational Linguistics and Lunch series for their suggestions, as well as the anonymous reviewers for ComputEL-2 who gave us useful comments. This research was funded by the DARPA LORELEI program under Agreement No. HR0011-15-2-0023.

References

Adam C Baker. 2009. Two statistical approaches to finding vowel harmony. Technical report, Citeseer.

Mathias Creutz and Krista Lagus. 2005. *Unsupervised morpheme segmentation and morphology induction from text corpora using Morfessor 1.0.* Helsinki University of Technology.

Eesti Kirjandusmuuseumi Folkloristika Osakond. 2005. Estnische sprichwörter.

Sharon Goldwater, Thomas L Griffiths, and Mark Johnson. 2006. Contextual dependencies in unsupervised word segmentation. In *Proceedings of the 21st International Conference on Computational Linguistics and the 44th annual meeting of the Association for Computational Linguistics*, pages 673–680. Association for Computational Linguistics.

Robert Thomas Harms. 1962. *Estonian grammar*, volume 28. Indiana University.

David Harrison, Emily Thomforde, and Michael OKeefe. 2004. The vowel harmony calculator.

Mikko Kurimo, Mathias Creutz, and Matti Varjokallio. 2007. Morpho challenge evaluation using a linguistic gold standard. In *Workshop of the Cross-Language Evaluation Forum for European Languages*, pages 864–872. Springer.

Mikko Kurimo, Sami Virpioja, Ville Turunen, and Krista Lagus. 2010. Morpho challenge competition 2005–2010: evaluations and results. In *Proceedings of the 11th Meeting of the ACL Special Interest Group on Computational Morphology and Phonology*, pages 87–95. Association for Computational Linguistics.

Peter Ladefoged and B Blankenship. 2007. The ucla phonetics lab archive - buryat.

Constantine Lignos. 2010. Learning from unseen data. In *Proceedings of the Morpho Challenge 2010 Workshop*, pages 35–38.

Tomas Mikolov, Ilya Sutskever, Kai Chen, Greg S Corrado, and Jeff Dean. 2013. Distributed representations of words and phrases and their compositionality. In *Advances in neural information processing systems*, pages 3111–3119.

Karthik Narasimhan, Regina Barzilay, and Tommi Jaakkola. 2015. An unsupervised method for uncovering morphological chains. *arXiv preprint arXiv:1503.02335.*

Haşim Sak, Tunga Güngör, and Murat Saraçlar. 2008. Turkish language resources: Morphological parser, morphological disambiguator and web corpus. In *Advances in natural language processing*, pages 417–427. Springer.

Nathan Sanders and K David Harrison. 2012. Discovering new vowel harmony patterns using a pairwise statistical model. In *Poster presented at the 20th Manchester Phonology Meeting, University of Manchester.*

Kairit Sirts and Sharon Goldwater. 2013. Minimally-supervised morphological segmentation using adaptor grammars. *Transactions of the Association for Computational Linguistics*, 1:255–266.

Gregory T Stump. 2001. *Inflectional morphology: A theory of paradigm structure*, volume 93. Cambridge University Press.

Stephen Swartz. 1997. *Warlpiri yimi kuja karlipa wangka.* Summer Institute of Linguistics, Australian Aborigines and Islanders Branch, Warlpiri Translation Project.

Endangered Data for Endangered Languages:
Digitizing Print dictionaries[*]

Michael Maxwell
Aric Bills
University of Maryland
{mmaxwell,abills}@umd.edu

1 Introduction

This paper describes on-going work in dictionary digitization, and in particular the processing of OCRed text into a structured lexicon. The description is at a conceptual level, without implementation details.

In decades of work on endangered languages, hundreds (or more) languages have been documented with print dictionaries. Into the 1980s, most such dictionaries were edited on paper media (such as 3x5 cards), then typeset by hand or on old computer systems (Bartholomew and Schoenhals. 1983; Grimes 1970). SIL International, for example, has nearly 100 lexicons that date from their work during the period 1937–1983 (Verna Stutzman, p.c.).

More recently, most dictionaries are prepared on computers, using tools like SIL's Shoebox (later Toolbox) or Fieldworks Language Explorer (FLEx). These born-digital dictionaries were all at one time on electronic media: tapes, floppy diskettes, hard disks or CDs. In some cases those media are no longer readable, and no backups were made onto more durable media; so the only readable version we have of these dictionaries may be a paper copy (cf. Bird and Simons 2003; Borghoff et al. 2006). And while paper copies preserve their information (barring rot, fire, and termites), that information is inaccessible to computers. For that, the paper dictionary must be digitized.

A great many other dictionaries of non-endangered languages are also available only in paper form.

It might seem that digitization is simple. It is not. There are two approaches to digitization: keying in the text by hand, and Optical Character Recognition (OCR). While each has advantages and disadvantages, in the end we are faced with three problems:

1. Typographic errors;

2. Conversion from the dictionary's visual layout into a lexicographically structured computer-readable format, such as XML; and

3. Converting each dictionary's idiosyncratic structure into some standard tagging system.

This paper deals mostly with the second issue (but see section 6 about the first issue, and section 7 about

the last issue). The information structure in a print dictionary is represented mostly implicitly, by formatting: white space, order, font and font style, and occasionally by numbering, bullets, or markup (such as 'Ex.' for an example sentence). The task addressed in this paper is that of converting this implicit information into explicit tags for lexical entries, parts of speech, glosses, example sentences, and so forth.

At present, the tools described here are very much in the development phase, and must be run on the command line. Ideally, we would go on to create a Graphical User Interface (GUI) which would serve as a front end to these tools. Whether we will achieve that goal within the limits of our funding remains to be seen. But even if we do, we do not envision the task of converting paper dictionaries into electronic databases to be a job that most field linguists will want to, or even should, undertake. Indeed, there are a limited number of paper dictionaries that need to be converted (all modern dictionaries, we believe, are being created electronically). Instead, we envision the user community for this software as being composed of a small number of experts in lexicography, who can learn enough about a particular language to reliably interpret the format of a dictionary of that language, and can therefore act as a sort of conservation corps for legacy dictionaries.

2 Print Dictionary Format

Figure 1 shows two lexical entries in a Tzeltal-English dictionary (Cruz, Gerdel, and Slocum 1999; this is a more detailed version of Slocum and Gerdel 1976). In this dictionary, headwords of major entries appear at the left margin of a column, in bold font. They are followed by a part of speech, identifiable by position, italic font, and the fact that they come from a small class of tokens ('s', 'vt', etc.). The Spanish glosses follow in regular font; individual glosses are separated by commas (not shown in this snippet). Cross references to other entries in the dictionary are bolded and preceded by the word 'Véase' (Spanish for "see"). Multiple senses (not shown in this example) are indicated by Arabic numerals. The entire entry is formatted with hanging indent. Finally, subentries are further indented, and otherwise follow much the same formatting as main entries, with a subset of the information (e.g. subentries lack part of speech).

[*]This material is based upon work supported by the National Science Foundation under grant number BCS1644606.

Proceedings of the 2nd Workshop on the Use of Computational Methods in the Study of Endangered Languages, pages 85–91,
Honolulu, Hawai'i, USA, March 6–7, 2017. ©2017 Association for Computational Linguistics

Figure 2 shows a lexical entry in SIL's Muinane-Spanish dictionary (J. W. Walton, J. P. Walton, and Buenaventura 1997).[1] As in the Tzeltal dictionary, headwords of major entries appear at the left margin of a column, in bold font. They are followed by a part of speech, identifiable by position, by a lighter (non-bold) upright font, and again by the fact that they come from a small limited class of tokens ('s.', 'v.i.', etc.), all ending in a period. The glosses follow in the same font, and consist of Spanish words; individual glosses are separated by commas, and the list of glosses ends with a period. If the list of glosses extends beyond the first line, it is indented by a bit over an em relative to the headword. Example sentences and their translations appear on separate lines, indented by perhaps two ems; the Muinane text of example sentences is in italics, while the Spanish translation is in an upright font. Within the Muinane text, the inflected form of the headword is underlined. Finally, subentries (as in the right-hand column) are indented by about one em, and otherwise follow the same formatting as main entries. Irregular inflected forms (not shown in the figure) are given in italics, preceded by their inflectional category, with square brackets enclosing the grammatical information and the irregular form. Elsewhere in this dictionary, multiple senses are provided with Arabic numerals in a bold font.

Note that in both of these dictionaries, lexical entries are represented as paragraphs with hanging indent. Significantly, there is no extra vertical space between these paragraphs; this makes automatic inference of lexical entries difficult, a problem to which we now turn.

3 Inferring Lexical Entries

In our experiments, we are concentrating on how the OCR form of a dictionary can be converted into a lexical database. We are not concerned here with the OCR process itself, which we treat as more or less a black box. Our reason for doing so should be obvious; much work has been done on converting paper documents into electronic form as streams of text, searchable by matching strings of characters. While some work has been done on formatting the streams of text to correspond with the position of that text on paper, so that a human user can be shown the location on the page of their search terms, apart from the issues of processing tables, very little work has been done on converting the OCR output of visually structured documents into structured databases. This is particularly true for dictionaries, which vary greatly in their format. The post-OCR conversion process is thus ripe for exploration, and is our topic here.

In order, then, to concentrate our effort on the conversion from OCR output to lexical database, rather than cutting up paper dictionaries and feeding them

through scanners, we are using for our experiments several dictionaries which are available on-line in image format:

- The Tzeltal-English dictionary mentioned above (Cruz, Gerdel, and Slocum 1999)

- The Muinane-Spanish dictionary mentioned above (J. W. Walton, J. P. Walton, and Buenaventura 1997)

- A Cubeo-Spanish dictionary (Morse, Jay K. Salser, and Salser 1999)

All three dictionaries use Latin script, although we did encounter issues with recognizing some characters (see section 6). Non-Latin scripts would of course introduce other issues, although most of those issues would have to do with training or adapting an OCR system to recognize those scripts, research which others have tackled (see e.g. Govindaraju and Setlur 2009; Smith, Antonova, and Lee 2009).

We converted the online images of these dictionaries into raster images, and then ran an OCR program on the result.

Most modern OCR systems include as one of their output formats the 'hOCR' form (`https://kba.github.io/hocr-spec/1.2/`. This XML format tags hypothesized words, lines, paragraphs, and columns, and provides additional information such as position on the page; some information on font and font style is also extractable. We have been using the open source program Tesseract (`https://github.com/tesseract-ocr`). An excerpt from the hOCR output of Tesseract showing the structure corresponding to the first line of figure 1 appears in figure 3.[2]

In this output, the 'bbox' indicates the coordinates of rectangles occupied by individual tokens, lines, paragraphs etc. Notice that this lexical entry has been correctly tokenized into the Tzeltal word 'ajan', the part of speech 's', and the Spanish gloss 'elote' (corncob), all as part of an `ocr_line`. Unfortunately, although lexical entries are represented as hanging indent paragraphs in this dictionary, neither the `<div>` (division) nor the `<p>` (paragraph) elements reliably parse this structure.[3] This is also true of the OCR output of the Cubeo dictionary which we have been working with (Morse, Jay K. Salser, and Salser 1999). It seems in general that we cannot rely on Tessearact's division into paragraphs, i.e. lexical entries.

Hence the first task for the user is to define the general shape of the page, including the approximate position of headers and/or footers, and columns. The user also needs to define the shape of a lexical entry, so that individual lexical entries can be parsed out from the

---

[1] A differently formatted version of this dictionary is available on-line: `http://www-01.sil.org/americas/colombia/pubs/MuinaneDictBil_49558-with-covers.pdf`.

[2] This has been simplified by removing some attributes, and formatted to clarify the structure.

[3] Also, while the OCR correctly captured the italicization of the part of speech, it usually fails to detect bolding, as seen for the headword.

ajan *s* elote
ajaw *s* rey de los indígenas *Véase*
  ajwalil

Figure 1: Some lexical entries from Tzeltal print dictionary

icánáaca adv. mientras.
Fíiciji úújóho icánáaca.
Voy a pescar mientras que estoy
  aquí.
Uújóho icánáaca táavaco tácójiti
múdúuhi.
Aunque estuve presente se comieron
  el pescado (sin compartirlo
  conmigo).

ífi s. cuerpo, naturaleza, vida.
ífíbaiji s. derechos de nacimiento (por
  viudez).
ífii s. su cuerpo (de él o de ella).
  ífííco báñihi v.t. engañarse (a sí
   mismo).
   Tafíico báñihi.
   Yo me engañé.
  ífííco ésicinihi v.t. recordarse de uno

Figure 2: Lexical entries from Muinane dictionary

```
<div class="ocr_carea"... title="bbox 526 577 1222 665">
  <p ... title="bbox 525 1459 1230 1655">
   <span class="ocr_line"... bbox 526 1459 794 1501...>
      <span class="ocrx_word" ... bbox 526 1460 607 1501...>
        ajan
      </span>
      <span class="ocrx_word" ... bbox 650 1471 667 1491...>
        <em>s</em>
      </span>
      <span class="ocrx_word" ... bbox 710 1459 794 1492...>
        elote
      </span>
   </span>
   ...
  </p>
</div>
```

Figure 3: Extract from hOCR output of Tzeltal dictionary (some details ellipted)

columns. A mechanism is therefore required to allow the user to define the shape of these entities, and then to apply this shape to the hOCR data so that successive lines (approximately) matching that shape can be either discarded (headers and footers) or grouped into lexical entries. This post-processing step is the first part of what we will call Stage 1.

There are several other steps needed to reliably group lines output by Tesseract into lexical entries. Tesseract does appear to correctly capture the division of lines between columns (without incorrectly joining lines across columns), but it does not create an actual column structure. This must be inferred in post-processing, so that lexical entries which are broken across columns can be re-joined. (Page breaks are of course correctly parsed.)

We have constructed a program (written in Python) to do this step of inferring the division of the OCRed text into components. A human supplies several parameters to the program, including:

- The number of columns on a page, and their left-hand margins relative to the page.[4]

- Any information that spans columns. These are typically headers and/or footers, but see below for other information which may fall into this category.

- Number of tab stops in lexical entries. Lexical entries are often formatted as hanging indent paragraphs; in such a case, the indent would be the first tab stop. For some dictionaries there may be additional tab stops (indents), as in the Muinane dictionary of figure 2. At present the user must also supply an approximate measure for each indent, but we hope to eliminate the need for that.

The output of Stage 1 is then an XML file whose structure below the root element consists of a sequence of inferred lexical entries. Within these lexical entries, the structure is a sequence of `<span class='ocr_line'...>` elements, unchanged from the original input.

Nevertheless, we expect there to be a need for manual intervention in this inference step. Figure 4 shows several potential instance of this in the Cubeo dictionary. First, while Tesseract is reasonably good at recognizing that images (such as the picture of the tree in the second column) are not text, and ignoring them, the captions of such figures are generally parsed as paragraphs, and must be omitted from the machine-readable dictionary.[5]

Second, observe that the letter 'B' constitutes a spanning element across both columns. That is, while elsewhere columns are usually continued at the top of the page, in this case, columns containing entries beginning with the letter 'A' appear above this spanning element, while the columns for words beginning with 'B' appear below this.

Finally, note that the upper first column, down to the spanning 'B', consists entirely of the continuation of a lexical entry on the previous page, and is thus indented to the first tab stop. In fact, this lexical entry continues in indented form onto the upper right-hand column. If our program incorrectly inferred that this indent is the level at which lexical entries start, instead of the level at which the second and following lines of a lexical entry are indented, then our program will infer that the upper columns consist of a number of entries, rather than being a single entry with some subentries.[6]

Our approach to manual correction is intended to allow the user to make corrections in a way that is preserved during processing, even during earlier stages of processing. The motivation for this is as follows: suppose that the user did not notice problems resulting from the layout of 4 until much additional processing and manual annotation had taken place. Insofar as this subsequent manual annotation is correct, we wish to preserve it, even if previous stages of automatic processing need to be re-applied. (Automatic annotation, on the other hand, can be easily and cheaply re-done, hence does not require preserving–indeed the reason for re-doing previous automatic stages would presumably be to introduce changes in their functioning.) Our programs therefore preserve human-supplied annotations so that the annotated file can be re-run through earlier steps of processing without loss of the user's work.[7]

We must therefore provide a means for human correction of the output at this point in the pipeline, and do so in a way that does not lose any subsequent annotation, particularly where that subsequent annotation is done by humans.

4 Inferring Substructure

Once the boundaries between lexical entries have been tagged, the next step is to build a finite state grammar giving the order of elements in the dictionary (referred to by lexicographers as the dictionary's 'microstructure'). This can be written as a regular expression by observing a sampling of lexical entries. Conceptually,

---

[4]This may of course differ for left- and right-hand pages. For dictionaries whose headwords are written in right-to-left scripts, this will probably need to be the right-hand margin of the columns.

[5]If pictures are to be included in the machine-readable dictionary, we assume that the process of capturing those images and linking them to an appropriate entry will be separate from the process of converting the text portion of the dictionary into database form.

[6]In fact the program looks for indents relative to a bounding box around all the text of the page; so in this example, the indents would probably be correctly determined, since the lower left-hand column establishes the full width of the text. However, if the long lexical entry had appeared on a page that did not have a spanning letter, the page width might have been incorrectly inferred.

[7]Another way to preserve human work would be to use stand-off annotation; but that would require ensuring that the stand-off annotation pointed only to structures present in the earliest stages of processing.

Figure 4: A page of the Cubeo print dictionary

for example, in the two lexical entries of figure 1, there are two structures:[8]

```
Headword POS GlossWord
Headword POS GlossWord GlossWord \
    GlossWord GlossWord `Véase' XRefWord
```

Hence the task for the user is to create a finite state grammar representing these two lexical entries, and to incrementally expand the grammar to match additional lexical entries. A grammar (still conceptual) combining the above two structures would be the following:

```
Headword POS GlossWord+ \
    (`Véase' XRefWord)?
```

Here we have used Kleene plus to indicate that the GlossWord can be repeated one or more times, parentheses for grouping, and '?' to indicate optionality.

The finite state grammar described above can be thought of as a finite state acceptor (FSA). But in order to transmute the hOCR file into a lexicographically structured dictionary, a finite state transducer (FST) is used to convert the elements found in the hOCR file into the elements needed for the dictionary. For example, what we have called 'Headword' in the above conceptual grammar is represented in the input by `<span class='ocrx_word'...> ... <strong> <span>`; this hOCR structure must be converted into lexicographic elements like `<form>...</form>`.[9] Similarly, the transducer converts a sequence of con-

ceptual glosswords, each represented by a `<span class='ocrx_word'...>...</span>`, into an element like

```
<def>
  <cit type="translation" xml:lang="sp">
      <quote>...</quote>
  </cit>
</def>
```

Further refinement of this grammar will capture the fact that the POS is one of a small number of possible words ('s', 'vt', etc.), and will take account of punctuation which (in some dictionaries) defines the end of certain elements.

The grammar is applied to the output from Stage 1 to parse as many lexical entries as it can; unparsed lexical entries are passed through as-is. Examination of unparsed lexical entries will reveal other patterns that need to be captured, which may include subentries, multiple senses, etc. semantic restrictions or explanations (such as 'trampa (compuesta de madera)' (= "trap (composed of wood)")), etc.

Recall that the hOCR representation tags each line of the original print dictionary. We have retained these tags in the output of Stage 1 because some line breaks may be relevant to parsing. (For example, subentries in the Tzeltal dictionary start on new lines.) However, line breaks can also be due to typesetting constraints. The FST therefore allows newlines between any two tokens, outputting an epsilon (nothing).

Application of the FST grammar to the output of Stage 1 produces a derived XML file in which (most) lexical entries have been transformed from a sequence of lines, each composed of a sequence of tokens, into lexicographically tagged entries. This constitutes the output of Stage 2.

The output of Stage 2 may contain a residue of lexical entries that do not parse. This may imply deficiencies in the grammar, but it may instead be a result of boundaries between lexical entries which have been incorrectly OCRed or inferred in Stage 1 processing. The input structure can be modified to correct such errors, and the grammar rules re-applied until some desired proportion of the lexical entries parse successfully.

Finally, the human may choose to parse some of these non-parsing entries–particularly complex ones– by hand, a process which we touch on in the next section.

5 Post-editing

Ideally, the grammar developed in section 4 will correctly account for all the lexical entries inferred in section 3. In practice, this may not always be the case. One source of noise which is likely to prevent full coverage is inconsistencies in the print dictionary; another is typos (treated in section 6, below) which are severe

---

[8] For purposes of this paper, we ignore the subentry.

[9] The `<strong>` tag represents bold font in this dictionary. For output, we use the Text Encoding Initiative (TEI) schema for dictionaries, see http://www.tei-c.org/release/doc/tei-p5-doc/en/html/DI.html.

enough to prevent correct parsing. But probably the main reason for incomplete coverage will be unique (or nearly unique) complex lexical entries, which are not erroneous per se, but which are enough unlike "normal" lexical entries that they resist parsing by normal means. Thus the output of Stage 2 may include some lexical entries in the line oriented format output by Stage 1 (figure 3), rather than as lexical entries parsed into lexical fields. At some point, it becomes more productive to convert such anomalous entries by hand, rather than further modifying the grammar to account for them.

We therefore allow post-editing of the output of Stage 2, so that the final output contains only those lexicographic elements appropriate to a dictionary database, without any of the formatting elements output by the OCR system. We are currently using a programmer's editor to do this post-editing; we may later substitute an XML editor specialized for dictionaries, which has been developed by David Zajic and others in our group.

6   Typo correction

As mentioned in section 1, OCR systems (and human typing) will produce typographic errors. This problem is particularly acute in dictionaries of minority languages, since it is unlikely that one can find an off-the-shelf OCR model tuned for such a language. Minority languages may also introduce unusual characters; Cubeo, for example, has a single (but frequent) verbal root that contains the only phonemically contrastive instance of a voiced interdental fricative, and the Cubeo dictionary writes it as a barred 'd', a letter not recognized by our OCR system.[10] The fact that such dictionaries are likely to be bilingual further exacerbates the problem, since at the time the OCR process runs, there is no indication of which words are in which language; so even if one did have a character-based language model to help discover typos, the system would not know which words to apply that to.

But of course the latter problem is solved once we have converted the OCR output into an XML dictionary file; we then know which fields encode which languages. At that point, various techniques can be employed to find possible typos, whether using a standard spell corrector for the glossing language, creating a character-based language model of the minority language, or manually searching in the minority language fields for particular sequences of characters (such as characters characterizing that one Cubeo verb root, using an ordinary 'd' for search in place of the desired barred-d). We therefore treat typo correction as a nearly last step, rather than an initial step.

---

[10]Morse and M. B. Maxwell 1999, p. 5 treats this as virtually allophonic, but the Cubeo dictionary writes it in this one morpheme with a distinct alphabetic character.

7   Conversion to standard XML schemas

The structure of the output of the processing described above should match the *conceptual* structure of the original print dictionary. For reasons which will not be discussed here, this is probably not the optimum structure for electronic dictionaries. For example, while print dictionaries frequently treat phrasal entries as subentries of one of the words found in the phrase, it is more common in lexicographic databases to treat phrasal entries as separate lexical entries, linked to each of the words of which they are composed. A view of a phrasal entry as a subentry of these words can then be created on the fly.

The Lexical Markup Framework (LMF, Francopoulo 2013; ISO TC37 2008) is a meta-schema finding increasing use for electronic dictionaries. There is no comparable standard for print dictionaries; however, the Text Encoding Initiative (TEI) Guidelines (TEI Consortium 2016), particularly chapter 9, contain an ample set of tags that should be usable for virtually any dictionary. While we cannot treat here the conversion between a custom XML file derived from a particular print dictionary (which might conform to the TEI) and other standards (such as LMF), we do consider that conversion to be a recommended practice.

8   Related work

To the best of our knowledge, there has been little published about how to convert OCRed (or hand-typed) lexical data into a database format. From what we can ascertain from personal communication and examination of errors in converted dictionaries, what is usually done is to process such data using a chain of scripts, using regular expressions to convert whatever information is available into a target format, generally SGML or (more recently) XML.

There is one documented project that developed a more general means of importing OCRed dictionaries. This is the earlier University of Maryland project, BRIDGE (Karagol-Ayan, D. Doermann, and Dorr 2003; Ma et al. 2003). Unfortunately, the software developed under that project had multiple dependencies which are no longer readily available, so the tools are not working; our attempts to re-create the workflow using more modern, freely available software did not succeed. Also, while that project relied heavily on machine learning, we are creating a more manual process, which we expect to be easier to maintain and modify.

In a series of papers, Zajic and his collaborators at our institution have explored error detection in digital dictionaries (Zajic, Bloodgood, et al. 2015; Zajic, D. S. Doermann, Bloodgood, et al. 2012; Zajic, D. S. Doermann, Rodrigues, et al. 2013; Zajic, M. Maxwell, et al. 2011). This work will inform our work on the parsing of lexical entries (4); as mentioned in section 5, we may also incorporate the specialized XML editor that group has developed.

9   Availability

We will make our software available as open source, although the exact license has not been determined.

References

Bartholomew, Doris A. and Louise C. Schoenhals. (1983). *Bilingual dictionaries for indigenous languages*. Mexico: Summer Institute of Linguistics.

Bird, Steven and Gary Simons (2003). "Seven dimensions of portability for language documentation and description." In: *Language* 79.3, pp. 557–582.

Borghoff, U.M., P. Rödig, J. Scheffczyk, and L. Schmitz (2006). *Long-Term Preservation of Digital Documents: Principles and Practices*. Berlin: Springer.

Cruz, Manuel A., Florence L. Gerdel, and Marianna C. Slocum (1999). *Diccionario tzeltal de Bachajón, Chiapas*. Serie de vocabularios y diccionarios indígenas "Mariano Silva y Aceves" 40. Coyoacán, D.F., Mexico: Instituto Lingüístico de Verano, A.C. URL: `http : / / www . sil . org / system / files / reapdata / 52 / 85 / 76 / 52857610164780871251544555610851968393 / S040_DicTzeltalFacs_tzh.pdf`.

Francopoulo, Gil, ed. (2013). *LMF: Lexical Markup Framework*. Hoboken, NJ: Wiley.

Govindaraju, Venu and Srirangaraj Setlur, eds. (2009). *Guide to OCR for Indic Scripts: Document Recognition and Retrieval*. London: Springer.

Grimes, Joseph E. (1970). "Computing in Lexicography." In: *The Linguistic Reporter* 12.5–6, pp. 1–5. URL: `http : / / citeseerx . ist . psu . edu / viewdoc/download;?doi=10.1.1.620.9976& rep=rep1&type=pdf`.

ISO TC37 (2008). *Language resource management — Lexical markup framework (LMF)*. Technical Report ISO 24613:2008.

Karagol-Ayan, Burcu, David Doermann, and Bonnie Dorr (2003). "Acquisition of Bilingual MT Lexicons from OCRed Dictionaries." In: *Machine Translation Summit IX*.

Ma, Huanfeng, Burcu Karagol-Ayan, David Doermann, Doug Oard, and Jianqiang Wang (2003). "Parsing and Tagging of Bilingual Dictionaries." In: *Traitement Automatique Des Langues* 44, pp. 125–150.

Morse, Nancy L., Jr. Jay K. Salser, and Neva de Salser (1999). *Diccionario Ilustrado Bilingüe: cubeo–español, español–cubeo*. Bogotá: Editorial Alberto Lleras Camargo. URL: `https : / / www . sil . org / resources/publications/entry/19008`.

Morse, Nancy L. and Michael B. Maxwell (1999). *Cubeo Grammar*. Studies in the Languages of Colombia 5. Dallas: Summer Institute of Linguistics.

Slocum, Marianna C. and Florence L. Gerdel (1976). *Diccionario tzeltal de Bachajón: castellano – tzeltal, tzeltal – castellano*. Serie de vocabularios y diccionarios indígenas "Mariano Silva y Aceves" 13. México, D.F.: Instituto Lingüístico de Verano.

Smith, Ray, Daria Antonova, and Dar-Shyang Lee (2009). "Adapting the Tesseract open source OCR engine for multilingual OCR." In: *MOCR '09: Proceedings of the International Workshop on Multilingual OCR*. New York: ACM. URL: `http : / / doi . acm.org/10/1145/1577802.1577804`.

TEI Consortium (2016). *TEI P5: Guidelines for Electronic Text Encoding and Interchange*. Technical Report. Charlottesville, Virginia. URL: `http : / / www . tei-c.org/Guidelines/P5/`.

Walton, James W., Janice P. Walton, and Clementina Pakky de Buenaventura (1997). *Diccionario Bilingüe muinane–español, español–muinane*. Bogotá: Editorial Alberto Lleras Camargo.

Zajic, David M., Michael Bloodgood, Benjamin Strauss, and Elena Zotkina (2015). *Faster, More Thorough Error Detection in Electronic Dictionaries*. Technical Report. University of Maryland: Center for Advanced Study of Language.

Zajic, David M., David S. Doermann, Michael Bloodgood, Paul Rodrigues, Peng Ye, Dustin Foley, and Elena Zotkina (2012). *A Hybrid System for Error Detection in Electronic Dictionaries*. Technical Report. University of Maryland: Center for Advanced Study of Language.

Zajic, David M., David S. Doermann, Paul Rodrigues, Peng Ye, and Elena Zotkina (2013). *Faster, More Accurate Repair of Electronic Dictionaries*. Technical Report. University of Maryland: Center for Advanced Study of Language.

Zajic, David M., Michael Maxwell, David S. Doermann, Paul Rodrigues, and Michael Bloodgood (2011). "Correcting Errors in Digital Lexicographic Resources Using a Dictionary Manipulation Language." In: *Proceedings of Electronic Lexicography in the 21st Century (eLex)*. Vol. abs/1410.7787. URL: `http://arxiv.org/abs/1410.7787`.

A Computationally-Assisted Procedure for Discovering
Poetic Organization within Oral Tradition

David Meyer
david.meyer@yahoo.com

Abstract

A procedure is described which is capable of detecting poetic organization within transcribed oral tradition text. It consists of two components: An automated process which generates recurring n-gram patterns, and a verification process of manual review. Applied to a corpus of Tahitian and Mangarevan oral tradition, it has led to discovery of a variety of uses of meter and parallelism; ranging from the universally common to the unanticipated. The procedure should be generalizable to the study of other of the world's oral poetries, having been designed to identify a wide range of organizational possibilities.

1   Introduction

Our knowledge of the many ways by which oral tradition may be organized poetically derives from an uneven study of mostly European, Middle-Eastern, and Asian traditions. On a positive note, descriptions of the oral poetry of Indo-European languages have been sufficient to spawn the field of comparative-historical poetics (see Watkins 1995). Unfortunately, much less effort has been applied to the remainder of the world's oral traditions, which tend to fade away well before their languages die off. In a homogenizing era, unless these vulnerable data are collected and their varied means of poetic organization discovered, much of what could have been learned with regard to oral poetics universally might be forsaken.

When venturing into the study of an undescribed poetic tradition, a purely manual approach is generally insufficient. The investigative path is likely to be lined with wide cognitive gaps from researcher prejudice as to what might be recognized as poetic.

The procedure described here attempts to remedy potential bias by informing the researcher of instances of parallelism which may not have been otherwise detected. The procedure consists of two components: An automated process which generates recurring n-gram patterns,

and a verification process of manual review. Manual verification is recommended given that a tradition may employ many different organizational methods, but the corpora which contain them are often small.

Some of the examples used below are drawn from application of the procedure to two sources of Polynesian oral tradition: A 50,000 word corpus of early 19th century Tahitian material representing multiple genres, and a 10,000 word corpus of early 20th century Mangarevan songs and chants. Treatment of the complete Tahitian corpus was successful at the discovery of two varieties of counting meter (one of which may be unique to Tahiti), complex patterns of meter and sound parallelism, and many uses of syntactic and semantic parallelism (see Meyer 2011 and 2013). Analysis of the Mangarevan data is still underway.

Due to space constraints, the automated procedure's functionality has only been summarized here. It is hoped that enough information will have been provided for the computational linguist reader to be successful at his or her own implementation.

2   Description of the Procedure

As mentioned, the procedure consists of an automated process which generates recurring n-gram patterns, followed by a verification process of manual review.

With regard to former, computationally-generated candidates consist of recurring n-grams of linguistic features,[1] any of which could potentially have application to poetic composi-

---

[1] Among the oral poetries of the world, a wide range of linguistic features have been found organized in uncountable creative ways. With respect to the phoneme, for instance, poetic organization may be of the phoneme itself, of a class of phonemes (e.g. as in an assonant pattern where only the vowels are significant), of a phonemic feature (e.g. a pattern of contrasting +*acute* and -*acute*), etc. The term *linguistic feature* here refers to any linguistic information detectable at the level of phoneme, syllable, word, or line that could serve to form a pattern of poetic meter or parallelism.

Proceedings of the 2nd Workshop on the Use of Computational Methods in the Study of Endangered Languages, pages 92–100,
Honolulu, Hawai'i, USA, March 6–7, 2017. ©2017 Association for Computational Linguistics

tion. The n-grams are sorted and counted, and then presented – in their original context – in multiple interactive reports as preparation for manual review.

The automated component initially attempts to accommodate any linguistic feature a poet may wish to employ. After an initial round of manual analysis, however, it is desirable to pare the feature set down to just those which demonstrate some degree of promise; in order to lighten the load of the overall endeavor.[2] The list in table 1, for example, contains the reduced linguistic feature set which was ultimately selected for treatment of the Polynesian data.

Table 1. Final set of linguistic features treated with regard to the Tahitian and Mangarevan data.

Relevant to meter

Primary word stress count
Primary and secondary word stress count
Word mora count
Word syllable count

Relevant to sound and syntactic parallelism

At the level of the phoneme, one or a series of:
Phoneme
Consonant
Vowel

At the level of the syllable, one or a series of:
Syllable form
Syllable-initial phoneme
Syllable onset
Syllable rhyme

At the level of the word, one or a series of:
Word form
Word consonants
Word vowels
Word lemma
Word part-of-speech
Word-initial syllable
Word-final syllable
Word-initial syllable onset
Word-final syllable onset
Word-initial syllable rhyme
Word-final syllable rhyme
Word-initial phoneme
Word-final phoneme

It may also be necessary to re-apply the procedure were it discovered during manual review

that the oral tradition specialist's poetic use of linguistic features differs from that of general language.[3]

In its implementation, the automated process need not be restricted to observation of a single feature in isolation (single-feature pattern detection), but should attempt to be sufficiently expansive so as to detect an oral poet's efforts to coordinate more than one feature (multi-feature pattern detection). It should also be capable of detecting patterns of inverted parallelism. Line,[4] word, and syllable boundaries may or may not be significant, and therefore all possibilities for boundary inclusion into a pattern should be permitted.

Concerning the raw output of candidate pattern generation, it was found during manual review of the Polynesian data that:

1. Some patterns suggested poetic organization, however the majority – around 90% – held little or no interest.

2. Some patterns pointed to a larger, more comprehensive pattern.

3. Some patterns pointed to a pattern that might be detected better at a different level of analysis.

Patterns demonstrating some degree of promise were filtered through the following criteria:[5]

1. Similar types of pattern should be either non-existent or significantly less frequent in prose.

---

[2] See also the discussion of combinatorial explosion in 2.4 below.

[3] For example, in the treatment of the Tahitian and Mangarevan passages which will be presented below, long and short vowels have been conflated, as it was discovered early on in manual analysis that patterns could be extended, or those near to each other joined, by permitting such an abstraction. It was also discovered that the Tahitian and Mangarevan diphthong /ae/ is poetically equivalent to /ai/, and the Tahitian /ao/ to /au/. Poetic equivalence of /ae/ to /ai/ has been similarly observed by Jacob Love to apply to Samoan rhyme (Love 1991:88). Finally, the glottal stop phoneme /ʔ/ was determined to serve no role in Tahitian poetic function.

[4] A tradition's poetic line must be established before line boundary may be included as a pattern element. Nigel Fabb suggests that the concept of line is a poetic universal (Fabb 2009:54-55). It generally represents a syntactic structure with a specific metrical count, although for some traditions it may be non-metrical, bounded by some indicator such as a pause or lengthened vowel. Its identification, perhaps through trial and error, should be accomplished early on in the analysis.

[5] These criteria were empirically motivated mostly from analysis of the Polynesian data, and so may evolve after the described process has found application to a wider variety of traditions.

2. A pattern should occur multiple times in the same text. A longer pattern need only occur twice in the same text.

3. The placement of the majority of a pattern's occurrences should appear intentional; for example, as when found principally in the same segment of a text, or when placement suggested some higher degree of coordination.

4. Similar types of pattern should be found in at least two other texts of the same genre, in order to filter out patterns which might be unrepresentative of the poetic tradition, or which were perhaps merely the result of chance occurrence.

Poetic intent might subsequently be asserted if either of the following were satisfied:

1. The candidate pattern was found to match any method of poetic organization documented for other of the world's poetic traditions.

2. For promising pattern types unspecified in the literature, a pattern might be esteemed to self-justify as poetic were it found to be sufficiently complex or repetitive so as to eliminate the likelihood of chance.

The following sections will discuss single-feature pattern detection, multi-feature pattern detection, and detection of inverted parallelism. Examples will be provided of application of the procedure to a passage from a familiar English children's poem, and to extracts from several of the transcribed Tahitian and Mangarevan oral texts.

2.1 Single-Feature Pattern Detection

In single-feature pattern detection, only one linguistic feature is analyzed at a time. As with the other detection methods, the possibility exists of poetic intent whenever an n-gram token recurs.

The first four lines of the well-known children's poem *Mary had a little lamb* will serve to initially demonstrate this type of analysis. The passage in (1) has been tagged for three word-level linguistic features: *IPA word form*, *simple part-of-speech*, and *word syllable count*.

(1) Passage from *Mary had a little lamb* tagged for word form, simple part-of-speech, and word syllable count

1.
Mary	*had*	*a*	*little*	*lamb*
mɛɹi	hæd	ə	lɪdəl	læm
NOUN	VERB	FUNC	MODIF	NOUN
2	1	1	2	1

2.
whose	*fleece*	*was*	*white*	*as*	*snow*
huːz	fliːs	wəz	waɪt	æz	snoʊ
FUNC	NOUN	VERB	MODIF	FUNC	NOUN
1	1	1	1	1	1

3.
and	*everywhere*	*that*	*Mary*	*went*
ænd	ɛvɹiwɛɹ	ðæt	mɛɹi	wɛnt
FUNC	NOUN	FUNC	NOUN	VERB
1	3	1	2	1

4.
her	*lamb*	*was*	*sure*	*to*	*go*
hɚ	læm	wəz	ʃɚ	tu	goʊ
FUNC	NOUN	VERB	MODIF	FUNC	VERB
1	1	1	1	1	1

The list of bi-gram word form tokens from this passage would begin:

mɛɹi-hæd

hæd-ə

etc.

The list of 4-gram simple part-of-speech tokens would begin:

NOUN-VERB-FUNC-MODIF

VERB-FUNC-MODIF-NOUN

etc.

From a tally of matching simple part-of-speech bigrams, we note in (2) below four occurrences of *NOUN-VERB*.

(2) Some bigram repetition in the *Mary had a little lamb* passage
Level of analysis: Word
Linguistic feature: Simple part-of-speech
Boundary relevance: Line boundary is significant.
Minimum pattern occurrences = 4

1.
Mary	*had*	*a*	*little*	*lamb*
NOUN	**VERB**	FUNC	MODIF	NOUN

2.
whose	*fleece*	*was*	*white*	*as*	*snow*
FUNC	**NOUN**	**VERB**	MODIF	FUNC	NOUN

3.
and	*everywhere*	*that*	*Mary*	*went*
FUNC	NOUN	FUNC	**NOUN**	**VERB**

4.
her	*lamb*	*was*	*sure*	*to*	*go*
FUNC	**NOUN**	**VERB**	MODIF	FUNC	VERB

With prior knowledge that English is an SVO language, however, the *NOUN-VERB* pattern candidate is dismissed during manual review as being common as well to English prose.[6]

In (3) below, we find repetition of the word syllable count 11-gram: *1-2-1-|-1-1-1-1-1-1-|*,[7] corresponding to *a little lamb | whose fleece was white as snow |*, and *that Mary went | her lamb was sure to go |*.

(3) 11-gram repetition in the *Mary had a little lamb* passage
Level of analysis: Word
Linguistic feature: Word syllable count
Boundary relevance: Line boundary is significant.
Minimum pattern occurrences = 2

1. *Mary   had   a   little   lamb*
   2   1   1   2   1

2. *whose   fleece   was   white   as   snow*
   1   1   1   1   1   1

3. *and   everywhere   that   Mary   went*
   1   3   1   2   1

4. *her   lamb   was   sure   to   go*
   1   1   1   1   1   1

It may be that parallelism of such a long pattern is metrically significant, although this would be difficult to confirm given just one recurrence. It should be reiterated that while patterns which emerge out of a single text are not always conclusively poetic, when compared with similar pattern organization in other texts, poetic intent often becomes clear.

In (4), we turn to analysis at the syllable level. Here, we discover the apparent end-rhyming bigram /oʊ/-| of *snow* |, and *go* |.

(4) Some bigram repetition in the *Mary had a little lamb* passage
Level of analysis: Syllable
Linguistic feature: Syllable rhyme
Boundary relevance: Line boundary is significant.
Minimum pattern occurrences = 2

1. *Mary   had   a   little   lamb*
   ɛ ɪ   æd   ə   ɪ əl   æm

2. *whose fleece   was   white   as   snow*
   uːz   iːs   əz   aɪt   æz   oʊ

3. *and   everywhere that Mary   went*
   ænd   ɛv   i   ɛɹ   æt   ɛ ɪ   ɛnt

4. *her   lamb   was   sure   to   go*
   ɚ   æm   əz   ɚ   u   oʊ

With prior knowledge that end-rhyme on alternating lines is common to English, French, and several other poetic traditions, we conclude that the intent here is poetic.

In (5), we encounter a passage of a Mangarevan song[8] which consists of a repeated syntactic frame, with the four nouns *vai, kukau, aʔi,* and *inaina* and the two adjectives *rito* and *ka* serving as its variable elements. We observe end-rhyme in lines 1 and 5 with the syllable rhyme pattern ***a-i|*** (in bold) corresponding to the nouns *vai* and *aʔi,* and note that ***a-i*** as a bigram is also contained within the name of the song's subject, the young woman Tai-tinaku-toro. We additionally observe assonant matching between the syllable rhyme bigram ***a-u*** (in bold underlined) of the noun *ku.ka.u* and the syllables *na.ku* of the woman's name. Finally, we note a match between the syllable rhyme bigram ***I-A*** (in bold small caps) of the noun *i.na~i.na* and the syllables *ti.na* of the woman's name.

(5) Some bi- and tri-gram repetition in an extract of a Mangarevan song (Buck 1938:170)
Level of analysis: Syllable
Linguistic feature: Syllable rhyme
Boundary relevance: Line boundary is significant.
Minimum pattern occurrences = 2

1. *ko   te   vai*
   o   e   **a.i**
   EXIST   the   fresh.water
   The water

2. *e   rito   nei*
   e   i.o   e.i
   IPFV   clear   here
   that is clear here,

3. *ko   te   kukau   ia*
   o   e   u.**a.u**   i.a
   EXIST   the   bath   ANAPH
   it is the bath

---

[6] With regard to languages for which common patterns of prose – part-of-speech or otherwise – are unknown, the analysis process should be applied as well to a prose corpus, and its findings subtracted, either by automated or manual means, from poetry analysis results.

[7] To ease readability, *line-boundary* is indicated in some pattern descriptions as a vertical bar |.

---

[8] In Tahitian and Mangarevan song, adjacent vowels are not heard to form diphthongs, and so the second vowel of each diphthong in this passage is treated as its own syllable.

4. *o*   *tai-tinaku-toro*
   o   **a.i I.<u>A</u>.u** o.o
   INALIEN.WEAK Tai-tinaku-toro
   of   Tai-tinaku-toro.

5. *ko*   *te*   *aʔi*
   o   e   **a.i**
   EXIST the   fire
   The fire

6. *e*   *ka*   *nei*
   e   a   e.i
   IPFV   lit   here
   that is lit here,

7. *ko*   *te*   *ina~ina*   *ia*
   o   e   **I.A I.A**   i.a
   EXIST   the   drying.agent   ANAPH
   it is the drying agent

8. *o*   *tai-tinaku-toro*
   o   **a.i I.<u>A</u>.u** o.o
   INALIEN.WEAK Tai-tinaku-toro
   of   Tai-tinaku-toro.

If similar use of assonance were discovered in several other texts of the same genre, such should warrant a claim that *assonant matching between a syntactic frame's variable elements and the poem's theme* is a method of Mangarevan poetic organization.

2.2 Multi-Feature Pattern Detection

In multi-feature analysis, n-gram patterns are comprised of cross-level linguistic feature information. This is motivated by a desire to be sufficiently expansive so as to detect a poet's efforts to coordinate more than one feature.[9]

In the *Mary had a little lamb* passage, the addition of a bit of manual semantic tagging reveals the following multi-feature tri-gram:

Semantics: lamb-part -
Word form: wəz -
Part-of-speech: MODIF

The tri-gram token is provided in context in (6):

(6) Some multi-feature trigram repetition in the *Mary had a little lamb* passage
Level of analysis: Word
Linguistic features: Word form, simple part-of-speech, and "Mary-part" and "lamb-part" semantic tagging
Boundary relevance: All boundaries are ignored.
Minimum pattern occurrences = 2

1. Mary   had   a   little   lamb
   mɛɹɪ   hæd   ə   lɪdəl   læm
   NOUN   VERB   FUNC   MODIF   NOUN
   Mary-part   lamb-part

2. whose   fleece   was   white   as   snow
   huːz   fliːs   **wəz**   waɪt   æz   snoʊ
   FUNC NOUN   VERB   **MODIF**   FUNC NOUN
   lamb-part

3. and   everywhere   that   Mary   went
   ænd   ɛvɹɪwɛɹ   ðæt   mɛɹɪ   wɛnt
   FUNC NOUN   FUNC   NOUN   VERB
                                         Mary-part

4. her   lamb   was   sure   to   go
   hɚ   læm   **wəz**   ʃɚ   tu   goʊ
   FUNC NOUN   VERB   **MODIF**   FUNC VERB
   lamb-part

Whether or not the recurrence of this tri-gram might be interpreted as poetic, it should be recognized that it would not have been detected by single-feature analysis.

From the Tahitian corpus, we find an 11-gram multi-feature token which combines information relevant to word form, syllable count, and word vowel:

Line boundary -
Word form: e -
Word form: noho -
Line boundary -
Syllable count: 1 -
Syllable count: 2 -
Line boundary -
Word form: i -
Word form: te -
Word vowels: a-o-a -
Line boundary

---

[9] Multi-feature detection was originally inspired by the bag of trees approach used by Data-Oriented Parsing, which permits assembling syntactic patterns from different levels of tree structure (see Bod 1998).

This token appears initially in lines 1 through 3 and then repeats in lines 4 through 6 of (7) below:

(7) Some multi-feature 11-gram repetition in an extract of "Warning by messengers of the pa'i-atua service" (Henry 1928:158-159)
Level of analysis: Word
Linguistic features: Word form, word vowel, syllable count
Boundary relevance: Line and word boundaries are significant.
Minimum pattern occurrences = 2

1. *e*   *noho*
 e   o o
 1   2
 IPFV sit
 Sit

2. *i*   *niʔa*
 i   i a
 1   **2**
 at   above
 on

3. *i*   *te*   *maːhora*
 i   e   a o a
 1   1   3
 at   the yard
 the yard,

4. *e*   *noho*
 e   o o
 1   2
 IPFV sit
 Sit,

5. *e*   *ʔupu*
 e   u u
 1   **2**
 IPFV recite.a.prayer
 recite

6. *i*   *te*   *ʔahoːʔa*
 i   e   a o a
 1   1   3
 DIROBJ the brush.clearing.prayer
 the brush clearing prayer.

It might be best to re-interpret this complex n-gram as simply providing evidence of two overlapping methods of organization: A *3-3-5* pattern of syllabic counting meter alongside an *a-o-a* pattern of end-rhyme. During manual review, an attempt should always be made to re-analyse candidates into more generalizable patterns.

From the Mangarevan material, we find a 15-gram multi-feature token which combines information relevant to word form, syllable form, syllable onset, and syllable rhyme:

Line boundary -
Word_form: ena -
Word_form: ʔana -
Line boundary -
Word_form: i -
Syllable_onset: t -
Syllable rhyme: a -
Syllable_form: vae -
Syllable_rhyme: e -
Syllable_rhyme: u -
Syllable_rhyme: a -
Line boundary -
Word_form: te -
Word_form: u -
Line boundary

In (8) below, this 15-gram comprises lines 1 through 3, and then repeats in lines 4 through 6:[10]

(8) Some multi-feature 15-gram repetition in an extract of a *rogorogo* chant (Buck 1938:114)
Levels of analysis: Word and syllable
Linguistic features: Word form, syllable form, syllable onset, syllable rhyme
Boundary relevance: Line, word, and syllable boundaries are significant.
Minimum pattern occurrences = 2

1. **ena**   **ʔana**
 e.na   ʔa.na
  n   ʔ n
 e.a   a.a
 DEM.PROX.2 now
 See there now

2. **i**   *tua-vai-heua*
 i   tu.a-**vai**-he.u.a
      t **v** h
 i   u.a a.i **e.u.a**
 at   Tua-vai-heua
 at Tua-vai-heua is

3. **te**   **u**
 te   u
 t
 e   u
 the milk
 the milk.

---

[10] Due to space considerations, the lines of the passage between these two matching sections have been omitted.

...

4. *ena*   *ʔana*
   e.na   ʔa.na
    n   ʔ n
   e.a   a.a
   DEM.PROX.2 now
   See there now

5. *i*   *te*   *vavae*   *ʔenua*
   i   e   va.**vae** ʔe.nu.a
     t   v v   ʔ n
   i   e   **a**.ae   **e.u.a**
   at the leg   land
   coming over land is

6. *te*   *u*
   te   u
   t
    e   u
   the milk
   the milk.

The repeated word forms within this 15-gram perhaps serve to bracket the sound parallelism which occurs between its variable elements.

It should be noted that, with regard to the Polynesian data, the discovery of poetic organization was generally achievable through single-feature analysis. Patterns only detectable through multi-feature analysis were uncommon.

2.3 Inverted Parallelism

In some poetic traditions, patterns of linguistic features are not always repeated as is, but rather by means of an inverted ordering. An example is *chiasmus*, which is an inversion of repeated semantic elements; very common to the Ancient Hebrew of the Old Testament.

Automated detection of inverted parallelism is accomplished by a simply comparing the linguistic feature n-grams of a given document with the n-grams generated from a reverse ordering of those features. As before, matching n-grams are sorted and counted, and then presented within the context of the non-reversed material.

In the Tahitian example given in (9) below, we find the 7-gram pattern of syllabic counting meter *6-4-5-3-3-3-4* which is followed, after a *5* count, by its inverted match *4-3-3-3-5-4-6*.

(9) Inverted 7-gram repetition in an extract of "The genealogies of the gods" (Henry 1928:355-359)
Level of analysis: Word
Linguistic features: Line syllable count
Boundary relevance: Line and word boundaries are significant.
Minimum pattern occurrences = 2

6   1.   *e*   *atua*   *anaʔe*
         1   3   3(2)[11]
         EXIST god   all
         They were all gods,

4   2.   *te*   *tahuʔa*
         1   3
         EXIST artisan
         the artisans

5   3.   *ʔe*   *te*   *ʔa:rere*
         1   1   3
         and the messenger
         and the messengers.

3   4.   *e*   *mana*
         1   2
         EXIST power
         Power

3   5.   *to:*   *ra:tou*
         1   2
         INALIEN.NEUT 3.PL
         was theirs

3   6.   *i*   *te*   *po:*
         1   1   1
         in the Realm.of.Darkness
         in the Realm of Darkness

4   7.   *ʔe*   *i*   *te*   *ao*
         1   1   1   1
         and in the world
         and in the world.

5   8.   *rahu-a*   *mai*   *ra*
         3   1   1
         conjure-PASS hither there
         He was conjured forth,

4   9.   *te*   *atua*
         1   3
         the god
         the god

---

[11] The syllable count for *anaʔe* in this context has been reduced to 2, as the last /a/ of the preceding word *atua* and the first /a/ of *anaʔe* merge to form a single long [a:], having a syllable count of 1.

10. *ʔo   raʔa*
3   1   2
        PROP   Raʻa
        Raʻa.

11. *e   moʔa*
3   1   2
        EXIST   sacredness
        Sacredness,

12. *e   mana*
3   1   2
        EXIST   power
        power,

13. *e   hana~hana*
5   1   4
        EXIST   glory
        glory,

14. *e   mau   riri*
4   1   1   2
        EXIST   to.hold anger
        the ability to hold anger

15. *to: raʔa   atua*
6   1   2   3
        INALIEN.NEUT   Raʻa   god
        belonged to the god Raʻa.

Due to the detection as well of many other patterns of inverted meter in the corpus, *inversion of the patterns which govern syllabic counting meter* was deemed to self-justify, under criteria mentioned above, as a method of Tahitian poetic organization.

2.4   Concerning Combinatorial Explosion

Inherent to the automated process is a combinatorial explosion of n-grams – particularly true with regard to multi-feature analysis. The total number of single- and multi-feature n-gram tokens generated for a given text may be determined as described in figure 1.

The number of word-level n-grams generated from a typical 1,000 word text, after restricting analysis to 10 layers of linguistic feature tagging, is the quite large 6.82×10^{501}. By reducing the number of tagged layers to four and maximum *n* to 10, however, the final count diminishes to a much more tractable 1.39 billion. It should be mentioned that foregoing multi-level analysis would permit maximum *n* to be set much higher.

It follows that a reduction in the interaction of linguistic features for a given pass would result in some patterns being missed by the automated

Figure 1. Calculation for all single- and multi-feature n-gram tokens of a text.[12]

Given:

C = The count of all single- and multi-feature n-gram tokens which might be generated from a text at a given level of analysis (e.g. *word level, syllable level*).

E = The number of linguistic elements in the text (e.g. in the passage from *Mary had a little lamb*, we analysed at the word level where there are 22 words and 5 instances of *line boundary*, for a total of 27 word-level elements).

N = The current n-gram *n* number.

Max N = The *n* number of the largest desired n-gram. For an n-gram token to be able to occur at least twice, and thereby potentially demonstrate a pattern, *max n* should not exceed half the total number of linguistic elements (e.g. for word-level analysis of the passage from *Mary had a little lamb*, it would not be useful for *n* to be larger than 13).

F = The number of tagged linguistic features (e.g. the passage from *Mary had a little lamb* in (1) is tagged for three features).

$$C = \sum_{N=1}^{Max\ N} (E - (N - 1)) \cdot F^{N}$$

process. Therefore, a certain degree of trial and error must be pursued in order to determine which combinations of four features at a time yield the best candidates. Furthermore, with a maximum *n* of just 10, it may become necessary to stitch together – either manually or through an automated process – adjacent and overlapping patterns.

3   Conclusion

Alongside grammatical description, dictionary compilation, language pedagogy, and the other efforts typically undertaken to assist in the preservation of an endangered language, it is important that documentation of a language community's oral tradition, and the poetics commonly embedded therein, be awarded full consideration as well. Both of these serve a significant role in language identity, and the realm of verbal

---

[12] To arrive at the count needed to include analysis of inverted parallelism as well, simply double the *C* result.

art is enriched through their study. Relevant to the level of detail required for such research, John Miles Foley asserts that "We must give the idiosyncratic aspects of each tradition their due, for only when we perceive sameness against the background of rigorously examined individualized traits can we claim a true comparison of oral traditions" (Foley 1981:275).

The procedure which has been described here is admittedly labor-intensive; especially with regard to its manual component. However, it is probably necessary that it be so in order to succeed at documenting the majority of a poetic tradition's *individualized traits*. Relevant to the Tahitian material, the procedure was successful at the detection of a syllabic counting meter based upon word stress (see Meyer 2013:88-105). Such was previously unattested among world poetries, and with its discovery our understanding of what is universally possible for meter became expanded.

References

Rens Bod. 1998. *Beyond grammar: An experience-based theory of language*. Center for the Study of Language and Information, Stanford, CA.

Peter H. Buck. 1938. *Ethnology of Mangareva*. Bernice P. Bishop Museum Bulletin 157. Bishop Museum Press, Honolulu, HI.

Nigel Fabb. 2009. Symmetric and asymmetric relations, and the aesthetics of form in poetic language. *The European English Messenger,* 18(1):50–59.

John Miles Foley. 1981. Tradition-dependent and -independent features in oral literature: A comparative view of the formula. In John Miles Foley, editor, *Oral traditional literature, a festschrift for Albert Bates Lord*, pages 263–281. Slavica Publishers, Columbus, OH.

Teuira Henry. 1928. *Ancient Tahiti*. Bernice P. Bishop Museum Bulletin 48. Bishop Museum Press, Honolulu, HI.

Jacob Wainwright Love. 1991. *Sāmoan variations: Essays on the nature of traditional oral arts.* Garland Publishing, New York, NY.

David Meyer. 2011. A computationally-assisted analysis of early Tahitian oral poetry. PhD Dissertation, Department of Linguistics, University of Edinburgh.

David Meyer. 2013. *Early Tahitian poetics*. De Gruyter Mouton, Boston, MA.

Calvert Watkins. 1995. *How to kill a dragon: Aspects of Indo-European poetics*. Oxford University Press, New York, NY.

Improving Coverage of an Inuktitut Morphological Analyzer Using a Segmental Recurrent Neural Network

Jeffrey C. Micher
US Army Research Laboratory
2800 Powder Mill Road
Adelphi, MD 20783
`jeffrey.c.micher.civ@mail.mil`

Abstract

Languages such as Inuktitut are particularly challenging for natural language processing because of polysynthesis, abundance of grammatical features represented via morphology, morphophonemics, dialect variation, and noisy data. We make use of an existing morphological analyzer, the Uqailaut analyzer, and a dataset, the Nunavut Hansards, and experiment with improving the analyzer via bootstrapping of a segmental recurrent neural network onto it. We present results of the accuracy of this approach which works better for a coarse-grained analysis than a fine-grained analysis. We also report on accuracy of just the "closed-class" suffix parts of the Inuktitut words, which are better than the overall accuracy on the full words.

1 Introduction

Inuktitut is a polysynthetic language, and is part of the Inuit language dialect continuum spoken in Arctic North America[1]. It is one of the official languages of the territory of Nunavut, Canada and is used widely in government and educational documents there. Despite its elevated status of official language, very little research on natural language processing of Inuktitut has been carried out. On the one hand, the complexity of Inuktitut makes it challenging for typical natural language processing applications. On the other hand, Inuktitut may only be spoken by around 23,000 people as a first language,[2] and as a result, receives minimal commercial attention. The National Research Council of Canada has produced a very important morphological analyzer for Inuktitut. We make use of this analyzer and propose a neural network approach to enhancing its output. This paper is organized as follows: first we talk about the nature of Inuktitut, focusing on polysynthesis, abundance of grammatical suffixes, morphophonemics, and spelling. Second, we describe the Uqailaut morphological analyzer for Inuktitut. Third, we describe the Nunavut Hansard dataset used in the current experiments. Forth, we describe an approach to enhancing the morphological analysis based on a segmental recurrent neural network architecture, with character sequences as input. Finally, we present ongoing experimental research results.

2 Nature of Inuktitut

2.1 Polysynthesis

The Eskimo-Aleut language family, to which Inuktitut belongs, is the canonical language family for exemplifying what is meant by polysynthesis. Peter Stephen DuPonceau coined the term in 1819 to describe the structural characteristics of languages in the Americas, and it further became part of Edward Sapir's classic linguistic typology distinctions.[3] Polysynthetic

---

[1] https://en.wikipedia.org/wiki/Inuit_languages

[2] http://nunavuttourism.com/about-nunavut/welcome-to-nunavut

[3] https://en.wikipedia.org/wiki/Polysynthetic_language

Proceedings of the 2nd Workshop on the Use of Computational Methods in the Study of Endangered Languages, pages 101–106,
Honolulu, Hawai'i, USA, March 6–7, 2017. ©2017 Association for Computational Linguistics

languages show a high degree of synthesis, more so than other synthetic languages, in that single words in a polysynthetic language can express what is usually expressed in full clauses in other languages. Not only are these languages highly inflected, but they show a high degree of incorporation as well. In Figure 1 we see an example of a sentence in Inuktitut, *Qanniqlaunngikkalauqtuqlu aninngittunga.*, consisting of two words, and we break those words down into their component morphemes.

Qanniqlaunngikkalauqtuqlu
qanniq-lak-uq-nngit-galauq-tuq-lu
snow-a_little-frequently-NOT-although-3.IND.S-and
"And even though it's not snowing a great deal,"

aninngittunga
ani-nngit-junga
go_out-NOT-1.IND.S
"I'm not going out"

Figure 1: Inuktitut Words Analyzed

In this example, two Inuktitut words express what is expressed by two complete clauses in English. The first Inuktitut word shows how many morphemes representing a variety of grammatical and semantic functions (quantity, "a_little", frequency "frequently", negation, and concession) as well as grammatical inflection (3rd person indicative singular), can be added onto a root ("snow"), in addition to a clitic ("and"), and the second word shows the same, but to a lesser degree.

2.2 Abundance of grammatical suffixes

Morphology in Inuktitut is used to express a variety of abundant grammatical features. Among those features expressed are: eight verbs "moods" (declarative, gerundive, interrogative, imperative, causative, conditional, frequentative, dubitative) ; two distinct sets of subject and subject-object markers, *per mood*; four persons; three numbers, (singular, dual, plural); eight "cases" on nouns: nominative (absolutive), accusative, genitive (ergative), dative ("to"), ablative ("from"), locative ("at, on, in"), similaris ("as"), and vialis ("through"), and noun possessors (with number and person variations). In addition, demonstratives show a greater variety of dimensions than most languages, including location, directionality, specificity, and previous mention. The result of a language that uses morphology (usually suffixes) to express such a great number of variation is an abundance of word types and very sparse data sets.

2.3 Morphophonemics

In addition to the abundance of morphological suffixes that Inuktitut roots can take on, the morphophonemics of Inuktitut are quite complex. Each morpheme in Inuktitut dictates the possible sound changes that can occur to its left, and/or to itself. As a result, morphological analysis cannot proceed as mere segmentation, but rather, each surface segmentation must map back to an underlying morpheme. In this paper, we refer to these different morpheme forms as 'surface' morphemes and 'deep' morphemes. The example below demonstrates some of the typical morphophonemic alternations that can occur in an Inuktitut word, using the word *mivviliarumalauqturuuq*, 'he said he wanted to go to the landing strip':

Romanized Inuktitut word: mivviliarumalauqturuuq
Surface segmentation   miv-vi-lia-ruma-lauq-tu-ruuq
Deep form segmentation   mit-vik-liaq-juma-lauq-juq-guuq
Gloss   land-place-go_to-want-PAST-3.IND.S-he_says

Figure 2: Morphophonemic Example

We proceed from the end to the beginning to explain the morphophonemic rules. 'guuq' is a regressive assimilator, acting on the point of articulation, and it also deletes. So 'guuq' changes to 'ruuq' and deletes the preceding consonant 'q' of 'juq.' 'juq shows an alternation in its first consonant, which appears as 't' after a consonant, and 'j' otherwise. 'lauq' is neutral after a vowel, so there is no change. 'juma' is like 'guuq', a regressive assimilator on the point of articulation, and it deletes. So 'juma' becomes 'ruma,' and the 'q' of the preceding morpheme is deleted. 'liaq' is a deleter, so the preceding 'vik' becomes 'vi.' Finally, 'vik' regressively assimilates a preceding 't' completely, so 'mit' becomes 'miv.'[4]

2.4 Dialect differences / spelling variation

The fourth aspect of Inuktitut which contributes to the challenge of processing it with a computer is the abundance of spelling variation seen in the electronically available texts. Three aspects of spelling variation must be taken into account. First, Inuktitut, like all languages, can be divided into a number of different dialects. Dorais, (1990) lists ten: Uummarmiutun, Siglitun, Inuinnaqtun, Natsilik, Kivallirmiutun,

---

[4] http://www.inuktitutcomputing.ca/Technocrats/ILFT.php#morphology

Aivilik, North Baffin, South Baffin, Arctic Quebec, and Laborador. The primary distinction between the dialects is phonological, which is reflected in spelling. See Dorais (1990) for a discussion of dialect variation. Second, a notable error on the part of the designers of the Romanized transcription system has produced a confusion between 'r's and 'q's. It is best explained in a quote by Mick Mallon:[5]

> *It's a long story, but I'll shorten it. Back in 1976, at the ICI standardization conference, because of my belief that it was a good idea to mirror the Assimilation of Manner in the orthography, it was decided to use **q** for the first consonant in voiceless clusters, and **r** for the first consonant in voiced and nasal clusters. That was a mistake. That particular distinction does not come natural to Inuit writers, (possibly because of the non-phonemic status of [N].) Public signs, newspaper articles, government publications, children's literature produced by the Department of Education, all are littered with **q**s where there should be **r**s, and **r**s where there should be **q**s. Kativik did the right thing in switching to the use of **r**s medially, with **q**s left for word initial and word final. When things settle down, maybe Nunavut will make that change. It won't affect the keyboard or the fonts, but it will reduce spelling errors among the otherwise literate by about 30%.*

Third, an inspection of the word types that cannot be analyzed by the Uqailaut analyzer reveals that transcribers and translators do not adhere to a single standard of spelling. As an example, the root for 'hamlet', borrowed from English, appears in a variety of spelling variations in the Nunavut Hansard dataset. The Uqailaut root unique ID is "Haammalat/1n", mapped to the surface form "Haammalat". However, in the dataset, surface forms abound: *Haamalaujunut, Haamlaujunut, Hamalakkunnit, Hammakkut, Hammalakkunnut, Hammalat,* and *Hmlatni.*

In sum, the combination of polysynthesis, abundance of grammatical morphemes, morphophonemics, and spelling variation, make Inuktitut a particularly challenging language for natural language processing. In this work, we hope to begin to develop methods to overcome these challenges.

[5]http://www.inuktitutcomputing.ca/Technocrats/ILFT.php#morphology

3   Related work

The work on morphological processing is abundant, so here we simply present a selected subset. Creutz and Lagus (2006) present an unsupervised approach to learning morphological segmentation, relying on a minimum description length principle (Morfessor). Kohonen et al, (2010) use a semi-supervised version of Morfessor on English and Finnish segmentation tasks to make use of unlabeled data. Narasimhan et al. (2015) use an unsupervised method to learn morphological "chains" (which extend base forms available in the lexicon) and report results on English, Arabic, and Turkish. Neural network approaches to morphological processing include a number of neural model types. Among then, Wang, et al. (2016) use Long Short Term Memory (LSTM) neural morphological analyzers to learn segmentations from unsupervised text, by exploiting windows of characters to capture context and report results on Hebrew and Arabic. Malouf (2016) uses LSTM neural networks to learn morphological paradigms for several morphologically complex languages (Finnish, Russian, Irish, Khaling, and Maltese). One recent work which may come close to the challenge of segmentation and labeling for Inuktitut is presented by Morita et al. (2014) who use a Recurrent Neural Network Language Model during morphological analysis of unsegmented, morphologically complex languages such as Japanese.

However, none of the studies to date have attempted to improve analysis for polysynthetic languages such as Inuktitut. Given the complexity of Inuktitut, we proceed initially by bootstrapping from an available analyzer.

4   The Uqailaut morphological analyzer

A morphological analyzer exists for Inuktitut called the Uqailaut analyzer. It was created by Benoît Farley at the National Research Council of Canada and is freely available for use from the Uqailaut website[6]. The analyzer was used as downloaded, with no alterations to the source code whatsoever. It is a finite state transducer, which takes a word as input and returns a set of analyses on multiple lines. Each morpheme returned in an analysis is delineated by curly braces and contains the surface form of the morpheme, followed by a colon, followed by a unique ID for that morpheme. The unique ID

[6] http://www.inuktitutcomputing.ca/Uqailaut/.

contains the deep (dictionary) form of the morpheme, followed by a forward slash, followed by any specific morphological information. For example, processing the word 'saqqitaujuq' yields:

```
{saqqi:saqqik/1v} {ta:jaq/1vn} {u:u/1nv} {juq:juq/1vn}
{saqqi:saqqik/1v} {ta:jaq/1vn} {u:u/1nv} {juq:juq/tv-ger-3s}
```

Figure 3: Sample Analyzer Output

See the README file provided with the Uqailaut analyzer for specifics about the codes used in the unique ID for a morpheme.[7]

5   Nunavut Hansard dataset

A parallel Inuktitut-English dataset originated during the ACL 2003 Workshop entitled "Building and Using Parallel Texts: Data-driven Machine Translation and Beyond[8]" and was made available during this workshop. The data was subsequently used for a shared task on alignment that took place in the same workshop in 2005[9]. The dataset was assembled and aligned, and is described in Martin et al., (2003). The dataset is available from the web[10], and was downloaded from there.

6   Morphological processing of the Nunavut Hansard dataset

Since the morphological analyzer is not sensitive to context, all of the unique types from the Inuktitut side of the Nunavut Hansard were collected and prepared for analysis. Punctuation was tokenized beyond the initial tokenization provided in the dataset to facilitate processing. Types that contained an alphabetic string concatenated with a numeral (either an unwanted processing error or a numeral with grammatical inflexion) which would have failed in morphological analysis, were filtered out. A total of 287,858 types were successfully processed by the analyzer, leaving 125,695 types unprocessed, of which 124,189 were truly not processed by the analyzer (the remaining 1506 types yielded various processing errors). The number of types not processed was around 30% of the total types collected from the corpus.

7   Enhancing the output of the analyzer

The goal of the current research is to provide an analysis for the 30% of word types that the analyzer fails on without completely rebuilding the underlying analyzer. The purpose of this approach is to determine whether morphological analysis for such a complex, polysynthetic language can be learned from annotated data when only limited annotated data or a less-than-optimal, incomplete analyzer is available. We make use of the word types that were successfully analyzed into one single, unambiguous analysis as training data for a neural network morphological analyzer for the remaining unanalyzed word types. Following Kong et. al (2015), we make use of a segmental recurrent neural network (SRNN) that can be used to map character input to analysis output. The input to the network is the individual characters of the word type to be analyzed. Output from the network is a sequence of labels annotated with the number of characters that each label covers. For example, the word type, "qauqujaujunu", is analyzed to "ROOT:3 LEX:2 LEX:2 LEX:1 LEX:2 GRAM:2" which then can be converted to qau/ROOT qu/LEX ja/LEX u/LEX ju/LEX nu/GRAM, to provide a surface segmentation and morphological analysis information in the form of a coarse-grained label. Thus the SRNN can be used to perform segment labeling in addition to simple segmentation.

We train two separate neural analyzers. The first outputs a coarse-grained label indicating the type of each analyzed morpheme, as in the example in the previous paragraph. The second outputs the unique ID of each morpheme (formatted slightly differently from what the Uqailaut analyzer produces due to processing constraints). The output from analyzing the word "qauqujaujunu" would be "qau_1v:3 qu_2vv:2 jaq_1vn:2 u_1nv:1 juq_1vn:2 nut_tn-dat-p:2." The fine-grained labels consist of various bits of grammatical information, such as root type, lexical postbase type, or grammatical ending type with noun case or verb mood indicators. Over the dataset used in the experiments here, 1691 fine-grained labels were counted.

Training data for the neural network is provided by the Inuktitut side of the Nunavut Hansard corpus. All word types were analyzed by the Uqailaut morphological analyzer. Word types having a single analysis were used in the training set, since this subset of word types can be argued to be the most correctly analyzed set out of what

---

[7] http://www.inuktitutcomputing.ca/Uqailaut/

[8] http://web.eecs.umich.edu/~mihalcea/wpt/

[9] http://www.statmt.org/wpt05/

[10] http://www.inuktitutcomputing.ca/NunavutHansard/ info.php

is available. (Further experiments could make use of the types that have ambiguous, i.e. two or more analyses, as the training data, for example.) This subset consists of approximately 26K word types. For the "Coarse-Grained" model, 25,897 types were used. The Uqailaut analysis for each type was converted into a simple "surface-form/label," for each morpheme. A total of sixteen labels resulted from this conversion (listed in Table 1). A development (dev) set and a test set of 1000 items each were randomly held out from training.

```
ROOT            root (noun or verb)
LEX             lexical postbase
GRAM            grammatical suffix
CL              clitic
ADV             adverb
CONJ            conjunction
EXCLAM          exclamation
PR, RP, PRP     pronoun
AD              demonstrative adverb
PD              demonstrative pronoun
RAD             demonstrative adverb root
RPD             demonstrative pronoun root
TAD             demonstrative adverb suffix
TPD             demonstrative pronoun suffix
```

Table 1: List of Coarse-Grained Labels

For the "Fine-Grained" model, the full unique ID was used, with 1691 labels present in the set of analyses. Because the SRNN program did not allow for unseen labels when running in test mode, selection of the dev and test sets was not random and proceeded as follows: First, under the assumption that the greatest variation of labels would occur in the roots of the word types, (the "open-class" morphemes, versus the "closed-class" lexical post-base, grammatical endings, and clitics), the selection proceeded based on root labels. Of the 1,198 unique root labels, 898 occurred in two or more word types. For example, the root label "qauq_1v" occurs in six types, "qaurniq," "qaunimautilik," "qauqujaujut," "qauqujaulluni," "qauqujaujunu" and "qauvitaq." At least 1 of each of these types per root label was placed in the dev/test pool, with the remaining types containing that root label being assigned to the train set. To select which of the two or more types to put into each set, the longest (in terms of number of morphemes in the type) was selected for the dev/test pool, with the remaining going into the train set. Then, the dev/test pool was split into two sets of 449 items each.

8 Results

The program implementing the SRNN reports precision, recall, and f-measure calculated over segmentations alone (seg), or segmentations with tagging (tag). Table 2 shows the results on the two held-out sets for the two different models.

Model	Set	seg/tag	Precision	Recall	F-measure
Coarse-Grained	dev	seg	0.9627	0.9554	0.9591
		tag	0.9602	0.9529	0.9565
	test	seg	0.9463	0.9456	0.9460
		tag	0.9430	0.9424	0.9427
Fine-Grained	dev	seg	0.8640	0.8647	0.8644
		tag	0.7351	0.7357	0.7354
	test	seg	0.8291	0.8450	0.8369
		tag	0.7099	0.7235	0.7166

Table 2: Accuracy scores on full words

As would be expected, the model producing a coarse-grained output performs better than the model producing a fine-grained output. The model only has to decide between 16 labels in the former, versus 1691 labels in the latter. In addition, it should be kept in mind that the dev and test sets for the two models are not the same, due to the processing constraints of the program implementing the SRNN.

8.1 Accuracy on non-root morphemes

Most of the mislabeling errors occurred in the root morphemes of the analyzed words. As was mentioned above, the set of root morphemes can be likened to the set of "open-class" vocabulary, whereas the remaining morphemes (suffixes) of words are "closed-class." In order to attempt to filter out the randomness effect of trying to identify "open-class" root morphemes, scores were calculated over the output of the Fine-Grained model leaving out the roots. Table 3 displays these results.

Model	Set	seg/tag	Precision	Recall	F-measure
Fine-Grained roots absent in scoring	dev	seg	0.8838	0. 8860	0.8849
		tag	0.8178	0.8199	0.8188
	test	seg	0.8560	0.8807	0.8682
		tag	0.7922	0.8151	0.8035

Table 3: Accuracy scores on suffixes only

As expected, these scores (suffixes only) are higher than those measured on the full words (root+suffixes), yet still fall below 90% accuracy.

9 Conclusion

In this work in progress, we have proposed a method of improving the coverage of an existing morphological analyzer for the Inuktitut language using an SRNN bootstrapped from a portion of the analyses of words in a corpus. We show accuracy scores on two models, yielding coarse-, or fine-grained labels. Accuracy scores are also calculated on just the "closed-class" suffix strings (removing the "open-class" roots) which show a slight improvement over accuracy on the full words. Further experimentation is needed to refine the accuracy of this approach and to begin to develop methods of processing this highly complex, polysynthetic language.

References

Creutz, M. and Lagus, K., 2006. Unsupervised models for morpheme segmentation and morphology learning. *ACM Transactions on Speech and Language Processing*.

Dorais, L., 1990. "The Canadian Inuit and their Language," in *Arctic Languages, An Awakening,* Ed. Dirmid R. F. Collins, Unesco, pp. 185-289.

Kohonen, O., Virpioja, S., and Lagus, K., 2010. Semi-supervised learning of concatenative morphology. In *Proceedings of the 11th Meeting of the ACL Special Interest Group on Computational Morphology and Phonology*, pp. 78-86. Association for Computational Linguistics.

Kong, L., Dyer, C., and Smith, N., 2015. Segmental recurrent neural networks, *arXiv preprint arXiv:1511.06018*.

Malouf, R., 2016. Generating morphological paradigms with a recurrent neural network, *San Diego Linguistic Papers 6*, 122-129.

Martin, J., Johnson, H., Farley, B., and Maclachlan, A., 2003, Aligning and Using an English-Inuktitut Parallel Corpus, HLT-NAACL Workshop: Building and Using Parallel Texts Data Driven Machine Translation and Beyond, pp. 115-118, Edmonton, May-June 2003.

Morita, H., Kawahara, D., and Kurohashi, S., 2015. Morphological Analysis for Unsegmented Languages using Recurrent Neural Network Language Model, Association for Computational Linguistics, *Proceedings of the Conference on Empirical Methods in Natural Language Processing*, pp. 2292–2297, Lisbon, Portugal.

Narasimhan, K., Barzilay, R., and Jaakkola, T., 2015. An Unsupervised Method for Uncovering Morphological Chains. *Transactions of the Association for Computational Linguistics*, [S.l.], v. 3, pp. 157-167.

Wang, L., Cao, Z., Xia, Y., and de Melo, G., 2016. Morphological segmentation with window LSTM neural networks. In Proceedings of AAAI.

Click reduction in fluent speech: a semi-automated analysis of Mangetti Dune !Xung

Amanda Miller
Department of Linguistics
The Ohio State University
miller.5592@osu.edu

Micha Elsner
Department of Linguistics
The Ohio State University
melsner0@gmail.com

Abstract

We compare click production in fluent speech to previously analyzed clear productions in the Namibian Kx'a language Mangetti Dune !Xung. Using a rule-based software system, we extract clicks from recorded folktales, with click detection accuracy about 65% f-score for one storyteller, reducing manual annotation time by two thirds; we believe similar methods will be effective for other loud, short consonants like ejectives. We use linear discriminant analysis to show that the four click types of !Xung are harder to differentiate in the folktales than in clear productions, and conduct a feature analysis which suggests that rapid production obscures some acoustic cues to click identity. An analysis of a second storyteller suggests that clicks can also be phonetically reduced due to language attrition. We argue that analysis of fluent speech, especially where it can be semi-automated, is an important addition to analysis of clear productions in understanding the phonology of endangered languages.

1 Introduction

We compare click production in fluent speech to previously analyzed clear productions in the Namibian Kx'a language Mangetti Dune !Xung (hereafter !Xung). This language contains the four coronal click types recognized by the IPA (Association, 2006). Most content words contain an initial click, making clicks an important marker for lexical identity and useful for marking the beginning of words for speech processing (Beckman, 2013). Miller and Shah (2009) show that temporal cues, burst duration (BD) and rise time to peak intensity in the click burst (RT); and spectral cues, Cen-

ter of Gravity (COG) and Maximum Burst Amplitude (MBA), differentiate the clicks in clear productions. We extend this analysis to fluent, naturalistic speech in a corpus of folktales (Augumes et al., 2011). Using a semi-automated rule-based method to locate the clicks in the acoustic data, we are able to inexpensively align a large enough portion of the corpus for acoustic analysis. We show that the cues identified by Miller and Shah (2009) are less effective in differentiating clicks in running speech, providing quantitative evidence that this rare class of consonants is subject to phonetic reduction. Finally, we provide an analysis of the acoustic cues which differentiate the clicks, showing that the best cues for discriminating productions vary among speakers, but that in general spectral cues work better than measures of amplitude. Overall, our results demonstrate that clicks, which are known for being unique in their loudness, are not always so loud, and that even sounds that are known for their loudness undergo reduction just like other speech sounds.

2 Background

2.1 Click Burst Amplitude

It has long been noted that clicks are louder than pulmonic stop consonants. Ladefoged and Traill (1994) note that clicks in !Xóõ often have a peak-to-peak voltage ratio that is more than twice that of the onset of the following vowel (about a 6 dB difference in intensity), which Traill (1997) compares to Greenberg (1993) description of pulmonic stops as typically "...40 dB less intense than the following vowel." This property of clicks should make them easy to recognize automatically, even with relatively unsophisticated methods. While Li and Loizou (2008) have shown that low amplitude pulmonic obstruents are degraded in noisy speech environments, clicks might be expected to differ in this regard due to their typically high amplitude

Proceedings of the 2nd Workshop on the Use of Computational Methods in the Study of Endangered Languages, pages 107–115,
Honolulu, Hawai'i, USA, March 6–7, 2017. ©2017 Association for Computational Linguistics

click	Alveolar, Lateral	Palatal	Dental
IPA Sym	!, ‖	≠	ǀ

Table 1: Intensity of nosiebursts for !Xóõ clicks (loudest to quietest) (Traill, 1997).

bursts.

Previous work on click amplitudes has also noted a large degree of variability, which could make both click recognition and differentation of different click types more difficult. Traill (1997) provides an intensity scale as in Table 2[1], but states that there is a great degree of variability. Miller-Ockhuizen (2003) shows similar results for Juǀ'hoansi, and also comments on the great degree of variability. Traill and Vossen (1997) note that there is a large degree of variability in the amplitude of click bursts. None of these studies has numerically quantified the variability or determined to what degree it makes clicks confusable with non-clicks or with each other.

Traill (1997) argues that non-pulmonic stop consonants are enhanced versions of pulmonic stops, given the high amplitude bursts that are typically louder than the following vowel in clicks and in intermediate intensity bursts found in ejectives, building on Stevens and Keyser (1989)'s theory of consonant enhancement. The theory suggests that clicks should be easier to identify in the acoustic signal than pulmonic consonants. However, clicks with lower amplitude should also result in lower perceptibility in human speech recognition and lower identification in automatic speech recognition. What remains unknown from this work is whether or how often low-amplitude clicks are actually produced.

2.2   Click Burst Duration

Click amplitudes are useful cues for extracting clicks from the speech stream, but in order to differentiate between click types, listeners must also attend to other features. Previous work agrees that these features indicate different manners of articulation, although they differ in their theoretical account of the underlying phonological contrasts. Beach (1938) referred to this difference as affricate vs. implosive. Trubetzkoy (1969) recouched the manner contrast among clicks as fricative vs. occlusive. Both articulatory based

and acoustically based phonological features have been proposed to capture this contrast.

There are several acoustic cues that differentiate stops vs. affricates. Burst duration, rise time to peak amplitude and frication duration differences are all part and parcel of the manner contrast. Kagaya (1978) quantified the burst duration differences among Naro clicks, and showed that bilabial [ʘ], dental [ǀ] and lateral [‖] click types have long burst durations, while alveolar [!] and palatal [≠] click types exhibit short burst durations. Sands (1990), Johnson (1993) and Ladefoged and Traill (1994) showed that there are similar differences in Xhosa and !Xóõ clicks. In addition to measuring click burst durations, Ladefoged and Traill (1994) measured Rise Time to Peak amplitude in the click bursts, following Howell and Rosen (1983), who showed that this measure differentiates pulmonic plosives from affricates. Ladefoged and Traill showed that the alveolar and palatal click types in !Xóõ exhibit short rise times, while the bilabial, dental and lateral click types exhibit longer rise times to peak amplitude. Johnson proposed the feature [+/-noisy], focusing on the acoustic properties of the releases, and Ladefoged and Traill proposed the feature as [+/-abrupt] to describe this phonological contrast in terms of the speed of the anterior release.

In Mangetti Dune !Xung, these click features were studied by Miller and Shah (2009), who show that the palatal click burst duration preceding [u] in Mangetti Dune !Xung exhibits interspeaker variation. One of the four speakers' productions that they studied exhibited longer burst durations for the palatal click type, suggesting that this speaker released the click less abruptly. Miller (to appear) explicitly compared the realization of clicks preceding [i] and [u], showing that the palatal click type in Mangetti Dune !Xung has two allophones. It is non-affricated (and thus presumably abruptly released) preceding [u] as in the other languages, but has a period of palatalization (palatal frication noise) following the click burst preceding [i]. Miller transcribes the palatalized allophone as [≠͡ɕ].

2.3   Click Discrimination

We know of one prior study using acoustic features for click discrimination. Fulop et al. (2004) applied discriminant analysis to the four coronal clicks in the Bantu language Yeyi on the basis

---
[1]Traill's scale also includes the bilabial click [ʘ], which is on average less intense than the others. This click does not occur in !Xung.

of the four spectral moments of the anterior click bursts, and showed that the classification for the laterals and palatals were much worse than the classification results for the alveolars and dentals. The alveolar clicks only displayed a 2.6% error rate, and the dental clicks an error rate of 24%, while the lateral and palatal clicks displayed an error rate of 93% and 67% respectively. The error rates given here represent measurements from isolated productions. In the present study, we give similar results for isolated productions in !Xung and compare these to results for productions from fluent speech. Like Fulop et al. (2004), we find relatively high degrees of confusion among the different clicks.

2.4 Click Reduction

Previous work on click reduction has distinguished two situations in which clicks are weakened: as an intermediate stage leading to click loss throughout a language, and as a prosodic phenomenon in ordinary speech. We find evidence of both these phenomena in our corpus data. Here, we review some prior work on them.

Traill and Vossen (1997) quantify a stage of "click weakening", which they claim is an intermediate stage before click loss (the change from a click consonant to a pulmonic consonant). They describe click weakening as a process of acoustic attenuation that effects only the abruptly released clicks [!] and [≠]. They compare the same click types in !Xóõ, a language that has not yet been described as undergoing any click loss, and G‖ana, a Khoe language where many of the alveolar clicks have been lost. They point out that the weakened G‖ana clicks are noisier, and have more diffuse spectra, than the strong !Xóõ clicks of the same type. They quantify the amplitudes of the clicks in the different languages by providing difference measures of click intensity based on the peak amplitude of the click minus the peak amplitude of the following vowel, which provides a scale of click amplitude relative to the vowel across the different languages. Further, they provide palataograms of some of the strong, and weakened clicks, which show that "weakened articulations have larger cavities and this is a result of reduction in the degree of tongue contact." They describe this weakening as a process of articulatory undershoot. They attribute the noisiness of the anterior releases in the weakened

clicks to more leisurely anterior releases, that lead to frication. They suggest that the affrication of the abruptly released alveolar and palatal clicks make them less perceptually distinct from the affricated dental and lateral clicks, and that full click loss would then resolve the perceptual ambiguity among the two classes of clicks.

Conversational reduction of clicks, meanwhile, is motivated not by language-wide change but by general articulatory concerns. Miller et al. (2007) provide qualitative evidence that nasal clicks have a stronger and longer duration of nasal voicing in their closures in weaker prosodic positions. Marquard et al. (2015) compared acoustic properties of voiceless oral plosives and clicks in three different phrasal positions (Initial, Medial and Final) in N|uu spontaneous speech. Their quantitative results showed that while the duration of pulmonic stop closures got shorter from initial, to medial, to final position, the clicks were shortest in initial position, and lengthened in medial and final positions. The clicks only showed reduction effects for Center of Gravity (lower COG values in phrase medial and phrase final positions, compared with phrase initial position), and in the acoustic energy level (degree of voicing) before the release burst, which is highest in phrase-final position, lower in medial position, and lowest in phrase-final position. Neither study investigated the effects of reduction on the distinguishability of clicks.

3 Materials

The corpus used in the current study consists of three folktales told by two different speakers, totaling about 45 minutes of speech (Augumes et al., 2011)[2]. One story, *Lion and Hare*, was told by one of the two oldest living speakers in Mangetti Dune, Namibia, Muyoto Kazungu (MK). Two additional stories, *Iguana* (BG1) and *Lion and Frog*(BG2) were told by Benjamin Niwe Gumi, (BG) who was a bit younger, but still a highly respected elder in the community. Our click identification tool does not require a transcript. The acoustic analyses of extracted clicks do require an orthographic transcript, since our tool assigns each detected click to its correct phonetic category by aligning the detections to the transcript. Two of the stories have existing ELAN transcripts in the archive, and the clicks of the third were transcribed by the first au-

---

[2]`https://elar.soas.ac.uk/Collection/`
`MPI178567`

thor.

The laboratory data used was a set of words recorded in a frame sentence that were previously analyzed by Miller and Shah (2009) and Miller (to appear).

4 Click Detection

We present a simple rule-based tool implemented using the acoustic analysis program Praat (Boersma and Weenink, 2016) to automatically detect clicks in the audio stream. This method is intended to locate clicks as a general class; we discuss the problem of separating the clicks by type below (Sec. 5). Because clicks are relatively short in duration and high in amplitude, the tool searches the acoustic signal in 1 ms frames.

At each frame, a potential click is detected if the raw signal amplitude exceeds 0.3 Pascal and the Center of Gravity exceeds 1500 Hz. If the region of consecutive frames which passes these filters has a duration less than 20 ms, it is labeled as a click. For MK, the center of gravity cutoff is changed to 1000 Hz and the durations allowed to extend to 25 ms. (These parameters were tuned impressionistically.)

We explored a few other measurements for identifying clicks. A relative measurement of amplitude (checking that the frame has higher amplitude than the one 15 ms back) improves precision but at the expense of recall. Since we hand-corrected the output of our tool, we opted to emphasize recall (it is easier for a human analyst to reject click proposals than to find clicks that the tool has not marked). We also attempted to reject short vowel sounds by checking for detectable formants within the high-amplitude region, but this proved unreliable.

Following click detection with the tool, a human analyst corrected all three transcripts. This process took less than $\frac{1}{2}$ hour for BG, who consistently produced his clicks at higher amplitudes, but 2-3 hours for MK, who varied his click amplitudes more widely. The corrected transcripts are used as a gold standard for evaluating the tool's stand-alone performance.

5 Acoustic Analysis

We compute 4 acoustic features known to differentiate coronal clicks: Burst Duration (BD), Rise Time to Peak Amplitude in the Burst (RT), Center of Gravity (COG) and the Ratio of the Maximum Amplitude in the Burst to the Amplitude at 20 ms into the vowel. These features were used in a previous study (Miller and Shah, 2009) and shown to separate !Xung clicks preceding [u]. We use the same dataset of 248 click tokens studied by Miller and Shah (2009), extracted from single content words produced in the focused position of a frame sentence, and compare the results to those for 197 clicks extracted from the folktales. The Miller and Shah (2009) dataset includes COG values only for clicks produced before [u], so we restrict our analyses of the folktales to the clicks produced before non-low back vowels [u] and [o] to make the two sets as comparable as possible. The [u] data from Miller and Shah (2009) are all bimoraic monosyllabic words containing the long vowel [u:], though they vary in terms of tone and phonation type. In the texts, both monosyllabic bimoraic and bisyllabic words with two short vowels occur. The vowels following the clicks in the monosyllabic words in the stories are either a long monophthong like [u:] or [o:], or are one of the diphthongs that commences with a non-low back vowel: [ui, oe, oa]. In CVCV words, both vowels are short. All laryngeal release properties (voiced, aspirated, glottalized) of clicks and vowels with non-modal voice qualities were included, as these don't effect the vowel quality (only the voice quality of the vowel). Both nasal and oral clicks are also included. Uvularized clicks were excluded, as were epiglottalized vowels, as these affect the vowel quality, and it is unknown, but possible, that they might affect the C.O.G. of the click bursts.

For the detection of clicks, and for the acoustic analysis of detected clicks, we measured the Rise Time to Peak Amplitude (RT) in the burst as the duration from the onset of the click burst to the maximum RMS amplitude during the click burst proper (transient, not including separate frication noise or aspiration noise that follows the transient), following Ladefoged and Traill (1994). The click burst duration was measured as the duration of the transient itself. The center of gravity was measured using the standard Praat measure on a 22,050 Hz spectrum that was calculated using a Hanning window. The relative burst amplitude was measured as the maximum RMS amplitude found in the click burst (release of the anterior constriction) divided by the RMS amplitude of the following vowel at a point 20 ms from the start of the vowel. The 20 ms point was chosen as it

Transcript	Clicks	Prec	Rec	F
MK 1	250	38.1	17.6	24.1
BG 1	180	66.8	61.6	64.2
BG 2	202	65.3	70.8	67.9
All	632	59.6	47.2	52.7

Table 2: Number of clicks and detection results for three transcripts.

was far enough into the vowel to allow the vowel to reach a higher amplitude, but contained completely within the first mora of the vowel. This assured that the vowel being measured was [u] or [o] in all cases.

5.1 Results

Our evaluation (Table 2) scores a system-annotated click as correct if it occurs within 10 ms of a true click. (Small variations in this number affect the result relatively little, since click bursts are typically short, distinctive events.) On the two transcripts of speaker BG, results are relatively good (precision around 65, recall between 60-70), enabling rapid post-correction by a human analyst. Performance is much poorer for MK (precision 38, recall 17) and post-correction took over four times as long.

Precision errors for BNG generally corresponded to other short, loud speech sounds: coronal ejectives: [ts'], [tʃ'] and the highest amplitude part of [i] vowels. Errors for MK were more varied; MK produced many quieter click bursts which were less distinct from the surrounding speech, and it was harder to set cutoffs that would distinguish the clicks from pulmonic stops and vowel sounds. See Figure 1 for example spectrograms. We believe these very low-amplitude clicks are a consequence of MK's linguistic background, a possibility we return to in more detail below (Sec. 7).

6 Acoustic Analysis of Clicks

Once the clicks have been extracted, we conduct an acoustic analysis of the four click types. The previous section focused on the task of distinguishing clicks from other sounds as an engineering application. Here, we build a model to discriminate between the four click types, in order to understand how much information they contribute for lexical identification in real speech processing. We conduct a linear discriminant analysis

Dataset	N Clicks	Disc. acc
Lab	248	75
Folktales	197	54
Lab (spkr JF)	75	87
Lab (spkr MA)	75	84
Lab (spkr TK)	74	92
Folktales (spkr BG)	142	73
Folktales (spkr MK)	55	56

Table 3: Linear discriminant analysis accuracies (leave-one-out) on folktale and laboratory clicks.

using the four acoustic features from Miller and Shah (2009), which were shown to differentiate among the four click types in clear productions. Here, we show that they are much less effective for fluent speech, suggesting that clicks, like other speech sounds, are reduced in fluent speech, blurring the primary acoustic cues that distinguish between them.

6.1 Features

Burst duration and Rise time to peak amplitude are both acoustic correlates of manner of articulation, indicating the click's degree of frication. Longer burst durations and rise times to peak amplitude both indicate more frication, while affricates have an immediate high-amplitude burst right after the release of the initial constriction. The relative burst amplitude reflects the size of the cavity and the abruptness of the release burst. The fourth acoustic attribute that was measured, Center of Gravity (COG), correlates with the the size of the lingual cavity of the click, and therefore is determined by the place of articulation of both constrictions.

6.2 Discriminant Analysis

Using linear discriminant analysis in the R package MASS (Venables and Ripley, 2013), we find that these features indeed differentiate clicks in the single-word lab productions, but are less diagnostic in fluent speech. Accuracies (Table 3) are computed with leave-one-out cross-validation. The lab speech clicks are classified with 75% accuracy, while performance on the folktale clicks is reduced to 54%. This gap is exaggerated by the poor discriminability of clicks produced by MK, whose atypically quiet clicks were also difficult to detect. However, a similar result can be obtained by comparing individual speakers. When a model is learned for each speaker individually, the

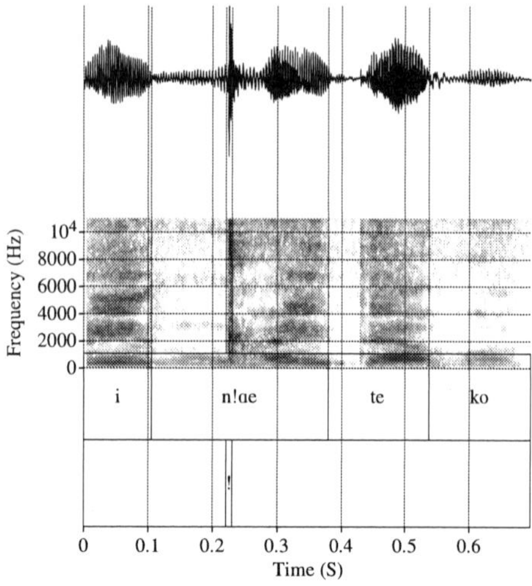 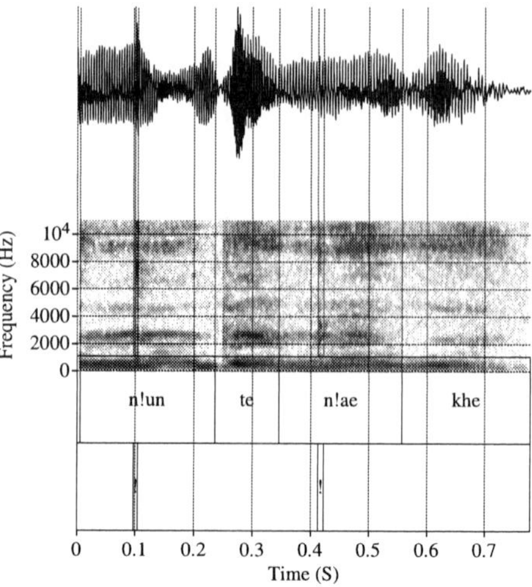

Figure 1: Spectrograms of the alveolar click in the word *n!ǎé* "lion" produced by BG (left) and MK (right) showing the difference in burst amplitudes.

three lab speakers' clicks are discriminated with 84-92% accuracy, while the folktale speaker BG's clicks are discriminated with only 73% accuracy. Thus, although intra-speaker variability decreases the accuracy of the classifier in both settings, it is still clear that the folktale clicks are harder to discriminate overall.

A visual explanation of the result is shown in Figure 2, where we plot the RT vs COG (the two most discriminative features for these speakers) for clicks from the folktale storyteller BG versus one laboratory elicitation speaker. The laboratory clicks show a clear separation among all four click types. Among the folktale clicks, only the dental [|] is cleanly separable from the others.

An examination of the learned discriminant functions shows the relative importance of the four acoustic cues. Each discriminant function is a linear combination of the cues; in our data, the first discriminant function captures most of the variance between the clicks for all speakers except MK, whose clicks were poorly classified to begin with. Table 4 shows the coefficients of the first discriminant function for several datasets. For the other speakers, COG is the most discriminative property of clicks, but the second-most discriminative function varies among speakers. Amplitude is a good cue for two of the laboratory speakers, MA and TK, but not for JF or the folktale speaker BG; rise time is also a good cue for MA

and TK but neither of the others. Interestingly, MK's atypical clicks are classified mainly based on their duration, a cue which was uninformative for the rest of the dataset. A small ablation analysis on BNG and MK's data tells the same story; COG is responsible for most of the classification performance for BNG (70% with COG alone vs 73% with all features). For MK, it is less useful but still captures over half of classifier performance (35% vs 56%).

7 Discussion

We can infer from the evidence provided that !Xung clicks are subject to phonetic reduction in fluent speech. The primary temporal and spectral cues for click identification become highly variable and less informative in rapid production. Listeners presumably use top-down information like lexical context to make up for increased confusability. Thus, !Xung clicks behave much like other speech sounds in rapid production, despite their canonical loudness, which makes them stand out from the speech stream in clear speech.

Although clicks in fluent speech are harder to discriminate from one another, our results do support the widespread idea that clicks as a class are easy to pick out of the speech stream, at least for speakers who produce them in the canonical way. Despite relying on a few features and hand-tuned threshold parameters, our click detection script

112

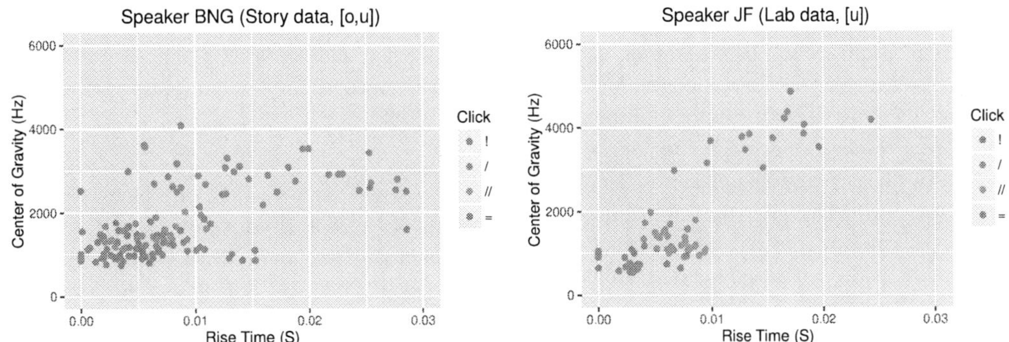

Figure 2: Folktale and laboratory clicks: RT vs. COG

	% var	Rise T	COG	Dur	Max amp	Spkr	Feats	Acc
Lab	92	0.41	1.63	0.03	-0.33	BNG	COG only	70
Lab (JF)	98	0.53	3.72	-0.25	-0.09	BNG	COG/rise	70
Lab (MA)	88	1.12	1.89	-0.17	-1.70	BNG	all	73
Lab (TK)	98	1.53	5.28	-0.03	-1.11	MK	COG only	35
Folk (BNG)	96	0.26	1.45	0.35	0.40	MK	COG/rise	47
Folk (MK)	67	0.03	-0.40	1.38	0.52	MK	all	56

Table 4: Left: Percent of variance captured and coefficients of four features in the first discriminant function learned in different datasets. Right: Ablation results for two speakers.

was able to automate enough of the acoustic analysis to save a substantial amount of transcriber time and effort. We expect that other non-pulmonic consonants like ejectives could also be detected with similar methods. These results are encouraging for corpus research in endangered languages.

The extremely low accuracy for click detections in the speech of MK should qualify this conclusion. There are a few possible reasons why MK's clicks are much lower in amplitude, harder to detect and harder to discriminate than those of the other speakers. First, MK is the oldest speaker in the dataset (in his 70s). Second, MK spent a large portion of his life in Angola living among speakers of an unknown Bantu language which did not include clicks. This Bantu language was an important mode of communication for much of his life, and indeed, he occasionally code-switched into it during the storytelling session. Perhaps because of this L2 background, MK produced some phonemic click consonants as pulmonic stops (primarily [k,g] for [!,∥], and [c,j] for [|, ≠]), and produced extremely variable amplitudes for many of the others.

Similar variability in click production is reported in langugage as a stage in click loss due to language endangerment (Traill and Vossen, 1997). It seems, therefore, that MK's clicks represent an initial stage of language loss and replacement with Bantu, which was reversed for the younger generation. BG's speech represents this revitalization of !Xung and its replacement of Bantu as the prestige language in the community.

The implication for speech technology and corpus research is that detection methods may vary in their accuracy from community to community. Methods developed for robust language communities may need to be recalibrated when working with severely endangered languages or features undergoing rapid change. Within a single community, however, the accuracy of a tuned detector might serve as a measure of language loss by quantifying the degree to which the target segments have been lost.

Our results reveal new facts about the discriminative features for clicks. For example, although Traill (1997) provided a scale of click burst intensity, shown in (1) above, the variability of the amplitude of the alveolar click bursts relative to the following vowel is so high, that it is clear that the amplitude alone can not be very useful in discriminating the four click types. As mentioned above, the relative perceptual weighting of the two temporal measures (click burst duration and rise time to peak amplitude) is completely unknown for clicks. Comparing our results to Fulop et al. (2004) Yeyi results, we can conclude that a combination of manner cues and place of articulation cues results in much better discriminability. Of course, we can not rule out the contribution of click reduction / loss to the poorer discriminability seen in the Yeyi results.

Machine learning can indicate how much information about click identity is carried by each of these cues, but this does not necessarily reveal which cues are important to human listeners. For instance, English fricatives and affricates are also differentiated by duration and rise time to peak amplitude (Howell and Rosen, 1983). Early studies assumed that Rise Time was the main acoustic feature of importance. However, Castleman (1997) showed that frication duration differences among the English contrast are more perceptually relevant than the rise time differences. While our results imply that COG is the most informative criterion for click identity, further perceptual experiments could tell whether this matches listeners' actual perceptual weightings. Of course, four manually selected features and a linear classifier do not tell the whole story of click discriminability. A more sophisticated model (King and Taylor, 2000) could discover features directly from the acoustic signal; however, we believe our features acceptably represent the major categories of cues.

8   Conclusion

Results suggest that phonetic studies of endangered languages must consider both clean productions and naturalistic speech corpora. It is important to discover not only the phonemic inventory of the language and the canonical landmarks that allow listeners to recognize speech sounds in clear speech, but also the range of phonetic variability displayed in fluent speech. In this study, investigation of connected speech led to the conclusion that the scale of click burst intensity is not very useful in distinguishing clicks, since the amplitude of alveolar click bursts is so variable. In studying natural data, rule-based extraction of particular segments may offer a low-cost alternative to developing a full ASR system for a language with little available data. The processed data could be used to supplement non-expert annotations (Liu et al., 2016; Bird et al., 2014) in training a full-scale ASR system, or to bootstrap a learning-based landmark recognition system (Hasegawa-Johnson et al., 2005).

Acknowledgments

We thank Mehdi Reza Ghola Lalani, Muyoto Kazungu and Benjamin Niwe Gumi. This work was funded by ELDP SG0123 to the first author and NSF 1422987 to the second author.

References

International Phonetic Association. 2006. The international phonetic alphabet (revised to 2005) [chart]. page 135.

Christine Augumes, Amanda Miller, Levi Namaseb, and David Prata. 2011. Mangetti Dune !Xung stories: In !Xung and English. The Ohio State University, the University of Namibia, and the Mangetti Dune Traditional Authority. Deposited at ELAR.

Douglas Martyn Beach. 1938. *The phonetics of the Hottentot language*. W. Heffer & Sons, ltd.

Jill N Beckman. 2013. *Positional faithfulness: an Optimality Theoretic treatment of phonological asymmetries*. Routledge.

Steven Bird, Lauren Gawne, Katie Gelbart, and Isaac McAlister. 2014. Collecting bilingual audio in remote indigenous communities. In *COLING*, pages 1015–1024.

Paul Boersma and David Weenink. 2016. Praat: doing phonetics by computer. Version 6.0.20 from http://praat.org.

Wendy Ann Castleman. 1997. *Integrated perceptual properties of the [+/-continuant] distinction in fricatives and affricates*.

Sean A Fulop, Peter Ladefoged, Fang Liu, and Rainer Vossen. 2004. Yeyi clicks: Acoustic description and analysis. *Phonetica*, 60(4):231–260.

Steve Greenberg. 1993. Speech processing: Auditory models. In R.E. Asher and S.M.Y. Simpson, editors, *Pergammon Encyclopedia of Language and Linguistics, Vol. 8*, pages 4206–4227.

Mark Hasegawa-Johnson, James Baker, Sarah Borys, Ken Chen, Emily Coogan, Steven Greenberg, Amit Juneja, Katrin Kirchhoff, Karen Livescu, Srividya Mohan, et al. 2005. Landmark-based speech recognition: Report of the 2004 Johns Hopkins summer workshop. In *Acoustics, Speech, and Signal Processing, 2005. Proceedings.(ICASSP'05). IEEE International Conference on*, volume 1, pages I–213. IEEE.

Peter Howell and Stuart Rosen. 1983. Production and perception of rise time in the voiceless affricate/fricative distinction. *The Journal of the Acoustical Society of America*, 73(3):976–984.

Keith Johnson. 1993. Acoustic and auditory analyses of Xhosa clicks and pulmonics. *UCLA Working Papers in Phonetics*, 83:33–45.

Ryohei Kagaya. 1978. Soundspectrographic analysis of Naron clicks: A preliminary report. *Annual Bulletin of Institute of Logopedics and Phoniatrics*, 12:113–125.

Simon King and Paul Taylor. 2000. Detection of phonological features in continuous speech using neural networks. *Computer Speech and Language*, 14(4):333–353.

Peter Ladefoged and Anthony Traill. 1994. Clicks and their accompaniments. *Journal of Phonetics*, 22(1):33–64.

Ning Li and Philipos C Loizou. 2008. The contribution of obstruent consonants and acoustic landmarks to speech recognition in noise. *The Journal of the Acoustical Society of America*, 124(6):3947–3958.

Chunxi Liu, Preethi Jyothi, Hao Tang, Vimal Manohar, Rose Sloan, Tyler Kekona, Mark Hasegawa-Johnson, and Sanjeev Khudanpur. 2016. Adapting ASR for under-resourced languages using mismatched transcriptions. In *Acoustics, Speech and Signal Processing (ICASSP), 2016 IEEE International Conference on*, pages 5840–5844. IEEE.

Carina Marquard, Oliver Niebuhr, and Alena Witzlack-Makarevich. 2015. Phonetic reduction of clicks–evidence from N|uu. In *Proceedings of the International Congress of Phonetic Sciences (ICPhS)*.

Amanda Miller and Sheena Shah. 2009. The acoustics of Mangetti Dune !Xung clicks. In *Proceedings of INTERSPEECH*, pages 2283–2286.

Amanda L Miller, Johanna Brugman, Bonny Sands, Levi Namaseb, Mats Exter, and Chris Collins. 2007. The sounds of N|uu: Place and airstream contrasts. *Working Papers of the Cornell Phonetics Laboratory*, 16:101–160.

Amanda Miller-Ockhuizen. 2003. *The Phonetics and Phonology of Gutturals: A Case Study from Ju|'hoansi*. Outstanding Dissertations in Linguistics Series. Routledge.

Amanda Miller. to appear. Palatal click allophony in Mangetti Dune !Xung: Implications for sound change. *Journal of the International Phonetic Association*.

Bonny Sands. 1990. Some of the acoustic characteristics of Xhosa clicks. *UCLA Working Papers in Phonetics*, (74):96.

Kenneth N Stevens and Samuel Jay Keyser. 1989. Primary features and their enhancement in consonants. *Language*, pages 81–106.

Anthony Traill and R Vossen. 1997. Sound change in the Khoisan languages: new data on click loss and click replacement. *Journal of African languages and linguistics*, 18(1):21–56.

Anthony Traill. 1997. Linguistic phonetic features for clicks: Articulatory, acoustic and perceptual evidence. *African linguistics at the crossroads: Papers from Kwaluseni*, pages 99–117.

Nikolai S. Trubetzkoy. 1969. *Principles of Phonology*. University of California Press.

William N Venables and Brian D Ripley. 2013. *Modern applied statistics with S-PLUS*. Springer Science & Business Media.

DECCA Repurposed: Detecting transcription inconsistencies without an orthographic standard

C. Anton Rytting and Julie Yelle
University of Maryland
Center for Advanced Study of Language (CASL)
College Park, MD
{crytting,jyelle}@umd.edu

Abstract

Most language resources and technologies depend on written text, while most endangered languages are primarily spoken. Transcribing speech into text is time consuming and error-prone. We propose a method for finding spelling inconsistencies without recourse to a standard reference dictionary or to a large training corpus, by repurposing a method developed for finding annotation errors. We apply this method to improve quality control of audio transcriptions, with particular focus on under-resourced, primarily oral language varieties, including endangered varieties.

1   Introduction

A critical part of documenting endangered languages is gathering and analyzing texts. In the case of many such languages, particularly ones without a long history of literacy or written literature, many if not most of these texts will be oral. Although recent work (Hanke & Bird, 2013) has explored ways of working with audio samples directly, most approaches to building additional resources (such as dictionaries and grammars, whether printed or digital) or human language technologies (such as part of speech taggers, morphological parsers, or automatic speech recognition systems) with audio text require transcription.

Even for languages with highly standardized spelling systems, maintaining transcription consistency is challenging. Inconsistencies in transcription can hamper the use of the corpus for other purposes, by distorting frequency counts and hiding patterns in the data. Transcription methodologies based on crowdsourced data collection have gained popularity in recent years due to their ability to deliver results at a fraction of the cost and turnaround time of conventional transcription methods (Marge, Banerjee, & Rudnicky, 2010) and collect linguistic data out of the reach of traditional methods of lexicography (Benjamin, 2015).

Yet crowdsourcing also carries a certain degree of risk stemming from the uncertainty inherent in the online marketplace (Saxton, Oh, & Kishore, 2013). While Marge, Banerjee, & Rudnicky (2010) found, for instance, that workers crowdsourced via Amazon Mechanical Turk (MTurk) had an average word error rate (WER) of less than 5% compared to in-house "gold-standard" transcription, Lee and Glass (2011) observed many MTurk transcriptions with a WER above 65%. Beyond concerns of authoritative knowledge and accuracy, the ability of crowdsourcing to open public lexicography to a "never-before-seen breadth of speaker input" from "the entire geographic range across which a language might vary" ushers in both insights and challenges related to language variation (Benjamin, 2015). More generally, any time the task of transcription extends beyond a small number of carefully trained transcribers, with limited resources for checking inter-transcriber agreement, the potential for inconsistencies arises.

We propose a simple, easy-to-apply method to examine transcriptions of audio corpora, including notes from elicitation sessions, for spelling errors and other inconsistencies that may arise in both conventional and crowdsourced data collection processes. While the proposed method is general enough to apply to any text input, we focus our experiments on transcriptions of spoken text. Our first set of experiments focus on transcriptions of spoken Arabic, including colloquial varieties; our second set focuses on the type of fieldwork we believe to be typical in building descriptions of (and resources for) endangered

Proceedings of the 2nd Workshop on the Use of Computational Methods in the Study of Endangered Languages, pages 116–121,
Honolulu, Hawai'i, USA, March 6–7, 2017. ©2017 Association for Computational Linguistics

languages. In both cases traditional approaches to spelling correction do not apply, because there is no standard spelling dictionary to which to refer.

It is our hope that this method could assist field linguists in pinpointing aspects of transcriptions or other texts in need of quality control, reducing the need for manual examination of textual data.

2   Related Work

Much of the work on expediting transcription or providing quality control has focused on the needs of high resource languages. For example, Lee and Glass (2011) and Vashistha, Sethi, and Anderson (2017) assume access to an automatic speech recognition system in the language. Such methods will have little relevance for endangered language description, particularly at early stages.

So far as we are aware, there has been little work published on automatic methods for detecting inconsistencies in fieldwork or other transcriptions of spoken language without recourse to a standard lexicon or a large training corpus. However, there has been some work on two related problems: first, dealing with spelling variation in historical corpora (e.g., Baron & Rayson, 2008); second, detecting inconsistency of linguistic annotations such as part of speech (POS).

One approach to inconsistency detection in corpus annotation, called Detection of Errors and Correction in Corpus Annotation (DECCA)[1], postulates two root causes for variation—ambiguity and error—and posits that "the more similar the context of a variation, the more likely it is for the variation to be an error" (Dickinson & Meurers, 2003). Variation is defined as the assignment of more than one label (e.g., POS tag) to a particular word type (or, in the case of labels on phrases, a phrase type). Ambiguity occurs when more than one tag is appropriate for a given word or phrase type (e.g., multiple POS tags for an ambiguous word like "can"); an annotation error is an instance of a tag that is not appropriate for a token in context (e.g., a verb tag on "can" in the phrase "the <u>can</u> of tuna").

Intuitively, if a sequence of words is repeated multiple times in an annotated corpus, and a

word within that sequence is tagged with different parts of speech in different instances of that sequence, it is likely that at least one of those tags is erroneous. Such a word sequence is called a *variation n-gram*.

3   Detecting Spelling Variants with DECCA

3.1   Defining the Task

In contrast to Dickinson and Meurers' interest in annotation errors, we are interested in detecting inconsistencies (or unwanted variation) in the text itself—the transcription of speech—without assuming the existence of any additional annotation layer such as POS.

Dickinson & Meurers' POS-tag error detection was performed in the context of a well-defined standard for annotation; thus, deviations from that standard may aptly be described as "errors." The tag set itself was a static, closed (and relatively small) set. In contrast, in our transcription-checking task, the list of words that may be used to transcribe a text is open and typically not pre-defined; even if dictionaries are used for guidance or reference, there may be words spoken (e.g., names, recent borrowings) that do not occur in the reference. For such words, at least, there may not be a pre-established standard spelling, and indeed for low-resourced languages there may be variant spellings for many words.

In this case, while finding spelling errors is still an issue, the larger question may be detecting variant spellings (such as "gray" vs. "grey" in English) that do not encode any semantic distinctions and hence are best conflated or unified to a single spelling for the purposes of (at least some types of) further analysis. Thus the detection either of a confirmed spelling error or of spelling variation like "gray" vs. "grey" that, in the judgment of a language expert, is not semantically meaningful (and hence can be conflated) would count as a hit for this task. Flagging a pair or set of words such as "pray" vs. "prey," which are legitimately distinct from each other, would be a false alarm.

3.2   Method

In order to apply DECCA to this purpose, we select some aspect of the speech transcription in which we suspect there may be inconsistencies—for example, whitespace or a particular spelling distinction—and we reformat the data such that that aspect of the transcription is removed from the context and treated as if it were a separate

---

layer of annotation. If some inconsistency of that aspect is observed in contexts where the transcription is otherwise identical, the observed variation ought to be flagged for human review and possible normalization.

For whitespace variation, the presence or absence of whitespace characters (and other punctuation indicating word or morpheme boundaries, such as hyphens) within an otherwise identical phrase of at least two words is flagged for examination.

For detecting variation in spelling, our proposed method requires prior knowledge (whether from a language expert or some other source) of sets of substrings that may be sources of variation. For example, a language expert in English may flag the substring pair "-ay" vs. "-ey" as a potentially conflatable substring pair for finding hypothesized variants. In this case, the words "gray" and "grey" would be conflated in the text and the original spellings treated as tags in the DECCA input (e.g., {gr<1>, gray} and {gr<1>, grey} rather than Dickinson & Meurers' {word, POS} pairs such as {grey, ADJ}). Similarly, "pray" and "prey" would be mapped to {pr<1>, pray} and {pr<1>, prey}, respectively. DECCA then flags conflation terms for which multiple spellings occur at least once in the corpus in identical contexts (e.g., {"the gray dog"; "the grey dog"}). The intuition behind the heuristic is that true variants like "gray" and "grey" are more likely to show up in identical contexts than semantically distinct pairs like "pray" and "prey." Of particular interest are contexts with at least one word preceding and one word following the variant word—what we might call "non-fringe" contexts (following Dickinson & Meurer's heuristic of "distrusting the fringe").

4 Experiments

To test the feasibility of this approach, initial experiments were performed on corpora of transcribed spoken colloquial Arabic available from the Linguistic Data Consortium (LDC). We report here on two types of variation: spelling and whitespace.

After confirming the basic feasibility of this approach for spelling variation, we proceeded to test it on field notes on Kenyah Lebu' Kulit, an endangered language variety spoken in Indonesian Borneo.

Because we do not have complete ground truth on all the spelling inconsistencies for these corpora, we are not able to report recall. For these experiments, we therefore report precision only, based on an expert's review of the DECCA output in the various experiments.

4.1 Spoken Colloquial Arabic Transcripts

We tested DECCA's ability to detect inconsistencies in speech transcription on four corpora: GALE Phase 2 Arabic Broadcast Conversation Transcript Part 1 (Glenn, Lee, Strassel, & Kazuaki, 2013); Levantine Arabic Conversational Telephone Speech, Transcripts (Appen Pty Ltd, 2007); CALLHOME Egyptian Arabic Transcripts (Gadalla, et al., 1997); and CALLHOME Egyptian Arabic Transcripts Supplement (Consortium, 2002). These corpora provide transcripts of speech from three varieties of Arabic and at least five countries.

In these transcriptions, which reflect the diglossic nature of Arabic, orthography that is reflective of the colloquial pronunciation of dialectal words for which there are direct, nearly identical equivalents in Modern Standard Arabic (MSA) coexists alongside MSA orthography. As a result, these corpora, taken together, attest a considerable number of instances of spelling variation.

Two in-house Arabic-speaking researchers, one of whom is the second author of this paper, performed the human review of variation observed in identical contexts. Both annotators are native speakers of English who hold Master of Arts degrees in Arabic and certifications of Arabic proficiency at the ILR 3/ACTFL Superior level.

4.1.1 Spelling Variation

We summarize here experiments on two kinds of spelling variation in colloquial Arabic. One is the result of a phonological merger of two phonemes in some dialects (but not in MSA). The other variation in the spelling of the glottal stop, which in MSA is subject to complicated spelling rules, and in colloquial usage is often omitted. In the phoneme merger experiment, we examine the role of context frames in the precision of DECCA's hypotheses.

In the phoneme merger experiment, 63 pairs of words differing only in د (*dāl*) vs. ذ (*dhāl*), appearing a total of 242 times in the corpus, were flagged by DECCA. Each of these appeared at least once in the same context frame (non-fringe contexts, consisting of at least one preceding and following word: i.e., [*ContextWord1* _____ *ContextWord2*]). Of these 63 pairs, one of our in-house Arabic language experts judged that 61 were variant spellings that ought to be conflated, one was a semantically distinct minimal pair, and one was indeterminate. Excluding the uncertain pair, the precision was 98%.

Adding two other context frames—[*ContextWord1 ContextWord2* _____] and [_____ *ContextWord1 ContextWord2*] in addition to [*ContextWord1* _____ *ContextWord2*]—yielded an additional 68 items (appearing a total of 348 times), of which 60 were conflatable spelling variants, seven were semantically distinct, and one was uncertain. The combined precision was 94%.

If the context restriction is relaxed completely, then 337 items are returned, with 251 items consisting of variant spellings, and 80 records consisting of semantically distinct minimal pairs. Thus the baseline precision on the *dāl/dhāl* conflatable substring pair, without any restriction by context frame, is 76%.

For the *hamza* variation experiment, the second author of this paper annotated the 175 most frequent sets of words differing in *hamza* spelling that appeared in identical [*Context-Word1* _____ *ContextWord2*] frames. These sets of words appeared a total of 1,107 times in the corpus. Of these 175 items in context, two were semantically distinct minimal pairs, while 149 were variations that deserved normalization. Excluding 21 uncertain cases, the precision was 98.7%.

4.1.2 Whitespace Variation

In our preliminary whitespace experiments, we evaluated a subset of the variation instances with at least 20 characters of otherwise identical context, including at least two other consistent space characters, one on either side of the whitespace variation. The second author of this paper examined 95 variation n-grams, of which 22 were categorized as legitimate whitespace differences justified by semantic distinctions and 54 were seen as non-semantically motivated variants (31 errors; 23 instances of free variation). Nineteen items were marked as indeterminate and excluded. This yielded a precision of 71%.

4.2 Kenyah Lebu' Kulit

Having seen utility of this approach in our experiments on spoken Arabic transcriptions, we then applied the method to Kenyah Lebu' Kulit, an endangered language variety spoken by about 8,000 people in Indonesian Borneo. We used a database of transcribed texts available from the Max Planck Institute for Evolutionary Anthro-pology Jakarta Field Station as part of the "Languages of North Borneo" project (Soriente, 2015).[2] The data were inputted by a community-based documentation team, most of whom were native speakers of Kenyah Lebu Kulit without formal training as linguists. We were fortunate to obtain this corpus at an intermediate stage prior to the corpus collector's completion of quality control efforts leading up to publication, which allowed us to test our inconsistency-detection method's utility as an automated approach to quality control.

The Kenyah Lebu' Kulit corpus consists of 5,665 utterances in 27 files, with 52,549 tokens. This is considerably smaller than the corpus used in the Arabic experiments. Therefore we would expect fewer variation n-grams for any given experiment. Although we did not have access to an in-house expert in this language, the corpus contains Indonesian-language glosses that provided us with a rough indication of accuracy. We also consulted the researcher who collected the Kenyah Lebu' Kulit corpus, asking her to review instances of the corpus in which apparent orthographic minimal pairs appeared in identical contexts, to obtain verification that each pair was in fact semantically distinct (as described below).

As we examined this corpus, we noted that the orthography used by the transcribers draws a distinction between {é} /e/ and {e} /ə/. As experience working with informal texts in other languages has shown that diacritics such as the acute accent are frequently omitted, we first tested for inconsistencies between these two letters.

DECCA returned 31 orthographic minimal pairs differing only between {e} and {é}, five of which occurred in non-fringe contexts:

- <s> {mémang/memang} kaduq
- ngan {sénganak-senganak/senganak-senganak} teleu
- tei {é/e} </s>
- seken {mé'/me'} kena janan
- tegen {né/ne} ka senteng

Of these, the corpus collector confirmed that one ({é/e}) was a legitimate (semantically distinct) minimal pair, three were mistakes (two resolving to {...e...} and one to {...é...}), and the last ({né/ne}) was a mistake of a different sort: {né} should have been {né'} /neʔ/.

---

[2] Available from http://jakarta.shh.mpg.de/data.php (as of February 15, 2017). In these preliminary experiments, we used a version obtained from Dr. Antonia Soriente and Bradley Taylor.

Following up on a comment by the corpus collector about possible inconsistencies in transcribing word-final glottal stops, we conducted a further experiment examining the presence or absence of glottal stop at the end of a word.[3] As with the previous experiment, only non-fringe contexts were examined. This experiment yielded 102 variation n-grams, including 37 unique orthographic minimal pairs differing only by absence vs. presence of word-final glottal stop {'}.

Of these 37 orthographic minimal pairs, the corpus collector confirmed that only two ({lu/lu'} and {ra/ra'}) were semantically distinct minimal pairs. The other 35 were instances of spelling variation, yielding a precision of 95%.

5   Conclusion

Initial experiments suggest that DECCA can find inconsistencies in transcription of spoken Arabic, including both orthographic variation (assuming some prior knowledge of which sets of substrings should be examined) and variation in whitespace. Further preliminary experiments suggest that DECCA can also be applied to corpora collected in fieldwork settings, even when those corpora are relatively small.

We anticipate that DECCA, being simple and easy to use, could be applied as part of a suite of tools that field researchers and transcribers use for quality control on their own collections. We also anticipate it could be applicable for crowdsourced or community-led transcription efforts, particularly if wrapped in a user interface that facilitates the selection of candidate conflatable substring pairs and the reviewing of returned results. For example, the DICER tool (Baron, Rayson, & Archer, 2009; Baron & Rayson, 2009) could provide a framework for generating candidate conflatable substring pairs which could be input into DECCA.

Even for more resourced languages, where standard orthographies and reference dictionaries exist, this approach may prove helpful for words that may be missing from those dictionaries, such as names (particularly transliterated foreign names) and recent borrowings and neologisms. It may also help in instances where a standard dictionary includes multiple variants as equally correct, but greater consistency is desired by the corpus creators.

Although the focus of the work is on identifying spelling variants for quality control, insofar as the identification of minimal pairs may be useful for writing descriptive grammars and for training transcribers, we note that the tool can be used to identify minimal pairs as a byproduct of quality control.

Further work could focus on alternative context filters to improve coverage while maintaining high precision, particularly in the context of small corpora. We also welcome conversations with those who wish to apply this approach to corpora they are building.

Acknowledgments

The authors express their gratitude to Dr. Antonia Soriente and her funders for granting us access to the Kenyah Lebu' Kulit corpus. We thank Dr. Soriente for her generosity in evaluating our method's output, making it possible for us to test our transcription inconsistency-detection method on an endangered language. We also thank Valerie Novak for writing the scripts used to prepare the DECCA output of the Arabic corpora for annotation. Any errors remain our own.

This work was supported in part with funding from the United States Government and the University of Maryland, College Park. Any opinions, findings and conclusions or recommendations expressed in this material are those of the authors and do not necessarily reflect the views of the University of Maryland, College Park and/or any agency or entity of the United States Government.

References

Appen Pty Ltd, S. A. (2007). Levantine Arabic Conversational Telephone Speech, Transcripts LDC2007T01. Web Download. Philadelphia: Linguistic Data Consortium.

Baron, A., & Rayson, P. (2008). VARD2: A tool for dealing with spelling variation in historical corpora. *Postgraduate conference in corpus linguistics*. Birmingham, England: Aston University.

Baron, A., & Rayson, P. (2009). Automatic standardisation of texts containing spelling variation: How much training data do you need? *Proceedings of the Corpus Linguistics Conference*. Lancaster, England: Lancaster University.

---

[3] The orthography for Kenyah Lebu' Kulit uses the single quote mark {'} to indicate glottal stop. However, as word-final quote marks caused issues for the software used to manage the corpus, a {q} was substituted for most instances of word-final glottal stop in the intermediate stage of the corpus we worked with. For simplicity, we treat {'} and {q} as equivalent here, mapping {q} to {'}, anticipating a global mapping of {q} to {'} in published versions of the corpus.

Baron, A., Rayson, P., & Archer, D. (2009). Automatic standardization of spelling for historical text mining. *Proceedings of Digital Humanities 2009.* College Park, MD: University of Maryland.

Benjamin, M. (2015). Crowdsourcing Microdata for Cost-Effective and Reliable Lexicography. In L. Li, J. McKeown, & L. Liu (Ed.), *Proceedings of AsiaLex*, (pp. 213-221). Hong Kong.

Dickinson, M., & Meurers, D. (2003). Detecting Errors in Part-of-Speech Annotation. *Proceedings of the 10th Conference of the European Chapter of the Association for Computational Linguistics (EACL-03).* Budapest, Hungary: Association for Computational Linguistics.

Gadalla, H., Kilany, H., Arram, H., Yacoub, A., El-Habashi, A., Shalaby, A., . . . McLemore, C. (1997). CALLHOME Egyptian Arabic Transcripts LDC97T19. Web Download. Philadelphia: Linguistic Data Consortium.

Glenn, M., Lee, H., Strassel, S., & Kazuaki, M. (2013). GALE Phase 2 Arabic Broadcast Conversation Transcripts Part 1 LDC2013T04. Web Download. Philadelphia: Linguistic Data Consortium.

Hanke, F. R., & Bird, S. (2013). Large-Scale Text Collection for Unwritten Languages. *IJCNLP*, (pp. 1134-1138).

Lee, C.-y., & Glass, J. (2011). A Transcription Task for Crowdsourcing with Automatic Quality Control. *ISCA*, (pp. 3041-3044). Florence, Italy.

Linguistic Data Consortium. (2002). CALLHOME Egyptian Arabic Transcripts Supplement LDC2002T38. Web Download. Philadelphia: Linguistic Data Consortium.

Marge, M., Banerjee, S., & Rudnicky, A. (2010). Using the Amazon Mechanical Turk for transcription of spoken language. *IEEE-ICASSP*.

Saxton, G. D., Oh, O., & Kishore, R. (2013). Rules of Crowdsourcing: Models, Issues, and Systems of Control. *Information Systems Management, 30*(1), 2-20.

Soriente, A. (2015). Language Documentation in North Borneo Database: Kenyah, Penan Benalui and Punan Tubu. A joint project of the Department of Linguistics, Max Planck Institute for Evolutionary Anthropology, the Center for Language and Culture Studies, Atma Jaya Catholic University and the University of Naples 'L'Orientale'.

Vashistha, A., Sethi, P., & Anderson, R. (2017). Respeak: A Voice-based, Crowd-powered Speech Transcription System. *CHI 2017.* Denver, CO: ACM.

Jejueo talking dictionary:
A collaborative online database for language revitalization

Moira Saltzman
University of Michigan
moiras@umich.edu

Abstract

This paper describes the ongoing development of the Jejueo Talking Dictionary, a free online multimedia database and Android application. Jejueo is a critically endangered language spoken by 5,000-10,000 people throughout Jeju Province, South Korea, and in a diasporic enclave in Osaka, Japan. Under contact pressure from Standard Korean, Jejueo is undergoing rapid attrition (Kang, 2005; Kang, 2007), and most fluent speakers of Jejueo are now over 75 years old (UNESCO, 2010). In recent years, talking dictionaries have proven to be valuable tools in language revitalization programs worldwide (Nathan, 2006; Harrison and Anderson, 2006). As a collaborative team including linguists from Jeju National University, members of the Jejueo Preservation Society, Jeju community members and outside linguists, we are currently building a web-based talking dictionary of Jejueo along with an application for Android devices. The Jejueo talking dictionary will compile existing annotated video corpora of Jejueo songs, conversational genres and regional mythology into a multimedia database, to be supplemented by original annotated video recordings of natural language use. Lexemes and definitions will be accompanied by audio files of their pronunciation and occasional photos, in the case of items native to Jeju. The audio and video data will be tagged in Jejueo, Korean, Japanese and English so that users may search or browse the dictionary in any of these languages. Videos showing a range of discourse types will have interlinear glossing, so that users may search Jejueo particles as well as lexemes and grammatical topics, and find the tools to construct original Jejueo speech. The Jejueo talking dictionary will serve as a tool for language acquisition in Jejueo immersion programs in schools, as well as a repository for oral history and ceremonial speech. The aim of this paper is to discuss how the interests of diverse user communities may be addressed by the methodology, organization and scope of talking dictionaries.

1. Introduction

The purpose of this paper is to present the ongoing development of the Jejueo Talking Dictionary as an example of applying interdisciplinary methodology to create an enduring, multipurpose record of an endangered language. In this paper I examine strategies for gathering extensive data to create a multimodal online platform aimed at a wide variety of uses and user groups. The Jejueo Talking Dictionary project is tailored to diverse user communities on Jeju Island, South Korea, where Jejueo, the indigenous language, is critically endangered and underdocumented, but where the population's smart phone penetration rate is 75% (Lee, 2014) and semi-speakers are highly proficient users of technology (Song, 2012). The Jejueo Talking Dictionary is also intended for Jejueo speakers of varying degrees of fluency in Osaka, Japan, where up to 126,511 diasporic Jejuans reside (Southcott, 2013). A third aim of the Jejueo Talking Dictionary is to create extensive linguistic documentation of Jejeuo that will be available to the wider scientific community, as the vast majority of existing documentary materials on Jejueo are published in Korean. The Jejueo Talking Dictionary will serve as an online open-access repository of over 200 hours of natural and ceremonial language use, with interlinear glossing in Jejueo, Korean, Japanese and English.

2 Background

2.1 Language context

Very closely related to Korean, Jejueo is the indigenous language of Jeju Island, South Korea. Jejueo has 5,000-10,000 speakers

Proceedings of the 2nd Workshop on the Use of Computational Methods in the Study of Endangered Languages, pages 122–129,
Honolulu, Hawai'i, USA, March 6–7, 2017. ©2017 Association for Computational Linguistics

located throughout the islands of Jeju Province and in a diasporic enclave in Osaka, Japan. With most fluent speakers over 75 years old, Jejueo was classified as critically endangered by UNESCO in 2010. The Koreanic language family consists of at least two languages, Jejueo and Korean. Several regional varieties of Korean are spoken across the Korean peninsula, divided loosely along provincial lines. Jejueo and Korean are not mutually intelligible, owing to Jejueo's distinct lexicon and grammatical morphemes. Pilot research (Yang, 2013) estimates that 20-25% of the lexicons of Jejueo and Korean overlap, and a recent study (O'Grady, 2015) found that Jejueo is at most 12% intelligible to speakers of Korean on Korea's mainland. [1] Jejueo conserves many Middle Korean phonological and lexical features lost to MSK, including the Middle Korean phoneme /ɔ/ and terms such as *pizʌp* : Jejueo *pusʌp* 'charcoal burner' (Stonham, 2011: 97). Extensive lexical and morphological borrowing from Japanese, Mongolian and Manchurian is evident in Jejueo, owing to the Mongolian colonization of Jeju in the 13th and 14th centuries, Japan's annexation of Korea and occupation of Jeju between 1910 and 1945, and centuries of trade with Manchuria and Japan (Martin, 1993; Lee and Ramsey, 2000). Several place names in Jeju are arguably Japonic in origin, e.g. Tamna, the first known name of Jeju Island (Kwen ,1994:167; Vovin, 2013). Moreover, several names for indigenous fruits and vegetables on Jeju are borrowed from Japanese, e.g. *miķaŋ* 'orange'. Mongolic speakers left the lexical imprint of a robust inventory of terms describing horses and cows, e.g. *mɔl* 'horse'. Jejueo borrowed grammatical morphemes from the Tungusic language Manchurian, e.g the dative suffixal particle **de < ti* 'to' (Kang, 2005).

2.2 Current status of Jejueo

The present situation in Jeju is one of language shift, where fewer than 10,000 people out of a population of 600,000 are fluent in Jejueo, and features of Jejueo's lexicon, morphosyntax and phonology are rapidly assimilating to Korean (Kang, 2005; Saltzman, 2014). Recent surveys on language ideologies of Jejueo speakers (Kim, 2011; Kim, 2013) show that a roughly diglossic situation is maintained by present day language ideologies. In a series of qualitative interviews on language ideologies, Kim (2013:33) finds common themes suggesting that Korean is used as a means of showing respect to unfamiliar interlocutors, as Korean "...is perceived as the language of distance and rationality". Likewise Jejueo is considered appropriate to use whenever interpersonal boundaries, such as distinctions within social hierarchies are perceived less salient than the intimacy and mutual trust two or more people share. (Kim, 2013).

Yang's (2013) pilot survey on language attitudes finds that while community members recognize Jejueo as a marker of Jeju identity worth transmitting to future generations, few speakers feel empowered to reverse the pattern of language shift to Korean. There are no longer monolingual speakers of Jejueo on Jeju or in Osaka. The examples below are samples of the same declarative construction produced by a fluent Jejueo speaker in (1), a typical younger Jejueo semi-speaker in (2), and the Korean translation (3). Jejueo morphemes in (2) are in boldface.

(1)
harmang   -jʌŋ sontɛi   -jʌŋ miķaŋ
grandmother-CONJ grandchild-CONJ orange-
-ul   tʰa -m   -su -ta
ACC pick-PRS[PROG]-FO-DECL
"The grandmother and grandchild are picking oranges."

(2)
harmang   *-koa sontɛa   -oa kjul*
grandmother-CONJgrandchild-CONJ
orange-
-ul ţa -ko   i   -su-ta
ACC pick-PROG-EXIST[PRS]-**FO.DECL**
"The grandmother and grandchild are picking oranges."

(3)
harmʌni   -oa sontɛa   -oa kjul
grandmother-CONJ grandchild-CONJ orange-
-ul ţa -ko   iş   -ʌjo
ACC pick-PROG EXIST[PRS]-FO.DECL

---

[1] In a 2015 study O'Grady and Yang found that speakers of Korean from four provinces on the mainland had rates of 8-12% intelligibility for Jejueo based on a comprehension task of a one-minute recording of Jejueo connected speech.

"The grandmother and grandchild are picking oranges."

While examples (1) and (3) have several cognate forms, the majority of grammatical particles are genetically unrelated. The accusative particle *-ul* is shared by Korean and Jejueo, although in Jejueo the nominative and accusative markers are most commonly dropped. In example (2) the construction the Jejueo morphemes have been replaced by Korean morphemes, save 'grandmother' and the verbal ending, a pattern typical of non-fluent speakers of Jejueo (Saltzman, 2014).

3 Jejueo lexicography and sustainability

Because most Korean linguists view Jejueo as a conservative dialect of Korean (Sohn, 1999; Song, 2012), lexical documentation of Jejueo has not been a scientific priority. The few Jejueo lexicographic projects have been carried out in the last 30 years by linguists native to Jeju Island and are all bilingual in Korean and Jejueo. Two large-scale Jejueo-Korean print dictionaries were published (Song, 2007; Kang, 1995), though Kang's oft-cited dictionary was given a small distribution to local community centers and libraries, and was not made commercially available. In 2011 Kang and Hyeong published an abridged Korean-Jejueo version of the dictionary. The remaining lexicographic studies of Jejueo are a handful of dictionaries tailored to individual semantic domains, such as 제주어 속담 사전 [Jejueo Idiom Dictionary] (Ko, 2002), 무가본풀이 사전 [Jeju Dictionary of Shamanic Terms] (Jin, 1991), and 문학 속의 제주 방언 [Jeju Dialect in Literature] (Kang et al., 2010), an alphabetized introduction to the Jejueo lexicon through Jeju folk literature. No major reference materials on Jejueo's lexicon or other linguistic features provide English glossing, although an English sketch grammar of Jejueo is currently in development (Yang, in preparation).

It is well established that lexicographic materials can contribute significant symbolic support to a given language variety (Corris et al., 2004; Crowley, 1999; Hansford, 1991), particularly for unwritten non-prestige codes. Bartholomew and Schoenhals (1983) note that publication of lexicographic materials may even help indigenous languages be perceived as 'real languages' in the sociolinguistic marketplace. The lexicographic materials alone, however, do not engender sufficient motivation for a speech community to maintain the use of their heritage language. Fishman (1991) warns against dictionary projects that become 'monuments' to a language rather than stimulating language use and intergenerational transmission.

A recent study by O'Grady (2015) found that the level of Jejueo transmission between generations shows a drastic decline. Given the task of answering content questions based on a one-minute recording of Jejueo connected speech, heritage speakers in the 50-60 age bracket demonstrated a comprehension level of 89%, while heritage speakers between 20 and 29 showed just 12% comprehension, equal to that of citizens of Seoul. In my previous field work in Jeju I found fluent Jejueo speakers and most semi-speakers unmotivated to access available Jejueo lexicographic materials. While these lexicographic works provide extensive data for the scholarly community, they arguably contribute to a growing body of Jejueo documentation and revitalization projects which are discrete, temporary and organized from the 'top-down' without community collaboration.

Sun Duk Mun, a Jejueo linguist with the Jeju Development Institute (JDI), reasons that Jeju parents must take pride in Jejueo and use it in the home, as Jeju teachers should allow Jejueo in classrooms, in order to expand Jejueo's declining domains of use (Southcott, 2015). However, in a highly competitive society where the majority of classroom hours are allocated to the Seoul-based national standard language (Song, 2012), and even entertainment media reflects the nation's emphasis on 'correct' usage of Korean, status planning for Jejueo revitalization is crucial. Beyond Kim's (2013) and Kim's (2011) studies on Jejueo language ideologies, no sociolinguistic research on Jejueo has been conducted, leaving issues like bilingualism, domains of use and the socio-historical factors for language shift speculative at most in the literature. A successful campaign for the reversal of Jejueo language endangerment will hinge on the development of tools for documentation and language learning which reflect the socio-historical background and desires of the speech communities involved. To initiate such a campaign, ideological clarification and collaboration between the Jeju provincial government, Jejueo scholars, native speakers and educators is needed. The aim of the Jejueo Talking Dictionary is to match the diverse desires of Jeju users with collaborative methodology for data collection, as we will see in the next section.

4 Methodology

4.1 Community-based data collection

A primary goal of the Jejueo Talking Dictionary project is to train language activists in field linguistics to create a sustainable infrastructure for data collection, analysis, publication and archiving. In this way, Jeju community members will drive the scope of the Jejueo Talking Dictionary, in terms of adding the types of linguistic data that are found most useful to Jejueo-speaking communities in Jeju and Osaka. By training community members in linguistic documentation, Jejueo speakers and semi-speakers will have a foundation in field linguistics from which to build collaborative networks for crowdsourcing and status planning with Jejueo scholars, the provincial government, educators and elderly fluent speakers. At present, the team of foreign and local linguists developing the Jejueo Talking Dictionary is training local college students and activists at Jeju Global Inner Peace. Members of the team record elderly fluent speakers of Jejueo, annotate the recordings, and upload files into an open-access working corpus of data using Lingsync, a free online program for sharable audio and video files of annotated linguistic data. Linguists from Jeju National University, Jejueo specialists from the Jejueo Preservation Society, and I analyze the Jejueo data and check its accuracy with native speakers, ensuring the quality of the corpus. In September, 2016 we will develop the corpus into a free online program and an Android application for smartphones.

4.2 Building an interdisciplinary network

A second goal of the Jejueo Talking Dictionary project is to build an interdisciplinary network for data collection. Our team of linguists from Jeju and abroad, language preservationists, activists and community elders have recruited ethnomusicologists, historians, experts in the indigenous religion and anthropologists to lend their expertise to the collection of lexemes and texts of various genres. In this way we aim to create a methodology of interdisciplinary data collection that builds a multidimensional record of Jejueo, to serve a wide range of uses and user groups. At present we have incorporated approximately 200 hours of previously unpublished annotated video data including Jeju oral history, shamanic rituals, indigenous music and cuisine preparation. Our team aims to enlist the support of ethnobotanists and ethnozoologists who can assist the team in collecting data on the indigenous flora and fauna of Jeju Island. In the future, data collection can be connected to language revitalization programs, such as master-apprentice programs (see Hinton, 1997), where semi-speakers join speakers of Jejueo in their usual activities farming, foraging for roots, herbs and vegetables in the mountains, picking seasonal fruit, and diving for seafood near Jeju's shores.

5 Contents of Jejueo Talking Dictionary

The Jejueo Talking Dictionary is intended to serve as a tool for both cultural education and language acquisition. With this in mind, we give equal attention to the collection of archaic and ceremonial speech, and the most frequently used lexemes and expressions. The Jejueo Talking Dictionary will compile existing annotated video corpora of Jejueo songs, conversational genres and regional mythology into a multimedia database, supplemented by original annotated video recordings of natural language use. Lexemes and definitions will be accompanied by audio files of their pronunciation, listings of frequent collocations, and occasional photos, for items native to Jeju. The audio and video data will be tagged in Jejueo, Korean, Japanese and English, allowing users to search or browse the dictionary in any of these languages. Like Korean, Jejueo features complex agglutination of case, TMA and discourse register particles on verbs and nouns (Sohn, 1999). Videos showing a range of discourse types will have interlinear glossing, so that users may search Jejueo particles as well as lexemes and grammatical topics, and find the tools to construct original Jejeuo speech. At the time of writing, we have recorded and annotated approximately 500 audio files of individual lexemes and 300 hours of video data. Below I itemize genres of Jejueo speech we have collected.

6.2 Inclusiveness versus usability

As the Jejueo Talking Dictionary is intended to serve a variety of uses, creating a cultural and linguistic repository of Jejueo stands somewhat at odds with developing a user-friendly dictionary for language education. We have found one solution to be to develop separate modules for the dictionary (see Vamarasi, 2013), so that it may be viewed according to individual purposes. In addition to viewing the dictionary page translated in Jejueo, Korean, Japanese and English, users can access separate modules from the main page. At present, these include modules for language lessons, browsing cultural topics, browsing photos, and browsing conversational genres and grammatical features. In the language education module, users access Jejueo lessons based around the most frequently used lexemes in the language, illustrated with photos. For this module we are also developing language-learning games and a 'word of the day' feature. All of the lexical entries in the dictionary and lexical items used in the narrative videos are tagged, so that searching a Jejueo word from any of the modules brings up a textual sample of the

lexeme in a grammatical construction, and videos featuring the lexeme in natural language use, where that data is available. Transcripts of all of the videos may be downloaded and printed, and users may select a transcript with interlinear glossing, the Jejueo transcription only, or a translation in Korean, Japanese or English.

6.3 Language standardization

It is important to note that the standardization of Jejueo orthography is still ongoing, and among the several regional varieties of Jejueo, none has been designated as the standard. For the Jejueo Talking Dictionary project we adopt the orthographic preferences of the most recent Jejueo lexicographic materials (Kang and Hyeon 2011; Kang, 2007), and list headwords and regional varieties in the order assigned in those materials.

7 Conclusion

An open-ended lexicographic resource such as an online talking dictionary lends itself well to incorporating a variety of data designed to serve diverse uses and user groups. The Jejueo Talking Dictionary can be continuously and cost-effectively modified as we obtain more data and gain feedback on the usability of the dictionary. We aim for the Jejueo Talking Dictionary to be an accessible multipurpose repository of the Jejueo language, where the content and the collection of linguistic data are both driven by the Jeju community. With Jejueo in a state of critical endangerment, incorporating community members in the development and dissemination of language-learning materials is key.

Audio recordings	Video recordings
anatomy	conversations focusing on discourse markers
common expressions	game playing
cuisine	oral histories of 4.3 Massacre, Japanese occupation, marriage rituals, farming, fishing
cardinal directions	preparation of native cuisine
flora	preparation of rituals (Buddhist, shamanic)
fauna	shamanic rituals: major public rituals for lunar year, family rituals
geography	stories of indigenous mythology (regional varieties)
grammatical suffixes	work songs, chants (regional varieties)
high frequency nouns, verbs, adjectives	
ideophones	
idioms	
kinship terminology	
mythological and shamanic terminology	
weather terminology (polysemic terms for wind, rain)	

Table 1. Jejueo Talking Dictionary corpus

References

Bartholomew, Doris and Louise Schoenhals. 1983. *Bilingual dictionaries for indigenous languages.* Hidalgo, Mexico: Summer Institute of Linguistics.

Corris, Miriam, Christopher Mannig, Susan Poetsch and Jane Simpson. 2004. How useful and usable are dictionaries for   speakers of Australian indigenous people. *International Journal of Lexicography*, 17(1): 33-68.

Crowley, Terry. 1999. *Ura: A disappearing language of Southern Vanuatu.* Canberra: Pacific Linguistics.

Fishman, Joshua. 1991. *Reversing language shift: Theoretical and empirical foundations of assistance to threatened languages.* Bristol: Multilingual Matters.

Hansford, Gillian. 1991. Will Kofi understand the white woman's dictionary? Some ways to make a bilingual dictionary more usable to a new literate. *Notes on Linguistics*, 52, 17-28.

Harrison, K. David and Gregory D.S Anderson. 2006. Tuvan Talking Dictionary. Retrieved from http://tuvan.talkingdictionary.org

Hinton, Leanne. 1997. Survival of endangered languages: The California master-apprentice program. *International Journal of the Sociology of Language,* 123, 177-191.

Jin, Seong-Gi. 1991. *Dictionary of Jeju Shamanic Terms.* Jeju: Minsokweon.

Kang, Jeong-Hui. 2005. *A study of morphological change in the Jeju dialect.* Seoul: Yeokrak.

Kang, Yeong-Bong. 1994. *The language of Jeju.* Jeju: Jeju Munhwa.

Kang, Yeong-Bong. 2007. *Jeju Language.* Seoul: National Folk Museum, Jeju Special Self-Governing Province.

Kang, Yeong-Bong, Kim, Dong-Yun and Kim Sun-Ja. 2010. *Jeju Dialect in Literature.* Jeju: Gukrimgukeoweon.

Kang, Yeong-Bong. & Hyeon Pyeong-Hyo. 2011. *Standard Language- Jejueo Dictionary.* Jeju: Doseochongpan Gak.

Kim, Soung-U. 2013. *Language attitudes on Jeju Island - an analysis of attitudes towards language choice from an ethnographic perspective.* Master's thesis, School of Oriental and African Studies, London.

Kim, Sun-Ja. 2011. *A Geolinguistic Study on the Jeju Dialect.* Ph.D. dissertation, Jeju National University, Jeju.

Ko, Jae-Hwan. 2002. *Jejueo Idiom Dictionary.* Jeju: Minsokweon.

Kwen, Sangno. 1994. *A diachronic dictionary of Korean place names.* Seoul: Ihwa Munhwa Chwulphansa.

Lee, Iksop and Robert Ramsey. 2000. *The Korean language.* Albany: SUNY Press.

Lee, Minjeong. 2014, December 12. Smartphone usage overtakes PCs in South Korea. *Wall Street Journal.*

Martin, Samuel E. 1993. *A reference grammar of Korean: A complete guide to the grammar and history of the Korean language.* Rutland, Vermont: Charles E. Tuttle.

Nathan, David. 2006. Thick interfaces: mobilizing language documentation with multimedia. In J. Gippert, N.P. Himmelmann, & U. Mosel (Eds.), *Essentials of Language Documentation* (pp. 363-390). Berlin: Mouton de Gruyter.

O'Grady, William. 2015. *Jejueo: Korea's other language.* Paper presented at ICLDC 5, Honolulu.

Saltzman, Moira. 2014. *Language contact and morphological change in Jejueo.* Master's thesis, Wayne State University, Detroit.

Sohn, Ho-Min. 1999. *The Korean Language.* Cambridge: Cambridge University Press.

Song, Sang-Jo. *Big dictionary of Jeju language.* Seoul: Hanguk Munhwasa.

Song, Jae-Jung. 2012. South Korea: language policy and planning in the making. *Current Issues in Language Planning,* 13. 1-68.

Southcott, Darren. 2013, September 10. The story of Little Jeju: Jaeil Jejuin. *The Jeju Weekly*, pp. 2A.

Southcott, Darren. 2015, May 13. Parents must take pride in Jejueo. *The Jeju Weekly,* pp. 3B.

Stonham, John. 2011. Middle Korean △ and the Cheju dialect. *Bulletin of the School of Oriental and African Studies,* 74. 97-118.

UNESCO Culture Sector. 2010. Concerted efforts for the revitalization of Jeju language. Retrieved from http://www.unesco.org/new/en/culture/themes/endangered-languages/news/dynamic-contentsingleviewnews/news/concerted_efforts

_for_the_revitalization_of_jeju_language/#.U1
WeFFeZi4Y. Accessed 10 February 2015.

Vamarasi, Marit. 2013. The creation of learner-
centred dictionaries for endangered languages: a
Rotuman example. *Journal of Multilingual and
Multicultural Development.*
doi:10.1080/01434632.2013.825266

Vovin, Alexander. 2013. From Koguryo to Tamna:
Slowly riding to the South with speakers of
Proto-Korean. *Korean Linguistics, 15.* 222–240.

Yang, Chang-Yong. 2013. *Reference grammar of
Jejueo.* Manuscript in preparation.

Computational Support for Finding Word Classes: A Case Study of Abui

Olga Zamaraeva[*], František Kratochvíl[**], Emily M. Bender[*], Fei Xia[*] and Kristen Howell[*]

[*]Department of Linguistics, University of Washington, Seattle, WA, U.S.A.
[**]Division of Linguistics and Multilingual Studies, Nanyang Technological University, Singapore
{olzama, ebender, fxia, kphowell}@uw.edu,   fkratochvil@ntu.edu.sg

Abstract

We present a system that automatically groups verb stems into inflection classes, performing a case study of Abui verbs. Starting from a relatively small number of fully glossed Abui sentences, we train a morphological precision grammar and use it to automatically analyze and gloss words from the unglossed portion of our corpus. Then we group stems into classes based on their cooccurrence patterns with several prefix series of interest. We compare our results to a curated collection of elicited examples and illustrate how our approach can be useful for field linguists as it can help them refine their analysis by accounting for more patterns in the data.

1 Introduction

Computational methods can play a major role in endangered language documentation by producing summaries of collected data that identify apparent patterns in the data as well as exceptions to those patterns. On the one hand, this can help identify errors in glossing (where apparent exceptions are merely typos or orthographic idiosyncrasies). On the other hand, it can help the linguist understand and model patterns in the data, especially in cases where the phenomena in question have overlapping distributions. In this paper, we undertake a case study of verb classes in Abui [abz] in light of the morphotactic inference system of the AGGRE-GATION project (Bender et al., 2014; Wax, 2014; Zamaraeva, 2016).

We begin with an overview of the phenomenon that is the focus of our case study (§2), formulate the problem and describe the steps to solve it (§3). Next we describe the tools and algorithms we apply to compare the output of the system (which summarizes what is found in the accessible corpus data) with a set of elicited judgments (§4). We

conclude with a discussion of where the results of our system differ (§5).

2 Abui verb classes

In this section, we provide a brief introduction to Abui verbs, with respect to what prefixes the verbs can take.

2.1 Abui and Undergoer Marking

Abui [abz] is an Alor-Pantar language of Eastern Indonesia. František Kratochvíl and colleagues have collected and transcribed a corpus comprising roughly 18,000 sentences, of which about 4,600 have been glossed (Kratochvíl, 2017).

Abui is notable for its argument realization, which Kratochvíl (2007; 2011) argues is sensitive to semantic rather than syntactic features. A key part of this system is a collection of five prefix series that can attach to verbs which index different undergoer-like arguments. For the most part, each undergoer type has a phonologically distinct paradigm (e.g. PAT prefixes tend to end in *a*); the full paradigm is given in Table 1.[1] The prefixes occur in both first and second (and in some cases, third) position with respect to the stem, though in this paper we will focus on the first position only.

PERSON	PAT	REC	LOC	GOAL	BEN
1S	*na-*	*no-*	*ne-*	*noo-*	*nee-*
2S	*a-*	*o-*	*e-*	*oo-*	*ee-*
1PE	*ni-*	*nu-*	*ni-*	*nuu-*	*nii-*
1PI	*pi-*	*pu-/po-*	*pi-*	*puu-/poo-*	*pii-*
2P	*ri-*	*ro-/ru-*	*ri-*	*ruu-/roo-*	*rii-*
3	*ha-*	*ho-*	*he-*	*hoo-*	*hee-*
3I	*da-*	*do-*	*de-*	*doo-*	*dee-*
DISTR	*ta-*	*to-*	*te-*	*too-*	*tee-*

Table 1: Abui person indexing paradigm

An example of the prefix attachment is given in (1) where the stem *mia* 'take' agrees in person and

---

[1]The 3I mostly create reflexives. The (DISTR) prefixes index reciprocals and distributive.

Proceedings of the 2nd Workshop on the Use of Computational Methods in the Study of Endangered Languages, pages 130–140,
Honolulu, Hawai'i, USA, March 6–7, 2017. ©2017 Association for Computational Linguistics

number with the noun *aloba* 'thorn'. The subject *na* (1SG.AGT) is not indexed on the verb.[2]

(1) Na   aloba   he-mia
     1SG.AGT [thorn]_{LOC} 3UND.LOC-take.IPFV
     'I am taking out the thorn.' [abz; N12.064]

The five undergoer prefix series mark distinctions among different undergoer-like roles. Many verbs can co-occur with different undergoer prefixes (Kratochvíl, 2014; Fedden et al., 2014; Kratochvíl and Delpada, 2015). Accordingly, the prefixes (and the role distinctions they mark) can be analyzed as contributing to the interpretation of the event. This is illustrated in alternations such as *he-komangdi* 'make it less sharp' ∼ *ha-komangdi* 'make it blunt'; *he-bel* 'pluck it' ∼ *ha-bel* 'pull it out'; *he-fanga* 'say it' ∼ *ha-fanga* 'order him' (Kratochvíl and Delpada, 2015).

In order to better understand the semantic contribution of these prefixes, we would like a rich, detailed description of their distribution in the corpus of naturally occurring speech. In particular, looking at verb classes defined in terms of undergoer prefix compatibility is a promising avenue for better understanding the semantic restrictions on and contributions of the prefixes themselves.

2.2 Abui Undergoer Prefix Glossing

Each prefix series marks one undergoer type, but varies by person and number. The undergoer type of the prefix can in principle be consistently inferred from its phonological form. Specifically, each series ends with a characteristic vowel pattern, at least in the singular, which seems to have a much higher frequency in the corpus. The patterns are shown in Table 2 together with the gloss labels typically used for each series. The *C-* at the start of each prefix form represents the consonants which vary with series. The gloss labels are suggestive of semantic patterns, but the exact semantic contribution of the prefixes is ultimately what we are working towards understanding and thus these labels should be interpreted as preliminary place-holders.

As is typical for active field projects, the glossing is not consistent across the corpus. Most relevantly for our purposes, *Co-* prefixes are sometimes glossed as GOAL (i.e. the same as the *Coo-*

Form	Gloss	Condition
Ø-	stem alone	I
Ca-	patient (PAT)	II
Ce-	location (LOC)	III
Cee-	benefactive (BEN)	III
Co-	recipient (REC)	IV
Coo-	goal (GOAL)	IV

Table 2: Prefix forms and glosses; Condition I is stem attested bare.

Stem	I	II	III	IV	Class
fil 'pull'	+	+	+	+	A (*1111*)
kaanra 'complete'	+	+	+	+	A (*1111*)
kafia 'scratch'	+	-	+	+	B (*1011*)
yaa 'go'	+	-	+	+	B (*1011*)
mpang 'think'	+	-	-	+	C (*1001*)
bel 'pull out'	-	+	+	+	D (*0111*)
luk 'bend'	-	-	+	+	E (*0011*)

Table 3: Examples of Abui verb classes

prefixes) and *Ce-* prefixes are sometimes glossed as BEN (i.e. the same as the *Cee-* prefixes). For the purposes of our present study, we work around these glossing inconsistencies by merging the prefix classes (treating *Ce-* and *Cee-* as one class and *Co-* and *Coo-* as one), effectively reverting (temporarily) to the older analysis in Kratochvíl (2007). This is indicated in Table 2 by the shared Condition numbers for these series. At this stage we also exclude any forms that do not end with *a-*, *o-*, or *e-*, from the analysis.

Together, Conditions I-IV define 16 possible verb classes,[3] where a class is defined by the property of being able to appear in each Condition. In Table 3, we illustrate this with seven verbal stems. We track whether these stems can occur freely (Condition I); whether they are compatible with the prefix *Ca-* (PAT), Condition II; prefix *Co-* (REC) or *Coo-* (GOAL), Condition III; prefix *Ce-* (LOC), or *Cee-* (BEN), Condition IV.

In Table 3, the first five stems (Row 1-5) can occur freely (without affixes—Condition I). Of these five, only the first two stems are also compatible with all other prefix series (Conditions II-IV). The remaining stems form three distinct inflectional classes, labeled with capital letters in the last column of the table and with a binary code which can be used to easily decipher the nature of the class (e.g. class *1111*: all combinations are possible).

---

[2] According to Siewierska (2013), systems marking undergoers alone (leaving actors unmarked) are rare, constituting only about 7% of her sample. In the Alor-Pantar family, undergoer marking is a common trait.

[3] In practice, we will have 15 classes, since class *'0000'* (no Condition applies) cannot be described without additional Conditions, such as a the presence of a light verb.

The question we are investigating here is which verbs appear to belong to which of these inflectional classes, according to the collected corpora. We have created a set of elicited judgments for 337[4] verbs regarding their compatibility with the different undergoer prefixes (Kratochvíl and Delpada, 2017). Our goal is to provide a summary of attested verb-prefix combinations, from both glossed and as yet unglossed corpus data, and compare it to the elicited judgments. In the following sections, we describe how the systems developed by the AGGREGATION project can be used to these ends.

3 Methods for computational support

Classifying verbal stems according to the Conditions we have outlined is a cooccurrence problem: given segmented and glossed IGT, we seek to determine which stems co-occur with which types of affixes. Presently, the Abui corpus is managed using the SIL Toolbox (SIL International, 2015), which allows simple concordance functions, but does not support the kind of distributional analysis we are engaging in here.[5] The AGGREGATION project machinery, which is concerned with building precision grammars, finds cooccurrence patterns of affixes as part of the morphological rules inference. Thus we are taking advantage of the existing pipeline and do not have to create an additional piece of software for this task.

In addition to providing the cooccurrence analysis, the AGGREGATION machinery offers a crucial benefit: It is building a full-fledged morphological analyzer, which we can use to automatically analyze words that have not yet been manually glossed. This gives us more data and helps find more instances of the hypothesized verb classes.[6] Inferring a morphological grammar automatically from IGT is one of the AGGREGATION

---

[4]There are actually 347 verbs in the set, but for the purposes of this paper we do not distinguish between homophones; we compare verbs by orthography only. This lets us compare between e.g. *fanga* ('say') in the curated set and *fanga* ('tell') in the corpus.

[5]The SIL Toolbox system also does not have a functioning consistency check function. Migration to other systems such as FLEX (SIL International, 2017) is not ideal, because the glossed part of the IGT (worth hundreds of man-hours) would be lost during the transfer. The FLEX system also does not support linked audio recordings which help to refine the transcription.

[6]There are further potential analyses facilitated by our methodology, including an exploration of cases where multiple prefixes occur together. We leave these to future work.

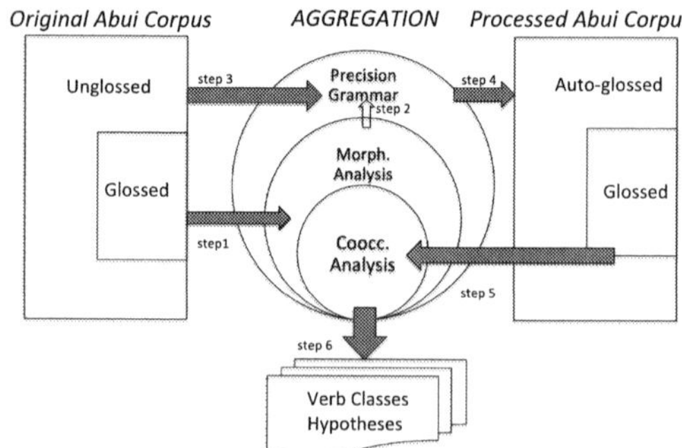

Figure 1: The components of the process. Cooccurrence and morphological analysis are separate processes which both belong to AGGREGATION pipeline. Morphological analysis is converted to a precision morphological grammar, which is used to parse the unglossed parts of the corpus.

project's principal subtasks (see e.g. Bender et al. (2014)), and in this paper we are taking it one step further by actually using the inferred grammar to help develop resources for Abui. The process is outlined in Figure 1 and explained in the next section.

4 System overview

In this section, we describe the systems we use to perform distributional analysis and the analysis of the unglossed corpus. We start with a brief description of precision grammars and systems for generating them from language descriptions (§4.1) before turning to software (dubbed 'MOM') for extracting such descriptions for the morphotactic component of precision grammars from interlinear glossed text (IGT; §4.2). We then describe how the system was straightforwardly extended to model verb classes in Abui (§4.3), and finally, how we used the resulting precision grammar to produce hypothesized glosses for parts of the unglossed corpus (§4.4).

4.1 Precision Grammars and the AGGREGATION project

A precision grammar is a machine-readable encoding of linguistic rules that supports the automatic association of analyses (e.g. morphological or syntactic parses or semantic representations) with strings. As argued in Bender et al. (2012), precision grammars can be useful for language documentation. Here we explore how they can help provide hypothesized glosses for as-yet unanalyzed text.

Precision grammars are expensive to build, requiring intensive work by highly trained grammar engineers. The Grammar Matrix project (Bender et al., 2002; Bender et al., 2010) aims to reduce the cost of creating precision grammars by producing a starter-kit that automatically creates small precision grammars on the basis of lexical and typological language profiles. The AGGREGATION Project (Bender et al., 2014) is further building on this by applying the methods of Lewis and Xia (2008) and Georgi (2016) to extract language profiles suitable for input into the Grammar Matrix grammar customization system from existing collections of IGT.

In this paper, we focus on the morphotactic component of these systems. The Grammar Matrix's morphotactic system (O'Hara, 2008; Goodman, 2013) allows users to specify position classes and lexical rules. Position classes define the order of affixes with respect to each other (and the stem) while lexical rules pair affix forms with morphosyntactic or morphosemantic features. The grammars created on the basis of this information contain morphological subcomponents that can recognize well-formed strings of stems and affixes and associate them with feature structures that represent the information encoded by the morphemes and are compatible with the rules for syntactic structures. Here we develop only the morphological component, and leave the syntax in an underspecified state. We take advantage of the embedded morphological parser by analyzing words individually. In the following two subsections, we describe the Matrix-ODIN-Morphology (MOM) system and how we use it both for distributional analysis of verb stems (vis à vis prefix classes) and to create a grammar which we then use to parse the unglossed portion of the corpus. Note that it is straightforward to find morpheme cooccurrences in segmented data, and the fact that we use MOM for it is a matter of convenience. However, using MOM to automatically gloss words is a novel approach which we describe in detail.

4.2 Matrix-ODIN Morphology

The goal of the Matrix-ODIN Morphology or 'MOM' system (Wax, 2014; Zamaraeva, 2016) is to extract, from a corpus of IGT, the information required to create a computational morpho-logical grammar of the regularized forms found in the IGT. Specifically, this information includes: (i) a set of affixes, grouped into position classes; (ii) for each affix, the form of the affix (and eventually, the associated morphosyntactic or morphosemantic features, as indicated by the glosses); (iii) for each position class, the inputs it can take (i.e. which other position classes it can attach to).

The MOM system first observes affix instances in the data (relying on the segmentation provided in IGT) and where in the word they are attached. Affix instances with the same form and the same gloss are considered to be examples of the same morpheme. Affixes are then recursively grouped into position classes on the basis of overlap in the sets of morphemes they are observed to take as input (attach to).[7] The degree of overlap is a tuneable parameter of the system.

The relationships between the affixes can then be expressed as a graph where groups of morphemes are nodes and input relations are directed edges. The graph can be used to specify the morphotactic component of a precision grammar.

Suppose our corpus of IGT consists of the one sentence in (2).

(2)   he-ha-luol   tila bataa ha-tang
      3LOC-3PAT-gather rope tree   3PAT-hand
      he-tilak-a   mai   neng nuku di
      3LOC-hanging-CONT and.then man one 3A
      mi ya ho-pun-a   ba
      take SEQ 3REC-grab.PFV-CONT SIM
      natea.
      rise.IPFV

      'In the next one, there was a rope hanging on the tree branch when a man came and took it and remained standing there holding it.' [abz]

Initially, MOM will collect affix instances and represent the data as the graph in Figure 2 shows. Then, since nodes *verb-pc3* and *verb-pc1* have 100% overlap in incoming edges, they will be merged into one position class, as Figure 3 shows.

Note that the grammar in Figure 2 cannot generate *he-ho-verb1-a*, but the grammar in Figure 3 can thanks to the merge. In other words, MOM

---

[7]MOM (Wax, 2014) models linear ordering of affixes as follows. In the string *p2-p1-stem-s1*, *p1-* will be assumed to apply first, then *p2-*, and finally *-s1*. Internally, *s1-* will be modeled to take *p2-* as input rather then the stem. Inputs (rather than outputs) are considered the defining property of the position class, which is consistent with the theoretical model of position class morphology as outlined in e.g. Crysmann and Bonami (2012).

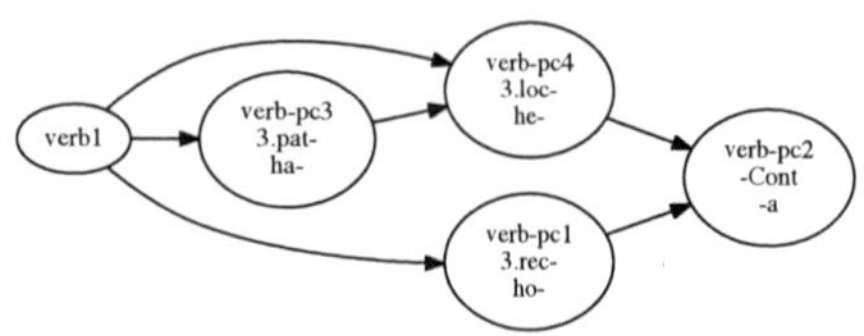

Figure 2: MOM-generated graph which groups affix instances seen in the data into types, and reflects the order in which the affixes were seen with respect to the stems and to each other. Prefixes and suffixes are distinct which is seen in their orthography in the figure.

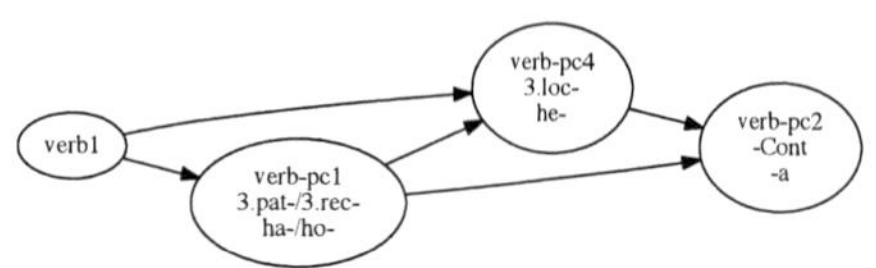

Figure 3: MOM-generated graph which has combined two affix types in Figure 2 into one position class, based on the overlap of their incoming edges.

generalizes patterns seen in the data based on its definition of position class to potentially increase the coverage of the precision grammar.

4.3 Extending MOM to model verb classes

The MOM system as implemented by Wax (2014) and developed further by Zamaraeva (2016) considers all stems of the same part of speech to belong to a single class, and then groups affixes based on what they can attach to (e.g. directly to the stem or to specific other affixes). Setting input overlap to 100% is equivalent to grouping affixes by their cooccurrence pattern (right-hand context for prefixes and left-hand context for suffixes).

We straightforwardly extended the system to model classes of stems (within parts of speech) based on which affixes attach to them. We modify MOM to initially put every new stem into its own node.[8] Then running the edge overlap algorithm described in §4.2 on the outgoing edges of the stem nodes with overlap set to 100% outputs

verb classes defined by their cooccurrence with the first attaching prefix. Finally, computing overlap only over the edges that represent the undergoer prefixes yields a set of hypothesized Abui verb classes as they are described in §1.

4.4 Applying a Morphological Grammar to the Unglossed Part of the Corpus

The goal of grouping verbs by their cooccurrence patterns could be achieved by a variety of simple methods and there is no specific benefit in finding these patterns using MOM. However, when we set out to aggregate the cooccurrence information, we found only about 8,000 verbs in the glossed portion of the Abui corpus (see Table 4). In order to extend our analysis to the unglossed portion, we took advantage of the ability to turn MOM output into a precision grammar via the Grammar Matrix customization system. This grammar, like all grammars output by the customization system, is compatible with the ACE parsing engine (Crysmann and Packard, 2012).

The specification for the morphological grammar is created by running MOM on the glossed portion of the corpus, exactly as described in §4.2, treating all stems as one class, with affix input overlap set to 100%. The grammar is customized by the Grammar Matrix customization system and loaded into ACE. Then, the unglossed portion of the corpus is converted into a list of words, and each word token from the unglossed portion is parsed with ACE and the derived grammar.

Of the 12,034 total unique words extracted from the unglossed part of the corpus, the ACE parser was able to find morphological analyses for 4,642 words. The remainder are either not verbs, based on verb stems not attested in the glossed portion of the corpus,[9] or affix combinations not anticipated by our derived grammar.

Because Abui has many short stems and affixes (e.g. consisting of one phoneme), there are typically many ways to segment a word, and the parser produces multiple analyses for most words for which there was a successful parse; we pick one parse based on the following heuristic.

As explained in §2, for the purposes of this paper there are three prefix series of interest, namely, the ones that end with *a-*, *o-*, and *e-*. Of them, some will end with *oo-* and *ee-*. We rank higher the

---

[8] A new stem for the system is the orthography, normalized by lowercasing and stripping punctuation, which has not been seen before.

[9] The ACE parser in principle allows unknown word handling which would allow us to extend our analysis to unseen verb stems. This is left for future work.

parses where the prefixes of interest are adjacent to the stem; furthermore, we rank higher the long vowel prefixes ending in *oo-* and *ee-* (Conditions III and IV), because initial experiments showed that they were least represented in the glossed data and led to the majority of errors (see Section 5 and Table 7). Error analysis later shows that this preference leads to higher accuracy for Conditions III and IV.

After this step, we have a mapping of $4,642$ word orthographies from successful parses to a segmented and glossed version, one per word. This mapping is used to automatically segment and gloss these words whenever they are found in the unglossed sentences in the corpus. The result is a new corpus combined from the original sentences that were fully glossed and the previously unanalyzed sentences, for which one or more words is now analyzed and glossed. Table 4 shows the amount of the segmented and glossed data before and after applying the morphological grammar to the unglossed part of the corpus.[10]

4.5 Summary

This section has explained our methodology for distributional analysis over glossed Abui text and for automatically glossing portions of the unglossed text. For the first goal, which is a simple cooccurrence problem, we use a module of the MOM system which, after minor modifications, outputs verb classes as defined in §2. For the second objective, we use the full functionality of the MOM system as well as other tools leveraged in the AGGREGATION pipeline, including the Grammar Matrix customization system and the ACE parser. In the next section, we quantitatively compare the results of this analysis based on attested forms with a data set based on elicited judgments and summarize an Abui expert's qualitative opinion about the results.

5 Results

5.1 Comparison with the curated set

We now turn to a comparison of our summary of the attested data with a curated set of elicited

judgments.[11] This curated set contains 337 verbal stems and documents their compatibility with Conditions I-IV discussed in §2, according to native speaker intuitions. Both the curated data set and our automatic output are represented as illustrated in Table 3, where each row represents a verb stem as belonging to a particular class.

To quantify the relationship between these two sources of information, we set the curated data as the target of comparison and then compute precision and recall per class for the automatic data.[12]

Only 12 of the 15 possible verb classes are found in the curated data set, but the system finds all 15 in the corpus. Thus the automatic processing of the forms attested in the corpus hypothesizes both additional verbs for known classes and additional classes.

It is important to emphasize that the curated data set that we compare our extracted data to is a work in progress, and the elicitation mostly relies on a small number of speakers. Even with further work, this curated data set will undoubtedly continue to contain gaps and possible mistakes.[13] Conversely, the corpus alone will probably never be enough: gaps in the corpus data can either be accidental or a result of grammatical incompatibility. This is the familiar tension between corpus and intuition data (see, for example, Fillmore (1992) and Baldwin et al. (2005)). Thus mismatches between the curated and automatically derived data sets do not necessarily indicate system errors (though we have performed error analysis in order to try to identify any). Instead,

---

[10]At this point, we do not know how accurate the morphological analyzer is; we assess the result by how useful the automatically glossed data ends up being for expert analysis. Evaluating the morphological analyzer by cross-validation will be part of future work.

[11]Code, data and instructions for reproducing the results can be found at http://depts.washington.edu/uwcl/aggregation/ComputEL-2-Abui.html

[12]Precision (P) and recall (R) are traditionally defined in terms of different types of mistakes that the system makes. For this paper, we define P and R with respect to the curated set as follows, per class. Let V_1 be the number of verbs in class A in the curated set classified as A by the system, e.g. a verb that was classified as *1111* by the system is also present as *1111* in the curated set. Let V_2 be the number of verbs in class A in system output which belong to a different class in the curated set, e.g. the verb that is *1111* in the system output is actually *1011* in the curated set. Then precision for class A is $P = \frac{V_1}{V_1+V_2}$. Let V_3 be the number of verbs in a class in the curated set which were not put in this class by the system, e.g. the verb is in the curated set as *1111*, but the system put it in *1011*. Then recall $R = \frac{V_1}{V_1+V_3}$. Precision and recall tend to compete, and F1-score is a harmonic mean of the two; the higher the F1-score, the better the system fares in both precision and recall. $F1 = 2 \cdot \frac{precision \cdot recall}{precision+recall}$.

[13]For example, a word form presented to a speaker in isolation or in an invented sentence might sound bad, while being perfectly fine in a naturally occurring context.

Code	IGT collection	IGT	IGT with verbs	Total word tokens	Total word types	Verb tokens	Verb types
GL	*Manually glossed*	4,654	2,120	33,293	4,487	8,609	2,712
AG	*Autoglossed*	13,316	11,538*	130,218	12,034	96,876*	4,642*
CB	*Combined*	17,970	13,406	163,511	13,948	105,485	5,939

Table 4: The corpus statistics. GL and AG refer to the glossed and unglossed portions of the corpus. The asterisks in the AG row indicate numbers that are based on the output of the morphological analyzer. The CB row shows the union of the GL and AG portions.

Class	Example	C	GL (in C)	CB (in C)
0001	*tatuk* 'have fever'	0	29 (1)	11 (0)
0010	*tahai* 'look for'	0	60 (4)	24 (1)
0011	*luk* 'bend'	25	4 (2)	4 (2)
0100	*buk* 'tie'	9	112 (10)	50 (4)
0101	*tok* 'drop'	0	3 (1)	8 (1)
0110	*weel* 'bathe'	1	2 (1)	6 (0)
0111	*bel* 'pull out'	10	1 (1)	1 (0)
1000	*king* 'long'	4	430 (38)	247 (19)
1001	*mpang* think	1	33 (8)	35 (6)
1010	*aai* 'add'	2	69 (17)	97 (15)
1011	*kafia* 'scratch'	184	25 (12)	50 (6)
1100	*toq* 'demolish'	19	59 (13)	121 (18)
1101	*kolra* 'cheat'	2	7 (1)	35 (6)
1110	*momang* 'clean'	3	13 (2)	62 (8)
1111	*buuk* 'drink'	75	7 (2)	103 (27)
	Total	337	854 (113)	854 (113)

Table 5: Class sizes. When there is no example in the curated set (C), an example is taken from the hypothesized set output by the system.

they represent cases in which corpus analysis can further our understanding of the language at hand.

5.1.1 Class sizes

Table 5 gives an overview of the class sizes. The size of a class is the number of unique verb stems that belong to that class. For each class (the 1st column), we provide an example of a stem in that class (the 2nd column), and show the number of unique stems in that class according to (i) the curated set (the 3rd column), (ii) the manually glossed (GL) portion of the corpus (the 4th column), and (iii) the combined (CB) data set of the corpus (the 5th column). For the last two columns, the numbers in the parentheses are the number of unique stems that appear in both the corpus (belonging to that class) and the curated set (belonging to any class).

The general trend is that adding more data leads to reclassifying some verbs from classes whose bit-vector definitions contain more 0s to classes whose bit-vector names contain more 1s. This is expected: the unglossed portion of the data may contain patterns that the glossed portion does not contain.

The total number of unique stems found in the originally glossed portion of the data is 854. The intersection between this set and the curated set, however, is only 113. We do not gain any new stems by adding previously unglossed data, since the ACE parser will not presently analyze a word with an unknown stem.[14]

The per class intersection between the corpus derived set and the curated set is often very small; only a few classes defined by the system have more than a few stems which also belong to any of the curated set classes. This means we can only compare the curated set to the system output with respect to a few verbs. Nonetheless, we report the results in §5.1.2 below.

5.1.2 Comparing class labels of stems

For the 113 stems appearing in both the curated set and the corpus, we compare their class labels in the two data sets. In Table 6, we pretend that the curated table is the gold standard, and report precision (P) and recall (R) of the system output. The system output is either based on the glossed portion only (GL) or the combined corpus (CB). The three rows with dash only correspond to the three classes which have zero members in the curated set in Table 5. In other rows, the precision or recall is zero when there is no match between system output and the curated set,[15] which is not surprising given that many verb classes contain only very few stems.

At a general level, Table 6 shows that adding more data by glossing it automatically helps discover more patterns. Specifically, the system now puts at least one verb into class *1001* that exactly matches one of the verbs in that class in the curated set. Since class *1001* contains only 2 verbs in the curated set but the corpus contains over 30, it is possible that further inspecting the system output can contribute to a fuller description of this class.

---

[14]See note 9.

[15]For the clarity of presentation, we define F1 score to be zero when P and R are equal to zero.

Class	Precision		Recall		F1 score	
	GL	CB	GL	CB	GL	CB
0001	-	-	-	-	-	-
0010	-	-	-	-	-	-
0011	0	0	0	0	0	0
0100	0	0	0	0	0	0
0101	-	-	-	-	-	-
0110	0	0	0	0	0	0
0111	0	0	0	0	0	0
1000	0	0	0	0	0	0
1001	0	**0.17**	0	**0.50**	0	**0.25**
1010	0	0	0	0	0	0
1011	0.58	**1.0**	0.13	0.12	0.21	**0.22**
1100	0.23	0.22	0.50	**0.67**	0.32	**0.33**
1101	0	0	0	0	0	0
1110	0	0	0	0	0	0
1111	0.50	0.35	0.04	**0.35**	0.07	**0.35**
micro-avg	0.10	0.19	0.10	0.19	0.10	0.19

Table 6: Precision, Recall, and F1-scores when comparing verb classes in the curated set and in the corpus (GL is for the glossed portion, CB is for the combined corpus). When the CB result is higher than the GL one, the former is in bold.

5.1.3 Comparing (stem, condition) pairs

In addition to comparing the class labels of stems, we can compare the (stem, condition) pairs in the curated set and in the corpus. The results are in Table 7. There are 113 stems that appear in both sets and four conditions; therefore, there are 452 possible (stem, condition) pairs. If a (stem, condition) pair appears in both data sets, it is considered a match. There are two types of mismatches: a pair appears in the curated set but not in the system output (type 1) or vice versa (type 2).

Condition	Match	Mismatch	
		Type 1	Type 2
Curated v. GL			
I	72	20	21
II	90	17	6
III	50	61	2
IV	36	75	2
Total	248	173	31
Curated v. CB			
I	**84**	8	21
II	83	4	26
III	**66**	43	4
IV	**54**	56	3
Total	**287**	111	54

Table 7: Numbers of matches and mismatches when comparing 452 (stem, condition) pairs in the curated and in the corpus (GL for glossed portion, and CB for the combined corpus). When the number of matches in CB is higher than in GL, we put it in bold.

Table 7 shows higher proportions of matches

(e.g., 285 out of 452 pairs in CB) than what is shown in Table 6 because it is making more fine-grained distinctions. For instance, if a verb belongs to class *1100* in the curated set and the system puts it in class *1110*, such a verb will get zero points towards precision and recall in Table 6, but it will get three matches (while getting one mismatch) in Table 7. Where comparison at the class level directly targets our research question, comparison at the (stem, condition)-level offers insights into which prefixes are more consistently glossed in the corpus, and conversely, which may need cleanup.

5.1.4 Mismatch Analysis

Our results show relatively low agreement between the curated data set and the automated distributional analysis, which is reflected by low F1-scores in Table 6. There are several sources for this disagreement: gaps in the collected corpus, gaps in the manually constructed analysis, and system-related issues.

Gaps in the collected corpus As discussed in §5.1.3, there are two types of mismatches between the curated set and the system output: type 1 (occurring in the curated set but not in the corpus) and type 2 (the opposite). Gaps in the collected corpus is what causes the type 1 mismatch. It is not a very informative kind of mismatch, because when something is not attested in a relatively small field corpus,[16] it does not mean it is not possible in the language. For this type of mismatch, the most likely explanation is that an example which would account for it has not yet been added to the corpus.

Gaps in the curated set In contrast, the type 2 mismatch means that there are examples in the corpus that indicate the combination is possible, but the curated set states otherwise. In this case, either the curated set needs to be refined or there are errors in the IGT corpus.[17] This is the more interesting type of mismatch. The counts in Table 7 show that, after adding more data, the type 2 count increases. Specifically, it gives rise to more mismatches with respect to Condition II (the PAT prefix). Most of these counterexamples are in fact spurious and are discussed below with respect to system-related issues, but there is at least one genuine discovery. The verb *kaang* ('to be good') was

---

[16]As opposed to huge raw-text corpora available for some high resource languages.

[17]Barring bugs in our system.

deemed to not be able to combine with the PAT prefix according to the curated set, but this type 2 mismatch led us to confirm that the (stem, condition) pair is in fact possible (with the meaning 'recover from disease'). Further analyzing this type of mismatches may lead to more discoveries.

System-related issues There are two main sources of noise in our system output: the morphological analyzer (i) mislabels nouns as verbs, and (ii) does not normalize words with respect to phonological variation.

Possessive prefixes in Abui often look like the PAT prefixes, and lexical categories are fairly fluid. Thus some word tokens that are automatically analyzed as verbs by the grammar might actually be nouns in context (and thus more appropriately analyzed as representing other sets of affixes). This affects the precision scores for classes *1100* and *1111*; analysis on the stem-prefix level (Table 7) shows that it is indeed the PAT prefixes that are "to blame" here, as the number of mismatches with respect to other conditions lowers when automatically glossed data is added.

Finally, there are stems from the curated set that are attested in the corpus but which the system was unable to find. This is most often due to lack of phonological normalization in the corpus. This problem is more prominent in the unanalyzed part of the data; by virtue of it having not been analyzed, there is no normalization with respect to phonological variation of forms such as 'tell', written as *anangra* and *anara*. This indicates an important direction for future work: in addition to segmenting and autoglossing, it will be valuable to train a phonological analyzer which would map stems to a single canonical representation.

5.2 Expert analysis

The second author, who is an expert in Abui, reviewed the verb classes output by our system from the combined dataset, e.g. the 11 verbs in class *0001*, the 24 verbs in class *0010*, etc. In general, the classes were found to contain noise, the sources for which include homophones, mistakes in the corpus,[18] and lack of phonological normalization. At the same time, *0001* appears to be a potentially true–previously unknown–class of verbs whose semantics may have something in common. Many of these verbs usually occur with an experiencer argument. Classes *0100* and *1011* were al-

ready known, but the system output helped find more verbs which truly belong to them. These refinements to the classes will help inform linguistic hypotheses about the inflection system as a whole and its interaction with the lexical meaning of the verbal stem. Further analysis of the results will provide a methodology for significantly improving and extending the treatment in Kratochvíl (2007).

6 Conclusion and Future Work

We performed a computational overview of a corpus to hypothesize inflectional verb classes in Abui. As a part of this process, we used precision grammar machinery to automatically gloss part of the previously unanalyzed corpus of Abui and thus obtained more data.

We compared two different types of analyses–manual, based on elicitation, and automatic, produced by our system–and found that the mismatches between the two, especially the type where a pattern is found in the corpus but not in the elicited set, help refine the understanding of the classes.

For future work, we can add a phonological analyzer to the automatic glossing procedure and refine the parse ranking for the automatic glossing. In addition, adding unknown stem handling to the morphological grammar may help further refine the understanding of the patterns of verb-prefix cooccurrence. Finally, the methods which we used here can be extended to perform a computational overview of the Abui verbs with respect to not only first, but also second and third position prefixes. While looking at verbs with first position prefixes only required no more than a simple cooccurrence table, looking at prefixes across all three positions increases the complexity of the problem and further highlights the value of being able to automatically derive and apply a full-scale morphological grammar to the task.

Acknowledgments

This material is based upon work supported by the National Science Foundation under Grant No. BCS-1561833 (PI Bender) and by the Singapore Ministry of Education under Tier 2 Grant MOE2013-T2-1-016 (PI Kratochvíl).

---

[18]The identification of these mistakes is also useful.

References

Timothy Baldwin, John Beavers, Emily M. Bender, Dan Flickinger, Ara Kim, and Stephan Oepen. 2005. Beauty and the beast: What running a broad-coverage precision grammar over the BNC taught us about the grammar — and the corpus. In Stephan Kepser and Marga Reis, editors, *Linguistic Evidence: Empirical, Theoretical, and Computational Perspectives*, pages 49–69. Mouton de Gruyter, Berlin.

Emily M. Bender, Dan Flickinger, and Stephan Oepen. 2002. The Grammar Matrix: An Open-Source Starter-Kit for the Rapid Development of Cross-Linguistically Consistent Broad-Coverage Precision Grammars. In John Carroll, Nelleke Oostdijk, and Richard Sutcliffe, editors, *Proceedings of the Workshop on Grammar Engineering and Evaluation at the 19th International Conference on Computational Linguistics*, pages 8–14, Taipei, Taiwan.

Emily M. Bender, Scott Drellishak, Antske Fokkens, Laurie Poulson, and Safiyyah Saleem. 2010. Grammar Customization. *Research on Language & Computation*, pages 1–50. 10.1007/s11168-010-9070-1.

Emily M. Bender, Sumukh Ghodke, Timothy Baldwin, and Rebecca Dridan. 2012. From Database to Treebank: Enhancing Hypertext Grammars with Grammar Engineering and Treebank Search. In Sebastian Nordhoff and Karl-Ludwig G. Poggeman, editors, *Electronic Grammaticography*, pages 179–206. University of Hawaii Press, Honolulu.

Emily M. Bender, Joshua Crowgey, Michael Wayne Goodman, and Fei Xia. 2014. Learning grammar specifications from IGT: A case study of Chintang. In *Proceedings of the 2014 Workshop on the Use of Computational Methods in the Study of Endangered Languages*, pages 43–53, Baltimore, Maryland, USA, June. Association for Computational Linguistics.

Berthold Crysmann and Olivier Bonami. 2012. Establishing order in type-based realisational morphology. In *Proceedings of HPSG*, pages 123–143.

Berthold Crysmann and Woodley Packard. 2012. Towards Efficient HPSG Generation for German, a Non-Configurational Language. In *COLING*, pages 695–710.

Sebastian Fedden, Dunstan Brown, František Kratochvíl, Laura C Robinson, and Antoinette Schapper. 2014. Variation in Pronominal Indexing: Lexical Stipulation vs. Referential Properties in Alor-Pantar Languages. *Studies in Language*, 38(1):44–79.

Charles J. Fillmore. 1992. "Corpus linguistics" or "computer-aided armchair linguistics". In Jan Svartvik, editor, *Directions in Corpus Linguistics: Proceedings of Nobel Symposium 82, Stockholm, 4-8 August, 1991*, pages 35–60. Mouton de Gruyter, Berlin, Germany.

Ryan Georgi. 2016. *From Aari to Zulu: Massively Multilingual Creation of Language Tools using Interlinear Glossed Text*. Ph.D. thesis, University of Washington.

Michael Wayne Goodman. 2013. Generation of machine-readable morphological rules with human readable input. *UW Working Papers in Linguistics*, 30.

František Kratochvíl and Benidiktus Delpada. 2015. Degrees of affectedness and verbal prefixation in Abui (Papuan). In Stefan Müller, editor, *Proceedings of the 22nd International Conference on Head-Driven Phrase Structure Grammar, Nanyang Technological University (NTU), Singapore*, pages 216–233, Stanford, CA. CSLI Publications.

František Kratochvíl and Benidiktus Delpada. 2017. Abui Inflectional Paradigms. Electronic Database. Nanyang Technological University, February.

František Kratochvíl. 2007. *A grammar of Abui: a Papuan language of Alor*. LOT, Utrecht.

František Kratochvíl. 2011. Transitivity in Abui. *Studies in Language*, 35(3):588–635.

František Kratochvíl. 2014. Differential argument realization in Abui. *Linguistics*, 52(2):543–602.

František Kratochvíl. 2017. Abui Corpus. Electronic Database: 162,000 words of natural speech, and 37,500 words of elicited material (February 2017). Nanyang Technological University, Singapore.

William D. Lewis and Fei Xia. 2008. Automatically identifying computationally relevant typological features. In *Proceedings of the Third International Joint Conference on Natural Language Processing*, pages 685–690, Hyderabad, India.

Kelly O'Hara. 2008. A morphotactic infrastructure for a grammar customization system. Master's thesis, University of Washington.

Anna Siewierska. 2013. Verbal person marking. In Matthew S. Dryer and Martin Haspelmath, editors, *The World Atlas of Language Structures Online*. Max Planck Institute for Evolutionary Anthropology, Leipzig.

SIL International. 2015. Field Linguist's Toolbox. Lexicon and corpus management system with a parser and concordancer; URL: http://www-01.sil.org/computing/toolbox/documentation.htm.

SIL International. 2017. Sil Fieldworks. Lexicon and corpus management system with a parser and concordancer, URL: http://software.sil.org/fieldworks/.

David Wax. 2014. Automated grammar engineering for verbal morphology. Master's thesis, University of Washington.

Olga Zamaraeva. 2016. Inferring Morphotactics from Interlinear Glossed Text: Combining Clustering and Precision Grammars. In *Proceedings of the 14th SIGMORPHON Workshop on Computational Research in Phonetics, Phonology, and Morphology*, pages 141–150, Berlin, Germany, August. Association for Computational Linguistics.

Waldayu and Waldayu Mobile:
Modern digital dictionary interfaces for endangered languages

Patrick Littell
Carnegie Mellon University
Language Technologies Institute
5000 Forbes Ave.
Pittsburgh PA 15213
`plittell@cs.cmu.edu`

Aidan Pine
University of British Columbia
Department of Linguistics
2613 West Mall
Vancouver, BC V6T 1Z4
`apine@alumni.ubc.ca`

Henry Davis
University of British Columbia
Department of Linguistics
2613 West Mall
Vancouver, BC V6T 1Z4
`henry.davis@ubc.ca`

Abstract

We introduce Waldayu and Waldayu Mobile, web and mobile front-ends for endangered language dictionaries. The Waldayu products are designed with the needs of novice users in mind – both novices in the language and technological novices – and work in tandem with existing lexicographic databases. We discuss some of the unique problems that endangered-language dictionary software products face, and detail the choices we made in addressing them.

1 Introduction

Lexicographers have noted that with the increase in access to digital technology, "lexicography is clearly at a turning point in its history" (Granger and Paquot, 2012). While the changes that technology presents to lexicography are relevant to non-endangered languages as well, there exists a unique set of challenges in developing lexicographic materials for endangered languages in particular. We identify and address two of these fundamental and perennial difficulties.

1. At least in the North American context (and likely elsewhere), there are relatively few potential users who are both fluent in the language and trained in a systematic orthography. Many users are students who have not yet achieved fluency in the language they are searching.

2. Lexicographic efforts have, in many communities, taken place over generations by various scholars, using a variety of formats, orthographies, and assumptions, leading to data sets that are often very heterogeneous.

To address these issues, we have developed *Waldayu* and *Waldayu Mobile*. Waldayu is an orthographically-aware dictionary front-end with built-in approximate search, and a plugin architecture to allow it to operate with a variety of dictionary formats, from the output of advanced back-ends like TLex (Joffe and de Schryver, 2004), to semi-structured HTML like online word lists, to simple word/definition spreadsheets. Waldayu Mobile is a mobile implementation of Waldayu which is compatible with both Android and iOS devices.

Waldayu and Waldayu Mobile were originally developed to provide online and mobile interfaces to a forthcoming Gitksan (Tsimshianic) e-dictionary, but are intended to be language-neutral and have since been expanded to St'at'imcets (Salish), Nuu-chah-nulth (Wakashan), Sliammon (Salish),

Proceedings of the 2nd Workshop on the Use of Computational Methods in the Study of Endangered Languages, pages 141–150,
Honolulu, Hawaiʻi, USA, March 6–7, 2017. ©2017 Association for Computational Linguistics

Squamish (Salish), Thangmi (Sino-Tibetan), and Cayuga (Iroquoian).

In Section 3, we discuss some of the user experience principles we have adopted, and in Section 4 discuss our challenges and solutions in adapting these to mobile devices. In Section 5, we discuss our implementation of approximate search.

2   A reusable front-end for novice users

Waldayu is primarily intended as a front-end solution to the perennial "Dictionary problem": that dictionaries are fundamentally a language-learning tool but require a certain level – sometimes an advanced level – of language knowledge to use in the first place. This is particularly apparent in our field context, the North American Pacific Northwest, where the sheer phonological and morphological complexity of the languages makes traditional print dictionary use particularly difficult (Maxwell and Poser, 2004).

We can observe this when, to give a real-life example, a user is trying to look up the word for "coyote" (snk̓y̓ep) in Thompson's monumental print dictionary of Nłeʔkepmxcín (Thompson, 1996). To successfully find this word, the user must know that it is alphabetized under k̓ rather than s or n (which are prefixes/proclitics) and that k̓ and y̓ are distinct from k and y for the purposes of collation. With thousands of nouns starting with s and about ten phonemes that might be confused with k (both pan-Salishan traits), most words in the dictionary cannot easily be found by novice users.

This is not a specific criticism of Thompson's lexicographic choices; complex languages require the lexicographer to make difficult decisions about orthography, morphology, morphophonology, and collation, and any decision they make about these will pose difficulty for some segment of novice users.

However, modern technology – particularly approximate search – allows us a way to meet the user halfway, by letting the system itself be aware of complications (prefixes/proclitics, easily-confused sounds, orthographic differ-

ence, etc.) that novices have yet to master.

Waldayu is not, however, intended to be a *replacement* for a mature, collaborative lexicographic software solution such as TLex, Kamusi (Benjamin and Radetzky, 2014), or the Online Linguistic Database (Dunham, 2014). Most lexicographic teams we have encountered already have preferred back-ends, file formats, and workflows; solving the "dictionary problem" for users should not require teams to abandon solutions into which they have already invested time, effort, and resources. Rather, Waldayu and Waldayu Mobile are intended to serve as a lightweight, unclutttered online front-end for novice users, while expert users can make use of more advanced functionality offered by a mature lexicographic database.

3   User experience and interaction

There are five user experience principles that we attempted to make consistent throughout both products, so as to remove barriers for novice users who may not be familiar with online dictionaries, or online interfaces in general.

3.1   Consistent control behaviours

Each control (button, search box, link, etc.) has only a single function, and no controls change their behaviour depending on the settings of other controls. For example, there is no Gitksan-English/English-Gitksan toggle that changes the behaviour of the search box; this convention, although ubiquitous in online bilingual dictionaries, is a frequent source of user error even for experienced users.

Rather, Waldayu utilizes a double search bar, in which user input in the left search box searches the primary language (e.g., Gitksan) while the left search box searches in the secondary language (e.g., English).[1] This parallels the two most frequent user tasks, using English as a query language to find an entry in

---

[1] This is superficially similar in appearance to the two-box interface used by Google Translate, but both boxes accept user input, and the user cannot swap the boxes or otherwise change what languages they represent.

Figure 1: Screenshot of Waldayu as the Gitksan/English Online Dictionary

Figure 2: Reduced Waldayu control layout embedded at the top of each page

a target language dictionary, and using a target language as a query language to find an English definition.

3.2 Immediate responses

In addition to the above, we try to avoid requiring other "two step" user inputs (e.g., typing a query and then hitting "search"). Instead, we attempt to provide user inputs with immediate feedback à la Google Instant search or other "AJAX"-style client and server interfaces (although as noted in Section 3.5, Waldayu does not in fact have a client-server architecture).

3.3 Consistent visual metaphors

In both controls and presentation, consistent visual metaphors are maintained. We borrow the fundamental metaphor from the FirstVoices online word lists (First Peoples' Cultural Council, 2009) – the online interface most familiar to our users – that the primary language (e.g., Gitksan) is always in the left column, and the secondary language (e.g., English) is always in the right column. This metaphor is maintained in the search interface (as seen in Fig. 1, the left search box searches the primary language, the right search box searches the secondary language), in browsing interfaces like the random word page (Fig. 3), and in entry pages (with primary language keywords and examples on the left, definitions and commentary on the right).

This horizontal visual metaphor is augmented by a colour scheme that presents the target language as green-blue (#066) and English as dark gray (#333); like other metaphors, these colours are preserved throughout the site.

10 random entries:	MORE
siigaiwii	associate
hasba	backwards
wilaks	introduce, make known
sip	bone
anyuust	cellar, storage pit
mis'moot'ixs	chickenhawk
ksaxw	exit
iuda'mixsxw	to hug
haguxsgait'amdinsxw	camera
sim'oo'git	chief

Figure 3: Position and colour metaphors maintained in a "browsing" page

3.4 Continued presence of controls

The major controls and links are present on every page, and work the same way on each page. The interface of the start page (a horizontal bar with links to free browsing, random browsing, etc., the page title, and the dual search bar) is embedded (with a reduced layout, as seen in Fig. 2) and fully functional at the top of every page.

This is intended to make it essentially impossible to "get lost" within the site; there is no question of how to return to the site's core functionality because every page has that functionality.

3.5 Connection-independence

Many of our user communities are located in remote regions of Canada, and some users do not have home internet connections or reliable mobile data access. While the initial connection to the Waldayu site, or the initial download of Waldayu Mobile, requires an internet connection, subsequent uses should not.[2]

While Waldayu appears to be a modern AJAX client-and-server web application, in actuality the Waldayu engine compiles a single HTML file, containing the dictionary itself in JSON format and JavaScript code that emulates a multi-page website. This way, the page can be downloaded and used offline on any platform; it has no installation steps, external files, or any prerequisites (save, of course, for a reasonably recent web browser).

4 The mobile user experience

Exporting Waldayu's user experience to mobile devices could not be done wholesale. While most laptop screens have a minimum of ~700px in width, mobile devices are typically in the ~300px range, with the result that maintaining the principles in Section 3 often required different interface decisions.

---

[2]Or, more precisely, as much functionality as possible should be retained even if the internet connection is lost. Some multimedia capability is lost when Waldayu loses internet access, but the basic search functionality remains.

4.1 Side menus

While a navigation bar that itemizes each individual page associated with the site was an appropriate organization for Waldayu, the navigation bar became too cluttered for mobile devices, especially considering Waldayu Mobile has additional pages such as a "Flashcards" page. For this reason, navigation for Waldayu Mobile was translated into a side-menu that is accessible by tapping the three-bar icon (what is sometimes called "hamburger" in mobile interface jargon) in the upper left corner of the screen, or swiping to the right on a touch screen. This is seen below in Figure 4.

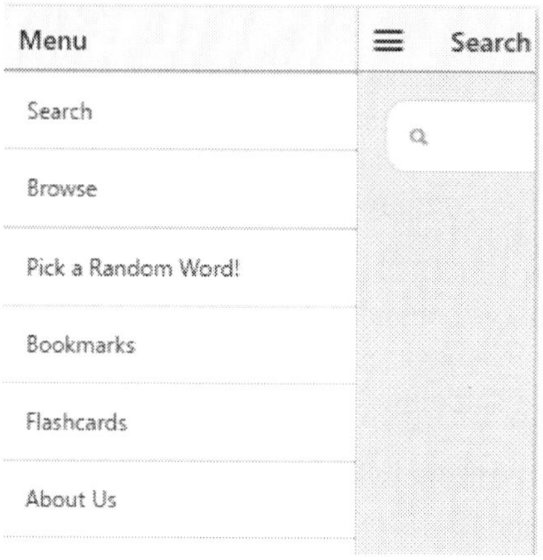

Menu | Search

Search

Browse

Pick a Random Word!

Bookmarks

Flashcards

About Us

Figure 4: Side menus

4.2 A unified search bar

Similarly, maintaining Waldayu's horizontal metaphor for search bars in Waldayu Mobile would force search bars to be too small (i.e., less than 150px wide) for a positive mobile user experience. The option to force users to turn their devices and search with a 'landscape' (horizontal) orientation was also not preferred because it would result in forfeiting being able to visualize results as queries are searched. This would mean that users would have to search with a horizontal orientation, and view results either by scrolling or switching to a vertical orientation which would go against our UX principles in Section 3.

Initially, two solutions were created. The first kept both search bars and dynamically changed their widths depending on whether a user tapped the left or right search bar. However, this still proved to limit the size of the search bar too severely.

The second solution was to use only a single search bar and a language selector; while this does not achieve the principle in Section 3.1, we hypothesized that increased attention to the visual metaphors in Section 3.3 might alleviate the difficulties this interface can cause. The language-selection radio buttons preserved the aforementioned horizontal metaphor (L1 on the left, L2 on the right) and dynamically changed the colour scheme of the search box to either the L1 or L2 colour.

While this solved the issues related to screen size, user testing revealed difficulties with the "two step" process, in which users first need to first consider what type of search they wished to perform and then select a button, which in turn changes the behaviour of the search bar. Likely, this is a result of the habituation to Google-style search bars where users can type any sort of query and expect accurate and relevant results.

Ultimately, this led us to develop a single search bar which searches the query term in both languages. The L1 and L2 results are presented together (still preserving the aforementioned visual metaphors), but with additional highlighting indicating, for each result, whether the match is on the L1 side or the L2 side. This is seen below in Figure 5.

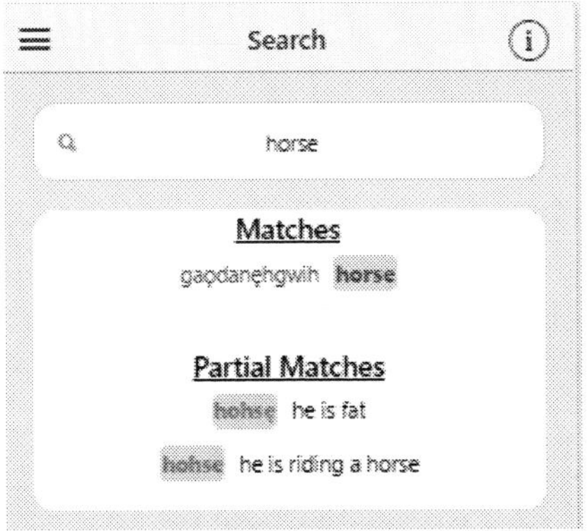

Figure 5: Highlighted search results in Cayuga (Ranjeet and Dyck, 2011) (left) and English (right)

5   Approximate Search

In this section, we consider the implementation of approximate search within Waldayu and Waldayu Mobile.

There are four primary reasons for why an approximate search is not simply a convenient feature for endangered language dictionaries, but a necessary one.

1. Some users, even if they can distinguish all the phonemes of the language (e.g., /k/ vs. /q/), do not always know the orthographic convention used to encode this difference.

2. Other users – particularly students – may know the orthographic convention but be unable to reliably discern certain phonological differences in their target language, resulting in systematic and predictable errors in spelling.

3. Many users will not have easy access to a keyboard which is able to type the required characters, whether for lack of a language-specific keyboard, difficulty with keyboard installation, or because they are using a mobile device.[3]

4. Many North American Indigenous languages have multiple orthographies, sometimes historical, but sometimes in current competition with each other. Different regions, generations, scholars, and schools have produced materials using different orthographic conventions, and users may have learned any of them, or may be attempting to enter data from material written in a different orthography.

Sometimes these issues are compounded, in that a user might type either "kl" or "tl" as an approximation of /ƛ/. Sometimes, though, the correct sequence of characters is perfectly valid using a standard English keyboard, but the user has difficulty hearing the distinction,

---

[3]FirstVoices (First Peoples' Cultural Council, 2009) recently developed an Android and iOS Keyboard app that allows users to type in over 100 endangered languages in Canada, the US and New Zealand.

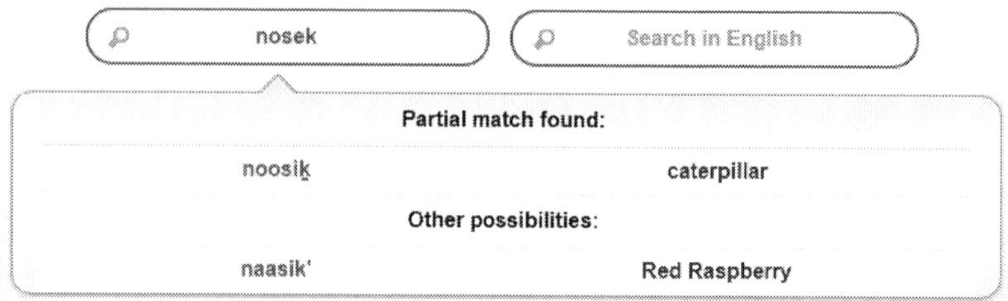

Figure 6: Gitksan-English Online Dictionary returning *noosik̲* and *naasik'* as possible matches to user query *nosek*.

as is the case with glottalized resonants (e.g. *'w* vs *w*) in many languages of the Pacific Northwest.

To address these issues, we implemented several approximate search algorithms. The most important criterion – aside from being fast enough to return results to users in a reasonable amount of time – was that this algorithm should either not require parameterization for a particular language, or should be able to be parameterized by a non-programmer (so that lexicographers can adapt the Waldayu software to a new language without hiring a programmer or having to contact the developers).[4] Ideally, a lexicographer should be able to adapt Waldayu using only familiar consumer software (like a spreadsheet program) rather than modifying the code or composing a structured data format directly.

5.1 Unweighted Levenshtein search

We began with a simple Levenshtein distance algorithm (Levenshtein, 1966), in which each word is compared to the user query and ranked according to the number of single-letter edits needed to change the query into the word. This comparison has the benefit that it can be expressed as a finite-state automaton (Schulz and Mihov, 2002) and, after construction of the automaton itself, run in linear time over the length of the query in characters, making search results nearly instantaneous re-gardless of the size of the dictionary.

Simple Levenshtein distance, however, is insufficiently discriminative to give useful results to users; for example, the Gitksan word for tree, *gan* (/Gan/), sounds similar to English "gun", but given the query *gun*, an unweighted Levenshtein algorithm has no reason to order the result *gan* above the result *din*, since these both differ from "gun" by two edits.

5.2 Weighted Levenshtein search

To address this, we then parameterized edit costs such that more similar and frequently-confused characters (*g̲* and *g*, *a* and *u*) accrue a lesser penalty, thereby ranking more-similar words higher, along the lines of Needleman and Wunsch (1970), Kondrak (2000), or Rytting et al. (2011).[5] Users could parameterize these penalties using a simple spreadsheet, in which they identified classes of similar sounds and chose [0.0-1.0] penalties within these classes.

While this approach proved adequate for our sample dictionaries, it did not scale well to larger dictionaries, leading to inappropriately long search times in practice, particularly on mobile devices.[6] Searching a five-letter word in a dictionary of about 9,000 words took up to 9 seconds on an iPhone 4.

---

[4]The third possibility is that the system learns appropriate parameters directly from the data. While this is promising for future work, we did not have, for any of our development languages, an appropriate corpus of user-transcribed data from which a system could learn orthographic correspondences.

[5]We also reduced the relative penalties for deletions and insertions at the beginnings and ends of words; this had the effect of allowing search for subword strings such as roots.

[6]As noted in Section 3.5, Waldayu ensures basic functionality even while offline. Search is therefore performed entirely on the client side, to ensure a consistent user experience online and offline.

5.3 Unweighted Levenshtein search on "comparison" forms

We therefore adopted a hybrid approach that leverages Waldayu's built-in orthographic conversion tools, in which we run an unweighted Levenshtein comparison between "orthographies" that purposely fail to represent easily-confused distinctions.

As background, Waldayu is designed to be orthography-independent, since it is designed to be able to take in heterogeneous resources that are not necessarily in the same orthography or the orthography that the user expects. Non-programmer lexicographers can specify orthographic correspondences using a simple table like that in Table 1, which Waldayu can read and compile into a finite state transducer.[7]

kw	k^w
k̲	q
k̲w	q^w
x	χ
x̲w	$χ^w$

Table 1: Sample orthographic correspondence table

In addition to specifying genuine orthographic transformations, the user can also specify transformations into one or more "comparison" orthographies, in which easily-confused (or difficult to enter on a keyboard) distinctions are not represented. Comparing words by collapsing similar sounds into a small number of equivalence classes is a technique of long standing in lexicography (Boas and Hunt, 1902)[8], information retrieval (Russell, 1918) and historical linguistics (Dogolpolsky, 1964).

In Waldayu, the user can specify a Soundex-like (Russell, 1918) transformation of entries and queries; by default Waldayu uses a transformation intended for North American Pacific Northwest languages ("PugetSoundex"), but it can straightforwardly be adapted to other languages. Table 2 illustrates a sample transformation.

k	KY
kw	KW
k̲	K
k̲w	KW
x	HY
xw	HW
x̲	H
x̲w	HW

Table 2: Sample correspondence table for approximate phonological comparison

For example, in the Gitksan development dictionary, the entry *noosik̲* ("caterpillar") undergoes a transformation into *NWSYK*, losing the distinctions between vowel length and height, the *u*/*w*/rounding and *i*/*y*/palatization distinctions, and the velar/uvular distinction. Meanwhile, a user input like *nosek* (Fig. 6) would undergo a similar transformation and likewise result in *NWSYK*. The results of these transformations are then compared using an unweighted Levenshtein distance; since the edit penalties are not continuous, we can implement this as a Levenshtein automaton using the `liblevenshtein` library (Edwards, 2014). As both orthographic transduction and Levenshtein automata operate in linear time, the resulting system returns results nearly instantaneously (dropping from the 9 seconds reported in Section 5.2 to less than 10 milliseconds).[9]

In practice, all entries in the development dictionary go through two transformations and comparisons, one to a very reduced form

---

[7]Programmer-lexicographers, on the other hand, can write orthographic transformation plugins if they require transformations more sophisticated than can be expressed in a tabular format.

[8]Presuming that he likely made mistakes in differentiating the similar sounds of Kwak'wala language, and that users of the dictionary would face similar confusions, Boas collated the glossary of the *Kwakiutl Texts* according to equivalence classes, so that, for example, all lateral fricatives and affricates were collated together.

[9]Qualitative evaluation of these approximate search algorithms (e.g, how often does a user query result in their intended word?) will require a larger collection of user-generated text than we currently have, and thus remains to be done.

like *NWSYK* and another to a more faithful (although still quite broad) phonological representation. The search algorithm ranks results according to a weighted average of these comparisons. This dual representation allows us to rank entries by both coarse and fine distinctions without using a continuous penalty function.

6 Conclusion and Future Research

Waldayu and Waldayu Mobile[10] are under continued development, although they are functional as-is and can be (and are being) adapted to additional languages.

Of the many features that remain to be implemented, several touch on unsolved (at least for this domain) research problems:

1. Incorporating algorithmic methods for determining the language of a given query term, along the lines of Cavnar and Trenkle (1994), could enhance the results of the "unified" search bar (Section 4.2, in order to dynamically prioritize L1 and L2 results according to which language the system decides the query is targeting. However, this is not a trivial task (Beesley, 1988), and the difficulties in Section 5 also pose difficulties for language identification, since many user queries will be attempts at L1 words but influenced by L2 phonology and orthography.

2. Combining phonological/orthographical approximate search with morphologically-aware subword search has proven problematic, when faced when long words composed of many relatively short morphemes. Take, for instance, the word for "telephone" in Gitksan:

   haluu'algyagamt'uuts'xw
   ha-luu-algya<u>x</u>-m-t'uuts'xw
   INSTR-in-speech-ATTR-wire
   "telephone" (Hindle and Rigsby, 1973)

The results returned from combined phonological/orthographical/morphological search, although "relevant" in the sense that the entries contain sequences of morphemes that are phonologically/orthographically close to the query, can seem very counter-intuitive from a user point-of-view. It remains to be seen what level of morphological analysis and what notion of distance produces results that are intuitively "correct" from a user point of view.

3. We need to move our assumptions about the efficacy of our UX and algorithms beyond anecdote. For search algorithm efficiency, we would like to develop both statistical methods and analytics for determining how often users are given correct or relevant search results. For UX, we would like to conduct controlled experiments with users who possess varying levels of linguistic knowledge and target language competency.

4. Finally, the conflicting demands of web and mobile interfaces has led to a degree of codebase fragmentation. This fragmentation was in part due to Waldayu's origin as a web-based application – where there are fewer constraints on the interface – and subsequent adaptation to more-constrained mobile applications. The next version of Waldayu, now well into development, seeks to unify the interfaces and codebase as much as possible by taking a "mobile first" approach and implementing all three versions (web, Android, and iOS) in AngularJS, using the Ionic framework[11] for Waldayu Mobile. This change reworks Waldayu into a responsive Single Page Application (SPA), as seen in Figure 7, and brings features of Waldayu Mobile (like automatic flashcard generation) back into the web-based interface.

These problems suggest interesting future

---

[10] `www.waldayu.org`

[11] `ionicframework.com`

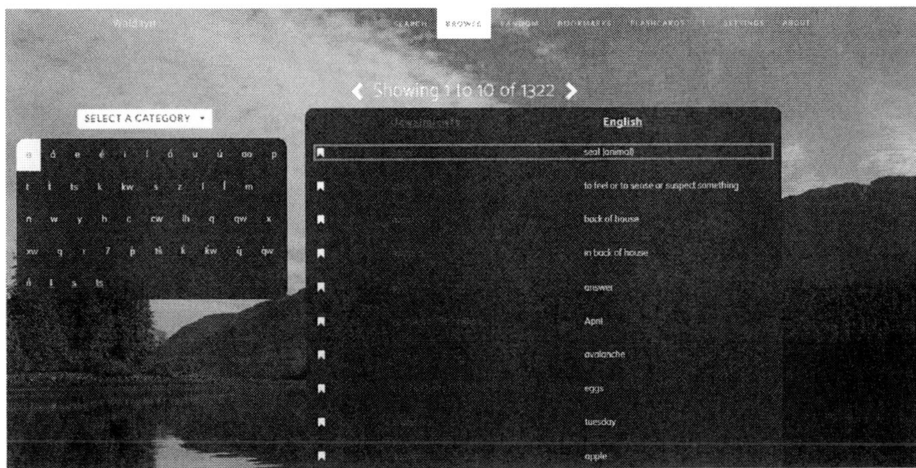

Figure 7: Browse state of Waldayu using AngularJS

research directions at the intersection of user experience, linguistics, and computation, and furthermore suggest that user-facing, novice-friendly interfaces may be valuable in generating novel data sets and research questions for endangered language research.

Acknowledgments

The development of Waldayu and Waldayu Mobile was supported by the SSHRC Insight Grant 435-2016-1694, 'Enhancing Lexical Resources for BC First Nations Languages'. Finally, we would also like to acknowledge our presence on unceded Coast Salish territory, where the majority of this work was inspired, created, and written about.

References

Kenneth Beesley. 1988. Language identifier: A computer program for automatic natural-language identification of on-line text.

Martin Benjamin and Paula Radetzky. 2014. Small languages, big data: Multilingual computational tools and techniques for the lexicography of endangered languages. In *Proceedings of the 2014 Workshop on the Use of Computational Methods in the Study of Endangered Languages*, pages 15–23.

Franz Boas and George Hunt. 1902. Kwakiutl texts. *Memoirs of the American Museum of Natural History*, 5.

William B. Cavnar and John M. Trenkle. 1994. N-gram based text categorization. In *In Proc. of SDAIR-94, 3rd Annual Symposium on Document Analysis and Information Retrieval*, pages 161–175.

Aron B. Dogolpolsky. 1964. Gipoteza drevnejego rodstva jazykovych semej severnoj evrazii s verojatnostej toky zrenija. *Voprosy Jazykoznanija*, 2:53–63.

Joel Dunham. 2014. *The Online Linguistic Database: Software for Linguistic Fieldwork*. Ph.D. thesis, University of British Columbia.

Dylon Edwards. 2014. liblevenshtein: A library for generating finite state transducers based on Levenshtein automata. Retrieved from https://github.com/universal-automata/-liblevenshtein.

First Peoples' Cultural Council. 2009. FirstVoices. Retrieved from http://www.firstvoices.com/.

Sylviane Granger and Magali Paquot. 2012. *Electronic lexicography*. Oxford University Press.

Lonnie Hindle and Bruce Joseph Rigsby. 1973. *A short practical dictionary of the Gitksan language*, volume 7. Department of Sociology/Anthropology, University of Idaho.

David Joffe and Gilles-Maurice de Schryver. 2004. Tshwanelex: A state-of-the-art dictionary compilation program. pages 99–104.

Grzegorz Kondrak. 2000. A new algorithm for the alignment of phonetic sequences. In *Proceedings of the 1st North American chapter of the Association for Computational Linguistics conference*, pages 288–295. Association for Computational Linguistics.

Vladimir I. Levenshtein. 1966. Binary codes capable of correcting deletions, insertions, and reversals. *Soviet Physics Doklady*, 10:707–710.

Michael Maxwell and William Poser. 2004. Morphological interfaces to dictionaries. In *Proceedings of the Workshop on Enhancing and Using Electronic Dictionaries*, ElectricDict '04, pages 65–68, Stroudsburg, PA, USA. Association for Computational Linguistics.

Saul B. Needleman and Christian D. Wunsch. 1970. A general method applicable to the search for similarities in the amino acid sequence of two proteins. *Journal of Molecular Biology*, 48:443–53.

Kumar Ranjeet and Carrie Dyck. 2011. Cayuga digital dictionary. Retrieved from https://cayugalanguage.ca.

Robert C. Russell. 1918. *U.S. Patent 1,261,167*. U.S. Patent and Trademark Office.

C. Anton Rytting, David M. Zajic, Paul Rodrigues, Sarah C. Wayland, Christian Hettick, Tim Buckwalter, and Charles C. Blake. 2011. Spelling correction for dialectal arabic dictionary lookup. 10(1):3:1–3:15, March.

Klaus U. Schulz and Stoyan Mihov. 2002. Fast string correction with Levenshtein-automata. *International Journal of Document Analysis and Recognition*, 5(1):67–85.

Laurence C. Thompson. 1996. *Thompson River Salish dictionary: Nłeʔkepmxcín*. University of Montana Occasional Papers in Linguistics.

Connecting Documentation and Revitalization:
A New Approach to Language Apps

Alexa N. Little

7000 Languages

12 Murphy Drive

Nashua, NH 03062

`alittle@7000languages.org`

Abstract

This paper introduces 7000 Languages, a nonprofit effort to adapt commercial language-learning software for free use by endangered language groups. We discuss the advantages and challenges of our approach and suggest ways of converting corpus and archive data into language-learning courses. We also demonstrate the capabilities of the software, both for the revitalization and the documentation of endangered languages. Finally, we discuss ideas for future expansion of our programs and seek feedback from others involved in endangered language work.

1 Introduction

Many endangered language communities are interested in producing "language apps": digital tools for teaching and learning their languages. Although these language apps are useful for language revitalization efforts, building them requires considerable time, funding, and technical skill. Even successful community projects may lack the resources for future updates to their language apps.

Researchers who study endangered languages also want to provide digital tools, so that their research and data will be helpful to communities. Creating and maintaining an entire language-learning system, however, is more than a researcher can reasonably accomplish.

The current compromise is the digital archive. In a digital archive, language data is secure, accessible, and generally portable. XML-formatted data could even, with some manipulation, be integrated into a language app. However, the time and expense of building the rest of such an application remains a challenge for both sides.

We introduce a nonprofit effort, 7000 Languages, that seeks to resolve this problem. Our approach uses technology donated by the language-learning industry to produce free commercial-grade language apps in partnership with endangered language advocates.

2 The Programs

We have organized our approach into two programs – one from a revitalization-first perspective, and one from a documentation-first perspective. Below is a brief description of these two programs, followed by an in-depth discussion of how projects starting from either perspective will ultimately benefit both sides.

2.1 Partnership Program

Our Partnership Program is a free program intended for groups, such as endangered language communities, who have a revitalization-first perspective. The system works as follows:

7000 Languages has an agreement with a for-profit language-learning company, Transparent Language. This agreement allows 7000 Languages to use Transparent Language's internal tools to develop online courses for endangered and low-resource languages. The tools include:

- a program that converts an Excel template filled with language content (text, images, and recordings) into a functioning course

- a program for designing a custom unit, lesson, and activity layout

- a graphical user interface (GUI) for creating individual lessons, ideal for those with limited technical experience (see Figure 1)

Proceedings of the 2nd Workshop on the Use of Computational Methods in the Study of Endangered Languages, pages 151–155,
Honolulu, Hawai'i, USA, March 6–7, 2017. ©2017 Association for Computational Linguistics

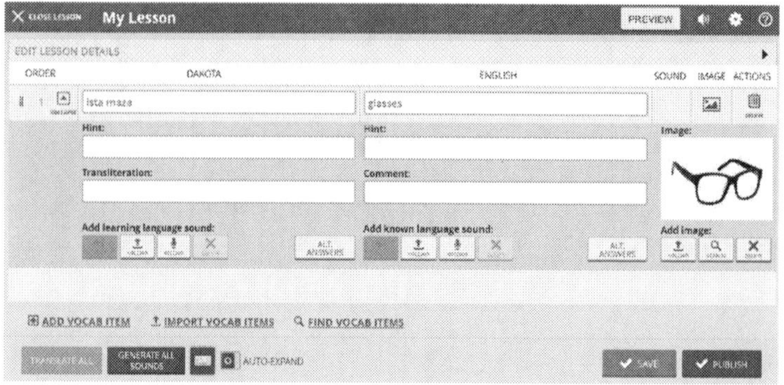

Figure 1. A GUI for lesson authoring.

7000 Languages trains interested groups, called Partners, to use these tools. The Partner decides what they want to teach, and they retain ownership rights of all the content they create. Once the course is finished, 7000 Languages contacts Transparent Language, who sets up a "node" for the Partner in their systems. This publishes the course online and lets the Partner create user accounts. The Partner can add as many users as they want, for free. The course will also be made available, for free, on the 7000 Languages website and published through Transparent Language's library and education subscriptions.

Published courses present an opportunity to produce documentation of the language. Because the courses accept and store language data from the tools in XML format, data can also be exported from the course in XML format. The XML entry for each item contains the phrase in the target language, a translation in the source language, a reference to the target language audio file, and a reference to the source language audio file (if available). See Figure 2 for a partial sample of an XML file exported from a lesson.

Once exported, the XML files can be submitted for archival, used to form a corpus, or reformatted and used in another digital application, such as a searchable dictionary. It is our hope that this will allow endangered language groups to focus on revitalization without having to sacrifice documentation and other uses of their language data.

```
- <card>
    <side1_phrase>blue</side1_phrase>
    <side2_phrase>pelung</side2_phrase>
    <guid>{26B1AD8D-7D64-49C4-BEB0-ADABB9F81418}</guid>
    <list_position>3</list_position>
    <side2_sound url="sounds/learn002.mp3"/>
    <is_video_sound_used>false</is_video_sound_used>
    <is_video_auto_played>false</is_video_auto_played>
  </card>
- <card>
    <side1_phrase>brown</side1_phrase>
    <side2_phrase>coklat</side2_phrase>
    <guid>{DB6B1A48-050F-4851-94EB-79A68C1968D3}</guid>
    <list_position>4</list_position>
    <side2_sound url="sounds/learn003.mp3"/>
    <is_video_sound_used>false</is_video_sound_used>
    <is_video_auto_played>false</is_video_auto_played>
  </card>
- <card>
    <side1_phrase>gray</side1_phrase>
    <side2_phrase>klau</side2_phrase>
    <guid>{C12DB5E5-B9EE-4943-9FD9-2A47F6BFCCDC}</guid>
    <list_position>5</list_position>
    <side2_sound url="sounds/learn004.mp3"/>
    <is_video_sound_used>false</is_video_sound_used>
    <is_video_auto_played>false</is_video_auto_played>
  </card>
```

Figure 2. Vocabulary items from a Balinese lesson, exported as an XML file.

2.2 Archives Program

Our Archives Program is a free program intended for groups, such as field linguists, libraries, and archivists, who have a documentation-first perspective, such as field linguists, libraries, and archivists. It assumes that some language materials already exist, and that both the group holding the data and the larger language community are interested in a language app. The focus of the program is manipulating the existing data to be usable in a language app.

Our goal for the Archives Program is to give documentation-focused researchers the opportunity to contribute, without much additional work, to language revitalization efforts in the relevant community.

The Transparent Language courseware (i.e., the technical components of the language app that make it interactive) generally requires content in a specific XML format. If the linguist or archivist who holds the data is familiar with rewriting XML, we ask them to rewrite their data to match those specifications. If not, 7000 Languages can often create the appropriate conversion programs. (In the future, we hope to create standard scripts capable of translating XML and other text schema commonly used for language documentation into courseware-compatible versions.)

Once the data has been reformatted into a compatible XML file, and we have verified it will integrate properly with the courseware, we can create interactive lessons simply by importing the data. Just as in the Partnership Program, those lessons can then be published online, and the community given control over a "node" where they can create unlimited free user accounts. The course will also be distributed by 7000 Languages, if the community permits, and made available through Transparent Language's library and education subscriptions.

3   The Software

We will not attempt to show the entire functionality of the software in this short paper. Rather, we present examples that demonstrate the broad capabilities of the technology.

7000 Languages Partners can choose from over 40 different activity types to create their courses. These include matching, multiple choice, and variations on reading, writing, listening, and speaking practice. Figure 3 shows examples of several core activities. The technology also supports simulated conversations (in which the learner provides audio for one of the roles), videos, and text-based reference materials. Lessons usually include assessments, and quizzes are also available as a type of practice drill.

The system allows learners to track their progress. Each vocabulary item that a learner studies is stored in her "learned items." Over time, learned items fade and must be "refreshed" with practice activities. The learner can also consult her list of learned items to see what words she has learned. This list is searchable both by source and target language.

Teachers can also use the system to monitor their students' progress; from the Instructor Portal, they can assign specific lessons and track student activity.

Finally, the online course connects to a smartphone app, which contains flashcard-based activities with the content from each lesson. See Figure 4 for an example. If the user's phone is online, the learned items automatically synchro-

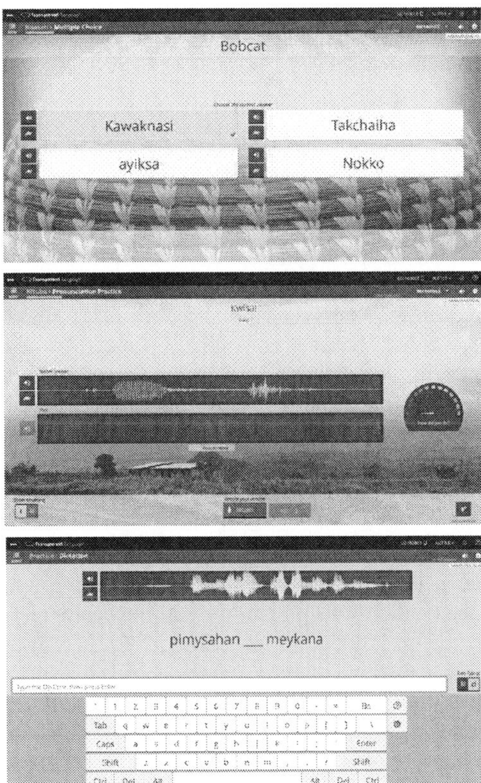

Figure 3. Sample activities on the web app.

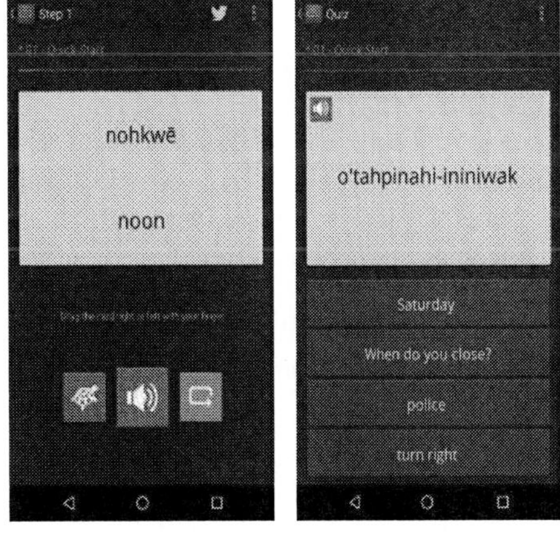

Figure 4. Flashcard-style activities on the mobile app.

nize between the online and mobile versions of the course. The flashcards can also be downloaded, then used even without an Internet connection. The next time the user is online, she can press the "sync" button to have her learned items synchronize between devices.

4 Benefits

We see several ways that our approach could benefit members and supporters of endangered language communities.

4.1 Functionality

As shown in Section 3, the software donated by Transparent Language offers a wide range of activity types and contains options for progress reporting, assessments, and mobile learning. All this functionality was originally funded by commercial interests and intended for commonly-taught languages. However, our approach allows endangered language communities to take advantage of this rich functionality as well.

4.2 Stability and Portability

As endangered language advocates strive to produce digital documentation and language apps, deprecation and portability has increasingly become an issue (Bird and Simons, 2003). An app that works on today's computer or smartphone may not work on the next generation model. And, with the speed of operating system updates, language apps must be updated frequently to remain functional. Finally, consumers can choose between several different operating systems, different types of smartphones, and even different web browsers. Ensuring that a language app will function on all of these systems is a significant challenge.

Because the courses produced under 7000 Languages rely on the same technology as Transparent Language's commercial courses, they benefit from the same updates. This reduces the financial and technical burden on communities to keep their individual language apps up-to-date, and helps ensure that the apps will remain usable across most common platforms.

4.3 Reduced Cost to Community

If the technology involved in creating a language app is available at no cost, communities can dedicate whatever resources they have to other purposes, such as hiring teachers, paying linguistic consultants, or developing additional learning materials.

4.4 Documentation and Revitalization

Because our approach allows language-learning lessons to be downloaded as archivable XML, and materials archived as XML can likewise be converted into language-learning lessons, it offers the potential for increased collaboration between revitalization-focused and documentation-focused groups. For example, an endangered language community could create a language course, then export the material for archival and linguistic analysis. Meanwhile, a linguist could conduct fieldwork, save their language documentation in XML format, and have that XML data converted into a usable language app for the community.

5 Challenges

Our work has been impacted by several challenging factors, and we are interested to hear the perspective of other endangered language advocates on these issues.

5.1 Licensing and Control

In order to use the technology of a for-profit language-learning company, we agreed to certain conditions. They are as follows:

- Transparent Language technology may only be used by 7000 Languages to produce courses for low-resource languages (i.e. not for commonly-taught world languages).

- Finished courses will be published on Transparent Language's library and education services. This means that users who pay to subscribe to Transparent Language courses will receive access to these courses, also.

- If a 7000 Languages Partner chooses to sell the course they created, they must pay a 20% royalty to Transparent Language for the use of its technology. However, if they distribute the course for free, there is never any royalty required.

- If Transparent Language ever chooses to sell a course created by a 7000 Languages Partner as a standalone course, they will pay a 20% royalty to the Partner.

Many communities are willing to accept these conditions in order to gain free use of Transparent Language's technology and the benefits we described in Section 4. However, we understand that some communities are not comfortable with a for-profit company controlling any aspect of their language, or with their language being widely available for anyone to learn. In such situations, our approach is not a good fit.

5.2 Sensitive Material

We have been approached by communities who wish to restrict access to some of their content, for cultural reasons. While we understand the need to both preserve this material and teach it only to the appropriate people, the technology does not have the sophisticated access controls required to make that possible. At the moment, we encourage these groups to design lessons with material that *can* be shown to the general public, and to use other resources to teach and archive sensitive material.

5.3 Grants

Although our approach greatly reduces the cost to endangered language groups by providing free access to a technological framework, it does not completely eliminate the costs of producing a language app. Designing a curriculum, making text and recordings, and learning to use the tools requires time and effort. Some of the groups who work with us have grant funding, but many do not—which means that they take on this work as volunteers.

5.4 Internet Access

Many of the communities facing language loss may also lack access to consistent, high-speed Internet service. Poor Internet infrastructure remains a problem in remote areas of the United States and Canada, even after 20 years (Carpenter et al., 2016). The inability to reliably access the Internet is a barrier for communities who are otherwise enthusiastic about adopting new technologies (Carpenter et al., 2016).

Transparent Language technology does function offline in the form of a mobile flashcard app. However, the fully-featured software generally requires a computer and an Internet connection, or an iPad onto which the software can be downloaded.

Because a computer and an Internet connection are used by Partners to develop courses in the first place, this has not yet been a major concern. However, some Partners may be unable to distribute their courses as widely as they wish because community members lack reliable Internet access. Furthermore, as the Archives Program expands, the course creators and course users are increasingly likely to be different groups altogether, with different levels of access to technology. We have anticipated these problems and are considering possible solutions now, before they become an active concern.

6 Future Work

The mission of 7000 Languages is to connect endangered language communities with the technology they need to teach, learn, and revive their languages. We recognize that the difficulty of creating language apps is not the only technological barrier that these communities face. In this paper, we have mentioned some possible future directions for increasing the impact of our program. We intend to make data exported from completed courses compatible with other technologies, such as dictionary apps or Natural Language Processing programs. We also plan to develop scripts to smooth the conversion process between documentation and language app. In planning our next steps, we look to the language revitalization and documentation field for suggestions, constructive criticism, and opportunities for collaboration.

7 Conclusion

In this paper, we introduced 7000 Languages, a nonprofit effort that uses technology donated by the language-learning industry to create free endangered language apps. We discussed the current approach of 7000 Languages, we described some features of the software, and we sought feedback from other endangered language advocates.

Acknowledgments

The programs described in this paper were made possible by the board of 7000 Languages, Transparent Language, and the individual donors who support our organization. Thanks to R. Regan and C. Graham for their assistance.

References

S. Bird and G. Simons. 2003. *Seven dimensions of portability for language documentation and description.* In Bojan Petek (ed.), Portability issues in human language technologies: LREC 2002.

Jennifer Carpenter, Annie Guerin, Michelle Kaczmarek, Gerry Lawson, Kim Lawson, Lisa P. Nathan, and Mark Turin. 2016. *Digital Access for Language and Culture in First Nations Communities.* Knowledge Synthesis Report for Social Sciences and Humanities Research Council of Canada. Vancouver, October 2016.

Developing a Suite of Mobile Applications
for Collaborative Language Documentation

Mat Bettinson[1] and Steven Bird[2,3]
[1]Department of Linguistics, University of Melbourne
[2]Department of Computing and Information Systems, University of Melbourne
[3]International Computer Science Institute, University of California Berkeley

Abstract

Mobile web technologies offer new prospects for developing an integrated suite of language documentation software. Much of this software will operate on devices owned by speakers of endangered languages. We report on a series of prototype applications that support a range of documentary activities. We present ongoing work to design an architecture that involves reusable components that share a common storage model and application programming interface. We believe this approach will open the way for a suite of mobile apps, each having a specific purpose and audience, and each enhancing the quality and quantity of documentary products in different ways.

1 Introduction

Documenting a language calls for a substantial collection of transcribed audio to preserve oral literature, epic narratives, procedural knowledge, traditional songs, and so on. Carrying out this program at scale depends on effective collaboration with speech communities. This collaboration spans the documentary workflow, starting with raising awareness and recruiting participants, followed by the core work of recording, transcribing and interpreting linguistic events, and finally the processes of preservation and access. The collaboration goes beyond individual workflow tasks to collaborative management, whereby the language community – as the producers and consumers of the material – help to shape the work.

Our vision is for a suite of applications supporting a variety of workflows, and contributing to a common store of language documentation, designed to support the kinds of remote and long-distance collaborations that arise when working with endangered languages. Emerging web technologies and proliferating mobile devices open the door to this future. Creating reusable components and a common application programming interface (API) will accelerate the process.

Instead of seeking consensus about a single documentary workflow enshrined in monolithic software, we envisage diverse workflows supported by multiple applications, built and rebuilt from shared components as local requirements evolve. Linguists should be able to customise an app by tinkering with a top level page, to make changes like moving a consent process from before to after a recording, or replacing the language selection component with a fixed choice, or requiring not just a portrait of the speaker but a second landscape view of the context in which a recording was made. However, rather than design the whole infrastructure, we have taken a bottom-up approach, developing components and specialised apps that help to clarify the requirements of the API.

This paper is organised as follows. First, we discuss the state of the art in section 2. Then in section 3 we describe the evolution of our thinking through a series of prototype applications. Next, in section 4, we discuss the data requirements for apps and their constituent components based on our prototyping experience, and suggest a common interface of components. Finally, in section 5 we describe further work in support of our goal of establishing a suite of interconnected language documentation applications and lay out our vision for a common language data API.

2 Mobile Apps for Language Documentation

Digital tools are widely used in documentary workflows, but they often require specialised training and are platform specific. In recent years there has been growing awareness of the importance of collaborating with language maintenance

Proceedings of the 2nd Workshop on the Use of Computational Methods in the Study of Endangered Languages, pages 156–164,
Honolulu, Hawai‘i, USA, March 6–7, 2017. ©2017 Association for Computational Linguistics

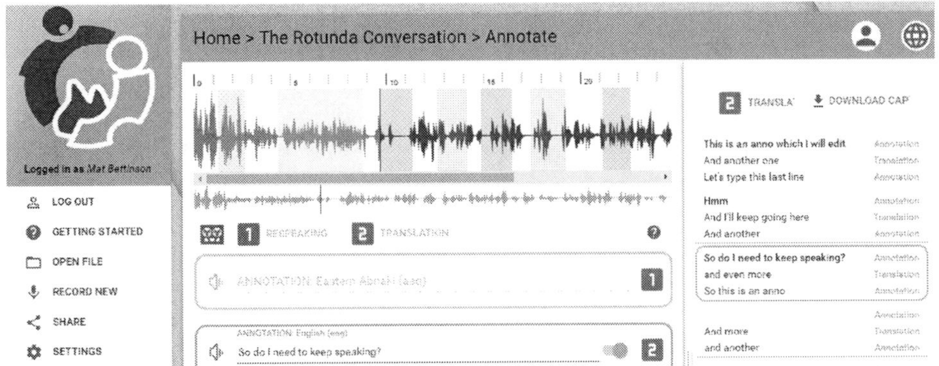

Figure 1: Aikuma-NG beta transcription web app, available from the Chrome Web Store

and revitalisation groups, particularly as we look to sustain activity and relationships beyond the 3-5 year window of a sponsored research project (Austin, 2010). The shift to mobile technologies is enabling this collaboration, and may ultimately transform the practice of documentary linguistics (Chatzimilioudis et al., 2012; Birch et al., 2013).

To date, dictionary and flashcard apps for language learning have been the most popular. For example, the suite of First Voices apps for iPhone in Canada, and the 'Ma' series of dictionary apps in Australia and the Pacific including Ma Iwaidja, Ma Gamilaraay and Ma Bena Bena (Carew et al., 2015). Taiwan's Council of Indigenous People's e-dictionary includes 16 Formosan languages, via a mobile-accessible website (Taiwan Indigenous Council, 2016). Apps have been used to conduct experiments on dialect variation, capturing linguistic judgements together with the location (Goldman et al., 2014; Leemann et al., 2016). The Android app Aikuma, a precursor of the work reported here, allows users to collect and translate spoken narrative (Bird et al., 2014).

Alongside these individual web apps there are web application suites for language documentation. LDC webann is an online annotation framework supporting remote collaboration (Wright et al., 2012). LingSync supports collaborative language documentation, and has been popular in North American linguistic fieldwork training (Cathcart et al., 2012). CAMOMILE is a framework for multilingual annotation, not specifically for linguistic research (Poignant et al., 2016).

These apps fall into two categories according to their audience and purpose: research apps for language documentation and 'community' apps for language development. The developer profile and funding sources are different, with research apps generally developed in academia, and community apps developed by commercial developers. This situation points to an opportunity for collaboration in the development of language apps that appeal to a broader audience.

3 Prototype Apps

This section reports on the development of three apps over the course of 2016. These apps represent an evolving understanding of methods to achieve modularisation through reusable components. One component in particular, for language selection, is required for all apps. We discuss this component in the context of each app to shed light on some options concerning web technologies and data models.

3.1 Transcription: Aikuma-NG

Aikuma-NG was developed to assess the feasibility of building mobile software using web technologies and delivering a similar feature set to desktop software (Figure 1). The app's audience is people who wish to transcribe speech, particularly community members and laypersons. The expected output is standard srt or vtt files for captioning YouTube videos. Aikuma-NG is a community app that requires no internet access post install.

Aikuma-NG incorporates basic metadata management and the ability to perform oral respeaking and translation, following the example of SayMore (Hatton, 2013).

Aikuma-NG's main feature is multi-tier transcription, making use of the additional audio from any respeaking or translation activities, in order to create transcriptions of a source and its translations. The app exports to common video subtitling formats as well as ELAN, and has been localised into English, Korean and Chinese.

Aikuma-NG was built as a Chrome App, because this provided a means to deliver a desktop-like experience. Chrome apps open full screen with no URL bars and have unlimited local data storage. We adopted the technology stack based on the JavaScript Model-view-controller (MVC) framework *Angular* and the UI framework *Angular Material*. The capacity for Angular Material to deliver a high quality UI was key factor in this choice. The Wavesurfer waveform visualisation package was adopted to handle visualisation and time series-based data structures (WaveSurfer, 2017). We found limited support in the JavaScript ecosystem for multimedia and local storage, requiring us to gain a deep knowledge of emerging web standards that had yet to be widely adopted in third-party software. Key challenges arose from acquiring experience of asynchronous programming, poor support for modularisation in the ES5 JavaScript and, in particular, the weak inter-component communication model of Angular 1.

3.1.1 The language selector

MVC frameworks such as Angular allow us to specify an app view with a template containing custom HTML tags. Figure 2 depicts four components in Aikuma-NG. An audio file visualiser/player based on Wavesurfer, and three selector components based on the touch-friendly Material Design UI to select languages, people and customisable tags. These components are used in a view template with markup as follows:

```
<ng-player ...></ng-player>
<ng-language-selector ...></ng-language-selector>
<ng-person-selector ...></ng-person-selector>
<ng-tag-selector ...></ng-tag-selector>
```

We chose the Angular and Angular Material-based stack recognising that the well-documented UI component examples represented a professional implementation of a UI, one that was recognisable by millions of users of Google's web tools and Android platform. Material Design's "chip" UI component was ideally suited to display a list of arbitrary categories or labels such as languages and tags. Angular Material's documentation included an implementation binding chips with text input auto-complete. Thiw was a good fit to facil-

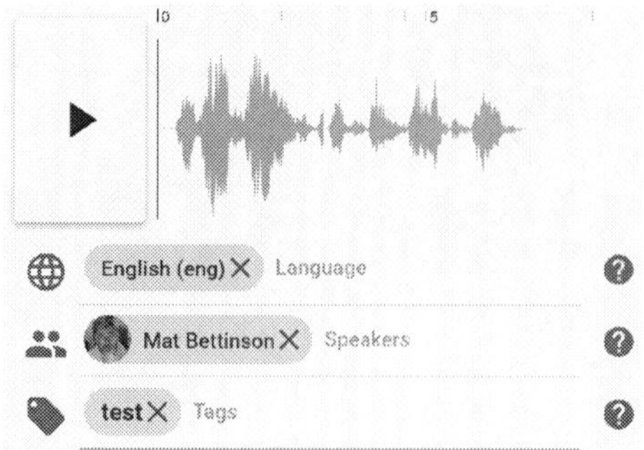

Figure 2: Aikuma-NG view from a template of sub-components

itate rapid selection from thousands of language names.

Experience from field testing showed that we must also allow users to create arbitrary names for their language. This is necessary to account for their language being unknown, or their preference to write the name of a language in another language such as the dominant language in the region. The consequence is that we must allow for auto complete over customised entries as well as ISO693 categorised labels.

Typical data flow involves passing an array of pre-populated languages to the component, if we are restoring a previous UI. The component accesses a data service to retrieve a list of ISO693 languages and custom languages for the auto-complete. Two-way data binding returned the data to a parent component.

3.1.2 Key findings

Web technologies can be used to build a full featured *desktop* app, as demonstrated by the ongoing popularity of Aikuma-NG. The Chrome App platform worked well for this application, but just months after the release, Google announced their intent to retire Chrome Apps. We believe Aikuma-NG can be implemented effectively as a progressive web app. Rapid iteration of UI designs in the field is particularly valuable, allowing us to find the best approach for our target audience.

3.2 AikumaLink: Task management

Aikuma-Link (Figure 3) is an online only *research* app that allows the researcher audience to recruit a remote participant to perform an activity of the linguist's choosing.

The app was motivated by the observation that researchers often return from the field with data

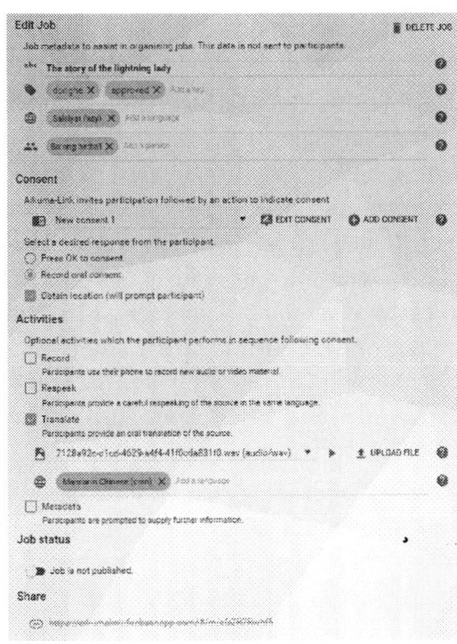

(a) Task creation

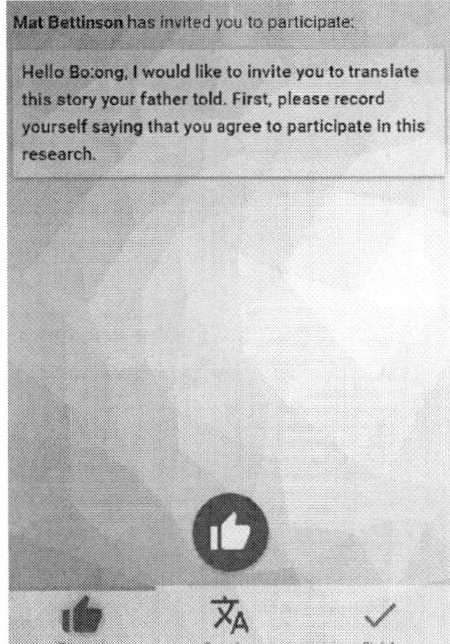

(b) Receiving a task

Figure 3: Aikuma-Link: Linguists define documentary tasks with supporting materials, the task is dispatched to participants to perform with a mobile app

that requires further interaction with native speakers to become useful. The same app offers desktop and mobile views and employed a real-time back end as a service (BaaS) as a common data model. The app was intended to investigate the ability of web apps to virtually eliminate the 'on-boarding' cost of recruiting participants to use research software.

Aikuma-Link is based on a process where the researcher first defines a task such as translating or respeaking audio recordings. From this task, the app generates a URL link which the researcher sends to the remote participant, typically by social media. Clicking the link on a phone launches the Aikuma-Link mobile app, which invites their participation and allows them to perform the prescribed tasks. The resulting data is then returned to the linguist. A stretch design goal is to facilitate crowdsourced experiments by crafting a single link which can invite any number of participants to perform the same activity.

3.2.1 The language selector

Material Design was originally chosen specifically because it was touch-friendly for mobile devices. Nevertheless, components based on text input (and therefore virtual keyboards) and long lists of autocomplete choices represent UI challenges of a different order to desktop. Where the component is used for the desktop browser linguist view, it can be used inline with many others because desktop users have large displays and scrolling in acceptable. For mobile, a component is better realised as one step in a wizard-like approach of multiple actions.

We were keen to improve upon inter-component communication and migrating to the commercial real-time backend Firebase turned out to be a great boon. We experimented with an approach where components accepted Firebase objects as arguments, effectively passing the component the means to read and write data to a specific database schema defined by the parent component. The language selector component was modified to read the current state and bind UI elements directly to the database.

In the following snippet, the language selector controller is adding an object specifying a language id directly to a Firebase array provided via the Firebase SDK. The 'then' syntax is a JavaScript asynchronous 'promise' pattern where the following will be evaluated when the promise to save the data is complete.

```
ctrl.selectedLanguagesFb.\$add({id: langId})
.then(function(ref) {
    chip.saved = true
})
```

Figure 4: Zahwa Procedural Discourse App prototype: Users narrate while swiping through photos

The UI "chip" saved property is set to true when the Firebase database write is complete. The saved property is used in the component template to apply a CSS class with the result that the chip colour changes to provide a visual indication that a save is complete.

The obvious issue with this component communication pattern is that it locks in a particular data system, or third-party vendor SDK in this case. Ideally a component should accept and return stand-alone data structures and leave parent components to decide how to retrieve and save such data. This was a general problem with the the current generation of MVC frameworks (Angular 1.x). We describe this pattern in the discussion of the Zahwa app to follow.

3.2.2 Key findings

Aikuma-Link's showed that, with care, web technologies could deliver a performant native app-like experience on relatively low-end phones. The link-share method of onboarding is promising and opens up a number of possibilities for crowd-sourced research. We found Firebase to be an excellent solution for rapidly prototyping mobile apps with collaborative data. Accounting for different sized displays, orientation changes and virtual on-screen keyboards is a significant challenge for mobile software development.

3.3 Zahwa: Procedural discourse

Zahwa is a *community* app (Figure 4) that has users take a series of photos and short videos from their device, then swipe through them while recording a voice-over. The app as conceived and designed with cooking recipes in mind but it is broadly applicable to documenting of any procedural discourse. Users who view the recipe, or instructions for making craft, etc, are able to interact with recipes, providing their own translation or reusing the media set for their own version.

Zahwa is a fully-featured mobile app built with web technologies (it is a progressive web app) and with robust offline capabilities. We first built a prototype out of a newer generation of our former framework but later adopted the Ionic 2 mobile framework, and with it Angular 2 and the Typescript variant of JavaScript. Migrating to this framework meant that all UI components would need to migrate from Angular Material to Ionic's native UI. Ionic offers both an iOS-like UI and Material Design (Android).

Broadly speaking, the reasons for adopting of Ionic 2 were threefold. First, Angular 2 brought substantial improvements in the methods to define components and views (pages), and inter-component communication. This virtually eliminated a slew of performance and reliability issues with Angular 1. Second, we realised that when building a full-scale mobile app, we are less interested in building common components for all mobile apps where we ought to concentrate on language documentation specific components. Finally, we found that Ionic had already demonstrated, through their user community, a realisation of our own goal to expand the base of potential app developers.

Ultimately, adopting Ionic allowed us to be more ambitious, and focus on technology components and user interfaces specific to our domain without needing to reinvent functionality that is common across mobile apps. This win turned out to be fortuitous because there was a substantial engineering challenge ahead. We had previously built offline-only and online-only apps, but had yet to combine the two, to craft a collaborative app that would use a network where available, while allowing for meaningful app usage offline.

After determining that there are no good off-the-shelf solutions, we retrofitted Zahwa with: offline storage based on PouchDB, a new service to synchronise local storage with Firebase, and a caching service to support offline behavior. These allow Zahwa to provide offline users with features to find salient recipes, e.g. geographically nearby, or use search such as languages and tags. The user can indicate that they would like to download a recipe when they have a connection. Creating new recipes and translating cached recipes can be performed offline. The work is sychronised when a

(a) Searching by Language

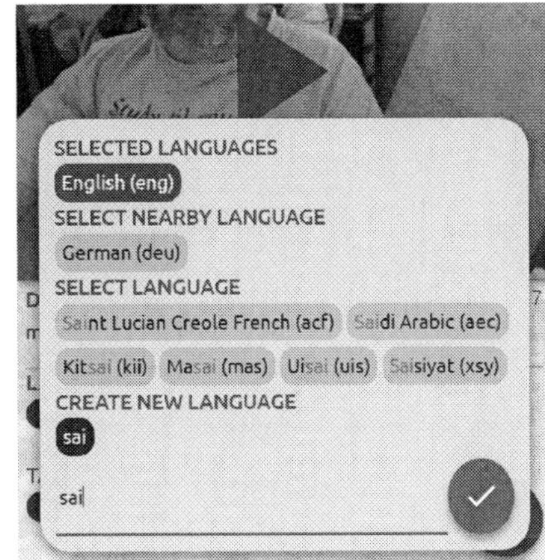

(b) Editing Languages with Popover

Figure 5: Zahwa: The language selector component used in different contexts. A simplfied in-line search mode and a more comprehensive popover mode to support the full range of the language selector's enhanced capabilities.

network reappears. Users may specify to limit this to WiFi rather than cellular data.

Zahwa has been a helpful vehicle to prototype a UI based on progressive enhancement of the data around a core activity. Given an existing recipe, community members may be motivated to translate it into another language, or record a new version of the same recipe by reusing the media. They may be motivated to tag the images of a recipe, contributing to an evolving lexicon. These enhancements may not be attractive to all users, but one could explore gamification as a way to encourage users to perform such tasks.

3.3.1 The language selector

Zahwa offers a more comprehensive demonstration of the ways in which a component may be utilised in different contexts within the same app (Figure 5). Users can discover recipes by language, even if offline, and mark the recipes for retrieval. The language selector in these cases simply presents chips to touch to select. With intelligent context, most users do not need to use the keyboard at all.

Mobile UIs should tend towards the minimal until the user has indicated they wish to engage in further detail. In Zahwa, the language selector offers a minimal list of languages but upon user interaction the component launches a pop up modal UI that is able to utilise most of the displays real-estate for the task at hand.

With there now being separate storage systems at play, child components ought now to act on pure data and let parent components load or save. Angular 2's component communication paradigm urges one-way binding for data inputs and an event-driven schema for data output as seen in this example from Zahwa:

```
<lang-edit [languages]="recipe.languages"
    (langsUpdated)="langsChanged(\$event)">
</lang-edit>
```

Zahwa's atomic components are children of activity components, usually represented as a page view. An example of an activity/page component is 'new recipe' and 'recipe edit'. Activity components create or modify higher order types, or documents, assembled or edited from child components. In the given example, the variable recipe is of type Recipe, which must have a property 'languages' of type Language. The function call langsChanged() would update the 'languages' property of the recipe document and execute a service call to persist the recipe to local and remote storage. While these were prototype services in Zahwa, this pattern corresponds well to more generalisable API calls as we'll discuss in section 5.

3.3.2 Key findings

Many of the challenges we faced over a year of development were challenges inherent in the state of web technologies, particularly MVC frameworks. Engineering software with the Ionic 2, Angular 2 and Typescript stack represents a dramatic

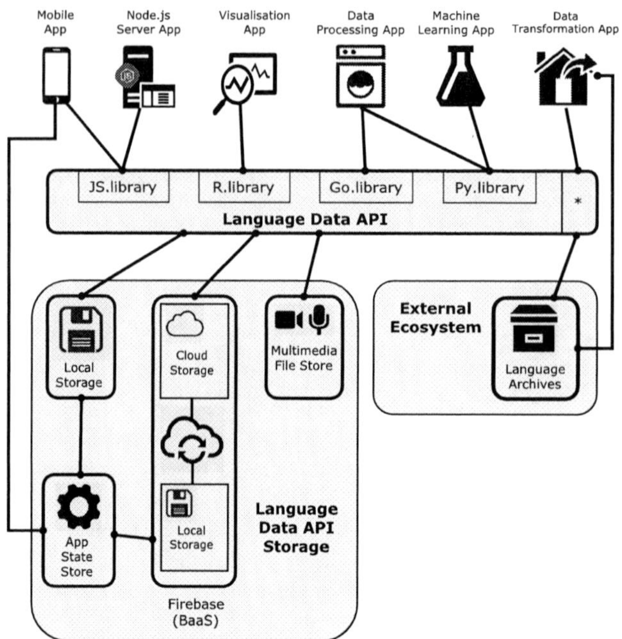

Figure 6: The ecosystem of a proposed Language Data API. Firebase is just one potential backend.

improvement at nearly every level, with fewer 'gotchas' requiring expert diagnostics. Ionic 2's definition of a 'page' as a type of component is a helpful counterpart for the notion of a language documentary *activity* combining several components toward one goal. A shift away from UI implementation details allowed us to focus on interaction design for higher level workflows.

4   A simple web component schema

We hope that the developers of language documentation technology will collaborate on a library of documentary components specific to the domain of language documentation. Adopting clean APIs on web-based components opens the door for others to modify open source apps to meet their requirements. Defining interfaces and providing a library of implementations is an effective way to build an open source community.[1] Current-generation JavaScript MVC frameworks offer a robust pattern for component communication based on attributes and event handelers passed as attributes on HTML templates. This can be demonstrated with this Angular 2 syntax example:

```
<type-select [input]="var" (output)="func($event)">
</type-select>
```

We suggest a simple selector name constructed from the name of a data type such as Language, and an implementation specific label based on the verb for the action such as 'select'. A example selector name is language-edit. [input] represents a one-way data binding from JavaScript variable 'var' of the type, e.g. Language. (output) specifies a local function to be executed when the component emits data. The function 'func' is passed an argument ($event) of schema {type: [Type...]}, e.g. a single property of the named type, with a value of an array of objects of this type. Occasionally components need to emit data other than the raw data type and those may be safely added as custom properties of the object.

With Typescript, we define a type Language as follows, noting that only 'name' is obligatory in this type:

```
export interface Language {
    name: string
    id?: string
    iso693?: string
}
```

A consequence of collaboration on shared components will be less duplication of effort, more reliable implementations, and ultimately, better user experiences and wider uptake of the software. Simultaneously, we lower the barrier to entry for would-be language app developers.

---

[1]This has been the model used in the computational linguistics community which has developed the *Natural Language Toolkit* (Bird et al., 2009).

5 Further Work

As we develop increasingly sophisticated apps, we require increasingly sophisticated manipulation of linguistic data. Supporting this in offline apps leads to a requirement for a JavaScript implementation. The API should also be implemented outside of the JavaScript ecosystem to facilitate data exchange and mobilising of data intensive capabilities into mobile applications.

Implementation of an API can be seen as an extension of defining language data types as the common interface for components as discussed earlier. We will develop the API as a JavaScript library initially, for use across mobile apps and server instances utilising NodeJS. Figure 6 illustrates the language data API in an ecosystem including research tools in other domains.

Our aim is for this API to encourage collaboration by facilitating data interchange between an array of language documentation apps for different audiences. A common API provides a gateway for other ecosystems to collect linguistic data and to mobilise existing data to new audiences via mobile devices.

6 Conclusion

In this paper, we have reported on our investigation of web technologies to craft a series of web and mobile apps in language documentation. We have shown with Aikuma-NG that it is feasible to use these technologies to migrate the well-established genre of audio transcription with waveforms to platform-independent web technologies. Aikuma-Link provides a glimpse of new capabilities arising from the low onboarding cost of mobile web apps, and the potential for a new generation of crowdsourcing applications. Finally with Zahwa, we developed a complete mobile app for a narrowly-defined linguistic task, and supported the online-offline requirement of many fieldwork situations.

Despite the inherent productivity gains of web technologies, our prototyping experience was occasionally frustrating due to the lack of maturity of some common technologies. We initially struggled to find a suitable pattern for component modularisation, data interchange and online-offline storage. However these common problems were and remain the target of significant engineering efforts by major players and the current situation is already much improved. A significant benefit of this prototyping work was reaching the point where we could collaborate with our target audience and deliver software people want to use.

There are many opportunities for collaboration in this space of app development, to unite existing initiatives and communities, and to share implementations. The work reported here has already served others as an effective starting point for quickly developing new mobile apps. For those who prefer to use other technologies, we nevertheless hope to collaborate on the design of a shared implementation-independent language data API. Our ultimate goal is to employ the web platform to connect tools outside of the web genre, improving the flow of data and the production of language documentation, while gaining rich new capabilities we have yet to explore.

Acknowledgments

We are grateful for support from the ARC Center of Excellence for the Dynamics of Language and from the National Science Foundation (NSF award 1464553).

References

Peter K Austin. 2010. Current issues in language documentation. In *Language Documentation and Description*, volume 7, pages 12–33. SOAS.

Bruce Birch, Sebastian Drude, Daan Broeder, Peter Withers, and Peter Wittenburg. 2013. Crowdsourcing and apps in the field of linguistics: Potentials and challenges of the coming technology.

Steven Bird, Ewan Klein, and Edward Loper. 2009. *Natural Language Processing with Python*. O'Reilly Media.

Steven Bird, Florian R Hanke, Oliver Adams, and Haejoong Lee. 2014. Aikuma: A mobile app for collaborative language documentation. In *Proceedings of the 2014 Workshop on the Use of Computational Methods in the Study of Endangered Languages*, pages 1–5.

Margaret Carew, Jennifer Green, Inge Kral, Rachel Nordlinger, and Ruth Singer. 2015. Getting in touch: Language and digital inclusion in australian indigenous communities. *Language Documentation and Conservation*, 9:307–23.

MaryEllen Cathcart, Gina Cook, Theresa Deering, Yuliya Manyakina, Gretchen McCulloch, and Hisako Noguchi. 2012. Lingsync: A free tool for creating and maintaining a shared database for communities, linguists and language learners. In *Proceedings of FAMLi II: workshop on Corpus Approaches to Mayan Linguistics*, pages 247–50.

Georgios Chatzimilioudis, Andreas Konstantinidis, Christos Laoudias, and Demetrios Zeinalipour-Yazti. 2012. Crowdsourcing with smartphones. *IEEE Internet Computing*, 16:36–44.

Jean-Philippe Goldman, Adrian Leemann, Marie-José Kolly, Ingrid Hove, Ibrahim Almajai, Volker Dellwo, and Steven Moran. 2014. A crowdsourcing smartphone application for Swiss German: Putting language documentation in the hands of the users. In *Proceedings of the 9th International Conference on Language Resources and Evaluation*, pages 3444–47.

John Hatton. 2013. SayMore: language documentation productivity. In *Proceedings of the 3rd International Conference on Language Documentation and Conservation*. University of Hawaii.

Adrian Leemann, Marie-José Kolly, Ross Purves, David Britain, and Elvira Glaser. 2016. Crowdsourcing language change with smartphone applications. *PloS one*, 11(1):e0143060.

Johann Poignant, Mateusz Budnik, Hervé Bredin, Claude Barras, Mickael Stefas, Pierrick Bruneau, Gilles Adda, Laurent Besacier, Hazim Ekenel, Gil Francopoulo, et al. 2016. The CAMOMILE collaborative annotation platform for multi-modal, multi-lingual and multi-media documents. In *Proceedings of the 10th International Conference on Language Resources and Evaluation*. European Language Resources Association.

Taiwan Indigenous Council. 2016. Taiwan Indigenous Council e-dictionary.

WaveSurfer. 2017. WaveSurfer.js. `https://wavesurfer-js.org`.

Jonathan Wright, Kira Griffitt, Joe Ellis, Stephanie Strassel, and Brendan Callahan. 2012. Annotation trees: Ldc's customizable, extensible, scalable, annotation infrastructure. In *Proceedings of the 8th International Conference on Language Resources and Evaluation*, pages 479–85. European Language Resources Association.

Cross-language forced alignment to assist
community-based linguistics for low resource languages

Timothy Kempton
SIL Nigeria, PO Box 953
Jos, Plateau State
Nigeria
tim_kempton@sil.org

Abstract

In community-based linguistics, community members become involved in the analysis of their own language. This insider perspective can radically increase the speed and accuracy of phonological analysis, e.g. providing rapid identification of phonemic contrasts. However, due to the nature of these community-based sessions, much of the phonetic data is left undocumented. Rather than going back to traditional fieldwork, this paper argues that corpus phonetics can be applied to recordings of the community-based analysis sessions. As a first step in this direction, cross-language forced alignment is applied to the type of data generated by a community-based session in the Nikyob language of Nigeria. The alignments are accurate and suggest that corpus phonetics could complement community-based linguistics giving community members a powerful tool to analyse their own language.

1 Background

1.1 Community-based linguistics

Fieldwork is traditionally directed by the linguist. It is the linguist who elicits data from members of a speech community. It is the linguist who phonetically transcribes a wordlist and makes an audio recording. It is the linguist who performs the analysis.

In community-based or participatory-based linguistics, members of the speech community participate in many of these stages (Czaykowska-Higgins, 2009). This includes linguistic analysis, with community members making discoveries and deepening their understanding of the patterns in their own language.

One particular approach to participatory-based phonological analysis is described by Kutsch-Lojenga (1996), Norton (2013), and Stirtz (2015). In this approach, members of the speech community write down words in their language on small cards. A trial orthography is used for the writing since the work is usually part of a language development project to help establish a writing system. The trial orthography may be no more sophisticated than a best-guess spelling using an alphabet of another language. Picking up each card, the language speaker calls out the word aloud and starts to arrange these cards into piles. The choice of pile depends on same/different judgments regarding a specific sound in the word. For example, during a session on the Nikyob[1] language of Nigeria where single syllable nouns were being investigated, the Nikyob speakers placed the words in six different piles representing six different tone patterns. Such piles represent the different contrastive categories of the phonological feature being investigated, e.g. tone might be investigated in one session, and voicing in another session.

The results of participatory-based linguistics are often presented as if they were generated purely from the language speakers' (insider) perspective. This is true most of the time. However, there is an interesting contribution from the (outsider) linguist which can be easily overlooked. Occasionally the linguist who is facilitating a session will hear a consistent difference that the language speaker does not at first notice, sometimes because the distinction is obscured by the trial orthography. For example, during the Nikyob session, speakers were so familiar with writing the five vowels of the

---

[1]The full name of the language is Nikyob-Nindem (ISO693-3 code kdp) covering two main dialects. The focus of this paper is on the dialect of of Nikyob [nĩŋkʲób]. The spelling of Nikyob has varied, both within the community and in the academic literature, due to the fact that the orthography is still developing. The Nikyob speaker recorded for this experiment is from the village of Garas.

Proceedings of the 2nd Workshop on the Use of Computational Methods in the Study of Endangered Languages, pages 165–169,
Honolulu, Hawai'i, USA, March 6–7, 2017. ©2017 Association for Computational Linguistics

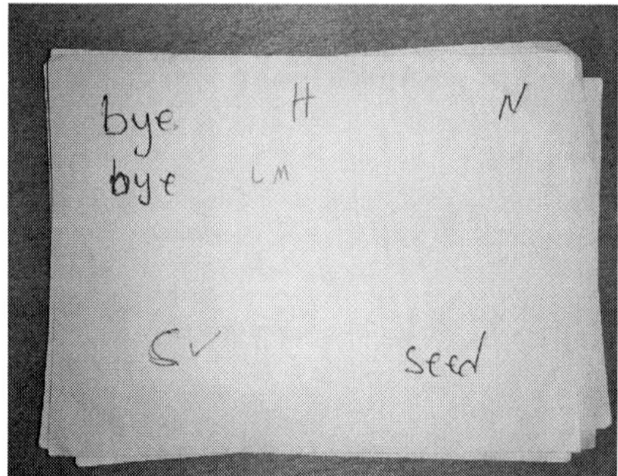

Figure 1: Card for the Nikyob word <bye> "seed"

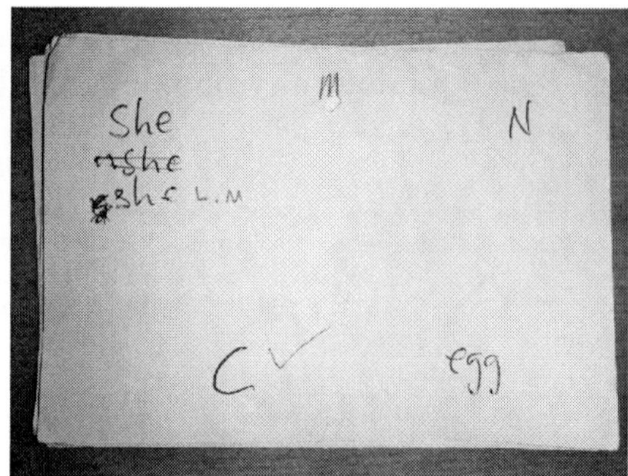

Figure 2: Card for the Nikyob word <she> "egg"

Hausa language /i,e,a,o,u/ they didn't always notice the extra vowel distinctions in Nikyob, i.e. /o/ versus /ɔ/ and /e/ versus /ɛ/. When the linguist suggested a distinction, the speakers quickly caught on and were soon able to hear their own distinction consistently. The speakers were also quick to recognise which phonological feature was being investigated, e.g. learning to focus on the vowel quality and ignoring the tone.

In these sessions, the primary contribution of the language speakers is their ability to make phonological distinctions, and the primary contribution of the linguist is her broad knowledge of phonetics and phonology. The speakers' language ability is often unconscious and the collaborative approach raises awareness of that ability. This then gradually accelerates the whole analysis process so that it is quicker than the linguist-only approach. There is also the added advantage that community members have greater motivation to continue in the language development project.

Annotations to the word cards, which are primarily a record of phonemic distinctions, form much of the documentation of these participatory sessions. This is valuable information reached by consensus by a group of speakers. However, the wealth of phonetic data generated in speaking the words is rarely recorded. This lost data limits analysis — not just analysis at the time, but particularly analysis in the future.

Figure 1 shows an example word card that the Nikyob speakers have written. First the singular form is written in the trial orthography <bye>. The "H" indicates the high tone, and "N" indicates a noun. The plural form is then given <bye> and

"LM" indicates a low tone rising to mid tone. "C" indicates that the data on the card has been entered on the computer. Finally there is the gloss: "seed". Note that the phonetic or the phonological representation ([bʲé], /bʲé/ respectively) is not used directly by the Nikyob speakers. Another example word card is shown in Figure 2 for a mid tone word.

1.2 Corpus phonetics

During the development of community-based linguistics in the area of fieldwork, there has been a separate interesting development in the area of phonetics. This is the rise of "corpus phonetics" which involves the "large-scale quantitative analysis of acoustic corpus data" (Yao et al., 2010). In a similar way that corpus linguistics has provided new insights into large collections of texts and transcriptions, corpus phonetics is providing new insights on large sets of acoustic data (Chodroff et al., 2015).

Much of this large-scale analysis is made possible with speech recognition technology and one of the fundamental tools is forced alignment — to automatically align phone transcripts with acoustic data.

2 A first step in combining these two approaches

Combining the participatory-based approach with corpus phonetics should be a fruitful method for analysing and documenting a phonology of the language. For example, corpus phonetics could help describe the phonetic character of the phonemic distinctions suggested from the participatory-based sessions and in turn suggest possible distinctions that may have been missed.

The work described in this paper takes the first step towards combining these two approaches. A fundamental tool of corpus phonetics, forced alignment, is evaluated to see if it can be successfully applied to the type of data generated by the participatory approach.

One characteristic of the data is that it is not adequate to train a forced alignment system. This is because the language has few resources, i.e. no labelled data or a pronunciation dictionary. However, it is still possible to use a forced alignment system trained on a different language. Having its roots in cross-language speech recognition (Schultz and Waibel, 1998), this is called cross-language forced alignment (Kempton et al., 2011), or untrained alignment (DiCanio et al., 2013).

Other characteristics of the data generated by the participatory approach include the lower quality of recording with background noise present and the transcription in a trial orthography.

3   Experimental set-up

An initial pilot corpus was elicited to simulate the data from a participatory-based session, a Swadesh 100 list in the Nikyob language. Each item elicited included an isolated word and the word in a frame sentence. The recording was made in the same room that would be used in a participatory-based session which was a slightly reverberant environment and no special effort was made to mask background noise.

Transcriptions in a trial orthography were taken primarily from a participatory-based tone workshop held in 2015. The trial orthography at the time was adapted from previous work by Kadima (1989), and corresponded with a tentative phoneme inventory derived from Blench (2005).

The cross-language forced alignment system uses a phone recogniser with a 21.5% phone error rate on the TIMIT corpus, so it is still fairly close to state-of-the-art (Schwarz, 2009, p46; Lopes and Perdigao, 2011). The artificial neural network uses a 310 ms window so it is implicitly context dependent (Schwarz, 2009, p39). The neural network produces phone posterior probabilities which are fed into a Viterbi decoder. This means that the system can easily be configured for forced alignment.

Phone set	BFEPP
Czech	0.27
Hungarian	0.49
Russian	0.62

Table 1: Expressing the Nikyob phoneme inventory: phonetic distance

Metric	Value
20 ms error	34%
Mean error	25 ms
Median error	15 ms

Table 2: Cross-language forced alignment on Nikyob Swadesh 100 list

Freely available phone recognisers trained on Czech, Hungarian and Russian were used (Schwarz et al., 2009). A phonetic distance measure, binary feature edits per phone (BFEPP) (Kempton, 2012), was used to predict which phone recogniser would be most suitable for the Nikyob language, and the same phonetic distance measure was used to automatically map the letter labels (reflecting the tentative phoneme inventory) from the Nikyob language to the phone recogniser. For example, the Nikyob <sh> letter represents the Nikyob /ʃ/ phoneme which can be automatically mapped to the Czech /ʃ/ phone recogniser. The Nikyob <w> letter represents the Nikyob /w/ phoneme. However, there is no Czech /w/ phone recogniser so the letter is automatically mapped to the closest recogniser which is the Czech /u/ phone recogniser.

The accuracy of the alignment was evaluated by comparing the boundary timings of the forced aligned labels with gold standard alignments. Gold standard alignments were created by a phonetician for the first 50 words of the Swadesh 100 list along with their frame sentences producing approximately 750 gold standard boundary alignments. The evaluation measure used in forced alignment is the proportion of alignments outside a particular threshold: 20 ms is a common choice. Some recent studies have used mean and median of the absolute timing error instead. In this paper all three evaluation measures are reported.

4   Results

Table 1 shows how close the phone sets of the different phone recognisers were able to express

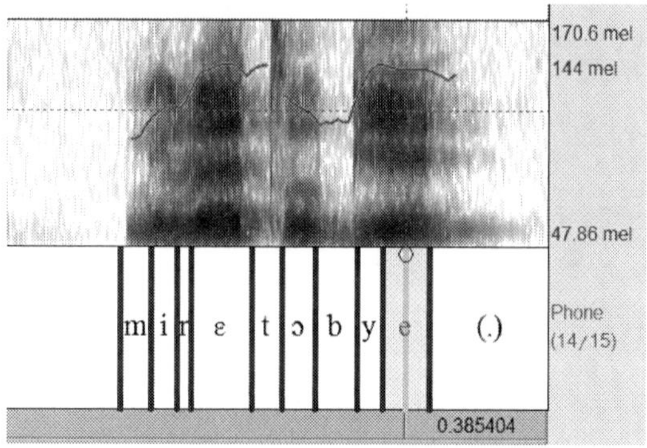
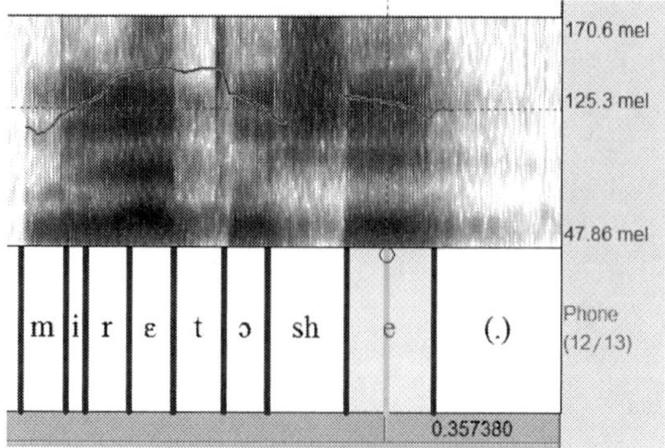

Figure 3: Forced alignment of high tone word <bye> "seed" with its frame sentence displayed in Praat

Figure 4: Forced alignment of mid tone word <she> "egg" with its frame sentence displayed in Praat

the Nikyob phoneme inventory. The phone set of the Czech recogniser was closest to the Nikyob phone inventory. So this recogniser was used in the forced alignment of Nikyob.

Results for the first 50 words in the Swadesh 100 list are shown in Table 2. These are the primary results of this paper.

Figure 3 shows an example forced alignment displayed in Praat (Boersma and Weenink, 2014). At the top there is a spectrogram with a pitch tracker and at the bottom there is the alignment of letter labels. Only the second half of the recording is shown where the word is included in the frame sentence: <mi rɛ tɔ bye>, /mī ɾɛ̃ tɔ̄ bʲé/, "I say seed". Another forced alignment example is shown in Figure 4.

5 Discussion

The results in Table 2 are encouraging when compared to previous studies on cross-language forced alignment. Previous 20 ms threshold results include a 39% error on isolated words (DiCanio et al., 2013), a 36% error on simple sentences (Kempton et al., 2011), and a 51% error on conversational speech (Kurtic et al., 2012). In a slightly different evaluation of word alignments within long utterances (Strunk et al., 2014), the error averaged across eight corpora revealed a mean error of 187 ms and a median error of 65 ms. There was also a measure of how much disagreement there was between human transcribers. The mean transcriber disagreement was 86 ms and the median transcriber disagreement was 34 ms.

These earlier studies have put forth the argument that such alignments are accurate enough to be usable, either as they are or with a small number of boundaries corrected. In the participatory-based linguistics scenario, there are many repetitions of words recorded and the subsequent aggregation of acoustic measurements would suggest that manual correction to the boundaries would be unnecessary.

The particular alignments reported in this paper are being used to assist with a tone analysis of the Nikyob language. For example, it is a straightforward mechanical process to extract pitch contours from the alignment shown in Figure 3 revealing that the high tone word <bye> "seed" has a pitch contour about 20 mels higher than the known mid tone in the frame sentence. Figure 4 shows that the mid tone word <she> "egg" has a pitch contour much closer to the known mid tone with a difference of about 1 mel. Forced alignment allows many such measurements to be taken. Figure 1 shows the word card for <bye> "seed" is actually part of a pile of word cards that have been judged by Nikyob speakers as high tone words. In the same way, Figure 2 shows a pile of mid tone words. Aggregated acoustic measurements can indicate the extent of phonetic differences within these piles and between these piles, i.e. the phonetic character of these phonemic distinctions can be documented.

Inspecting all the 50 forced aligned utterances indicates that about 8% of the utterances contain alignment errors that would produce erroneous pitch contour measurements. It seems unlikely that this would cause problems in the analysis but further investigation would be needed to confirm this.

6 Conclusion and future work

The results of this paper indicate that cross-language forced alignment can be applied to the data produced in a participatory-based session. With this promising first step, the prospect of combining participatory-based linguistics and corpus phonetics looks viable.

One could imagine a future scenario where the piles of paper cards are simulated on a touchscreen tablet, and as participants select words and speak them, the computer associates a set of recordings with each transcribed word. Phonemic distinctions could be easily tracked along with acoustic data. This would give speech communities a powerful tool to help them discover the phonology of their language.

Acknowledgments

I am grateful to Dushe Haruna who was recorded speaking the Nikyob words and Laura Critoph who produced the gold standard alignments. I appreciate the feedback from Gary Simons, Linda Simons and Matthew Harley on an earlier draft of this paper. This work is partially funded by the SIL International Pike Scholars Program.

References

Roger Blench. 2005. The Ninkyop language of central Nigeria and its affinities (Draft).

Paul Boersma and David Weenink. 2014. Praat: doing phonetics by computer. *Version 5.3.77* [Software].

Eleanor Chodroff, John Godfrey, Sanjeev Khudanpur, and Colin Wilson. 2015. Structured variability in acoustic realization: A corpus study of voice onset time in American English stops. *The Scottish Consortium for ICPhS*.

Ewa Czaykowska-Higgins. 2009. Research models, community engagement, and linguistic fieldwork: Reflections on working within Canadian indigenous communities. *Language Documentation & Conservation* 3(1).

Christian DiCanio, Hosung Nam, Douglas H Whalen, H Timothy Bunnell, Jonathan D Amith, and Rey Castillo García. 2013. Using automatic alignment to analyze endangered language data: Testing the viability of untrained alignment. *The Journal of the Acoustical Society of America* 134(3):2235–2246.

Hauwa Kadima. 1989. iByan Rwɛ wa Ninkyob 1 (a first alphabet of the Ninkyob language). Kadima.

Timothy Kempton. 2012. *Machine-assisted phonemic analysis*. Ph.D. thesis, University of Sheffield.

Timothy Kempton, Roger K. Moore, and Thomas Hain. 2011. Cross-language phone recognition when the target language phoneme inventory is not known. *Proc. Interspeech, Florence, Italy* .

Emina Kurtic, Bill Wells, Guy J. Brown, Timothy Kempton, and Ahmet Aker. 2012. A Corpus of Spontaneous Multi-party Conversation in Bosnian Serbo-Croatian and British English. *International Conference on Language Resources and Evaluation, Istanbul, Turkey* .

Constance Kutsch-Lojenga. 1996. Participatory research in linguistics. *Notes on Linguistics* (73):13–27.

Carla Lopes and Fernando Perdigao. 2011. Phone recognition on the TIMIT database. *Speech Technologies/Book* 1:285–302.

Russell Norton. 2013. The Acheron vowel system: A participatory approach. *Nuba Mountain Language Studies. Cologne: Rüdiger Köppe* pages 195–217.

Tanja Schultz and Alexander Waibel. 1998. Multilingual and Crosslingual Speech Recognition. *Proc. DARPA Workshop on Broadcast News Transcription and Understanding* pages 259–262.

Petr Schwarz. 2009. *Phoneme recognition based on long temporal context*. Ph.D. thesis, Brno University of Technology.

Petr Schwarz, Pavel Matějka, Lukáš Burget, and Ondřej Glembek. 2009. Phoneme recognition based on long temporal context. *phnrec v2.21* [Software].

Timothy M Stirtz. 2015. Rapid grammar collection as an approach to language development. *SIL Electronic Working Papers* (2015-004).

Jan Strunk, Florian Schiel, Frank Seifart, et al. 2014. Untrained forced alignment of transcriptions and audio for language documentation corpora using WebMAUS .

Yao Yao, Sam Tilsen, Ronald L Sprouse, and Keith Johnson. 2010. Automated measurement of vowel formants in the Buckeye corpus. *UC Berkeley Phonology Lab Annual Reports* .

A case study on using speech-to-translation alignments for language documentation

Antonios Anastasopoulos
University of Notre Dame
aanastas@nd.edu

David Chiang
University of Notre Dame
dchiang@nd.edu

Abstract

For many low-resource or endangered languages, spoken language resources are more likely to be annotated with translations than with transcriptions. Recent work exploits such annotations to produce speech-to-translation alignments, without access to any text transcriptions. We investigate whether providing such information can aid in producing better (mismatched) crowdsourced transcriptions, which in turn could be valuable for training speech recognition systems, and show that they can indeed be beneficial through a small-scale case study as a proof-of-concept. We also present a simple phonetically aware string averaging technique that produces transcriptions of higher quality.

1 Introduction

For many low-resource and endangered languages, speech data is easier to obtain than textual data. The traditional method for documenting a language involves a trained linguist collecting speech and then transcribing it, often at a phonetic level, as most of these languages do not have a writing system. This, however, is a costly and slow process, as it could take up to 1 hour for a trained linguist to transcribe the phonemes of 1 minute of speech (Thi-Ngoc-Diep Do and Castelli, 2014).

Therefore, speech is more likely to be annotated with translations than with transcriptions. This translated speech is a potentially valuable source of information as it will make the collected corpus interpretable for future studies. New technologies are being developed to facilitate collection of translations (Bird et al., 2014), and there already exist recent examples of parallel speech collection efforts focused on endangered languages (Blachon et al., 2016; Adda et al., 2016).

Recent work relies on parallel speech in order to create speech-to-translation alignments (Anastasopoulos et al., 2016), discover spoken terms (Bansal et al., 2017; Godard et al., 2016), learn a lexicon and translation model (Adams et al., 2016), or directly translate speech (Duong et al., 2016; Bérard et al., 2016). Another line of work (Das et al., 2016; Jyothi and Hasegawa-Johnson, 2015; Liu et al., 2016) focuses on training speech recognition systems for low-resource settings using mismatched crowdsoursed transcriptions. These are transcriptions that include some level of noise, as they are crowdsourced from workers unfamiliar with the language being spoken.

We aim to explore whether the quality of crowdsourced transcriptions could benefit from providing transcribers with speech-to-translation word-level alignments. That way, speech recognition systems trained on the higher-quality probabilistic transcriptions (of at least a sample of the collected data) could be used as part of the pipeline to document an endangered language.

2 Methodology

As a proof-of-concept, we work on the language pair Griko-Italian, for which there exists a sentence-aligned parallel corpus of source-language speech and target-language text (Lekakou et al., 2013). Griko is an endangered minority language spoken in the south of Italy. Using the method of Anastasopoulos et al. (2016), we also obtain speech-to-translation word-level alignments.

The corpus that we work on already provides gold-standard transcriptions and speech-to-translation alignments, so it is suitable for conducting a case study that will examine the potential effect of providing the alignments on the crowdsourced transcriptions, as we will be able to compare directly against the gold standard.

Proceedings of the 2nd Workshop on the Use of Computational Methods in the Study of Endangered Languages, pages 170–178,
Honolulu, Hawai'i, USA, March 6–7, 2017. ©2017 Association for Computational Linguistics

We randomly sampled 30 utterances from the corpus and collected transcriptions through a simple online interface (described at §3) from 12 different participants. None of the participants spoke or had any familiarity with Griko or its directly related language, Greek. Six of the participants were native speakers of Italian, the language in which the translations are provided. Three of them did not speak Italian, but were native Spanish speakers, and the last 3 were native English speakers who also did not speak Italian but had some level of familiarity with Spanish.

The 30 utterances amount to 1.5 minutes of speech, which would potentially require 1.5 hours of a trained linguist's work to phonetically transcribe. The gold Griko transcriptions include 191 Griko tokens, with 108 types. Their average length is 6.5 words, with the shortest being 2 words and the longest being 14 words.

The utterances were presented to the participants in three different modes:

1. `no` mode: Only providing the translation text.

2. `auto` mode: Providing the translation text and the potentially noisy speech-to-translation alignments produced by the method of Anastasopoulos et al. (2016).

3. `gold` mode: Providing the translation text and the gold-standard speech-to-translation alignments.

The utterances were presented to the participants in the exact same order, but in different modes following a scheme according to the utterance id (1 to 30) and the participant id (1 to 12). The first utterance was transcribed by the first participant under `no` mode, by the second participant under `auto` mode, the third participant under `gold` mode, the fourth participant under `no` mode, etc. The second utterance was presented to the first participant under `auto` mode, to the second participant under `gold` mode, to the third participant under `no` mode, etc.

This rotation scheme ensured that the utterances were effectively split into 3 subsets, each of which was transcribed exactly 4 times in each mode, with 2 of them by an Italian speaker, 1 time by a Spanish speaker, and 1 time by an English speaker. This enables a direct comparison of the three modes, and, hopefully, an explanation of the effect of providing the alignments. The modes under which each participant had to transcribe the utterances changed from one utterance to another, in order to minimize the potential effect of the participants' learning of the task and the language better.

The participants were asked to produce a transcription of the given speech segment, using the Latin alphabet and any pronunciation conventions they wanted. The result in almost all cases is entirely comprised of nonsense syllables. It is safe to assume, though, that the participants would use the pronunciation conventions of their native language; for example, an Italian or Spanish speaker would transcribe the sounds [mu] as `mu`, whereas an English native speaker would probably transcribe it as `moo`.

3   Interface

A simple tool for collecting transcriptions first needs to provide the user with the audio to be transcribed. The translation of the spoken utterance is provided, as in Figure 1, where in our case the speech to be transcribed was in Griko, and a translation of this segment was provided in Italian. In a real scenario, this translation would correspond to the output of a Speech Recognition system for the parallel speech, so it could potentially be somewhat noisy. Though, for the purposes of our case study, we used the gold standard translations of the utterances.

Our interface also provides speech-to-translation alignment information as shown in Figure 2. Each word in the translation has been aligned to some part of the spoken utterance. Apart from listening to the whole utterance at once, the user can also click on the individual translation words and listen to the corresponding speech segment.

For the purposes of our case study, our tool collected additional information about its usage. It logged the amount of time each participant spent transcribing each utterance, as well as the amount of times that they clicked the respective buttons in order to listen to either the whole utterance or word-aligned speech segments.

4   Results

The orthography of Griko is phonetic, and therefore it is easy, using simple rules, to produce the phonetic sequences in IPA that correspond to the transcriptions. We can also use standard rules for

Figure 1: Interface that only provides the translation `non deve mangiare la sera` *[he/she shouldn't eat at night]*, with no alignment information.

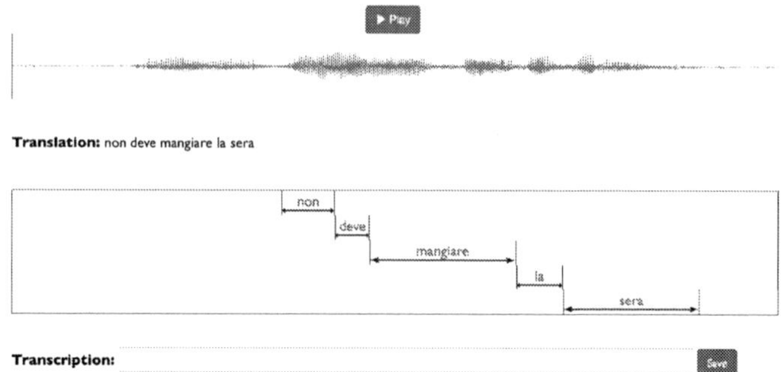

Figure 2: Interface that provides the translation `non deve mangiare la sera` *[he/she shouldn't eat at night]*, along with speech-to-translation alignment information. Clicking on a translation word would play the corresponding aligned part of the speech segment.

Spanish (LDC96S35) and Italian,[1] depending on the native language of the participants, in order to produce phonetic sequences of the crowdsourced transcriptions in IPA.

For simplicity reasons, we merge the vowel oppositions /e∼ɛ/ and /o∼ɔ/ into just /e/ and /o/ for both the Italian and Griko phonetic transcriptions, as neither of the two languages makes an orthographic distinction between the two.

For the transcriptions created by the English-speaking participants, and since most of the word-like units of the transcriptions do not exist in any English pronunciations lexicon, we use the LO-GIOS Lexicon Tool (SpeechLab, 2007) that uses some simple letter-to-sound rules to produce a phonetic transcription in the ARPAbet symbol set. We map several of the English vowel oppositions to a single IPA vowel; for example, IH and IY both become /i/, while UH and UW become /u/. Phonemes AY, EY, and OY become /ai/, /ei/, and /oi/ respectively. This enables a direct comparison of all the transcriptions, although it might add extra noise, especially in the case of transcriptions produced by English-speaking participants.

Two examples of the resulting phonetic transcriptions as produced by the participants' transcriptions can be found in Tables 1 and 2.

On our analysis of the results, we first focus on the results obtained by the 6 Italian-speaking participants of our study, which represent the more realistic crowdsourcing scenario where the workers speak the language of the translations. We then present the results of the non-Italian speaking participants. In order to evaluate the transcriptions, we report the Levenshtein distance as well as the average Phone Error Rate (PER)[2] against the correct transcriptions.

4.1 Italian-speaking participants

Transcription quality As a first test, we compare the Levenshtein distances of the produced transcriptions to the gold ones. For fairness, we remove the accents from the gold Griko transcriptions, as well as any accents added by the Italian speaking participants.

The results averaged per utterance set and per mode are shown in Table 3. We first note that

---

[1]Creating the rules based on (Comrie, 2009)

[2]The Phone Error Rate is basically length-normalized Levenshtein distance.

participant	acoustic transcription	distance
it1	bau tʃerkianta ena furno e tranni e rustiku	9
it2	pau tʃerkianta ena furna kanni e rustiku	7
it3	pau tʃerkianta na furno kakanni rustiko	5
it4	po ʃerkieunta na furna ka kanni rustiku	6
it5	pau tʃerkeunta en furno ganni rustiku	6
it6	pa u tʃerkionta en na furno kahanni rustiko	5
es1	pogurʃe kiunta en a furna e kakani e rustiku	12
es2	pao ʃerkeonta ena furna ka kani rustigo	5
es3	bao tʃerke on ta e na furno e kagani e rustiko	6
en1	paoje kallonta e un forno e grane e rustiko	15
en2	pao tʃerkeota eno furno e kakarni e rustiku	5
en3	pouʃa kianta e a forno e tagani e rustiku	14
average	pao tʃerkionta ena furno kaanni e rustiku	3
correct	pao tʃerkeonta ena furno ka kanni rustiku	

Table 2: Transcriptions for the utterance pào cerkèonta èna fùrno ka kànni rùstiku *[I'm looking for a bakery that makes rustic (bread)]* and their Levenshtein distance to the gold transcription.

the three utterance sets are not equally hard: the first one is the hardest, with the second one being the easiest one to transcribe, as it included slightly shorter sentences. However, in most cases, as well as in the average case (last row of Table 3) providing the alignments improves the transcription quality. In addition, the gold standard alignments provide more accurate information that is also reflected in higher quality transcriptions.

We also evaluate the precision and recall of the word boundaries (spaces) that the transcriptions denote. We count a discovered word boundary as a correct one only if the word boundary in the transcription is matched with a boundary marker in the gold transcription, when we compute the Levenshtein distance.

Under no mode (without alignments), the transcribers achieve 58% recall and 70% precision on correct word boundaries. However, when provided with alignments, they achieve 66% recall and 77% precision; in fact, when provided with gold alignments (under gold mode) recall increases to 70% and precision to 81%. Therefore, the speech-to-translation alignments seem to provide information that helped the transcribers to better identify word boundaries, which is arguably hard to achieve from just continuous speech.

Phonetic transcription quality We observe the same pattern when evaluating using the average PER of these phonetic sequences, as reported in Table 4: the acoustic transcriptions are generally better when alignments are provided. Also, the gold alignments provide more accurate information, resulting in higher quality transcriptions. However, even using the noisy alignments leads to better transcriptions in most cases.

It is worth noting that out of the 30 utterances, only 4 included words that are shared between Italian and Griko (ancora *[yet]*, ladro *[thief]*, giornale *[newspaper]*, and subito *[immediately]*) and only 2 of them included common proper names (Valeria and Anna). The effect of having those common words, therefore, is minimal.

4.2 Non-Italian speaking participants

The scenario where the crowdsourcers do not even speak the language of the translations is possibly too extreme. It still could be applicable, though, in the case where the language of the translations is not endangered by still low-resource (Tok Pisin, for example) and it's hard to find annotators that speak the language. In any case, we show that if the participants speak a language related to the translations (and with a similar phonetic inventory, like Spanish in our case) they can still produce decent transcriptions.

Table 5 shows the average on the performance of the different groups of participants. As ex-

	transcription	distance
it1	o ladro isodzeem biabiddu	5
it2	o ladro isodʒenti dabol tu	6
it3	o ladro i so ndze mia buttu	5
it4	o ladro isodzeembia po tu	2
it5	o ladroi isodʒe enbi a buttu	4
it6	o ladro idʒo dzembia a buttu	7
es1	o la vro ipsa ziem biabotu	9
es2	ola avro isonse embia butu	7
es3	o ladro isosen be abuto	9
en1	o labro ebzozaim bellato	13
en2	o laha dro iso dzenne da to	12
en3	o ladro i dzo ze en habito	11
average	o ladro isodʒe mbia buttu	3
correct	o ladro isodʒe embi apo ttu	

Table 1: Transcriptions for the utterance o làdro ìsoze èmbi apo-ttù *[the thief must have entered from here]* and their Levenshtein distance to the gold transcription. The word ladro *[thief]* is the same in both Griko and Italian.

pected, the Italian-speaking participants produced higher quality transcriptions, but the Spanish-speaking participants did not perform much worse. Also in the case of non-Italian speaking participants, we found that providing speech-to-translation alignments (under auto and gold modes) improves the quality of the transcriptions, as we observed a similar trend as the ones shown in Tables 3 and 4.

The noise in the non-Italian speaker annotations, and especially the ones produced by English speakers, can be explained in two ways. One, it could be caused by annotation scheme employed by the English speakers, which must be more complicated and noisy, as English does not have a concrete letter-to-sound system. Or two, it could be explained by the fact that English is much more typologically distant from Griko, meaning, possibly, that some of the sounds in Griko just weren't accessible to English speakers. The latter effect could indeed be real, as it has been shown that a language's phonotactics can affect what sounds a speaker is actually able to perceive (Peperkamp et al., 1999; Dupoux et al., 2008). The perceptual "illusions" created by one's language can be quite difficult to overcome.

utterance set	Levenshtein distance			all modes
	no	auto	gold	
set 1	14.1	13.5	13.9	13.8
set 2	10.0	10.6	8.7	9.8
set 3	11.8	10.1	10.5	10.8
average	12.0	11.4	11.0	11.5

Table 3: Breakdown of the quality of the transcriptions per utterance set. The value in each cell corresponds to the average Levenshtein distance to the gold transcriptions. Despite the differences in how "hard" each set is, the transcription quality generally improves when alignments are provided, as shown by the average in the last row.

utterance set	PER			all modes
	no	auto	gold	
set 1	23.0	25.1	23.8	24.0
set 2	25.8	26.0	23.3	25.0
set 3	32.1	26.0	24.5	28.1
avg	27.0	25.7	24.5	25.7

Table 4: Phone Error Rate (PER) of the phonetic transcriptions produced by the Italian-speaking participants per utterance set. In the general case, the quality improves when alignments are provided, as shown by the averages in the last row.

participants	PER
Italian	25.7
Spanish	28.3
English	34.3
all	28.5
best	22.8
worst	37.0

Table 5: Breakdown of the quality of the transcriptions per participant group. As expected, the group of participants that speak the language closest to the target language (Italian) produces better transcriptions.

4.3 Overall discussion

From the results, it is clear that the acoustic transcriptions are generally better when collected with the alignments provided. Also, the gold alignments provide more accurate information, resulting in higher quality transcriptions. However, even using the noisy alignments leads to better transcriptions in most cases.

One simple explanation for this finding is that our interface changes when we provide alignments, giving the participants an easier way to listen to much shorter segments of the speech utterance. Therefore, our observations of improved transcriptions might not be caused because of the alignments, but because of the change in the interface. This can be tested by comparing results obtained by two interfaces, one that is similar to ours, providing the alignments, and one that also provides the option to play shorter segments of the speech utterance, randomly selected. We leave however this test to be performed in a future study.

The results in Tables 3 and 4 are indicative of how, on average, we can collect better transcriptions by providing speech-to-translation alignments. However, we could obtain a better understanding by comparing the transcription modes on each individual utterance level.

For each utterance we have in total 12 transcriptions, 4 for each mode. We therefore have 48 possible combinations of pairs of transcriptions of the same utterance that were performed under a different mode. This means that we can have $48 \times 30 = 1440$ pairwise comparisons in total (so that the pairs include only transcriptions of the same utterance). In the overwhelming majority of these comparisons (73%) the transcriptions obtained with alignments provided, were better than the ones obtained without them.

In addition, for the about 380 pairs where the transcription obtained without alignments is better than the one obtained with alignments, the majority corresponds to pairs that include a combination of an Italian speaking participant (without alignments) and a Spanish or English speaking participant (with alignments). For example, the very meticulous participant it4 (who in fact achieves the shortest distance to the gold transcriptions) provides in several cases better transcriptions than almost all English and Spanish speaking participants, even without access to speech-to-translation alignments.

Time It took about 36 minutes on average for the 12 participants to complete the study (shortest was 20 minutes, longest was 64 minutes). This is less time than what trained linguists typically require (Thi-Ngoc-Diep Do and Castelli, 2014), at the expense, naturally, of much higher error rates.

At an utterance level, we find that providing the participants with the alignment information does not impact the time required to create the transcription. When provided with alignments, the participants listened to the whole utterance about 30% fewer times; instead, they chose to click on and play alignment segments almost as many times as opting to listen to the whole utterance. There was only one participant who rarely chose to play the alignment segment, and in fact the average quality of their transcriptions does not differ across the different modes.

5 Averaging the acoustic transcriptions

A fairly simple way to merge several transcriptions into one, is to obtain first alignments between the set of strings to be averaged by treating each substitution, insertion, deletion, or match, as an alignment. Then, we can leverage the alignments in order to create an "average" string, through an averaging scheme.

We propose a method that can be roughly described as similar to using Dynamic Time Warping (DTW) (Berndt and Clifford, 1994) for obtaining alignments between two speech signals, and using DTW Barycenter Averaging (DBA) (Petitjean et al., 2011) for approximating the average of a set of sequences. Instead of time series or speech utterances, however, we apply these methods on sequences of phone embeddings.

We map each IPA phone into a feature embedding, with boolean features corresponding to linguistic features.[3] Then, each acoustic transcription can be represented as a sequence of vectors, and we can use DBA in order to obtain an "average" sequence, out of a set of sequences. This "average" sequence can be then mapped back to phones, by mapping each vector to the phone that has the closest phone embedding in our space.

The standard method, ROVER (Fiscus, 1997), uses an alignment module and then majority voting to produce a probabilistic final transcription. The string averaging method that we propose here is quite similar, with the exception that our alignment method and the averaging method are tied together through the iterative procedure of DBA. Another difference is that our method operates on phone embeddings, instead of directly on phones. That way, it is more phonologically informed, so that the distance between two phones that are often confused because they have similar characteristics, such as /p/ and /b/, is smaller than the distance between a pair of more distant phones such as eg. /p/ and /a/. In addition, the averaging scheme that we employ actually produces an average of the aligned phone embeddings, which in theory could result in a different output compared to simple majority voting. A more thorough comparison of ROVER and our averaging method is beyond the scope of this paper and is left as future work.

Using this simple string averaging method we combine the mismatched transcriptions into an "average" one. We can then compute the Levenshtein distance and PER between the "average" and the gold transcription in order to evaluate them. Examples of "average" transcriptions are also shown in Tables 1 and 2. In almost all cases the "average" transcription is closer to the gold one than each of the individual transcriptions. Table 6 provides a more detailed analysis of the quality of the "average" transcriptions per mode and per group of participants.

We first use the transcriptions as produced by all participants, and report the errors of the averaged outputs under all modes. Again, the transcriptions that were produced with alignments

provided, when averaged, have lower error rates. However, the `gold` mode corresponds to an ideal scenario, which will hardly ever occur. Thus, we focus more on the combination of the `no` and `auto` modes, which will very likely occur in our collection efforts, as the alignments we will produce will be noisy, or we might only have translations without alignments. We also limit the input to only include the transcriptions produced by the Italian and Spanish speaking participants, as we found that the transcriptions produced by English speaking participants added more noise instead of helping. As the results in Table 6 show, using our averaging method we obtain better transcriptions on average, even if we limit ourselves to the more realistic scenario of not having `gold` alignments. The best result with an average PER of 23.2 is achieved using all the transcriptions produced by Italian and Spanish speaking participants. Even without using gold alignments, however, the averaging method produces transcriptions that achieve an average PER of 24.0, which is a clear improvement over the average PER of the individual transcriptions (25.7).

The reason that the "average" transcription is better than the transcriptions used to create it is intuitive. Although all the transcriptions include some level of noise, not all of the transcribers make the same errors. Averaging the produced transcriptions together helps overcome most of the errors, simply because the majority of the participants does not make each individual error. This is, besides, the intuition behind the previous work on using mismatched crowdsourced transcriptions. In addition, one of the bases of the Aikuma approach (Bird, 2010) to language documentation is re-speaking of the original text. Our averaging method could potentially also be applied to transcriptions obtained from these re-spoken utterances, further improving the quality of the transcriptions.

6 Conclusion

Through a small case-study, we show that crowdsourced transcriptions improve if the transcribers are provided with speech-to-translation alignment information, even if the alignments are noisy. Furthermore, we confirm the somewhat intuitive concept that workers familiar with languages closest to the language they are transcribing (at least phonologically) produce better transcriptions.

---

[3]The features were taken from the inventories of `http://phoible.org/`

transcriptions used to create average		avg. distance to gold	
mode	participants' native language	Lev/tein	PER
no	all	8.41	27.0
auto	all	7.82	25.9
gold	all	7.58	24.3
all	Ita+Spa	**7.21**	**23.2**
gold	Ita+Spa	7.55	23.6
no+auto	Ita+Spa	7.62	24.0

Table 6: Average Levenshtein distance and PER of the "average" transcriptions obtained with our string averaging method for different subsets of the crowdsourced transcriptions. The "average" transcriptions have higher quality than the original ones, especially when obtained from transcriptions of participants familiar with languages close to the target language. Providing alignments also improves the resulting "average" transcription.

The combination of the mismatched transcriptions into one, using a simple string averaging method, yields even higher quality transcriptions, which could be used as training data for a speech recognition system for the endangered language. In the future, we plan to investigate the use of ROVER for obtaining a probabilistic transcription for the utterance, as well as explore ways to expand our phonologically aware string averaging method so as to produce probabilistic transcriptions, and compare the outputs of the two methods.

We plan to consolidate our findings by conducting case studies at a larger scale (collecting transcriptions through Amazon Turk) and for other language pairs. A larger collection of mismatched transcriptions would also enable us to build speech recognition systems and study how beneficial the improved transcriptions are for the speech recognition task.

This work falls within an envisioned pipeline where we first align speech to translations, then crowdsource transcriptions, and last we train an ASR system for the endangered language. However, this is not the only approach we are considering. Another approach could replace crowdsourcing with multiple automatic phone recognizers (or even a "universal" one) that would output candidate phonetic sequences, which we would then use to train an ASR system. Our main aim is to start a discussion about whether any additional information like the translations or the speech-to-translation alignments contain information that would help a human to interpret an endangered language, and how they could be used alongside the collected parallel speech for documentation efforts.

We are also interested on how the annotation interfaces could be better designed, in order to facilitate faster and more accurate documentation of endangered languages. For example, our proposed interface, instead of just providing the alignments for each translation word, could also supply the transcriber with additional information, such as other utterance examples that this word has been aligned to. Or we could even attempt to suggest a candidate transcription, based on previous transcriptions that the transcriber (or others) have produced. This could potentially further improve the quality of the transcriptions, as providing several examples should improve consistency. Expanding our interface, so as to provide such additional information to the transcriber, is also part of our plans for future larger scale case studies.

References

Oliver Adams, Graham Neubig, Trevor Cohn, Steven Bird, Quoc Truong Do, and Satoshi Nakamura. 2016. Learning a lexicon and translation model from phoneme lattices. In *Proc. EMNLP*, pages 2377–2382.

Gilles Adda, Sebastian Stüker, Martine Adda-Decker, Odette Ambouroue, Laurent Besacier, David Blachon, Hélène Bonneau-Maynard, Pierre Godard, Fatima Hamlaoui, Dmitry Idiatov, et al. 2016. Breaking the unwritten language barrier: The BULB project. *Procedia Computer Science*, 81:8–14.

Antonios Anastasopoulos, David Chiang, and Long Duong. 2016. An unsupervised probability model for speech-to-translation alignment of low-resource languages. In *Proc. EMNLP*, pages 1255–1263.

Sameer Bansal, Herman Kamper, Sharon Goldwater, and Adam Lopez. 2017. Weakly supervised spoken term discovery using cross-lingual side information. In *Proc. ICASSP*.

Alexandre Bérard, Olivier Pietquin, Christophe Servan, and Laurent Besacier. 2016. Listen and translate: A proof of concept for end-to-end speech-to-text translation. In *Proc. NIPS End-to-end Learning for Speech and Audio Processing Workshop*.

Donald J. Berndt and James Clifford. 1994. Using dynamic time warping to find patterns in time series. In *Proc. KDD*, pages 359–370.

Steven Bird, Lauren Gawne, Katie Gelbart, and Isaac McAlister. 2014. Collecting bilingual audio in remote indigenous communities. In *Proc. COLING*, pages 1015–1024.

Steven Bird. 2010. A scalable method for preserving oral literature from small languages. In *Proc. ICADL'10*, pages 5–14.

David Blachon, Elodie Gauthier, Laurent Besacier, Guy-Noël Kouarata, Martine Adda-Decker, and Annie Rialland. 2016. Parallel speech collection for under-resourced language studies using the Lig-Aikuma mobile device app. *Procedia Computer Science*, 81:61–66.

Bernard Comrie. 2009. *The world's major languages*. Routledge.

Amit Das, Preethi Jyothi, and Mark Hasegawa-Johnson. 2016. Automatic speech recognition using probabilistic transcriptions in swahili, amharic, and dinka. *Proc. Interspeech*, pages 3524–3528.

Long Duong, Antonios Anastasopoulos, David Chiang, Steven Bird, and Trevor Cohn. 2016. An attentional model for speech translation without transcription. In *Proc. NAACL-HLT*, pages 949–959.

Emmanuel Dupoux, Núria Sebastián-Gallés, Eduardo Navarrete, and Sharon Peperkamp. 2008. Persistent stress deafness: The case of french learners of spanish. *Cognition*, 106(2):682–706.

Jonathan G Fiscus. 1997. A post-processing system to yield reduced word error rates: Recognizer output voting error reduction (rover). In *Procc. IEEE Workshop on Automatic Speech Recognition and Understanding*, pages 347–354.

Pierre Godard, Gilles Adda, Martine Adda-Decker, Alexandre Allauzen, Laurent Besacier, Helene Bonneau-Maynard, Guy-Noël Kouarata, Kevin Löser, Annie Rialland, and François Yvon. 2016. Preliminary experiments on unsupervised word discovery in mboshi. In *Proc. Interspeech*.

Preethi Jyothi and Mark Hasegawa-Johnson. 2015. Transcribing continuous speech using mismatched crowdsourcing. In *Proc. Interspeech*.

Marika Lekakou, Valeria Baldiserra, and Antonis Anastasopoulos. 2013. Documentation and analysis of an endangered language: aspects of the grammar of Griko.

Chunxi Liu, Preethi Jyothi, Hao Tang, Vimal Manohar, Rose Sloan, Tyler Kekona, Mark Hasegawa-Johnson, and Sanjeev Khudanpur. 2016. Adapting asr for under-resourced languages using mismatched transcriptions. In *Proc. ICASSP*, pages 5840–5844.

Sharon Peperkamp, Emmanuel Dupoux, and Núria Sebastián-Gallés. 1999. Perception of stress by french, spanish, and bilingual subjects. In *Eurospeech*. Citeseer.

François Petitjean, Alain Ketterlin, and Pierre Gançarski. 2011. A global averaging method for dynamic time warping, with applications to clustering. *Pattern Recognition*, 44(3):678–693.

SpeechLab. 2007. Speech at cmu, logios lexicon tool. *http://www.speech.cs.cmu.edu/tools/lextool.html*, Accesed Oct 2016.

Alexis Michaud Thi-Ngoc-Diep Do and Eric Castelli. 2014. Towards the automatic processing of yongning na (sino-tibetan): developing a 'light' acoustic model of the target language and testing 'heavyweight' models from five national languages. In *Proc. SLTU*, pages 153–160.

Author Index